THE STRUGGLE FOR THE GEORGIA COAST

THE STRUGGLE FOR THE GEORGIA COAST

JOHN E. WORTH

THE UNIVERSITY OF ALABAMA PRESS

TUSCALOOSA

Copyright © 2007
The University of Alabama Press
Tuscaloosa, Alabama 35487-0380
All rights reserved
Manufactured in the United States of America

∞

The paper on which this book is printed meets the minimum requirements of American National Standard for Information Sciences-Permanence of Paper for Printed Library Materials, ANSI Z39.48-1984.

Library of Congress Cataloging-in-Publication Data

Worth, John E.
The struggle for the Georgia coast / John E. Worth.
p. cm.
Includes bibliographical references and index.
ISBN-13: 978-0-8173-5411-4 (pbk. : alk. paper)
ISBN-10: 0-8173-5411-5 (pbk. : alk. paper)
ISBN-13: 978-0-8173-8386-2 (electronic)
1. Georgia—History—Colonial period, ca. 1600–1775—Sources. 2. Missions, Spanish—Georgia—History—17th century—Sources. 3. Spaniards—Georgia—History—17th century—Sources. 4. Indians of North America—Georgia—History—17th century—Sources. 5. Florida—History—Spanish colony, 1565–1763—Sources. I. Title.
F289.W67 2007
975.8'02—dc22

2006016070

To Concha

CONTENTS

FIGURES AND TABLES

FIGURES

TABLES

PREFACE TO THE NEW EDITION

In 1733, General James Edward Oglethorpe formally established the English colony of Georgia by landing settlers at the mouth of the Savannah River to form the new town of Savannah. Within three years, a string of English forts had been placed along the Atlantic coast as far south as modern Amelia Island. Over the course of Georgia's first decade, a series of battles waged on paper and on land and sea would negate Spanish territorial claims to the Atlantic coast north of the St. Marys River. As an inconclusive diplomatic struggle led ever more surely to open hostilities, each side began preparations for war. In an effort to garner further justification for Spain's stance, King Philip V ordered the governor of Florida to remit documentary evidence proving the historical "right and legitimacy" of Spanish claim to the territories within the new English colony of Georgia.

During the summer of 1739, the Governor of Spanish Florida Don Manuel de Montiano instructed his governmental notary Francisco de Castilla to scour the archives of St. Augustine in a search for the requested documentary proof. As Castilla compiled the documents included in the present volume, General Oglethorpe was deep in the interior on an expedition to the Chattahoochee River busily reinforcing English alliances with the Lower Creek Indians. When Montiano's package was finally completed in mid-August, a declaration of open war between England and Spain was only two months away, and the frontier would soon erupt into violence and bloodshed.

On August 18, 1739, Governor Montiano sent his formal report and documentation (dated August 14), along with an addendum including a set of three orders found after the completion of the main package (dated August 18), addressing his short cover letter to Don Joseph de la Quintana, the King's fiscal. "I pass to the hands of Your Grace all the papers that I have been able to discover in this archive of government and in the [archive] of the convent of San Francisco justifying the right, dominion, and ownership that the King has to the provinces of Guale and Mocama, which bear to the north of this post, and which are fifty leagues distant from it according to their latitude, so that Your Grace is served to place them in his royal hands, including the two reports regarding the same matter." Montiano's main package and its addendum were received and reviewed, and on May 24, 1740, Quintana penned a brief reply to Montiano, the draft of which was filed with the original Montiano package. "Having placed the one and the other [report] in the understanding of His Majesty, informed about what they demonstrate and about what Your Grace expresses for the better understanding of the right that they deal with, he has commanded that they should be present for what happens in the occasions that it might be suitable to make use of the news that they express, and I notify Your Grace that they are found in this understanding." In effect, the receipt of Governor Montiano's extensive report was politely acknowledged, and the package was filed away for possible use in the future. There it remained as the struggle for the Georgia coast raged thousands of miles away.

Perhaps the most well-known treatise produced as a result of this "War of Jenkins' Ear" was the 1742 manuscript "Historiographic Demonstration of the Right of Spain to New Georgia," written by the Spanish engineer Antonio de Arredondo (1742). This monumental work summarized the historical evidence for Spain's claim to Georgia and presented detailed arguments relating to the diplomatic struggle of the late 1730s. Herbert Bolton (1925) published an edited translation of Arredondo's manuscript nearly two centuries later, which, along with Bolton's introduction, is frequently cited in secondary literature relating to this period. Nevertheless, although Arredondo provides a useful insight into the history of the Spanish presence on the Georgia coast, the text is itself a secondary work, and thus must be considered an 18th-century historical monograph with only a few citations or footnotes, referring largely to documentary sources in the now-missing archives of St. Augustine.

Unlike Arredondo's 1742 treatise, Governor Montiano's 1739 package, an entirely different type of documentary source comprising original and transcribed documents dating to the 16th, 17th, and 18th centuries, remained effectively unknown to most modern researchers until the publication of this volume in 1995. Although undoubtedly viewed on occasion by various investigators (and indeed copied in the 1920s by John B. Stetson), the full significance of Montiano's package does not seem to have been recognized until the spring of 1991, when its 233 folios of text were located, reviewed, and microfilmed during my first research trip to the Archivo General de Indias in Seville, Spain.

The stack of documents sent to Spain by Governor Montiano rested quietly in Spanish archives for just over two and a half centuries in an obscure corner of the section relating to the Audiencia of Santo Domingo, within Legajo 2584, entitled "Expedientes e instancias de partes [Legal Proceedings and Petitions]." Montiano's package stands out from other documents in the stack due to its color, which mixes the off-white tone of the rest of the 18th-century pages with the darker and more deteriorated folios of original 17th-century documents extracted by the notary Castilla from the archives of St. Augustine. The package contains a marvelous assortment of documentary sources pulled or transcribed from both the official governmental archives of St. Augustine and the religious archives of the Franciscan convent in St. Augustine. Inasmuch as the contents of both of these archives remain lost to modern researchers, the following translations provide a rare glimpse of some of the internal documentation of Spanish Florida during its first two centuries.

The selections include not only the more commonly available royal cédulas sent to the governors of Florida but also other internal governmental documents such as official gubernatorial titles, commissions, and orders to individual soldiers and sailors in Florida; a census of the Christian and pagan Indians in the Guale and Mocama mission provinces; an original visitation record of Guale and Mocama; a criminal case against the provincial lieutenant of Guale; testimony relating to the return of Spanish raiders from their expedition against Scottish and English settlers to the north; and two 18th-century retrospective investigations of Spanish territorial holdings usurped by the English. Also included were transcribed extracts from a Franciscan book describing the history of Spanish Florida, records in Latin from a Franciscan chapter meeting in St. Augustine, a set of original letters from the friars of Guale, and an original Franciscan patent with notes signed by each Franciscan friar from all the missions of Florida.

Although the contents of Montiano's package touch on a multitude of topics, the common theme underlying the entire set of documents is the governor's attempt to demonstrate the historical time depth of Spain's presence on the Georgia coast and northward and to provide evidence for some of the depredations by English colonists and pirates during the latter half of the 17th century. Although Montiano's coverage is by no means complete, he did manage to assemble a number of crucial documents pertaining to the later history of the Guale and Mocama provinces, filling many of the gaps in our previous understanding of this period. Indeed, based on the contents of the following translated documents, supplemented with my own ancillary historical investigations of additional sources (many largely unused in the past), a markedly clearer and somewhat revised picture has emerged of the southward retreat of Guale and Mocama between 1655 and 1685.

Consequently, the present volume begins with an introductory overview synthesizing some of the new conclusions reached in part using the translated documents that follow. This overview details the historical background of the eventual abandonment of the Georgia coast by the Spanish, which paved the way for the establishment of the Georgia colony nearly half a century later. Following the Overview are the translations of Governor Montiano's 1739 package, beginning with his own cover letter and index, and followed by translations of the 15 numbered documents included by Montiano in his dispatch to the king, along with the addendum. Each translated document is preceded by an introduction placing it in historical context, and notes and tables are provided as necessary (particularly in the case of documents not extensively covered in the Overview).

English translations were made from handwritten transcriptions of microfilm copies of the original documents, supplemented by notes made in Seville while working with the originals. For the purposes of this volume, I have endeavored to present in English the closest possible translation of the original Spanish text. Writing styles varied considerably with the author and date of each document, but in general, the following translations are more literal than literary, with the emphasis being on accuracy rather than rendering each passage in modern idiomatic English. Nevertheless, some alterations in structure and wording were necessary in order to preserve the readability of each document. Punctuation and capitalization have been added using modern conventions. Where passages were especially confusing or difficult to read, my interpolations appear in brackets, as do any clarifications or original Spanish terms. The spellings of Indian names applied to people, towns, and geographic features are identical to each individual appearance in the original manuscripts, but Spanish names were made consistent and modernized in most cases. Page designations for the original manuscripts are also bracketed in the translations, indicating both folio number and side (e.g. [f.1, vto.] signifies the back [vuelto] side of the first folio [f.1]).

The present volume was originally developed with financial support from the Edward John Noble Foundation and the St. Catherines Island Foundation for the initial research and publication, and with the support of David Hurst Thomas at the American Museum of Natural History in New York, whose interest and encouragement assured the prompt publication of this group of previously unavailable documents relating to Guale and Mocama. The original work was published as monograph number 75 in the *Anthropological Papers of the American Museum of Natural History.*

RECENT WORK

More than eleven years have passed since the completion of the original manuscript for this book. The intervening years have witnessed a considerable amount of new research into the Guale and Mocama Indians and the missions of Spanish Florida in general, not only by myself but also by a wide range of other investigators, including a newer generation of scholars whose work has continued to build and expand on existing work. On the occasion of this new printing by The University of Alabama Press, it therefore seems appropriate and important to expand the original preface to provide an update on the state of current research regarding the Guale and Mocama of the Spanish colonial era and on the world in which they found themselves during the late 17th and early 18th centuries. More than a few of the predictions and conclusions in the 1995 edition have survived the test of time thus far, ranging from archaeological site locations to interpretations regarding ethnic identity and cultural history, for which reason alone an update is warranted. Beyond this, however, my own thinking about the nature of the colonial era and its impact on indigenous populations in the Southeast have grown and evolved through a combination of extensive new archival research and continual re-examination and analysis of these data in the light of many other discoveries and interpretations by colleagues in this and other disciplines. In order to bring the 1995 edition into the context of current thinking and also to provide citations to more recent publications, which bear directly on some of the issues discussed here, the following remarks are offered.

Perhaps one of the most significant interpretations that has emerged and been more thoroughly explored since 1995 is the degree to which the indigenous—chiefly social—organization of the Guale, Mocama, and other missionized groups within Spanish Florida persisted in the face of radical changes in settlement systems, material culture, and religious practice (see pp. 47–50, this volume). As I have since elaborated in greater depth (Worth 2002a; 2006), the political and economic underpinnings of the Spanish mission system actually tended to foment and reinforce existing patterns of chiefly inheritance and public finance for chiefly power, resulting in a considerable degree of longevity for chiefly sociopolitical systems. Indeed, the failure of mission chiefdoms to evolve and adapt in the face of far more fundamental and widespread transformations in the broader economic and political landscape of the eastern United States (associated with the spread of Northern European capitalism through the agency of the Indian slave trade and the firearms revolution, noted below) may ultimately have contributed to their stagnation and ruin in direct contrast to unmissionized groups of the northern interior, many of which still exist.

Apart from the recognition of the longevity of Guale and Mocama sociopolitical organization within the mission system, my 1995 assertion that the Guale and Mocama provinces in 1655 could be described as "syncretic societies that took shape within the expanding Spanish colonial system centered at St. Augustine" (see pp. 9–13) has also been borne out by subsequent research. In large part, as a consequence of the complex interplay between structural assimilation into the colonial system of Spanish Florida and the consequences of ongoing demographic collapse, by 1655 the Atlantic coastal mission provinces of Guale and Mocama were indeed profoundly shaped by the new world order in which they found themselves. An in-depth exploration of the underlying features of the colonial system of Spanish Florida and the fundamental role the mission chiefdoms played within that system ultimately became the cornerstone for my two-volume book *The Timucuan Chiefdoms of Spanish Florida* (Worth 1998a, 1998b). Although the point of departure for this work was an analysis of the interior Timucuan chiefdoms missionized during the 17th century, my broader analysis of the political and economic structure of colonial Spanish Florida fully incorporated the Guale and Mocama provinces along the northern mission chain, particularly with respect to the importance of agricultural labor and surplus corn production, as well as the Atlantic maritime trade based in St. Augustine. This broader colonial system also took center stage in Jerald T. Milanich's (1999) *Laboring in the Fields of the Lord: Spanish Missions and Southwestern Indians*. Archaeological evidence for its biological impact on native populations across Guale, Mocama, and the rest of Spanish Florida was examined in Clark Spencer Larsen's (2001) edited volume *Bioarchaeology of Spanish Florida: The Impact of Colonialism,* in which I also provided an ethnohistorical overview that summarized this system (Worth 2001). Paul Hoffman (2002) also explored historical dimensions of the Spanish colonial system within his recent volume *Florida's Frontiers*.

One of the most important contributions of the original 1995 volume was the synthesis of a detailed and substantially revised interpretation of the locations of original and relocated Guale and Mocama mission communities throughout the late 17th century (more recently supplemented by late 16th-early 17th-century locations set forth in Worth 2004a). This portrait not only differed from earlier interpretations, including not just the famous but flawed *The Spanish Missions of Georgia* (Lanning 1935), but also some of the more recent scholarship of that time (e.g. Jones 1978; Hann 1990:442–443, 463–464). Almost immediately after the publication of this volume, the revised landscape and chronology for Guale and Mocama began to be accepted within the scholarly community (e.g. Milanich 1995:172; Hann 1996:177; Saunders 2000b:30), and since that time at least a handful of these predicted site locations have produced archaeological evidence for mission-era occupation. Two ongoing projects include testing at the likely site of the relocated Santa Cruz y San Buenaventura de Guadalquini mission on Black Hammock Island (see pp. 45, 198, present volume), as well as fieldwork on a likely mission-era occupation near the Sapelo Island shell ring, possibly associated with mission San Joseph de Sapala or one of its three refugee Guale neighbors (Thunen and Whitehurst 2005; Jefferies and Thompson 2005; and see pp. 45, 194, 198 in the present volume).

General ethnohistorical and archaeological work regarding both the Guale and Mocama has continued throughout the past decade, adding considerably to what was known in 1995 when this volume was first issued. I extended my own ethnohistorical analysis of the Guale chiefdom into the sixteenth century for my chapter in Volume 14 (Southeast region) of the *Handbook of North American Indians* (Worth 2004a) and also as part of a broader ethnohistorical analysis of the question of indigenous corn agriculture among Atlantic coastal chiefdoms (Worth 1999b). Jerald Milanich (1999) penned an excellent summary of early Spanish contact with the Guale in his volume above. John H. Hann (1996) provided similar details regarding 16th-century French and Spanish interaction with the Mocama Indians, and their subsequent fate during the mission era, in *A History of the Timucua Indians and Missions,* and Jerald Milanich (1996, 2000, 2004) also explored the ethnohistory and archaeology of the Mocama in several recent works on the Timucua Indians in general. I included ethnohistorical information on several of the interior Mocama chiefdoms and missions as a part of my *Timucuan Chiefdoms* volumes (Worth 1998a, 1998b). Both Guale and Mocama Indians likewise figured prominently in John Hann's (2001) translation of *An Early Florida Adventure Story: The Fray Andrés de San Miguel Account,* which details the 1595 shipwreck of a young sailor along the Georgia coastline.

Recent advances in Guale archaeology have also been published by Rebecca Saunders in her book *Stability and Change in Guale Indian Pottery, A.D. 1300–1702* (Saunders 2000b), and shorter but comprehensive overviews of Guale archaeology and ethnohistory have also appeared (Saunders 2000a; Worth 2004a). Recent archaeological work in the Mocama area has included extensive and ongoing research into the precise ceramic chronology of that region from the late prehistoric to early colonial era, including the definition of the San Pedro ceramic series for the early historic Mocama province (Ashley and Rolland 1997; Rolland and Ashley 2000; Ashley 2001). In addition, my own ethnohistorical analysis of documented residence and migration patterns for the Mocama region during the 17th century has provided substantial evidence for the indigenous Mocama adoption of Guale-derived Altamaha/San Marcos ceramics prior to 1650, reversing earlier assumptions that any such ceramics within the Mocama region were necessarily made by immigrant Guale or Yamasee Indians (Worth 1997).

Guale and Mocama Indians were not the only groups explored in this volume; what was considered by historian Amy Turner Bushnell on the back cover of the 1995 edition to be a "bold thesis about the little known Chichimecos and their connection to slaving and the firearms revolution" has since been expanded with considerable additional research to produce a far more detailed and definitive work relative to the Chichimeco-Westo, entitled *The Westo Indians: Slave Traders of the Early Colonial South,* by Eric E. Bowne (2005). Indeed, the entire subject of Indian slavery has recently been evaluated in-depth using primarily English sources by Alan Gallay (2002) in *The Indian Slave Trade: The Rise of the English Empire in the American South, 1670–1717,* and I and others have independently delved extensively into the substantial impact of this institution across greater Spanish Florida (Worth 1998b, 2002, 2003; Hann 1996). Robbie Ethridge (2006) has more recently expanded the geographic range of this research to posit the existence of a widespread "shatter zone" that produced a ripple effect across much of the Eastern United States during the 17th and early 18th centuries.

My own initial research for this volume into the origins of the Yamasee Indians, which were one of the earliest products of the geopolitical struggle embodied by the Indian slave trade, also became a springboard for substantial new ethnohistorical work relative to the Yamasee (Worth 1999a, 2000b, 2004b). Archaeological work relative to the Yamasee has also blossomed in recent years, including not only extensive work in lower South Carolina, but also excavations at the Yamasee refugee mission community of La Punta near St. Augustine (e.g. Greene and DePratter 2000; Green et al. 2002; White 2002; Boyer 2005).

The shadowy images portrayed in this volume of the late-17th-century interior groups, later to be known as the Lower Creeks, have since been illuminated and explored in considerable new depth, including not only my own chapter-length ethnohistorical and archaeological overview of their origins and early history (Worth 2000), but also a dissertation and subsequent book by Steven Hahn (2000, 2004) entitled *The Invention of the Creek Nation, 1670–1763*. Thomas Foster's (2006) volume *Archaeology of the Lower Muskogee Creek Indians, 1715–1830* provides fresh insights into Lower Creek archaeology, as does John Hann's (2006) *The Native American World Beyond Apalachee: West Florida and the Chattahoochee Valley* relative to Lower Creek ethnohistory.

The origins and history of the Chisca Indians, noted only briefly in the present volume, have since been explored peripherally in several publications (e.g. Hann 1996:238–240; Beck 1997:165–166; Worth 1998b:18–21, 34–35, 2002a:47, 281–282) including my brief summary entry for the *Handbook* volume noted above (Galloway et al. 2004).

THE FATE OF THE GUALE AND MOCAMA

One area that was not explored in depth for the 1995 volume was the ultimate fate of the refugee Guale and Mocama after their 1702 retreat south of the St. Johns River. While details regarding the intervening years of Guale and Mocama presence in northeastern Florida between 1685 and 1702, as well as their short stay at Pilijiriba on the south bank of the St. Johns River through 1704, were subsequently explored by Hann (1996:287–293, 296–298), what has also been poorly understood until fairly recently are the details of Guale and Mocama survivorship after their withdrawal as refugees to St. Augustine, including most particularly the 1763 emigration of 89 surviving Florida mission Indians to Cuba. Two overviews of these final decades of refugee missions around St. Augustine have appeared in recent books (Hann 1996:298–325; Worth 1998b:147–156), but a more specific summary of the Guale and Mocama experience during this era is nonetheless instructive here as an update to the 1995 edition.

By the end of May, 1706 the last of Florida's missions had been withdrawn to St. Augustine, and as of January of 1711, the entire refugee population of Guale and Mocama seems to have been reduced to two mission communities: Santa Catalina de Guale with 61 inhabitants and San Juan del Puerto with 40 inhabitants, not counting the Guale population of 45 in the previously-relocated Nuestre Señora de Guadalupe de Tolomato mission, as well as the older coastal Timucuan populations (possibly including some relocated Mocama) living in mission Nombre de Dios, with 38 listed inhabitants (Worth 1998b:147–149). This total of 184 inhabitants increased to 295 in these same mission communities during the 1717 census following the Yamasee War of 1715, not counting an additional 82 aggregated individuals of interior Timucuan, Apalachee, Yamasee, Chachise, and other unspecified origin (Worth 1998b:149–150). While some of this Guale and

Mocama population growth can likely be attributed to natural population growth or intermarriage with members of other nearby mission communities, it also may reflect the return of Guale and Mocama Indians who may have initially fled the missions during the turbulent years after the 1702 English assault and siege on St. Augustine.

By 1726 the collective population of these four mission communities had risen to 319, augmented by 75 others including interior Timucuans, Macapiras from southern Florida, and other recent converts. Nevertheless, just two years later the four towns were enumerated with only 251 inhabitants (a few of which were unspecified Yamasee Indians), together with 15 interior Timucuans (Worth 1998b:151–152). Just a decade later, by the late-1730s, these towns were variously estimated to contain between 160 and 237 residents in total, probably reflecting a certain degree of population mobility during this era (Worth 1998b:152–155). Administratively, the principal mission convents were still designated as Santa Catalina de Guale and San Juan del Puerto, despite the fact that the four refugee missions held common names ranging from Chiquito (old Santa Catalina) and Tolomato for the Guale to Palica (old San Juan del Puerto) and Macaríz (Nombre de Dios) for the Mocama.

By 1752 only two of these towns still existed (Tolomato and Palica, with 26 and 29 residents, respectively), and by 1759 the inhabitants of Palica had been combined with those of Tolomato to form a total population of only 30 remaining residents who, curiously, were united more by geographic and historical origin rather than linguistic origin within the surviving community at Tolomato (Gelabert 1752; Truxillo 1759). Of this final number, detailed census records reveal that 11 were either half or fully Guale, and 14 were half or fully Mocama. In the nearby town of Nuestra Señora de la Leche (at Nombre de Dios), there were another 7 half or fully Guale Indians as well as a single Mocama (Ruíz 1759), bringing the grand total to 18 Guale and 15 Mocama Indians in these two towns in 1759.

Four years later, the surviving members of these communities embarked on ships and joined the 1763 Spanish evacuation of Florida to Cuba, ultimately settling in the villa of Guanabacoa, just east of Havana harbor (see Gold 1969:66–76). Recently, I have been fortunate to conduct direct archival investigations in the parish of Nuestra Señora de Asunción in Guanabacoa and, combined with extensive work in Cuban materials located in the Archivo General de Indias in Seville, the preliminary results of this ongoing research are extremely encouraging (Worth 2004c). A substantial number of the 89 Florida Indian evacuees were Guale or Mocama, including 5 predominantly Guale households originally from the Tolomato mission and 3 predominantly Mocama households originally from the Palica mission, all out of a grand total of 22 households enumerated in early census records in Guanabacoa (Anonymous n.d.a, n.d.b., n.d.c.). Though death rates were astonishingly high during the first years after their settlement in Guanabacoa, comprising greater than 50 percent population loss among all 89 immigrants prior to 1770 (including at least 14 members of these Guale and Mocama households), there are a few instances of survivorship that are noteworthy.

A Guale Indian named María Ursula Pérez, born about 1736 and living in Tolomato with her brother in 1752 and 1759, married Guanabacoa native Julian de la Rosa Aguilar (a "pardo libre" of African and possibly mixed Cuban Indian ancestry) on July 7, 1764, and subsequently had two children—María Josepha de la Concepción Aguilar in 1765 and Julian Joseph Aguilar in 1768—before her death in 1769 (Casares y Borjes 1764; Arteaga 1765, 1768, 1769b). Maria's 27-year-old brother Miguel Phelipe Pérez later married Yamasee Indian immigrant Maria Rosa Sánchez on October 28, 1766, and they had a daughter named Catalina de la Luz Pérez in 1767 shortly before the mother's death in 1769, which was followed by the death of Miguel himself in 1774 (Arteaga 1766, 1767, 1769a; Jorge 1774). None of these three half-Guale children born in Guanabacoa are documented to have died in childhood, leaving the possibility that some or all might have survived to have descendants of their own. Though research is still ongoing, living descendants of these African-Guale and Guale-Yamasee cousins may yet be discovered in modern Cuba. In addition, there is clear evidence for the survival of a number of other Florida Indian immigrants through at least 1800, suggesting that other Guale or Mocama lines of descent may also persist to the present day. This possibility, though perhaps remote, represents a tantalizing postscript to the present volume in that Guale and Mocama descendants may still exist in modern Cuban or even Cuban-American populations and may yet be unaware of their connection to the peoples whose lives and histories were part of the struggle for the Georgia Coast.

REFERENCES CITED

Anonymous

n.d.a. Families from Florida: Indians (families, names, pension amounts, death dates, ca. 1764). Archivo General de Indias, Papeles de Cuba 548.

n.d.b. List of families of Indians who came from Florida and find themselves placed in Guanabacoa (families, names, relationships, health status, ca. 1764). Archivo General de Indias, Papeles de Cuba 416.

n.d.c. List of families of Indians who came from Florida and find themselves placed in Guanabacoa (families, names, gender, ca. 1764). Archivo General de Indias, Papeles de Cuba 416.

Arredondo, Antonio de

1742. Demostración historiographica del derecho de España a Nueva Georgia. Archivo General de Indias, Santo Domingo 2593.

Arteaga, Melchor Antonio de

1765. Baptism record for María Josepha de la Concepción, November 17, 1765. Archivo Parroquial, Church of Nuestra Señora de la Asunción (Guanabacoa), Registro de Bautismos, Book 5P, Folio 65, No. 92.

1766. Marriage record for Miguel Phelipe Pérez and María Rosa Sánchez, October 28, 1766. Archivo Parroquial, Church of Nuestra Señora de la Asunción (Guanabacoa), Registro de Matrimonios, Book 3P, Folio 24v, No. 72.

1767. Baptism record for Cathalina de la Luz, daughter of Miguel Phelipe Pérez and Rosa María Sánchez, May 2, 1767. Archivo Parroquial, Church of Nuestra Señora de la Asunción (Guanabacoa), Registro de Bautismos, Book 5P, Folio 106, No. 596.

1768. Baptism record for Julian Joseph, son of Julian de la Rosa Aguilar and María Ursula Pérez, January 14, 1768. Archivo Parroquial, Church of Nuestra Señora de la Asunción (Guanabacoa), Registro de Bautismos, Book 5P, Folio 123, No. 681.

1769a. Burial record for Rosa María Sánchez, wife of [illegible] Pérez, May 25, 1769. Archivo Parroquial, Church of Nuestra Señora de la Asunción (Guanabacoa), Registro de Difuntos, Book 2P, Folio 60v, No. 830.

1769b. Burial record for Ursula María Pérez, wife of Julian de Aguilar, October 14, 1769. Archivo Parroquial, Church of Nuestra Señora de la Asunción (Guanabacoa), Registro de Difuntos, Book 2P, Folio 64v, No. 561.

Ashley, Keith H.

2001. Beyond Potsherds: A Technofunctional Analysis of San Pedro Pottery from the North Beach Site (8SJ48). *The Florida Anthropologist* 54(3–4):123–149.

Ashley, Keith H., and Vicki L. Rolland

1997. Grog Tempered Pottery in the Mocama Province. *The Florida Anthropologist* 50(2):51–66.

Beck, Robin A., Jr.

1997. From Joara to Chiaha: Spanish Exploration of the Appalachian Summit Area, 1540–1568. *Southeastern Archaeology* 16(2):162–169.

Bolton, Herbert

1925. *Arredondo's Historical Proof of Spain's Title to Georgia*. Berkeley: University of California Press.

Bowne, Eric E.

2005. *The Westo Indians: Slave Traders of the Early Colonial South*. Tuscaloosa: University of Alabama Press.

Boyer, Willet A., III

2005. Nuestra Senora del Rosario de La Punta: Lifeways of an Eighteenth-Century Colonial Spanish Refugee Mission Community, St. Augustine, Florida. Unpublished Master's Thesis, Department of Anthropology, University of Florida, Gainesville.

Casares y Borjes, Francisco

1764. Marriage record for Julian de Aguilar and María Ursula Pérez, July 7, 1764. Archivo Parroquial, Church of Nuestra Señora de la Asunción (Guanabacoa), Registro de Matrimonios, Book 3P, Folio 8, No. 31.

Ethridge, Robbie

2006. Creating the Shatter Zone: Indian Slave Traders and the Collapse of Southeastern Chiefdoms. In *Light on the Path: The Anthropology and History of the Southeastern Indians,* ed. by Thomas J. Pluckhahn and Robbie Ethridge, pp. 207–218. Tuscaloosa: University of Alabama Press.

Foster, Thomas
2006. *Archaeology of the Lower Muskogee Creek Indians, 1715–1830*. Tuscaloosa: University of Alabama Press.

Gallay, Alan
2002. *The Indian Slave Trade: The Rise of the English Empire in the American South, 1670–1717*. New Haven: Yale University Press.

Galloway, Patricia, Marvin D. Jeter, Gregory A. Waselkov, John E. Worth, and Ives Goddard
2004. Small Tribes of the Western Southeast. In *Handbook of North American Indians,* Volume 14: *Southeast,* pp. 174–190. Washington, D.C.: Smithsonian Institution Press.

Gelabert, Josef Antonio
1752. Transcript of Franciscan Census for Towns of Tolomato, Pocotalaca, Palica, and Punta, January 10, 1752. Archivo General de Indias, Santo Domingo 2604.

Gold, Robert L.
1969. *Borderland Empires in Transition: The Triple-Nation Transfer of Florida.* Carbondale: Southern Illinois University Press.

Green, William G., and Chester B. DePratter
2000. Ten Years of Yamasee Archaeology in South Carolina: A Retrospective and Guide for Future Research. Paper presented in the symposium "A Synthesis of Mississippian and Historic Period Native Americans in South Carolina" at the 57th Annual Southeastern Archaeological Conference, Macon, Georgia.

Green, William G., Chester B. DePratter, and Bobby Southerlin
2002. The Yamasee in South Carolina: Native American Adaptation and Interaction along the Carolina Frontier. In *Another's Country: Archaeological and Historical Perspectives on Cultural Interactions in the Southern Colonies,* ed. by Joseph W. Joseph and Martha Zierden, pp. 12–29. Tuscaloosa: University of Alabama Press.

Hahn, Steven C.
2000. The Invention of the Creek Nation: A Political History of the Creek Indians in the South's Imperial Era, 1540–1763. Ph.D. Dissertation, Department of History, Emory University, Atlanta.
2004. *The Invention of the Creek Nation, 1670–1763*. Lincoln: University of Nebraska Press.

Hann, John H.
1990. *Summary Guide to Spanish Florida Missions and Vistas with Churches in the Sixteenth and Seventeenth Centuries*. Washington, D.C.: Academy of American Franciscan History. Reprint (with illustrations) from *The Americas* 46(4):417–513.
1996. *A History of the Timucua Indians and Missions*. Gainesville: University Press of Florida.
2001. *An Early Florida Adventure Story: The Fray Andrés de San Miguel Account*. Gainesville: University Press of Florida.
2006. *The Native American World Beyond Apalachee: West Florida and the Chattahoochee Valley.* Gainesville: University Press of Florida.

Hoffman, Paul E.
2002. *Florida's Frontiers*. Bloomington: Indiana University Press.

Jefferies, Richard W., and Victor D. Thompson
2005. Contact Period Native American Settlement and Interaction on Sapelo Island, Georgia. Paper presented at the 62nd annual meeting of the Southeastern Archaeological Conference, Columbia, South Carolina.

Jones, Grant D.
1978. The Ethnohistory of the Guale Coast through 1684. In *The Anthropology of St. Catherines Island: 1. Natural and Cultural History,* ed. by David Hurst Thomas, Grant D. Jones, Roger S. Durham, and Clark Spencer Larsen, pp. 178–210. Anthropological Papers of the American Museum of Natural History 55(2).

Jorge, Alexandro Luís
1774. Burial record for Miguel Phelipe Pérez, widower of María Locaria Sánchez, November 14, 1774. Archivo

Parroquial, Church of Nuestra Señora de la Asunción (Guanabacoa), Registro de Difuntos, Book 2P, Folio 95v, No. 864.

Lanning, John Tate
1935. *The Spanish Missions of Georgia.* Chapel Hill: University of North Carolina Press.

Larsen, Clark Spencer, ed.
2001. *Bioarchaeology of Spanish Florida: The Impact of Colonialism.* Gainesville: University Press of Florida.

Milanich, Jerald T.
1995. *Florida Indians and the Invasion from Europe.* Gainesville: University Press of Florida.
1996. *The Timucua.* Cambridge, Mass.: Blackwell Publishers.
1999. *Laboring in the Fields of the Lord: Spanish Missions and Southwestern Indians.* Washington, D.C.: Smithsonian Institution Press.
2000. The Timucua Indians of Northern Florida and Southern Georgia. In *Indians of the Greater Southeast: Historical Archaeology and Ethnohistory,* ed. by Bonnie G. McEwan, pp. 1–25. Gainesville: University Press of Florida.
2004. Timucua. In *Handbook of North American Indians,* Volume 14: *Southeast.* Raymond D. Fogelson, vol. ed.; William C. Sturtevant, gen. ed., pp. 219–228. Washington, D.C.: Smithsonian Institution Press.

Rolland, Vicki L. and Keith H. Ashley
2000. Beneath the Bell: A Study of Mission Period Colonoware from Three Spanish Missions in Northeast Florida. *The Florida Anthropologist* 53(1):36–61.

Ruíz, Alonso
1759. Census of the Town of Nuestra Señora de la Leche, February 10, 1759. Archivo General de Indias, Santo Domingo 2604.

Saunders, Rebecca
2000a. The Guale Indians of the Lower Atlantic Coast: Change and Continuity. In *Indians of the Greater Southeast: Historical Archaeology and Ethnohistory,* ed. by Bonnie G. McEwan, pp. 26–56. Gainesville: University Press of Florida.
2000b. *Stability and Change in Guale Indian Pottery, A.D. 1300–1702.* Tuscaloosa: University of Alabama Press.

Thunen, Robert L., and John C. Whitehurst
2005. Cedar Point Survey: The 2005 Field School. Paper presented at the 62nd annual meeting of the Southeastern Archaeological Conference, Columbia, South Carolina.

Truxillo, Augustín
1759. Census of the Town of Nuestra Señora de Guadalupe de Tolomato, February 3, 1759. Archivo General de Indias, Santo Domingo 2604.

White, Andrea P.
2002. Living on the Periphery: A Study of an Eighteenth-Century Yamassee Mission Community in Colonial St. Augustine. Unpublished Master's Thesis, The College of William and Mary, Williamsburg, Virginia.

Worth, John E.
1997. Integrating Ethnohistory and Archaeology among the Timucua: An Overview of Southeast Georgia and Northeast Florida. Paper presented in the symposium "Late Prehistoric through Mission Period Research in the Coastal Timucuan Region" at the 54th annual meeting of the Southeastern Archaeological Conference, Baton Rouge.
1998a. *The Timucuan Chiefdoms of Spanish Florida,* Volume I: *Assimilation.* Gainesville: University Press of Florida.
1998b. *The Timucuan Chiefdoms of Spanish Florida,* Volume II: *Resistance and Destruction.* Gainesville: University Press of Florida.
1999a. Yamassee Origins and the Development of the Carolina-Florida Frontier. Paper presented at the fifth annual conference of the Omohundro Institute of Early American History and Culture, Austin, Texas.
1999b. Coastal Chiefdoms and the Question of Agriculture: An Ethnohistorical Overview. Paper presented at the 56th annual meeting of the Southeastern Archaeological Conference, Pensacola.
2000a. The Lower Creeks: Origins and Ear-

ly History. In *Indians of the Greater Southeast: Historical Archaeology and Ethnohistory,* ed. by Bonnie G. McEwan, pp. 265–298. Gainesville: University Press of Florida.

2000b. The Yamassee in Florida: An Ethnohistorical and Archaeological Overview. Paper presented in the symposium "A Synthesis of Mississippian and Historic Period Native Americans in South Carolina" at the 57th annual meeting of the Southeastern Archaeological Conference, Macon, Georgia.

2001. The Ethnohistorical Context of Bioarchaeology in Spanish Florida. In *Bioarchaeology of Spanish Florida: The Impact of Colonialism,* ed. by Clark Spencer Larsen, pp. 1–21. Gainesville: University Press of Florida.

2002a. Spanish Missions and the Persistence of Chiefly Power. In *The Transformation of the Southeastern Indians, 1540–1760,* ed. by Robbie Ethridge and Charles Hudson, pp. 39–64. Jackson: University Press of Mississippi.

2002b. Reign of Terror: The Indian Slave Trade and the Devastation of Spanish Florida, 1659–1715. Paper presented in the symposium "The Social History of the Southeastern Indians: The Seventeenth-Century Indian Slave Trade and the Creation of a Shatter Zone" at the 59th annual meeting of the Southeastern Archaeological Conference, Biloxi, Mississippi.

2003. The Evacuation of South Florida, 1704–1760. Paper presented at the 60th annual meeting of the Southeastern Archaeological Conference, Charlotte, North Carolina.

2004a. Guale. In *Handbook of North American Indians,* Volume 14: *Southeast.* Raymond D. Fogelson, vol. ed.; William C. Sturtevant, gen. ed., pp. 238–244. Washington, D.C.: Smithsonian Institution Press.

2004b. Yamasee. In *Handbook of North American Indians,* Volume 14: *Southeast.* Raymond D. Fogelson, vol. ed.; William C. Sturtevant, gen. ed., pp. 245–253. Washington, D.C.: Smithsonian Institution Press.

2004c. A History of Southeastern Indians in Cuba, 1513–1823. Paper presented at the 61st annual meeting of the Southeastern Archaeological Conference, St. Louis, Missouri.

2006. Bridging Prehistory and History in the Southeast: Evaluating the Utility of the Acculturation Concept. In *Light on the Path: The Anthropology and History of the Southeastern Indians,* ed. by Thomas J. Pluckhahn and Robbie Ethridge, pp. 196–206. Tuscaloosa: University of Alabama Press.

THE STRUGGLE FOR
THE GEORGIA COAST

ABSTRACT

This volume examines the late 17th-century transformation and retreat of the Spanish mission provinces of Guale and Mocama in the face of English-sponsored hostility from the north. The central focus of the text is the presentation of English translations of the recently identified 1739 package of historical documentation assembled by the Governor of Florida Don Manuel de Montiano in an attempt to demonstrate Spain's prior ownership of the new English colony of Georgia. This package comprises a rich variety of original and transcribed documents dating to the 16th, 17th, and 18th centuries, including gubernatorial orders, legal proceedings and investigations, internal Franciscan documentation, royal decrees, and a detailed census and visitation record for Guale and Mocama. Based on these documents, supplemented by extensive new historical research, an in-depth introductory overview provides a detailed and somewhat revised portrait of the retreat of Guale and Mocama between 1655 and 1685. Although the aggregation and relocation of aboriginal settlements to the south and toward the sea ultimately failed to halt the onslaught of slave-raiders and pirates, chiefly lineages remained largely intact throughout this period, attesting to the remarkable persistence and adaptability of Guale and Mocama culture.

INTRODUCTION

David Hurst Thomas

This is the fourth monograph in our series dealing with the archaeology of Mission Santa Catalina de Guale. Because this volume was generated as part of this long-term project, we begin with a word about the archaeological research program on St. Catherines Island, Georgia.

EXCAVATIONS AT MISSION SANTA CATALINA DE GUALE

In 1972, the American Museum of Natural History (AMNH) entered into an agreement with the Edward John Noble Foundation to encourage and facilitate scientific research on St. Catherines Island, a barrier island off the coast of Georgia. The resulting long-term program has enabled hundreds of scientists and students to carry out research on various aspects of the natural and cultural history of the island. Each year since 1974, field crews from the AMNH have conducted intensive and extensive archaeological investigations as part of this research. The results of these inquiries have been published in the Anthropological Papers of the American Museum of Natural History. The first volume in this series (Thomas et al., 1978) provides an overview of the natural and cultural history of St. Catherines Island, and can be viewed as a backdrop for this monograph as well.

We began our search for Mission Santa Catalina in 1977 with an extensive program of reconnaissance and site evaluation for all of St. Catherines Island and have been excavating the 16th- and 17th-century archaeological deposits ever since. The first monograph in this series dealing with the archaeology of the mission describes our motivation for seeking Santa Catalina and sets out our overall research strategy (Thomas, 1987).

The second volume (Larsen, 1990) describes the biocultural and bioarchaeological study of 17th-century Native American inhabitants of St. Catherines Island and the Georgia coast. The human remains recovered from Mission Santa Catalina de Guale represent one of the best-documented and most extensive series of human remains from an early contact site in North America. The study of these remains and comparisons made with other late precontact populations in the region provide an important opportunity to examine the impact of the arrival of Europeans on American Indians.

The third volume, by historian Amy Turner Bushnell, sets out the primary documentary back-up for these mission excavations, (Bushnell, 1994). Explicitly oriented toward the archaeologist's need for material culture information, Bushnell's extraordinary volume deals with the support system the Spanish set up for their mission chain of which Mission Santa Catalina de Guale was the northern terminus. Bushnell situates Mission Santa Catalina within Spain's overarching colonization scheme for the entire New World; her text ranges from narrative and specific illustration to full-blown historiographic analysis. The narrative chapters constitute the first real attempt to write a general history of the provinces of La Florida. Analytical and illustrative sections provide the detail needed by archaeologists encountering the archaeological record of Spanish Florida.

HOW THIS MONOGRAPH EVOLVED

In this, the fourth volume in the series, we present a large body of primary archival documentation, translated and supplemented by a series of important interpretive essays prepared by Dr. John E. Worth. Like Bushnell's previous contribution, this volume develops a historical framework against which to array the extensive new data resulting from the mission excavation. But unlike Bushnell's long-term and painstakingly articulated documentary research, the present volume arose from a totally unexpected, serendipitous discovery that took place in the spring of 1991.

As part of his doctoral research in the Archivo General de Indias (Seville, Spain), John E. Worth—then a graduate student at the University of Florida—made an amazing discovery. Here, amidst a stack of notary records dealing with St. Augustine was a long-forgotten package of 16th-, 17th-, and 18th-century documents. As Worth describes in the Preface, this "marvelous assortment" of documentary sources had been pulled together in 1739 at the behest of Don Manuel de Montiano, governor of Spanish Florida. Acting upon orders from King Philip V of Spain, Governor Montiano had assembled the primary sources documenting Spain's claim to territories contained within James Oglethorpe's new English colony of Georgia.

Contained within Governor Montiano's extraordinary parcel was a wealth of previously unavailable documentation. Beyond the well-known reports of earlier governors there were a variety of internal Spanish correspondence (including a census of Indians living in the Guale and Mocamo mission provinces); various Franciscan mission records, including a record of a heretofore unknown visitation; letters from the friars stationed in Guale; and an original patent with notes signed by each Franciscan friar serving in these missions.

Amazingly, Montiano's archival package had escaped the view of modern historians until it was discovered by John Worth, less than three years ago. Historians and archaeologists working on the early contact period in the coastal Southeast have long suffered from a lack of published historical sources, and, through the good offices of Professor Jerald T. Milanich (Florida Museum of Natural History), we were made aware of Worth's extraordinary good fortune.

It was immediately evident that the newly discovered Montiano report had tremendous potential for shedding fresh light on the mission period in Georgia—especially when combined with the results of our Mission Santa Catalina excavations. After a brief period of discussion, John Worth agreed to prepare a complete set of translations of these documents, illuminated by his own interpretive synthesis of the findings. As part of our St. Catherines Island archaeological research program, we provided support and assistance for Worth during the lengthy period required to prepare the translations and narratives.

The final product is a major contribution to our understanding of the Spanish missions along Georgia's coast, particularly during the second half of the 17th century. The previously untranslated documents form the backbone of the volume, providing contemporary accounts of labor practices, demography, population replacement and migration.

The value of these firsthand accounts and records is significantly enhanced by Worth's extraordinary introductory essay, in which he addresses a number of important and previously unresolved issues—particularly the circumstances and timing of the movement of mainland Guale missions and villages to new Sea Island locales. Worth's overview also provides new information and fresh interpretations, integrating earlier historical syntheses with newly available data on Native Americans living in the coastal Southeast. This work greatly enhances our knowledge of how the Sea Island missions were driven southward into Florida. Worth has painstakingly traced the 30-year retreat down the coast, producing a fine set of accompanying maps.

This volume also complements the historical account by Grant D. Jones, which appeared in an earlier volume of our St. Catherines series (Jones, 1978). In his synthesis, Jones dealt mostly with the period from first European contact to 1606; he only briefly summarized subsequent events to 1684, noting that considerable additional research was required to illuminate the 17th-century mission period in Georgia. Worth's manuscript does much to fill this void, and carries the documentation forward into the 18th century as well.

As we began preparing these translations for publication, we explored the notion of reproducing transcripts of the original Spanish text alongside Worth's translations. But the costs of publishing in this fashion forced us to abandon the side-by-side format. However, the original Spanish transcripts prepared by Worth during his research at the Archivo General de Indias have been accessioned into the Archives of the American Museum of Natural History, and any scholar interested in checking Worth's translations against the original Spanish transcripts can do so by contacting the Director of Archives, Department of Anthropology, American Museum of Natural History. The Spanish transcripts will be provided at cost.

The historical studies by Grant Jones, Amy Bushnell, and John Worth were initiated to provide badly needed supportive documentation for ongoing excavations at Mission Santa Catalina. But in each case, the final result has appeal to a much broader group of scholars. We think that archaeologists, anthropologists, geographers, and missiologists working throughout the Americas will be drawn to the newly available demographic data and the detailed account of how native labor was recruited. We are delighted with the final product, and feel certain that the volume will become an indispensable source for all scholars studying the aboriginal people of Georgia and the experience of those who came to establish and operate the coastal missions.

REFERENCES

Bushnell, Amy Turner
1994. Situado and sabana: Spain's support system for the presidio and mission provinces of Florida. Anthrop. Pap. Am. Mus. Nat. Hist. 74: 249 pp.

Jones, Grant D.
1978. The ethnohistory of the Guale coast through 1684. In David Hurst Thomas, Grant D. Jones, Roger S. Durham, and Clark Spencer Larsen, The anthropology of St. Catherines Island: 1. natural and cultural history. Anthrop. Pap. Am. Mus. Nat Hist. 55(2): 178–210.

Larsen, Clark Spencer (ed.)
1990. The archaeology of Mission Santa Catalina de Guale: 2. biocultural interpretations of a population in transition. Anthrop. Pap. Am. Mus. Nat Hist. 68: 150 pp.

Thomas, David Hurst
1987. The archaeology of Mission Santa Catalina de Guale: 1. search and discovery. Anthrop. Pap. Am. Mus. Nat Hist. 63(2): 47–161.

Thomas, David Hurst, Grant D. Jones, Roger S. Durham, and Clark Spencer Larsen
1978. The anthropology of St. Catherines Island: 1. natural and cultural history. Anthrop. Pap. Am. Mus. Nat Hist. 55(2): 155–248.

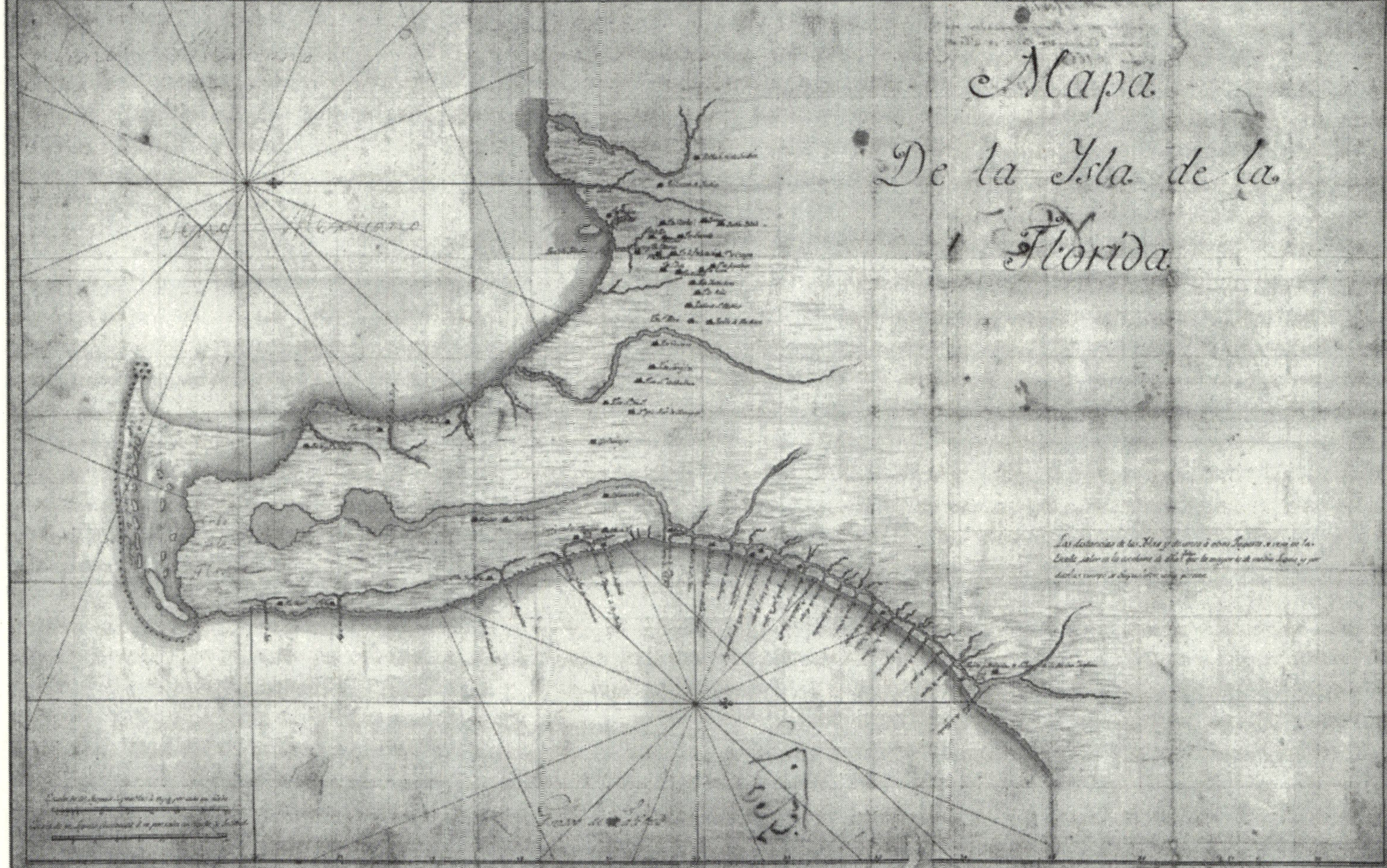

“Map of the Island of Florida,” expanded version. (See Fig. 3, p. 38 for full caption.)

OVERVIEW
THE RETREAT OF GUALE AND MOCAMA, 1655–1685

INTRODUCTION

The 1733 establishment of Savannah represented not simply the beginning of the creation of an English colony known as Georgia, but rather the final stage of an English/Spanish territorial struggle that had begun nearly three quarters of a century earlier. Indeed, the coastal region into which the Georgia colonists flooded soon thereafter had remained a virtual no-man's land for nearly 50 years prior to the arrival of General Oglethorpe. The effective abandonment of the Georgia coast by missionaries, soldiers, and Indians under the Spanish crown, which ultimately paved the way for English colonization, actually occurred in 1684, culminating a 23-year retreat in the face of repeated invasions by English-backed Indians and pirates.

The coast of modern Georgia had been home to aboriginal societies for thousands of years prior to the Columbian encounter of 1492. The first European exploration and missionization of the Precolumbian inhabitants of the coastal region of northeastern Florida and southeastern Georgia by Spanish soldiers and missionaries spanned the late 16th and early 17th centuries. During this time numerous aboriginal villages and societies were gradually incorporated into the Spanish colonial system centered in the garrison town of St. Augustine, founded in 1565. The unfolding of this process in the mission provinces of Guale and Mocama, inextricably linked with the expansion and development of the colonial system throughout all of Spanish Florida, has been examined in some detail by historians and archaeologists, and will not be recounted for this essay (e.g., Lanning, 1935; Geiger, 1937; Deagan, 1978; Jones, 1978; Thomas, 1987; Larsen, 1990). Nevertheless, it should be noted that the establishment of these mission provinces did not occur without substantial impact to the Indian societies involved, and that the very process of assimilation into the broader Spanish colonial system brought about significant transformations to Precolumbian cultures, as will be discussed below.

The present discussion centers on a later period, postdating the era of exploration and missionization and beginning at the midpoint of the 17th century, or more precisely in 1655, when an important list of all the Florida missions was compiled by Juan Díez de la Calle (1655, 1659). This list represents the first synthetic overview of the provinces of Guale and Mocama after the initial decade of the 17th century (when no less than three formal visitations were conducted between 1603 and 1606), and furthermore constitutes what is perhaps the last view of Guale and Mocama before the retreat southward. In this sense, the 1655 list provides a benchmark against which the turbulent events of the next three decades may be compared. This essay will thus examine the details and trends of the retreat of Guale and Mocama in the face of repeated attacks from their neighbors to the north (English colonists and Indians set in motion by their actions) and from seaborne raiders on the Atlantic (English and French pirates). Ultimately, this overview should serve to clarify the final chapter in the Spanish period on the Georgia coast, setting the stage for James Oglethorpe's arrival half a century later.

GUALE AND MOCAMA PROVINCES AT MID-CENTURY

The 1655 mission provinces of Guale and Mocama represented 17th-century Indian societies that had formed under conditions of Spanish missionization and colonization. In this sense, Guale and Mocama were not purely aboriginal social entities with an overlay of Spanish presence, but rather syncretic societies that took shape within the expanding Spanish colonial system centered at St. Augustine. Guale and Mocama were thus in actuality more a product of the colonial era than a victimized relic of the Precolumbian past. The societies that form the benchmark for this essay were different in several ways from those encountered in the same region by early Spanish and French explorers and colonists of the 16th century, and the process of retreat described below marks only one of the final stages in the transformation of the Indians who inhabited the Georgia coast.

This said, the task remains to probe the character of Guale and Mocama in the mid-17th century. In 1655, the Guale and Mocama provinces were evidently composed of 10 primary mission towns, 8 of which had resident Spanish friars. Six of these were within the province of Guale, and four were in Mocama. Although there appears to be little question that each of these towns had once been only the political head of a cluster of subordinate villages, by the late 17th century this dispersed settlement distribution had become substantially centralized (see below), and thus only these central mission towns will be used to trace the aggregation and retreat of Guale and Mocama between 1655 and 1685. Nevertheless, it should be recognized that many of the chiefly lineages of former satellite villages persisted within these centralized mission towns, resulting in a curious collection of titular aboriginal leaders lacking actual roles as village headmen (see below). The principal missions of these coastal provinces are presented in figure 1, along with their projected locations in the mid-17th century. More detailed evidence for the specific locations of these towns in 1655 and during their successive moves to the south is provided in Appendix A.

The northernmost province of Guale was composed of six primary mission towns extending from the mouth of the modern Ogeechee River drainage to the mouth of the Altamaha River drainage. The northernmost of these was San Diego de Satuache (or Chatuache), located 10 leagues to the north of Guale's provincial capital at Mission Santa Catalina. This mainland mission town was probably situated at or near the mouth of the Ogeechee River. San Phelipe de Alave, another mainland mission, was apparently located 9 leagues north from Mission San Joseph de Sapala (on Sapelo Island), and from San Phelipe one could descend 4 leagues to Mission Santa Catalina. Based on the projected track of this circuitous route from Sapala to Santa Catalina, Mission San Phelipe was probably located along the inland waterways of the Newport River (see Appendix A).

Proceeding to the south, the third mission in the Guale province was Santa Catalina de Guale, the location of which has been established with considerable confidence to be at the Wamassee Head archaeological site on St. Catherines Island (Thomas, 1987). Indeed, it is this location that serves as a benchmark against which much other locational information is compared. To the south lay Mission San Joseph de Sapala, probably located toward the northern end of Sapelo Island, perhaps at the Bourbon Field site. Another five leagues away, but this time to the southwest, was the southernmost mission town in Guale, Santo Domingo de Talaje/Asajo, another mainland mission located at the Fort King George site on the north bank of the mouth of the Altamaha River.

Although at this time there was a sixth principal mission town in the Guale province, Santa Clara de Tupiqui, it does not seem to have had a resident friar during this period, and thus was not included in the 1655 list. In the early 1660s it was apparently included on the visitation round of the friar stationed at Santa Catalina de Guale, the nearest mission. Tupiqui also continued to appear as a separate town within the Guale province on the yearly labor draft orders well into the late 1660s (see below), suggesting it was still at its original location along the inland waterways of the Sapelo River opposite Sapelo Island through this period, and very probably at the Pine Harbor site.

The four principal mission towns in the Mocama province extended from St. Simons Island on the north to the mouth of the St. Johns River on the south.[1] The northernmost mission was San Buenaventura de Guadalquini, situated on the southern tip of St. Simons Island some 8 leagues south of Santo Domingo (because previous scholars have consistently located Guadalquini on Jekyll Island to the south, detailed arguments regarding the location of this town are presented in Appendix A). Much farther to the south was Mission San Pedro de Mocama, probably located near the southern tip of Cumberland Island, another 12 leagues south of San Buenaventura. Although not listed on the 1655 list, Mission Santa Maria, at the Harrison Homestead site on Amelia Island,

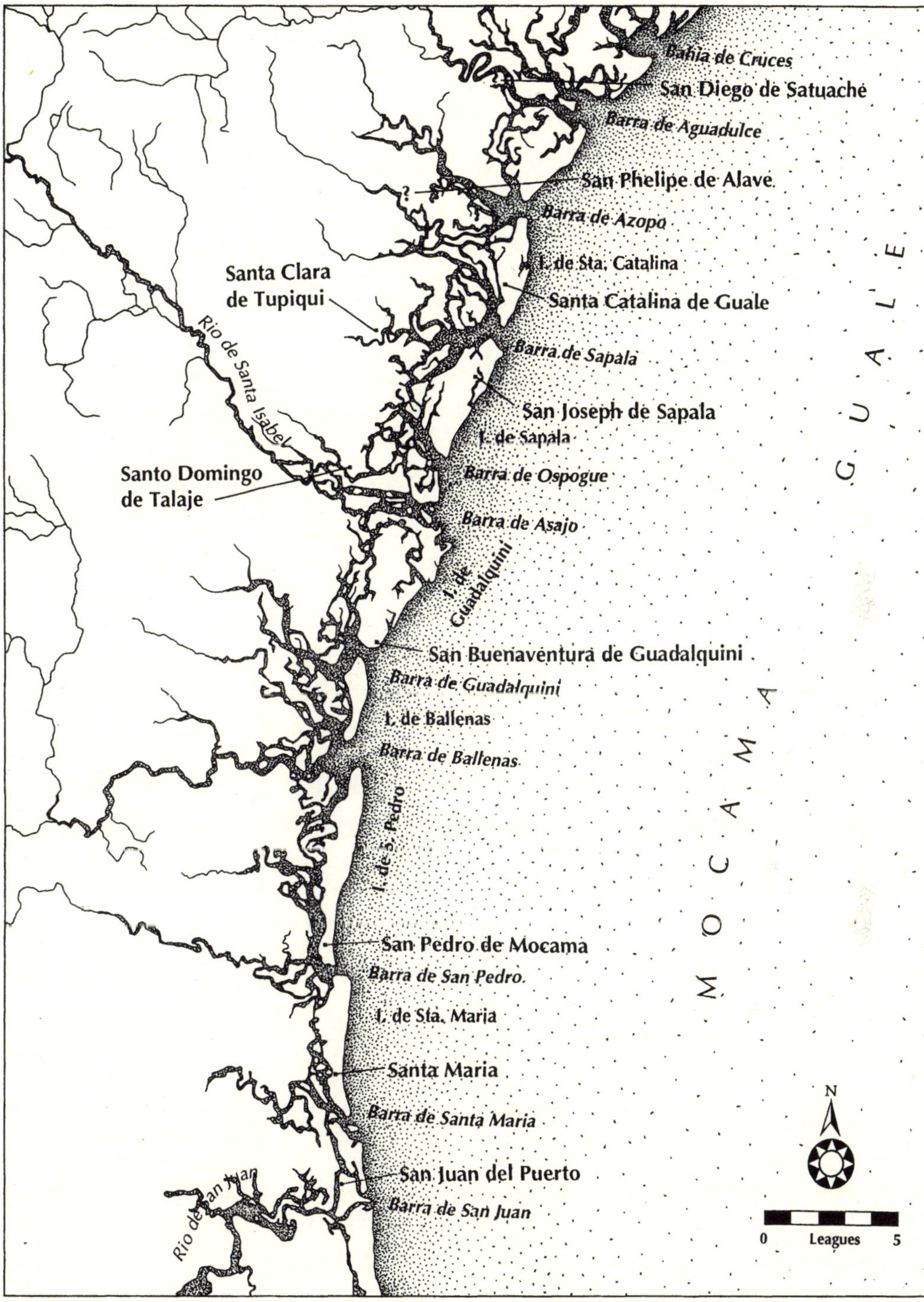

Fig. 1. Projected locations of principal Guale and Mocama missions in the mid-17th century, based on the mission list by Juan Díez de la Calle (1655) and supplementary documentary information (see Appendix A).

was evidently still in existence at this time, but apparently without a resident friar. The southernmost Mocama mission was San Juan del Puerto, 8 leagues south of San Pedro on Fort George Island at the mouth of the St. Johns River.

How does this portrait of Guale and Mocama differ from that of half a century earlier? An examination of ethnohistorical information compiled during the official Spanish visitations of this same region during the first decade of the 17th century reveals significant sociopolitical changes prior to 1655. Just after the turn of the century, there were indeed two important aboriginal societies along the Georgia and northern Florida coast, and their geographical extent roughly corresponded to that of the Guale and Mocama provinces of 1655. Nevertheless, the societies that were eventually to become the Guale and Mocama provinces described above were somewhat different in character just after the turn of the century.

Significantly, the political leadership of each province was situated in a different location. At the start of the 17th century (just after the tumultuous 1597 Guale rebellion), the northern Georgia coast was divided into three small chiefdoms, each of which comprised something on the order of a dozen subordinate towns (which themselves may have been less towns than clusters of villages with central administration). In 1606, however, the northernmost chiefdoms led by the towns of Guale and Espogache were politically subordinate to the chiefdom of Asajo/Talaje at the mouth of the Altamaha River, ruled by the brothers Don Domingo and Don Mateo (Avila, 1606). This contrasts with the sociopolitical organization of the mid-17th century, when the towns of Talaje and Tupiqui (apparently the successor to the old Espogache chiefdom) were evidently subject to the *mico* of Santa Catalina de Guale, Don Alonso Menéndez. It should be noted, however, that the island town of Guale had earlier been an important political center during the late 16th century, although the preeminent settlement during this period (1580s and 1590s) was the neighboring mainland town of Tolomato. The temporary shift of political power to the south (to Asajo/Talaje) during the early 17th century undoubtedly related to the Guale rebellion of 1597, after which Tolomato never regained its important status.

To the south, a similar shift in political power seems to have occurred during the first half of the 17th century. While the cacica Doña Maria of San Juan was subject to San Pedro's Doña Maria Meléndez in 1606 (on Cumberland Island), and the province of Mocama was commonly referred to as that of San Pedro throughout the early 17th century, San Juan's Clemente Bernal ultimately rose to preeminence over all of Mocama by the time of his death in 1665 (see below). Furthermore, as San Pedro declined and ultimately vanished in the early 1660s,[2] its former satellite town of Santa Maria appears to have risen in its stead, eventually becoming the heir apparent to the powerful cacique of San Juan (see below).

In part, these shifts in the administrative centers of the Guale and Mocama regions may be attributed to the complexities of traditional chiefly inheritance within each aboriginal society. Nonetheless, other concurrent sociopolitical transformations become readily evident by comparing the documentary information dating to these two periods. A simple glance at the late 17th-century mission lists (see Appendix B) for Guale and Mocama reveals a striking contrast with the long lists of subject towns and villages comprising the early 17th-century chiefdoms in the same region (see, for example, Jones, 1978: 205–209). There is good evidence that during the first half of the 17th century the provinces of Guale and Mocama underwent a remarkable shift in settlement systems, inasmuch as chiefdoms composed of a multiplicity of apparently separate settlements had by the last half of the century been reduced to only a handful of distinct towns.

The few towns comprising Guale and Mocama during the late 17th century seem to have been more or less spatially discrete populations living together as a community. Nevertheless, as is clear in many of the documents in this volume, many of the names of the villages that once made up the early 17th-century chiefdoms in this region seem to have persisted throughout the late 17th century, generally as hereditary titles possessed by individuals living together in these core towns. Furthermore, these titular leaders seem also to have had "vassals" of their own, although presumably mixed within the general population of the town. How can this phenomenon be explained?

The difference appears to lie more in the physical location of each former satellite village, and not necessarily in its human composition or leadership. What changed during the early 17th century was not so much the overall sociopolitical organization of Guale and Mocama, but the distribution of population across the landscape. Specifically, while outlying satellite villages did not completely disappear, they seem to have physically relocated to central towns, where they apparently maintained a distinct identity within the general population of each town. As a result, each of the core towns traced in the discussion below seems to have been composed of the remnants of chiefly lineages from many or all of the numerous early 17th-century satellite villages that formed the five chiefdoms noted above.

What were the processes leading to the reduction and aggregation of the population of the Guale and Mocama areas during the first half of the 17th century? In all likelihood, the transformation along this coastal region north of St. Augustine was not unlike that experienced by the Timucua mission province of interior northern Florida at about the same time (Worth, 1992). Population loss within the context of massive epidemics and the stresses of the draft labor system resulted in increasingly dysfunctional aboriginal societies, and whether by Spanish or Indian intent (and probably by a combination of both), settlement systems became increasingly centralized within the context of the colonial system of Spanish Florida. The interior Timucua province of the late 17th century bore a remarkable resemblance to Guale and Mocama at the same time, inasmuch as each society had been reduced to just a few central towns along the primary transportation corridors west and north of St. Augustine.

That Guale had been subject to these same stresses is clear from the 1657 petition of the cacique Don Alonso Menéndez of Santa Catalina and four other Guale caciques,[3] which reveals among other things that "this province of Guale has been left destitute of human forces on account of so many deaths" (Menéndez et al., 1657).[4] Indeed, that year Governor Diego de Rebolledo lumped Timucua and Guale together, noting that there were "very few Indians" left in either province due to plagues (Rebolledo, 1657). Such overwhelming stresses had undoubtedly contributed to outbreak of unrest in both provinces during the spring and summer of 1656, when Governor Rebolledo ordered the formal activation of the Indian militia in all the mission provinces. Responding to a perceived threat of foreign attack, Rebolledo demanded as many Guale warriors as could be sent (particularly those who were trained in the use of firearms),[5] and ordered the purchase on credit of as much corn as could be spared (Rebolledo, 1656). Although the leaders of Guale readily complied, the subsequent outbreak of the Timucuan Rebellion as a result of this same order ultimately led the governor to seize all the Guale firearms and send the warriors home, leaving the Guale caciques disgusted with Rebolledo (see Worth, 1992: 244–246). Rumor had it that had Timucua succeeded, the Guale province would have risen up as well.

In 1658, Governor Rebolledo sent Captain Nicolás Estevez de Carmenatis to conduct what would be the last formal visitation of the provinces of Guale and Mocama before the beginning of their retreat southward only three years later. Although the written record of this visitation has yet to be discovered, the text of the governor's original order for the visitation provides a broad overview of the status of Guale and Mocama during the mid-17th century. In particular, the following commission reveals some of the major concerns within these mission provinces in 1658, including the installation of caciques, the recovery of Christian fugitives from the surrounding unconverted provinces, the acquisition of a precise census relative to the standing Indian militia and the labor draft, and the maintenance of justice and good government in Guale and Mocama.

> Inasmuch as His Majesty (whom God preserve) charges me to visit all the provinces of my jurisdiction, and having done so in person in that of Timuqua and Apalache, and being now at the point of departure in order to do so in the [province] of Guale, I find myself with such a great number of occupations, such as the prep-

aration of this post and the dispatch of ships to the kingdom of New Spain for supplies for the sustenance of the infantrymen who serve His Majesty in this presidio, and because I am informed by some missionaries who serve in the said province, and likewise by the soldiers who frequent it, that it is necessary to place a remedy for many things, from which some inconveniences could result, and for what relates to the growth of the conversion and conservation of its natives and the tranquility of the said missionaries, and so that the towns that there are in the said province should have a code of regulations [*aranzel*][6] in each head [town] that might be necessary, so that through it they might know how they are to govern, and it is necessary for this effect, on account of the aforementioned causes, to send a person of satisfaction and sufficient qualities, and with much experience in these [provinces] so that in the name of His Majesty and mine he should place in execution what is ordered of him, and because these and other [qualities] concur in the [person] of Captain Nicolás de Carmenatis, who is [captain] of artillery in this presidio, I name him for my lieutenant governor and captain general, so that as such, upon receiving this [title] he should depart for the provinces that are designated to him, and being in them with the authority of my own person, he should execute the orders that he carries and whatever he might find suitable for its good discourse and for the conservation and good government of the natives, as is hoped from his person, and for all of this in His Royal Name I give him complete power, as sufficient as is necessary, to pacify and punish if it should be needed, to put casiques in possession [of their caciquedoms], if there are vacancies, taking declarations legally before a notary from the principals, as is accustomed, and to recover fugitive *cimarrones*, offering them on my behalf that those who appear to the said Captain in the first instant, within fifteen days at most, without much delay in recovering themselves and asking for pardon for their crimes, will be relieved of punishment, and if not, those who he can have at his hands he will punish, or send them to this city well-guarded, where they will be given the punishment that is suitable, for being obstinate and little fearful of God Our Lord, living among pagans, and the said Captain, as [stated] in a chapter of the regulatory code, will advise them to take particular caution with taking a census of [*enpadronar*] all the Indians who are vassals of His Majesty in the villages where they are with their families, bringing upon his return a relation of those who, if it were necessary, could take up arms,[7] and whom he will obligate to have and hold [their weapons] in all places, without any lack in this, on pain of being punished, and he will likewise bring a relation of the people who can remain in each one of the said villages for their guard, and for the labor,[8] attending to all the aforementioned with the selfless punctuality and faithfulness that is suitable to royal service, without following any other opinion, [and the captain will] hear the complaints from each particular person, and having heard them, he will do justice, always reserving for me what I should hand down in grave crimes, because in not doing so in affairs of such importance, in these consists the good government of the said provinces, and the affairs should remain once and for all settled, in order to report on it to His Majesty, and in falling short in something of this, proceedings will be made against him, and in this conformity I command to all the *micos*, casiques, their heirs, governors of casiquedoms, principal Indians, *mandadores*, *chacales*,[9] and the rest of the populus, and to the infantry he takes at his charge, and to any other people who find themselves in the said province of Guale, as well as that of Mocama, or who go to them on other matters, that they should obey and hold the said Captain Nicolás de Carmenatis for my lieutenant governor and captain general, and obey the orders he gives them in writing or verbally, giving him all the help and favor that might be needed during the time that this commission lasts, until returning to this city, which will be with the greatest brevity that he can, because I will order he who does not do so to be punished in public, and the said captain is likewise charged above all with the good treatment of the Indians on all occasions, not consenting that any aggravation be done to them, for thus is suitable to the royal service of His Majesty.

Since in 1658 there was as yet no provincial military garrison in Guale, Governor Rebolledo named Captain Estevez de Carmenatis his provincial lieutenant for the duration of his visitation, giving him the authority to settle all but the most serious matters (which would be concluded by the governor himself). This contrasts with later visitations, when the resident lieutenant of Guale and Mocama was temporarily suspended for the duration of the visitation (see Document 9).

The visitation order above is perhaps most significant with respect to this volume for what it does *not* mention. Specifically, in 1658, the mission provinces of Guale and

Mocama were characterized by concerns that were largely internal to Spanish Florida—the maintenance of orderly chiefly inheritance, the effect of population decline on the Indian militia and on the *repartimiento* labor draft, the status of the religious conversion in the mission towns, and the preservation of justice and effective government within the provinces. Though experiencing severe and often traumatic stresses as a result of regional depopulation (as were many other provinces within Spanish Florida), Guale and Mocama existed in a state of relative tranquility with respect to the outside world, particularly when compared with the next three decades. Only with the arrival of raiders from the north three years later would attention shift toward external concerns, as the indigenous societies of the Georgia coast were thrust into the fringes of a global conflict.

What is perhaps most remarkable about the Guale and Mocama provinces at mid-century is the apparent persistence of chiefly lineages within the context of regional population loss and localized settlement aggregation. Even as outlying satellite villages appear to have been drawn in to the political centers of Guale and Mocama, the distinctive identity of their hereditary chiefly lineages appears to have survived, at least in name. The core towns that made up the Guale and Mocama provinces of the mid-17th century thus represented aggregations of originally dispersed local clusters of villages, reflecting a remarkable degree of cultural adaptability under stress. In this sense, the Guale and Mocama of 1655 were truly syncretic societies, having formed out of the remnants of a declining aboriginal culture within the dynamics of the colonial system of Spanish Florida. Nevertheless, these products of the process of Spanish colonization and missionization would soon enter into a period of rapid and violent changes, which would sweep these aboriginal inhabitants of the Georgia coast from their homeland in less than a quarter of a century.

CHICHIMECO INVASION OF GUALE, 1661

The year 1661 marked the beginning of the end for the Guale and Mocama mission provinces. Late that spring, news arrived in St. Augustine that "a nation of warrior Indians" had struck Guale from the mainland, "sacking the churches and convents and killing the Christian Indians" (Menéndez Márquez, 1673; Sánchez de Urisa, 1672). On November 15 of that year, Governor Aranguiz y Cotes (1661a) sent the following letter (only partially preserved)[10] to the Crown, describing the events of the past months:

> By letter of the tenth of this past September, sixteen fifty [–] I gave account to Your Majesty how by the [–] of these provinces which borders with [–] walked a nation of a great number of Indians who said they were Chichumecos [and among] them some Englishmen with firearms,[11] and this year of sixteen sixty [one] on the twentieth of the month of June they made an *entrada* in the province of Guale [–] of this presidio minus Guale [–] and it was so unexpected that there descended [the river] that is called Santa Ysabel[12] [–] two hundred canoes, and they entered [–] of Talaxe, the first town [–] province of Guale, from which the Indians [–] village and a missionary [–] such a great number of Chichumeco [–] more than two thousand, they abandoned [–] village and retreated to [the village] of [–] with all the remaining Indians [–] and missionaries [–] the enemies / [—-] with all the [–] which according to what is understood [–] a nation which [borders?] from which [?] [–] me horror in all the [–] that I received the news from [–] a frigate with infantry [–] equipment of war and [–] promised other aid and [–] an occasion those that [–] parts [?] [–] of Zapala, and they carried off [–] the province for not having rushed to their assistance [–] promptly, and seeing [–] that they resisted their [–] they placed themselves in flight [with?] [–] some prisoners and [–] wounded from a bullet [–] Major Juan Sánchez [–] the infantry that [–] help [—-] with enemies and this [–] of enemies hunger and [–] I have advised Your Majesty [–].

Another account of the assault reveals that they "overpowered the village of Santo Domingo de Talaxe, which was a doctrina of the missionaries of San Francisco, and that more than 500 men, among Indians and other nations that use firearms, had descended in rafts [*valsas*] and canoes through the River of Santa Ysavel and had overpowered the said town" (Menéndez Márquez, 1673).

Although the details of this assault are only fragmentary, it seems clear that a body of perhaps as many as two hundred canoes and rafts, carrying between 500 and 2000 Chichimeco warriors armed with firearms, descended the modern Altamaha River from the interior of Georgia and attacked the first town of Guale, Talaje, situated on the northern bank of the river near the modern town of Darien. Based on the accounts above, this mission appears to have been abandoned as a direct result of the attack on June 20, with its inhabitants fleeing to Mission San Joseph de Sapala, situated only 5 leagues distant in a more protected barrier island location off the coast.

When news of this assault arrived several days later (probably June 26), Governor Aranguiz y Cotes immediately dispatched Sergeant Major Juan Sánchez de Uriza northward by land, "in order to stay in the town of Guadalquini and find out about the designs of the enemy" (Menéndez Márquez, 1673). Discovering that the survivors of the assault were in Sapala, and that the Chichimeco had reinforced for a fresh attack and were only half a day's march from Guadalquini (Aranguiz y Cotes, 1661b), on June 29 the governor dispatched Captain Antonio Menéndez Márquez (1673) in charge of a detachment of troops

> to go to the said town of Guadalquini in order to incorporate himself with the said sergeant major, with respect to the bristling number of the enemy, and he charged him to be under his [Sánchez de Uriza's] orders, assisting him, and that they should endeavor to pass to the town and village of Sapala, where all the missionaries and Indians of that province had retreated to, and that they should guard them until the frigates of His Majesty might arrive with the rest of the infantry, and all together they should endeavor to eject the enemy from that province and leave its natives in peace and tranquility.

Apparently at the same time, Captain Antonio de Argüelles was sent with even more troops by way of San Juan del Puerto to join the frigate sent by the governor at Guadalquini, with instructions to join Captain Francisco de la Rocha in Sapala (Aranguiz y Cotes, 1661b). The two were to work together in planning an appropriate defense against further depredations.

Mission San Joseph de Sapala, by then flooded with refugees, seems to have been the target of a second assault by the Chichimeco soon after the abandonment of Mission Santo Domingo. Having constructed "a boat that they made from the boards of the church and convent of Talaje" (Barreda, 1663), the Chichimeco apparently endeavored to follow their initial victory with an attack on Sapala, probably navigating along the inland waterways to the Bar of Ospogue (modern Doboy Sound), just across from Sapelo Island. Filling the vessel with 70 warriors, the Chichimecos launched their construction into the open water, at which point "the current of the Bar of Ospogue drew them out to sea, and they drowned in view of everyone, with no little sentiment from the enemy, through the said people being among those of most valor." Other Chichimecos, including "some of their principal leaders," were killed in battle with the Guale Indians, and they lost "many more, who in their retreat and flight died of hunger on the roads."

Largely frustrated in their continued assault on Guale, the Chichimeco raiders "turned around to retreat through where they came" and "went away to the [province] of Tama and to that of Catufa" (Aranguiz y Cotes, 1662a). Based on this statement, the Chichimeco seem to have withdrawn by way of the Altamaha River, evidently heading north along the Oconee River to the interior provinces noted.[13] Not far behind was Captain Juan Sánchez de Uriza leading a force of Spanish soldiers pursuing the Chichimeco into the interior and engaging them at least once, resulting in some wounded (Aranguiz y Cotes, 1661a; Sánchez de Urisa, 1672; Santos, 1672).[14] Probably using forces based in the Apalachee province, the Spaniards finally managed to capture 4 Chichimeco prisoners in the province of Apalachicola, some 180 leagues distant from St. Augustine, and their subsequent interrogation revealed much regarding their identity and origins (Aranguiz y Cotes, 1662a).

Bringing Chisca Indians from the western interior as interpreters for the four Chichimecos, the Spaniards learned from their captives that they had come from Jacán (Virginia), and that "very near to their lands, which were not more than one very large river in between, was fortified a nation of white people who made war on them every day, and who were approaching these provinces" (Aranguiz y Cotes, 1662a). The prisoners also related that the Chichimeco were at that time situated in the provinces of Tama and Catufa following their raid on Guale. This information evidently confirmed the governor's earlier intelligence, which suggested that these Chichimeco originated far to the north, and were in some way involved with the English.

There seems little doubt that the Chichimeco of the Spanish sources were in fact one and the same as the Rechahecrians, a group of Indians who settled at the falls of the James River in Virginia in 1656 (Swanton, 1922: 294–296; Crane, 1956: 5–6,16-17; Smith, 1987: 131–133). Following early hostilities with these English colonists and their Indian allies, the immigrants seem to have established peace with the Virginians. If, as others have argued, these Rechahecrians were indeed the displaced Erie of the Great Lakes region, forced to the south in the mid-1650s during the Iroquois wars, then they almost certainly had been armed with firearms prior to their arrival on the Virginia frontier (Smith, 1987: 132). Nevertheless, there is sound evidence that a trade in firearms and munitions soon developed between the Rechahecrians and the English colonists of Virginia during the late 1650s, and that these Chichimeco arrived with their weapons in the interior of modern Georgia within only three years (Swanton, 1922: 294–295).

In the fall of 1659, Governor Aranguiz y Cotes received notice from his lieutenant in the Apalache province of northwestern Florida of the arrival of enemy warriors in the interior:

> [E]ighty leagues from there [Apalache] there had arrived by a large river some striped Indians, and with them white people, and that they brought some firearms and among them two campaign pieces, and they came doing much damage, and the quantity is up to a thousand men and whites suspected to be some of those Englishmen who reside toward Jacán, but the design which they bring is unknown (Aranguiz y Cotes, 1659a).

During an investigation of the necessity for constructing a fort in Apalache, the governor elaborated that

> today His Grace finds himself with very abundant news that through the provinces of Apalachocoli and that of the Chacatos, bordering on that of Apalache, people are coming in great quantity, and those who they could be has not been well understood, due to the little capacity of the Indians, more than that they are white and blond people, and they bring in their company many warrior Indians, their faces striped, and who use firearms and come laying waste to the land (Aranguiz y Cotes, 1659b).

Although at that early date the identity of these Indian intruders was unknown, the governor later referred to these warriors from the north as the very same Chichimeco who carried out the 1661 attack on Guale (Aranguiz y Cotes, 1661a; translated above).

While there is no independent confirmation of the actual presence of Virginia traders among the Chichimeco along the northern Spanish frontier, it seems clear that such traders did provide both firearms and munitions for use by the Chichimeco raiders. When the first Englishman from Charles Town reached the town of the Chichimeco (known as the Westo by the Carolinians) in 1674 (see below), he was greeted with a volley of "fify or sixty small arms" (Woodward, 1674), confirming that not only were the Chichimeco in possession of firearms prior to contact with the Carolinians, but also powder and shot, which could only have been supplied on a regular basis by English traders to the north.

The Chichimeco were probably the first[15] in a long line of Indian groups recruited into the burgeoning northern trade in Christian Indian slaves captured from the Spanish missions. Upon first contact with Carolinians more than a decade after the assault on Guale, the Westo were described to be "well provided with arms, ammunition, tradeing cloath and other trade from the northward for which at set times of the year they truck drest deare skins furrs and young Indian Slaves" (Woodward, 1674). The little direct extant evidence regarding the Chichimeco suggests that their arrival in the Georgia interior during 1659 may have been directly motivated by the demand for slaves in Virginia, and that their assault of June 1661 was in effect a slave raid. The governor's later comment that these Chichimeco "ate human flesh" (Aranguiz y Cotes, 1662a) almost certainly reflects the very real fears of Guale survivors who had witnessed their relatives and neighbors carried off alive.

Such rumors persisted into the 1670s among Carolina Indians also victimized by Chichimeco raids.

The invasion of Guale in 1661 represented the first major assault on the Georgia coastal missions that directly resulted from the English colonial presence to the north.[16] It also marked the first step in a series of relocations that would ultimately leave the Georgia coast largely vacant. The destruction and abandonment of Mission Santo Domingo de Talaje at the mouth of the Altamaha River was followed by the reestablishment of the mission on nearby St. Simons Island under another name, Santo Domingo de Asajo, probably located at Cannons Point on the northern end of the island. Although this southernmost Guale mission was now situated on the same island as the northernmost Mocama mission, San Buenaventura de Guadalquini, the island location provided far greater security from raids originating in the interior, and probably easier access by boat.

Significantly, the raid on Guale was evidently only one of the least successful of a series of raids carried out by the Chichimeco during the early 1660s, most of which occurred deep in the interior of modern Georgia, beyond the scope of Spanish documentation. A year after the Guale assault, Governor Aranguiz y Cotes (1662a) noted regarding the Chichimeco that "had I not rushed to resist their design, they might have laid waste to it [the province of Guale], as notice has been had from other [provinces] of pagan Indians who came fleeing from them." If the Chichimeco had instilled fear in the mission province of Guale, they seem to have inspired true terror among the provinces of unconverted Indians still living in the interior, who may well have been subjected to even greater depredations without the assistance of the Spanish infantry. The old province of Tama, along with others along the upper Oconee River of northeastern Georgia and other regions, was rapidly laid waste, and the Spanish missions would soon feel the full impact of the Chichimeco raids.

ARRIVAL OF THE YAMASSEE

Soon after the first assault of the Chichimeco upon Guale, the coastal regions of modern Georgia and South Carolina were subjected to yet another invasion, but this time not by enemy warriors. The immigrants were pagan Indians, who instead arrived as refugees, apparently fleeing the very same type of depredations to which Guale had been subjected in the summer of 1661. A new geographic order had been established in the interior as a result of the arrival of the Chichimeco, and political allegiances were rapidly polarizing. The Chichimeco had relocated; by early April of 1663, the friars of Guale reported news that the Chichimeco had "left the place where they were living when they descended to this said province of Guale, and went much farther away to the mouth of another river by which one can only descend upon the province of Cofitachique or to that of Escamaçu, distant from this [province] of Guale" (Anguiano, 1663; Campaña, 1663). Although the phrasing of this passage is somewhat ambiguous, in all probability the location being described lies within the bounds of modern South Carolina, perhaps even in the same location along the middle Savannah River visited by Carolina explorer Henry Woodward in 1674 (see below). This location would place the Chichimeco south of the deep interior province of Cofitachequi, in central South Carolina, and northwest of the province of Escamaçu, which provided the only buffer between Guale and the enemy warriors.

The arrival of the Chichimeco in the Savannah River valley may date to late 1662, for in October of that year Governor Aranguiz y Cotes learned of fresh attacks just north of Guale, prompting the dispatch of the following order:

> Inasmuch as today, Tuesday, at three in the morning on the twenty-fourth day of this present month of October, news and notice came to me from the province of Guale by a letter which they wrote me in which they give account how there newly arrived at that province the Indian warriors that they call Chichimecos, who were the same who last year laid siege to the village and doctrina of Santo Domingo de Talaje, and today find themselves in the village which they call Huyache, five leagues distant from Guale, which they destroyed and put to the knife as many people as they found in it, and because it is presumed that they return laying waste to the land, and so that they do not

> make a new assault on the villages and doctrinas of the province of Guale, causing in it new anxieties like the past ones, and being the cause of perturbing the conversion, and for the great suitability to the service of Both Majesties, divine and human, to intercept and impede the passes from then with soldiers who should serve in garrison in the said province, so that they might not raze and destroy it, violating the temples and convents of the missionaries as they did in the [convent] of Talaje, a remedy which ought to be attended to with the diligence and punctuality which a case as important as the present requires, . . . I have commanded to loan a group from the infantry of this presidio with the preparation of their arms, munitions, and equipment of war, and the rest necessary for it, so that they might remain as escort in those villages, in defense and guard of the missionaries and natives who live in it, so that in this manner they might remain with all security (Aranguiz y Cotes, 1662b).

The remaining part of the governor's order named Captain Don Matheo Pacheco y Salgado as the leader of this garrison, commanding him to "go with the greatest brevity which he can to the province of Guale, where he will serve in garrison, electing for the guard station [*la custodia de guardia*] of that province the village which seems to him the most appropriate and suitable" (Aranguiz y Cotes, 1662b). Although the dispatch of soldiers to Guale was relatively common (temporary provincial lieutenants had even been named for Guale, at least in the years of 1651 and 1658),[17] the 1662 order may represent the point at which Mission Santa Catalina de Guale was selected as the permanent garrison headquarters for the Guale province.[18]

The order above also reveals that in the fall of 1662 the Chichimeco assaulted and largely destroyed the town of Huyache, described as 5 leagues from Guale. Inasmuch as this town was not noted to be a part of the Guale province, and the mission town of Guale (Santa Catalina) was located perhaps 10 leagues within the northern boundary of the province, the governor's statement probably refers to Huyache's distance from Guale's provincial border at San Diego de Satuache. This would place the location of Huyache near the mouth of the Savannah River, perhaps just to the south. Consequently, the attack on Huyache might have been occasioned by the arrival of the Chichimeco upstream along the middle Savannah River.

The identity of the inhabitants of Huyache is unclear. The similarity in ending between Satuache and Huyache suggests that the town may have been an indigenous unconverted town along the northern frontier of Guale, or perhaps some sort of outlier of the Satuache mission. Probably as a direct result of the assault on Huyache, Mission San Diego de Satuache was relocated to the south, where by 1666 it had already been aggregated to Santa Catalina de Guale on St. Catherine's Island. The inhabitants of Satuache would remain attached to the population of Santa Catalina throughout the rest of the 17th century, including two more relocations yet to come. It is possible that refugees from the nearby town of Huyache also retreated to Santa Catalina simultaneously, although the following spring this location was noted to be inhabited by members of a new group of Indians, called the Yamassee.

The small garrison established in the fall of 1662 seems to have been withdrawn by the following spring, for during early April of 1663, Captain Antonio de Argüelles was in Guale by order of Governor Aranguiz y Cotes (1663a) in an effort to get the opinions of the Indian *micos* and caciques of Guale regarding the establishment of a permanent military garrison in the province. Concurrently, the friars of Guale were ordered to provide written statments relative to the current status of the province, and to give their opinions as well. Their letters (see Document 6, this volume) provide crucial details regarding this enigmatic group of Indians named Yamassee.

Not only did the friars report that the Chichimeco had retreated deeper into the interior, but also that the province of Escamaçu, bordering Guale on the north, was at that time completely populated by a group of Indians known as "Yamasis," stretching across the mainland all the way from the village of Colon to a place called Uyache Eslaçu (most likely the above-mentioned Huyache). They seem to have been located in a number of villages (more than five), described as being located "six, eight, four, three, two, and more days by road from these provinces" (Anguiano, 1663), and were positioned directly between the enemy Chichimecos and the coastal missions of Guale.

Who were the Yamassee? Although during the following decades the Yamassee would figure prominently in the history of Guale and Mocama, the name itself appears for the first time in these letters, and without any substantial hint as to its derivation. This fact in itself is instructive, inasmuch as the Yamassee seem to represent an aggregation of Indian towns of diverse origins, forced together by necessity along the lower coast of South Carolina in the region previously known as the province of Escamaçu. The Yamassee did not come into existence as a more or less unified social entity until the early 1660s, but they soon became major players on the sociopolitical landscape of the Georgia coastal zone.

As will be seen below, the group of Indians known as Yamassee comprised a remarkable variety of aboriginal towns, some of which seem to have been indigenous to the Escamaçu region, and others of which had retreated there in the face of Chichimeco aggression in the deep interior. The original inhabitants of this region had long enjoyed a limited relationship with the Spanish, as Escamaçu was the site of frequent trading voyages by Spanish vessels out of St. Augustine during the first half of the century, but they were never effectively missionized. The sojourn of the newly formed Yamassee in the old province of Escamaçu would last only a short time, however, for continued attacks from the middle Savannah River valley soon forced them deeper into the Spanish colonial realm, and indeed briefly into Guale and Mocama proper.

GUALE AND MOCAMA DURING THE LATE 1660s

Following the turbulent years of the early 1660s, Guale and Mocama appear to have settled into a more or less stable routine for the next few years. The remaining five Guale missions of San Phelipe de Alave, Santa Catalina de Guale (with Santo Domingo de Satuache aggregated), Santa Clara de Tupiqui, San Joseph de Sapala, and the relocated Santo Domingo de Asajo appear to have remained relatively free from external hostility, although internal disputes and the arrival of more and more refugees continued during these years. The first four missions were consistent contributors to the *repartimiento* labor draft, sending four laborers from each town during the late winter for tasks in the soldiers' cornfields in St. Augustine, not counting four more sent from Satuache at Santa Catalina (Guerra y Vega, 1665a, 1666, 1667a, 1668a, 1669). Asajo was evidently excluded from the labor draft until 1669, perhaps in an effort to permit the town to establish itself in its new location on the northern end of St. Simons Island.

Of the four Mocama missions noted for the 1655 period, only San Buenaventura de Guadalquini and San Juan del Puerto seem to have persisted into the late 1660s. As an indigenous Mocama mission town, San Pedro de Mocama was last mentioned on the 1655 list, and Santa Maria was only noted once in 1665, when its cacica Juana was noted to be the legitimate heir to Clemente Bernal, the deceased cacique of San Juan and principal cacique of all Mocama (Guerra y Vega, 1665b). Since Santa Maria does not appear again as an indigenous Mocama mission after this date, the cacica Juana may have simply relocated her town to San Juan when she assumed the caciquedom of Mocama. The abandoned sites of both San Pedro and Santa Maria were eventually to be reoccupied by immigrant Yamassees, filling the void left by the consolidation of the Mocama missions (see below).

Only Guadalquini was included in the yearly *repartimiento* draft between 1665 and 1669, consistently contributing the largest number of laborers of any town in the entire coastal region, set at five laborers annually. San Juan was typically excluded from *repartimiento* duties due to its labor burden resulting from its location at the principal crossing point of the St. Johns River, serving as the gateway to the northern provinces.

Perhaps the most intriguing feature of the labor draft during the late 1660s is the fact that Governor Guerra y Vega specifically requested that "the Yamase caciques who find themselves in that province" of Guale should send "as many Indians of their nation as they can" (Guerra y Vega, 1666, 1667a, 1668a, 1669). Indeed, the fact that all labor draft orders between 1665 and 1669 explicitly state that the majority of the Indians drafted for *repartimiento* labor were pagans suggests that the Yamassee made up a significant part of the labor force from Guale and Mocama at least as early as 1665. This contrasts with the latest labor draft order known prior to 1665, which made no mention of either pagans or Yamassee in January of 1663 (Aranguiz y Cotes, 1663b). The increasing reliance on these immigrant laborers is evident from Governor Guerra y Vega's 1668 dispatch of Captain Antonio de Argüelles to Guale and Mocama in order to replace a number of fugitive Yamassee laborers, whose absence left the St. Augustine fields "impossible to cultivate" (Guerra y Vega, 1668a).

The reason the Yamassee began to contribute to the Spanish labor draft for Guale and Mocama almost certainly relates to their increasing resettlement inside the territory of these two mission provinces. In 1673, nearly half (24 of 50) of the *repartimiento* laborers extracted from the Guale/Mocama provinces were Yamassee, and at least by 1675, the Indian population living in pagan Yamassee villages within the old Mocama region outnumbered the total number of mission Indians in both Guale and Mocama (see Addendum, Document 1, and below). The process by which this massive influx occurred was probably similar to that described in a 1667 order detailing the petition of two unconverted towns to resettle inside Guale (see Document 7). In this case the caciques of the towns of Santa Elena and Abaya, both from the province of Escamaçu,[19] arrived unexpectedly at the northernmost Guale town of Santa Catalina in the summer of 1667, fleeing from the recent depredations of the Chichimeco. The pagan caciques then formally petitioned the governor of St. Augustine to be given lands on which to settle as refugees, pleading that "today they find themselves without having one settlement, or land assigned to them to be able to make one" (Guerra y Vega, 1667b).

Intriguingly, the cacique of Santa Elena had during the previous four years been involved in dealings with English explorers along the South Carolina coast, and probably had the young English doctor Henry Woodward in his town at the time of this petition. In September 1663, Captain William Hilton from Barbados arrived along the coast near Santa Elena, and was involved in some tense negotiations for the return of several shipwrecked English sailors (incidentally exchanging several letters and some meat and brandy with the other Argüelles brother, Alonso, who had been sent north to Santa Elena in search of the survivors). During this time, the son of the cacique of Santa Elena, named Wommony, was captured and taken to Barbados (Hilton, 1664).

On a second expedition dating to July of 1666, Lt. Colonel Robert Sandford arrived again at Santa Elena (termed Port Royal), and was involved in more amicable dealings with the elderly cacique (Sandford, 1666). Beyond returning the cacique's son Wommony, Sandford agreed to a formal exchange, in which the surgeon Henry Woodward remained behind at Santa Elena in order to learn the language of the Indians, and the son of the cacique's sister (and thus perhaps his heir) was sent away on Sandford's ship. Although the cacique wanted Sandford to return in three or five months, Sandford promised to return in 10 months, and the Indian's sister promised to care for Dr. Woodward so that her brother would receive good treatment. The cacique even went so far as to place Woodward on his "throne," granting him "possession of the whole country" in the name of the English Lords Proprietors (Sandford, 1666).

When May 1667 had passed, and the English explorers had not returned with his nephew, the cacique of Santa Elena seems to have given up hope of his earlier English alliance. Apparently at about that time, the Chichimeco made a final devastating raid on Santa Elena. Described three years later to the first Carolina colonists by Indians farther north along the coast, it was said of Santa Elena ("St. Hellena") that "ye Westoes a rangeing sort of people reputed to be the man eaters had ruinated [that] place killed sev'all of those Indians destroyed & burnt their habitations & that they had come as far as Kayawah doeing the like there" (Swanton, 1922: 66). Faced by the destruction of his town, the cacique of Santa Elena joined with the nearby cacique of Abaya and fled south to Santa Catalina, petitioning the Spanish for protection.

Inasmuch as Henry Woodward eventually found himself in St. Augustine, befriending the parish priest until he made his escape during the 1668 Searles raid on the city, it seems likely that Woodward was either turned over at that time by the cacique of Santa Elena or simply took advantage of the change in circumstances to save his life.

In August 1667, Governor Guerra y Vega granted permission for the relocation of these two towns within Guale, dispatching the experienced Captain Antonio de Argüelles with an order to "see and identify the locations and lands which can be given to the said pagan caciques of Santa Elena and Abaya so that they might form towns with their vassals and make their fields" (Guerra y Vega, 1667b). The order further stipulated that "the lands which are thus given and assigned to the said pagan caciques be with the approval of the caciques of the said province of Guale, and not in harm of them or their vassals." Although among the stated reasons for granting permission to settle in Guale was the possibility that "because by having communication with the Catholic Indians of the said province of Guale some of the said pagans could reduce themselves to our sacred Catholic faith," the later dominance of pagan refugees in the *repartimiento* labor draft from Guale and Mocama suggests that their arrival was seen as a revitalization of population levels (and thus the labor pool) in the northern mission provinces.

Based on census figures from the 1670s and 1680s, it is clear that substantial numbers of pagan refugees were allowed to settle in Guale and Mocama during these turbulent decades. Nevertheless, the names Santa Elena and Abaya are not among the towns mentioned. While it is possible that the remnants of these two towns joined the many others who became known as the Yamassee, later evidence hints that these particular towns might never have actually settled in Guale, or perhaps left soon after their arrival (see below). As will become evident below, the aboriginal group known as the Yamassee Indians comprised a variety of constituent towns, evidently forced together by necessity. Their individual identity became increasingly less visible in the historical documentation, with the name Yamassee taking precedence for both the Spanish and the English.

As noted above, beginning in the mid-1660s, incessant slave raiding by the Chichimeco on the middle Savannah River appears to have forced a variety of once separate aboriginal towns and villages from the unconverted interior and coastal regions of Georgia and South Carolina to take refuge on the margins of the Spanish sphere of influence. One of these areas of aggregation was the old province of Escamaçu, north of Guale and southeast of the Chichimeco. Although at first (ca. 1663) these refugees apparently endeavored to take advantage of their proximity to the Spanish without actually entering the mission provinces, continued hostilities from the nearby Chichimeco soon forced many groups to flee southward, and petition the Spanish for permission to settle within the then largely depopulated provinces of Guale and Mocama.

Once there, the benefits of protection by the Spanish infantry were paid for by substantial yearly contributions to the *repartimiento* labor draft. In this way, the Yamassee soon took on a central role in the political struggle for the Georgia coast. As recent and largely unconverted arrivals to the Spanish colonial system, their long-term allegiance was ephemeral at best, and yet they soon became the backbone of the Indian labor pool from the northern mission provinces, contributing half of each year's *repartimiento* draft. Partly as a consequence of this fact, the collection of refugee towns known as the Yamassee soon became a more and more cohesive confederacy, contributing to the formation of yet another syncretic society within the context of European colonization. Just as the Guale and Mocama provinces of the late 17th century represented a specific response to the conditions of missionization, so too did the Yamassee form out of the ruins of a Precolumbian aboriginal social order. The brief union of these three groups—Guale, Mocama, and Yamassee—would dominate the history of the Georgia coast for some two decades, although their future destinies lay along different paths.

ARRIVAL OF THE CAROLINIANS

In 1670 a major new player in the geopolitics of the 17th-century southeast arrived some distance north of Guale and Mocama.

In April of that year, a group of 150 English colonists sailed into the mouth of the Ashley River to found Charles Town, the first permanent settlement of the new Carolina colony. Whereas during the previous half century the English colonies along the northern Atlantic coastline had only had a more or less indirect and occasional effect on the Spanish colony of Florida, the establishment of Charles Town marked the beginning of direct and increasingly constant competition between English and Spanish colonists, with modern Georgia falling precisely along the zone of dispute.

During these last decades of the 17th century, two primary regions of conflict developed between Carolina and Florida. The first, forming the focus of the present essay, was the coast of Georgia, or more specifically the old mission provinces of Guale and Mocama. Here would unfold a short-lived but devastating competition between Carolina and Florida, in which the indigenous inhabitants of the Georgia coast, along with their Spanish allies, would be forced to retreat in under 15 years. The second region was deep in the interior, in western Georgia and present-day Alabama, where the battle for control of the emerging Creek confederacy would subsequently be fought between the Spanish, the English, and their respective Indian allies.

Although the specific reasons are unclear, at about the time when Charles Town was established, Mission San Phelipe de Alave was relocated far to the south, moving to the midpoint of modern Cumberland Island, perhaps near Table Point or Brickhill Bluff (see Appendix A).[20] The effective result of this move was the relocation of the northernmost Guale mission town to the middle of the Mocama province. The fact that San Phelipe was moved far away from Santa Catalina might have been related to a political dispute between these two towns which seems to have emerged during 1665 (see Document 5, Order 4). Regardless of this, however, the relocation itself was probably a preemptive strategic move, inasmuch as the removal of San Phelipe left the garrison town of Guale, Santa Catalina (with Satuache already aggregated), on the exposed northern frontier of Spanish Florida. Furthermore, the placement of San Phelipe on the northern part of Cumberland Island filled a major gap in the northern mission chain, establishing a way station along the more or less abandoned coastline between the remaining Mocama missions of San Buenaventura de Guadalquini and San Juan del Puerto.

Yet another move which was carried out somewhat later during this period was the relocation of Santa Clara de Tupiqui to the site of Mission San Joseph de Sapala, accomplishing the removal of the final mainland Guale mission to the barrier islands. These missions would remain joined until the final retreat from the Georgia coast. Although the exact date of this relocation is not clear, Tupiqui and Sapala were apparently still separate as late as 1673 (see Addendum, Document 1), but were together in the town of Sapala prior to 1675, when Tupiqui was not listed on either mission list (see Appendix B). Although the aggregation of Sapala and Tupiqui may largely have stemmed from their historical connection, and perhaps may have been related in some way to the 1668 death of the *mico* of Sapala, and his subsequent Spanish-administered replacement (Guerra y Vega, 1668b), in a larger perspective this move seems to have again been a strategic one, particularly in light of the fact that the overall Spanish/Indian policy along the Georgia coast during this time was to relocate mainland missions to the more sheltered barrier islands.

Direct competition between Carolina and Florida did not erupt immediately following the establishment of Charles Town, although Governor Guerra y Vega did in fact launch an abortive seaborne attempt to extinguish the fledgling English colony in 1670.[21] The increase in English traffic along the mid-Atlantic coast did lead to occasional minor confrontations between English vessels and the residents of Guale during this period, such as the accidental arrival of a Barbadian sloop at Mission Santa Catalina in May of 1670 (see Crane, 1956: 10; Bushnell, 1994), and a similar incident at Sapala in late 1674 (Ponce de León, 1675), but it was not until the end of the decade that Guale and Mocama became the direct targets of English-sponsored hostility. The reasons for this are complex, but a major factor in this delay was the Chichimeco themselves, who indirectly blocked the southward advance of the Carolinians during their first decade.

The polarizing effect of the immigrant Chichimeco (known to the Carolina colonists as Westo), who had used the middle Savannah River as their slave-raiding base since the early 1660s, soon effectively split the Indian groups along the Georgia/South Carolina coast. Coalescing along the northern coastal fringe of Guale after the violent arrival of the Chichimeco, the Yamassee soon came to be regarded as Spanish allies, and by the time Charles Town was founded to the north, Indian groups in this area were effectively walled in to the south and west. Referring to the neighboring Cusabo Indians, William Owen declared in September 1670 that "to ye southward they will not goe, fearing the Yamases Spanish comeraro [*camarada*] as ye Indian termes it. Ye Westoes are behind them a mortall enemie of theires whom they say are ye man eaters of them they are more afraid then ye little children are of ye Bull beggers in England" (Crane, 1956: 12). In effect, the Indians of the present-day South Carolina coast were thus more or less forced into an alliance with their new English neighbors, further polarizing the regional social landscape.

Probably very soon after the foundation of Charles Town, during the closing year of Governor Guerra y Vega's term, yet another garrison was placed in Santa Catalina under the command of Captain Nicolás Fernández de Goyas,[22] and this post was continued during the term of succeeding Governor Don Manuel de Cendoya, who replaced the sick Fernández de Goyas less than a week after his installation (Cendoya, 1671). On January 12, 1672, Governor Cendoya officially raised the post to that of lieutenant governor, appointing Captain Francisco Pacheco as the first in a long and continuous line of provincial lieutenants for Guale. With this act, Santa Catalina became the formal garrison headquarters for Guale, and probably at or near the same time became the northernmost defensive post against the new English colony of Carolina (with the withdrawal of San Phelipe).

Within only two months following the formal establishment of the Santa Catalina garrison, Squad Leader Pedro de Arcos (at that time acting lieutenant of the Guale province) was visited by two Indians from the province of Santa Elena, who reported that they had visited the new English settlement of San Jorge (Charles Town) the previous month. Returning from Mission Asajo, where he had gone "to arrange [*componer*] the pagan Indians who had arrived there,"[23] Lieutenant Pacheco interviewed the Indians, said to be "of those that they call Chiluques" (Arcos, 1672; Cendoya, 1672; Pacheco, 1672). Although the text of this first interview and a later one done in St. Augustine focused on the population and fortifications of the fledgling English colony to the north, details within the text are revealing regarding the Indian inhabitants of the English/Spanish frontier.

The primary informant was a Christian Indian named Diacun (1672), who was said to be a "native of Santa Elena," and who spoke the Guale language.[24] He indicated that early in February 1672, he and four companions had gone to Charles Town, where they saw several ships carrying new settlers, and about thirty houses and limited fortifications. Both on the way to Charles Town and on his return voyage to Santa Elena, Diacun indicated that he had spoken with the cacica of Ospo (indeed, her brother accompanied the group to the English settlement), who had provided intelligence regarding the English to the Spaniards in 1671. The cacica did not wish to go to St. Augustine again, since "the other time she had arrived down to Santa Catalina to see the Spaniards, and they had sent her to St. Augustine, and thus she did not wish to come because she was very afraid" (Diacun, 1672; Pacheco, 1672). After returning to Santa Elena, Diacun proceeded southward to Santa Catalina without his first companions, because "upon arriving at his land he found that the cacique of Santa Elena and other principals had died, and thus the rest [of the Indians] counseled the others not to come here [to Santa Catalina] since they would occupy a long time" (Pacheco, 1672).

The testimony above indicates that the town of Ospo, previously located within the Guale province (and twice burned for participation in the Guale rebellions of 1576 and 1597), was evidently located at that time between Santa Elena and Charles Town, and its leaders seem to have been acting as agents for the English during the early 1670s. Diacun testified that the cacica had deceived the

Governor in 1671, lying about the existence of "three castles" in Charles Town, when he had seen "no more than four poles placed there, and several others fallen to the ground" (Pacheco, 1672). The cacica of Ospo was apparently exaggerating the strength of the English colony, as Diacun's testimony revealed that the settlers were dying (he personally witnessed five English settlers die during his stay), and that they were unable to provide him even with food for the return journey, since the neighboring "Indians of Cofatachiqui" were killing the "cows and pigs and whatever they had" (Diacun, 1672; Pacheco, 1672). The brother of Ospo's cacica was even reported to have gone to the English, offering that "I will dare to take you to Santa Catalina, for there are few Spaniards, and we will seize them."

The incident above confirms that the Carolina/Florida frontier, and specifically the lower coast of present-day South Carolina, was home to quite a diversity of Indian groups during the first years following the arrival of the Chichimeco in the early 1660s, and that the inhabitants of such towns regularly visited both English and Spanish settlements. The existence of a town named Ospo, presumably related to the late 16th-century Guale town of the same name, in this region suggests that at least some of the settlements comprising the emergent Yamassee confederacy had originated on the Georgia coast to the south (Huspah was one of the Yamassee towns allied to the English during the late 17th and early 18th centuries [Swanton, 1922; Crane, 1956; Green, 1991]). The fact that the chiefly lineage of Ospo (also referred to as Ospogue) persisted throughout this period and beyond within the Guale mission province implies that a division may have occurred at some point among the inhabitants of the former town of Ospo. Some seem to have relocated to the north of Santa Elena, while others eventually became attached to Mission San Phelipe in the Guale province (see Document 9).

The identity of the Indians referred to as Chiluque during the 1670s is even less clear. Minimally, the Indian town of Santa Elena was within the grouping known at that time as the Chiluque "nation" (Medina, 1678). The testimony above is supplemented by later evidence that confirm the identity of the inhabitants of Santa Elena as Chiluque. In September of 1678, Squad Leader Bernardo de Medina, stationed at Mission Santa Catalina, greeted "two medium-sized canoes with people of the nation that they call Chiluques, and in each canoe came one cacique." Having come "from their towns of Santa Elena and from San Jorge," the Indians arrived to trade "deer meat, bear fat [*manteca de oso*], and other animals" (Medina, 1678). A pagan Indian "native of the settlement of Sancta Helena" had arrived in Santa Catalina the previous year on a similar mission, trading "beans, acorns, nuts, roasted deer [*benado asado*], and fat, which is an ancient custom among them, and most of the Christians do it, and they trade it for clothes or beads" (Hita Salazar, 1677). This latter Indian was interviewed in the Guale language, confirming the fact that the inhabitants of Santa Elena spoke a language at least similar to that of Guale.

The cultural identity of the Indians living in and around Santa Elena during the 1660s and 1670s is far from clear based on a variety of English and Spanish sources. As discussed above, although in 1663 this region was still described as the province of Escamaçu (a name associated with the unconverted Indians in this region throughout the early 17th century), it was at that time inhabited by the recently arrived Yamassee. The 1663 English expedition of William Hilton and the 1666 expedition of Robert Sandford found an important Indian town located at Santa Elena, but the subsequent destruction of the town by Chichimeco raiders seems to have led its cacique to seek refuge in 1667 among the Spanish missions to the south. In 1670, the town of Santa Elena was described by the English as ruined. However, in 1672, a Christian Indian native of Santa Elena was described as a Chiluque Indian (apparently the earliest application of this name), and at that time the cacique of Santa Elena was reported to have died along with several principals of the town. Subsequent trading visits to Guale by Indians (including two caciques) from Santa Elena in 1677 and 1678 confirmed that the Chiluque understood the Guale language. Nevertheless, with the backing of their recent English neighbors, the Chiluque were one of three groups that assaulted and destroyed

Mission Santa Catalina in 1680, even though they were described at that time as having been former allies of the Spanish (see below).

Although the name Chiluque strongly resembles that of the Cherokee of the Appalachian highlands, later evidence suggests that these were two separate groups. In his 1681 census of Guale and Mocama, Francisco de Fuentes listed both the Ohiluques (Chiluques) and the Chalaques (presumably Cherokee) among the English-allied enemies of Guale, suggesting that he considered them to be distinct from one another (see Document 7). The term Chiluque was instead used consistently during the 1670s to describe the residents of Santa Elena, immediately to the north of Guale, and as yet there is no other evidence to suggest that Cherokees from the deep interior were living in the old province of Santa Elena along the coast at this time. In fact, Chiluque may well derive from the same Muskhogean term as Cherokee, meaning "people of a different language," which would simply suggest that the inhabitants of Santa Elena during this period spoke a different language or dialect (although they clearly understood the Guale language, uniformly used by interpreters when speaking to the Chiluque of Santa Elena). Such a possibility would indeed be consistent with the interpretation of the old province of Escamaçu/Santa Elena being a haven for refugees from a variety of regions, most or all of which came to be known as Yamassee Indians. Nevertheless, whether these Chiluque of Santa Elena were identical with, part of, or distinct from the emerging Yamassee confederacy is presently unclear based on existing documentation.

Bishop Díaz Vara Calderón's 1675 description of the region to the north of Guale provides further information regarding the Santa Elena hinterland. Beginning at Mission Santa Catalina, the bishop noted that

> from there one goes two leagues to the Bar of Asopo, and from there behind banks and outside of bars and rivers, in fourteen leagues of distance, in the province of Escamaçu, today subject to the *Mico* of Cofatache, near the village of Oristan, is that of Santa Helena, which was of Christians, and at twenty-four leagues the port of San Jorge, today a settlement of Englishmen, eighty-four [leagues] distant from St. Augustine.

Although the bishop's description is somewhat convoluted, the structure of the Spanish text suggests that he located the town of Santa Elena 14 leagues from the Bar of Asopo (between St. Catherines and Ossabaw Islands, just 2 leagues north of Mission Santa Catalina) and 24 leagues south of Charles Town, and that it was within the province of Escamaçu, considered at that time to be politically subject to the province of "Cofatache," or probably Cofitachequi (located deep in the interior of Carolina). Whether or not this last reference is reliable (the bishop apparently did not visit this northern region), Santa Elena clearly remained an important town within the Escamaçu province north of Guale, and its Chiluque inhabitants would soon play an important role in the southward retreat of Guale (as the brother of Ospo's cacica had proposed in 1672).

Although the Carolina colonists began exploring the frontier soon after their arrival, making contacts with various Indian groups in their vicinity, including the famed interior province of Cofitachiqui in 1670 (Crane, 1956: 13), it was not until October 1674 that the ambitious Dr. Henry Woodward made first contact with the Chichimeco/Westo. Prior to that time, the Westo had been regarded as hostile enemies even by the Carolinans. Nonetheless, Woodward traveled a week into the interior in the company of a group of returning Westo Indians, arriving at their palisaded town on the western bank of the middle reaches of the present-day Savannah River (Woodward, 1674). His description of the town, including the long bark-covered houses with Indian scalps hanging from long poles, provides further evidence for the northern origins of the Chichimeco, and leaves no doubt as to their role as slave raiders armed and supported by more northerly English colonies (almost certainly Virginia; see above).

Beyond this, Woodward's account further suggests that the Chichimeco/Westo raided far and wide in the Southeast, antagonizing a variety of Indian groups to the north and west, including "Cowatoe" (Coweta), "Chorakae" (Cherokee), "Cussetaws" (Kasihta), "Checsaws" (Chickasaw), and "Chiskers" (Chisca), all of which were reported to be hostile enemies. Indeed, the early raids in the interior of Georgia and the 1661 assault on

Guale were but the first in a series of raids that would span two decades. Perhaps in large part due to the protection of the Spanish infantry, Guale remained largely secure during most of this period, and the Yamassee aggregated just north of Guale soon retreated under the protection of Spanish guns. Slaves were to be found in plentiful quantities in other areas, however, and the Chichimeco seem to have boasted great success with their direct supply of guns, powder, and shot from Virginia. When the Virginia explorer John Lederer penetrated the North Carolina interior from Virginia in 1670, he found that the Ocaneechee and Catawba Indians were well aware of these Chichimeco, known as "Rickohockan" or "Oustack" (Westo),[25] and regarded them as extremely hostile (Swanton, 1922: 296).

The situation of the Chichimeco only became easier with the establishment of Charles Town, however, for following Dr. Woodward's contact in 1674 they shifted their trading connections to the south, circumventing the earlier Virginia connection. For the rest of the decade, the Chichimeco/Westo played a pivotal role in Carolina Indian policy. Although their depredations seem to have been directed more toward unconverted Indian groups largely beyond the realm of Spanish protection, the Chichimeco became notorious to the Spaniards. In 1675, a Chisca Indian woman who had escaped from slavery in Charles Town reported that the Chichimeco were in fact being aided by the Carolinians, and had designs on the mission provinces, testifying that

> the English are united and confederated with another nation of thieving Indians called Chichimecos, so that these make war on and disturb the natives already converted to the Catholic religion, and who find themselves under obedience to His Majesty, entering in the provinces of this jurisdiction to do all evil and damage to them, induced by the said English (Hita Salazar, 1675).

The Chisca woman had been "taken to be sold [in exchange] for a shotgun at the settlement of the English that is on this coast, called San Jorxe" (Escovedo, 1675). During his visitation of Guale that same year, Bishop Gabriel Díaz Vara Calderón (1675) described the territory inland from the Atlantic coast as being inhabited by scattered settlements of "the nation of the Chichimecos, very numerous pagans so barbarous and cruel that their only goal is to assail the villages of Christians and pagans alike, taking away their lives without pardoning age, sex, or estate, roasting and eating them." Two years later, an Indian from Santa Elena testified that in Charles Town "he heard that the Indians of the Chuchumeco nation have trade and friendship with the settlement of the said Englishmen on the mainland, and they trade deerskins [*gamusas*] for shotguns, gunpowder, bullets, and clothing," indicating that slaves were not the only element of this trade with the Carolinians (Hita Salazar, 1677). What the mission Indians and Spaniards were only beginning to become aware of at that time, however, was that the Chichimeco were direct agents of the English, preying on the southern frontier using Carolina guns in search of slaves.

Although the early 1670s represent a substantial gap in the documentary record for the missions of Guale and Mocama, the *repartimiento* labor draft from 1673 supplements data from the 1675 and 1677–1678 mission lists to suggest that during this time a substantial demographic transformation was in progress. Specifically, the flow of Yamassee into the mission provinces continued well into the 1670s, and by 1675, the total Indian population of the old provinces of Guale and Mocama was heavily skewed in favor of the new arrivals. By 1673, some 24 of the total of 50 laborers drafted from the coastal provinces north of St. Augustine were identified as Yamassee, living in two primary settlements within the old province of Mocama (see Addendum, Document 1). Half of the Yamassee laborers (12 Indian men) were drawn from "the island and village of Santa Maria de los Yamazes," and the other 12 laborers were to be turned over by the "Yamaze caciques" situated on the island of Guadalquini (St. Simons Island). Two years later, one of two mission lists compiled at that time reveals remarkable details regarding this transformation of Guale and Mocama, and provides yet another benchmark in the story of the retreat from the Georgia coast (Arcos, 1675).

As can be seen in figure 2 (also see Appendix B), in 1675 only four Guale mission towns remained, and only three of these were on or near their original locations. Santa Catalina, with Satuache aggregated, was the northernmost frontier, with the highest population of all the towns in Guale and Mocama, Christian or pagan. San Joseph de Sapala, with Tupiqui almost certainly aggregated by this time, was located on the next island to the south, and Santo Domingo de Asajo (relocated since 1661) occupied the northern end of St. Simons Island. San Phelipe, relocated several years earlier, was situated far to the south, in the middle of the old Mocama province. The two remaining Mocama missions, San Buenaventura de Guadalquini and San Juan del Puerto, were still situated in their original locations, but widely separated. The gap between them was partially filled by the Guale mission of San Phelipe, but the vast majority of the old Mocama province had by 1675 been settled by unconverted Yamassee Indians, scattered across much of the Georgia and northern Florida coast.

These recent immigrants were settled in six distinct villages and towns in 1675, stretching from St. Simons Island in the north to Amelia Island in the south. As suggested by the 1673 labor draft order, one primary concentration was the boundary region between Guale and Mocama, on the middle of present-day St. Simons Island. Here, situated directly between the missions of Asajo and Guadalquini, were two towns containing some 160 pagan Indians. One, given the name of San Simón but apparently not a mission as such, was evidently situated on the inland side of the island, probably in the immediate vicinity of the later Fort Frederica.[26] Evidence from later documents (see below) indicates that its inhabitants were known as Colones, and thus almost certainly originally came from the town in the province of Escamaçu called Colon, which was described as a Yamassee town in 1663 (see above). The second and much larger pagan town was situated only a league from San Simón, and was called Ocotonico. Inhabited by 120 residents in 1675, this group formed the largest aggregation of unconverted Indians on the Georgia coast at that time, and the second largest in both Guale and Mocama.

The other concentration of unconverted immigrants in Mocama was on Amelia Island, where Arcos (1675) listed four separate pagan towns. The northernmost, inhabited by 60 Yamassee, was located on the tip of the island, followed by the town of Ocotoque a league to the south, with 40 residents. Two leagues southward was the town of La Tama, containing 50 pagan Indians, and half a league away was the town of Santa Maria, recently resettled by Yamassee immigrants after the disappearance of the original Mocama mission during the 1660s (see above). In total, the immigrant Yamassee population of Amelia Island reached 190 individuals, making it the second most populous island of Guale and Mocama in 1675, exceeded only by the combined Christian and pagan population of St. Simons Island, which was home to a total of 230 Indians.

The combined figures provided by Arcos reveal a total Indian population of 676 individuals living in Guale and Mocama in 1675, broken down into 350 enumerated non-Christian Yamassee and only 326 Christians living in missions (of which at least a few were pagans living in the Sapala and San Phelipe missions). In the space of just over a decade, the once-ravaged indigenous population of the Guale and Mocama mission provinces had been augmented and even surpassed by an influx of unconverted refugees fleeing the depredations of Chichimeco warriors. The Guale and Mocama provinces of the middle 17th century, already transformed and reshaped after decades of population decline in the context of the Spanish colonial system, had further contracted and reorganized under the weight of English colonial pressure from the north.

Not only were there fewer distinct towns, and in different locations than before, but these missions were also intermingled with a considerable number of immigrant refugee towns from a variety of areas in the interior. Guale and Mocama had become the site of a remarkable ethnic mix, including the remnants of a number of aboriginal societies from the coast and the interior. Apart from the towns of Guale and Mocama, this coastal region now included at least some former residents of the province of Escamaçu on the South Carolina coast (Colon, and probably Santa Elena and Abaya), as well as the deep interior province of Tama, or Altamaha (La

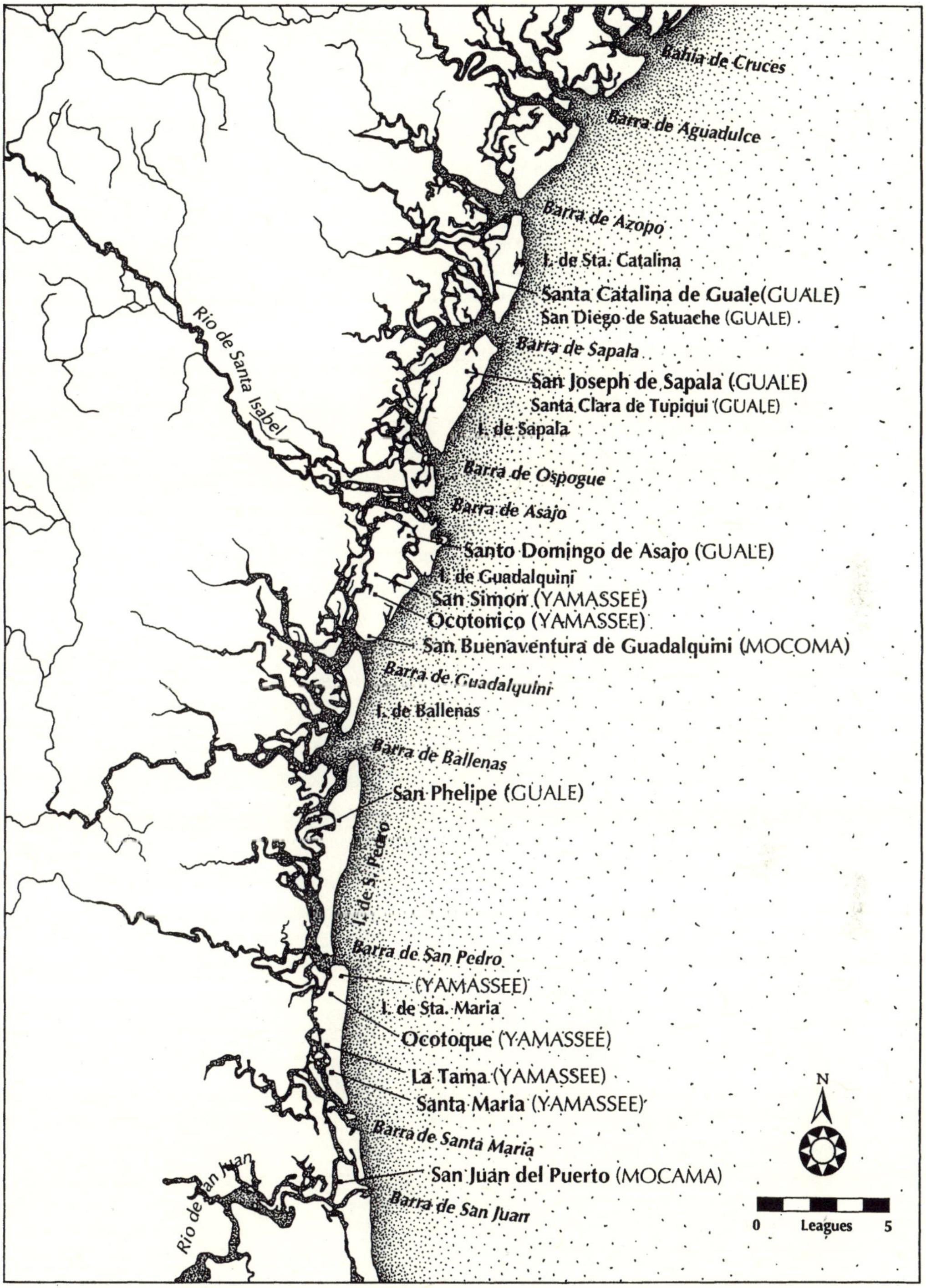

Fig. 2. Projected locations of principal Guale and Mocama missions and aggregated Yamassee towns in 1675, based on mission lists by Pedro de Arcos and Bishop Gabriel Díaz Vara Calderón.

Tama), and a variety of others provinces or towns which are either unnamed, or which have names of as yet undetermined origin (such as Ocotonico and Ocotoque). All of these latter groups seem to have spoken a Muskhogean dialect like the Guale, and were commonly known as the Yamassee Indians, despite their diverse origins.

During the winter of 1677–78, Captain Antonio de Argüelles made a formal visitation of Guale and Mocama, and the documentation resulting from this visit provides yet another benchmark in the retreat from the Georgia coast. Starting on the northern frontier, all four Guale and both Mocama mission towns were visited, including Santa Catalina/Satuache, San Joseph de Sapala/Tupiqui, Santo Domingo de Asajo, San Buenaventura de Guadalquini, San Phelipe, and San Juan del Puerto. In addition to these missions, however, the Yamassee inhabitants of Amelia Island were also treated to a formal visitation in the old Mocama mission town of Santa Maria. As a former mission occupied by immigrant and unconverted Yamassee Indians (its cacique Finge does not seem to have had a Christian name), Santa Maria does not seem to have been a true mission as such, and had no resident friar. Nevertheless, perhaps due to the substantial participation of the Yamassee in the *repartimiento* labor system, Santa Maria was included in the visitation.

The large Yamassee population of St. Simons Island does not seem to have been left out either, since the caciques attending the visitations of both missions Santo Domingo de Asajo and San Buenaventura de Guadalquini were noted to be "both Christian and heathen," suggesting that these visitations were attended by representatives of the Yamassee towns on the middle of the island. San Joseph de Sapala was also host to unconverted Indians during the visitation, probably Yamassee. Ultimately, no significant group in the region was left out of the visitation process, further reinforcing the increasing integration of the Yamassee into the Guale and Mocama mission provinces.

The comparatively brief details of the visitations in each mission town also hint at some of the problems associated with the aggregation and garrisoning of Guale. The leaders of Santa Catalina complained that the military garrison posted in their town was now being supported solely by the inhabitants of Santa Catalina, without substantial help from the rest of the Guale towns, in direct violation of the agreement reached when the soldiers were first stationed there. Furthermore, the Indians in the town of Santa Catalina were said to be "passing from one council house to another with slight cause," again in violation of earlier mandates for good government (Argüelles, 1678). Though ambiguous, this passage might refer to the council houses of the two distinct towns aggregated in Santa Catalina (Santa Catalina and Satuache), suggesting an attempt to maintain the separate identities of the two towns in the context of aggregation.

The other dual town in the Guale province, San Joseph de Sapala, was also involved in internal disputes as to the relationship between the two aggregated towns of Sapala and Tupiqui. During the visitation, the *mica*[27] of Tupiqui, Ana Estasia, complained that although the caciques of Sapala were her vassals, they refused to pay her tribute (in the form of a field of corn), and when asked, Sapala's cacique Phelipe refused to do so unless ordered to by the Spaniards. Although the determination was left to the judgement of all of the caciques of the province, the political dispute in Sapala, along with the problems noted above, reveal that Guale's transformation during this period was not without its stresses.

Just two years later, during January 1680, yet another mission list for Guale indicated that Franciscan friars were stationed at all six remaining mission towns in the Guale and Mocama provinces, including two at San Joseph de Sapala (Barreda, 1680). This was to be the calm before the storm, however, for in just over three months, the Chichimeco would make a final and devastating strike at the heart of the Guale province, stepping up the pace of retreat, and ushering in the last five years of indigenous occupation on the Georgia coast.

RETURN OF THE CHICHIMECO

In the spring of 1680, the Chichimeco joined forces with two Indian groups in the deep interior, including the Uchise (ancestral to the Lower Creeks) and the Chiluque (situated just north of Guale around Santa Elena), and led yet another raid against the mission provinces on the Georgia coast. As recounted immediately following the attack:

> [A]ll were at war, and the Chiluques and Uchizes sociable, treating and trading with these provinces in good friendship, and only the Chichumecos were always enemies, and last year they all made peace and established friendship with the English, which they conserve, and this year these three nations have been declared enemies (Hita Salazar, 1680a).

Some time in late April, a group of warriors descended on the Island of Guadalquini (St. Simons), assaulting the pagan town of San Simón, inhabited by the Colones (Hita Salazar, 1680a; 1680b; 1680c). Why this town in particular was chosen may never be known, but the fact that Guale's provincial Lieutenant at that time, Captain Francisco de Fuentes, later referred to this as the second attack by the Chichimeco on the inhabitants of San Simón (see below) implies that the first attack may have been at the original location of Colon in the province of Escamaçu (forcing their original flight), and that the Chichimeco might thus have considered them an easy target. On the other hand, San Simón might even have been a diversion tactic, particularly considering their next target.

What little information that exists regarding this first strike suggests that after only a few casualties, Captain Fuentes appeared with local Indian warriors to defend San Simón, and the Chichimeco, Uchise, and Chiluque retreated to prepare for their next attack (Hita Salazar, 1680a). The second wave of the assault took place at none other than Santa Catalina de Guale, the garrison headquarters for the entire Georgia coast. Governor Hita Salazar (1680a) related that:

> the first time they entered together on the Island of Guadalquini, in the said province, and caused some deaths, and the natives coming forth with my Lieutenant to the defense, they withdrew, and within a few days they entered on the Island of Santa Catalina, the capital and frontier to these enemies, with a force of more than three hundred men[28] they killed the first sentinel, which comprised six men, with one escaping to fire a shot, and the residents of that town, who were up to forty natives and five Spaniards from this presidio, were able to put up a defense, and occupied the convent of the missionary of that doctrina, where Captain Francisco de Fuentes, my lieutenant in that province, had arrived days before, and who arranged to defend himself with such preparation and valor that he defended himself from dawn until four in the afternoon with sixteen Indians who entered with firearms (on this occasion I have considered it important that the Indians have them). With the news I had I immediately arranged to send aid, the first of which was three days in advance, and then I sent a body of up to thirty soldiers and a vessel with up to eighteen men with the sailors, and when they arrived the enemies had already withdrawn. They assure me that among them came some Englishmen who instructed them, and all with long shotguns, which have caused much horror to these natives, who abandoned the Island of Santa Catalina.

In a later certification of Fuentes's military service, the Govenor provided further details regarding the heated battle at Mission Santa Catalina, noting that "the multitude of the [enemies] having rushed the convent, he [Fuentes] entered within the fence [*cerca*], which was made of boards [*tablas*], and there he defended himself with five Spaniards that he had and up to 40 Indians with some firearms . . . and the enemies retreated with the loss of some dead and wounded, with which the families of women and children, who were gathered within the fence, were secured" (Hita Salazar 1681). In a later account Governor Hita Salazar (1680c) noted that the Chichimeco burned the town before retreating.

The first reinforcements sent northward by the governor were apparently those under the command of Captain Juan Saturnino de Abaurrea,[29] who arrived four days after the initial assault on Santa Catalina. In a later certification of the captain's military service, Governor Hita Salazar (1687) recalled that after Saturnino de Abaurrea had already served once as provincial lieutenant in Guale,

> it occurred that the pagan Indian enemies of the Chichimeca nation and others invaded the said province [of Guale and Mocama], where I sent him [Saturnino de Abaurrea] with infantry and munitions in order to aid Captain Francisco de Fuentes, my lieutenant, who at the time found himself surrounded by the said enemies in the village of Santa Catalina, where he [Saturnino

de Abaurrea] arrived four days later, facilitating and overcoming some inconveniences that happened to him in the bars, rivers, and villages through which he passed, and the enemy having retreated, I ordered him to stay in garrison as assistance in the said province in the village and island of Guadalquini, so that with the said infantry he should exhort and make its Indian natives attend to their towns and the labor of their plantings.

Although Saturnino was apparently largely successful in convincing most of the inhabitants of St. Simons Island (the island of Guadalquini, where the first raid had occurred) to return to their towns and work their fields, the residents of Mission Santa Catalina were more deeply shaken by the assault on their town. In the aftermath of the battle, Fuentes was obliged to submit to the desire of the inhabitants of Santa Catalina to retreat southward, "seeing the said Indians with their wives and children disconsolate, and without having anywhere to take shelter, showing little valor and making many entreaties" (Hita Salazar, 1680c). The destroyed town was abandoned, never again to be occupied by its indigenous inhabitants. Now refugees themselves, the combined populations of Santa Catalina and Satuache moved 2 leagues to the south, joining the populations of Sapala and Tupiqui in the mission town of San Joseph de Sapala on Sapelo Island.[30]

On May 17, Sergeant Manuel Gómez was sent by land with munitions for the soldiers already stationed in Guale (Hita Salazar, 1680d). Hoping to dislodge the Chichimeco from St. Catherines Island, where they seem to have regrouped following Fuentes's retreat, Governor Hita Salazar called a meeting on May 23, 1680, in an effort to decide on a course of action (Hita Salazar, 1680e; Cigarroa, 1681). The decision made was one of offense, regarding it advisable to strike back at the enemy and uproot them from the island. Captain Nicolás Estebedes de Carmenatis was immediately dispatched with troops to be turned over to Captain Fuentes in Guale (Hita Salazar, 1680e; 1680f). Within three days, Captain Don Enrique de Ribera was sent north in the presidio's own vessel with even more troops and supplies, all supplementing the force under Fuentes' direct control (Hita Salazar, 1680e). These forces were directed to dislodge "the enemies who find themselves entrenched in the place of Cofunufo," located on the northern tip of St. Catherines Island, "or any other place in the said province" (Hita Salazar, 1680f).

Although there are no details of the events which followed, the Chichimeco seem to have abandoned the island soon thereafter, for within a month Governor Hita Salazar (1680g) sent orders to Captain Fuentes to convince the Indians to resettle Santa Catalina. Arguing that the abandonment of St. Catherines would not only result in the loss of a valuable and productive island, but would also leave it open for enemy occupation, the governor ordered Fuentes to convene the inhabitants of Santa Catalina in Sapala in order to make a case for their return. Admitting that "this will not be the most trivial vexation for them," Hita Salazar nevertheless insisted that if the Indians did not relent, their leaders should be sent to St. Augustine for a final determination by the governor.

In late October, while awaiting the arrival of newly installed Governor Don Juan Márquez Cabrera, who was on the road from Apalachee to St. Augustine, Governor Hita Salazar (1680c) further investigated the possibility of resettling of Santa Catalina, "by being the best and most fertile island, and where the most products are gathered." Captain Fuentes declared that there were several points on the island where a fortification might be constructed:

> I say that in two places one could make a fortification; one musket-shot from the said village [of Santa Catalina] in a place that they call Yusifizliçu, or in Cufunufu, one league distant to the north of the said village, by the terrain being higher, and closer to the landings of greater risk, without making mention of the two points of the said Island of Santa Cathalina, where the two Bars of Azopo[31] and Zapala enter, and the said fortification or fort should have twenty-one Spaniards in garrison (Fuentes, 1680).

Fuentes, however, was not of the opinion that a return to St. Catherines Island would necessarily be in the best interests of Guale, due to the fact that

> returning to settle Santa Catalina does not secure the rest of the villages and islands, because

the said enemies can traverse from whichever part of the mainland to the village that they might wish without being able to impede them or find out until after the fact, and there are places where it could be that one does not find out in six days, and in sum one can only somewhat secure the said province by making an expedition in search of the said enemies up to their own land, and making a frontier of the island that has less posts and places to guard with some type of fortification (Fuentes, 1680).

Instead, Fuentes recommended that Sapala be fortified, since "this place is the heart of the said province, and it ought to be garrisoned with all care for the security and consolation of everyone, and the greater part of the pagans will be assured." Ultimately, Fuentes's conclusion would be confirmed by the decision of the caciques themselves, who soon transmitted their unwillingness to return to Santa Catalina in the face of danger.

Within only days after Captain Fuentes expressed his opinion regarding the resettlement of St. Catherines Island, word arrived from Captain Saturnino de Abaurrea, the new provincial lieutenant of Guale, that the caciques of Santa Catalina had met on the morning of November 1, expressing complete refusal to his request, saying that

> they were resolved not to return to the said village of Santa Catalina, with the awareness that they are subject to the possibility of having whatever punishment that might be done to them, and that they will support it all in the love of God, because in going would follow exceedingly great damages, and also by having heard their vassals say that they will first make use of the *bejuco* before going another time to their land, even if there might be many conveniences in it. They also allege that the villages of San Felipe, Satuahe, Tupique, and Asajo have moved from the mainland to settle these islands without the señores governors having hindered their passage, and this objection is only made against them, having much more reason to leave their village, and that they do not know what this [objection] consists of, being thus that they have always taken great pains to be very obedient regarding what has been commanded of them in the service of His Majesty. They also told me to request Your Lordship to pity them and let them live in this village [of Sapala]. I advertise to Your Lordship that if you force these Indians to return another time, great disgraces would happen to some women, because they execute what they say, since for less cause they are accustomed to take this infernal venom (Saturnino de Abaurrea, 1680).

Governor Hita Salazar clarified the term *bejuco* in the 1680 response to charges in his *residencia*, recalling that Captain Saturnino de Abaurrea wrote that the inhabitants of Santa Catalina "were resolved that if I obligated them to make the said settlement again, they would take *bejuco* in order to kill themselves, an ancient custom among them" (Hita Salazar, 1680h). Evidently, the residents of Santa Catalina threatened mass suicide if they were forced to return to their former town. The governor's reply to Captain Saturnino de Abaurrea, written two weeks later on the back of his original correspondence, indicated that he would comply with the wishes of the Indians, expressing the hope that with the arrival of the new governor the Chichimeco might soon be repulsed in their own territory with a Spanish military strike.

The passages above effectively summarize both the overall Spanish strategy in defending Guale and Mocama since 1661 and the difficulties in implementing such a strategy. Specifically, the entire defense of Guale was directed against enemy assaults from the mainland. This strategy, however, was remarkably difficult for the Georgia coastal region, given the multiplicity of potential avenues of attack and the limited resources available to the Spaniards. The implementation of this policy during the previous two decades reflected a clear awareness of these problems, inasmuch as the guiding principles in settlement relocation were aggregation for mutual defense and even distribution for rapid communication and movement. As outlying towns and villages were withdrawn and aggregated, open gaps in the north–south distribution of settlements were gradually filled, resulting in a chain of more or less evenly spaced centralized towns, all of which had ready access to coastal waterways.

Ultimately, however, this strategy would prove fatal for the Guale and Mocama provinces, for within a few short years, the character of the enemy threat along the Georgia coast would change altogether. New assaults from the sea would replace the old land-based attacks, leaving Guale and Mocama in an even more vulnerable position than before.

The first half of the 1680s would eventually witness the final retreat from the Georgia coast, pushing Guale and Mocama toward their final aggregation to the south.

CALM BEFORE THE STORM

In the aftermath of the Chichimeco-led raid of 1680, Guale and Mocama settled into an uncomfortable stability over the next three years. A census compiled only a year after the withdrawal of Santa Catalina revealed the results of the assault (Fuentes, 1681; see Document 7). Guale and Mocama were now effectively composed of only five mission towns, with the northernmost Guale town of San Joseph de Sapala comprising the populations of four separate towns: Santa Catalina, Satuache, Sapala, and Tupiqui, all served by a single Franciscan friar.[32] The Guale mission of Santo Domingo de Asajo and the Mocama mission of San Buenaventura de Guadalquini were still located on either end of St. Simons Island, and both San Phelipe and San Juan del Puerto remained in their earlier locations, and each of them possessed a resident missionary.

Interestingly, census figures provided by Captain Fuentes reveal an overall increase in the Christian population of the mission towns, some of which experienced substantial expansion. Although the combined population of Santa Catalina and Satuache dropped, that of Sapala and Tupiqui increased, leaving the total figure for all four missions roughly equal. Asajo and San Juan del Puerto experienced only modest increases, but Guadalquini and San Phelipe effectively doubled in population, jumping from 40 and 36 to 87 and 71 respectively. The total Christian population living in the mission towns of Guale and Mocama jumped from 326 in 1675 to 420 in 1681. The reasons for this are undoubtedly complex, but they almost certainly have something to do with population shifts among the unconverted Indians living along the coast. Specifically, apart from the net increases in population among both Christian and non-Christian Indians living in Guale and Mocama, many of the immigrant Yamassee probably became Christians and relocated to the mission towns, inflating the number of Christians and decreasing the number of non-Christians.

The Fuentes census of 1681 shows that the mission provinces were still home to a substantial number of pagan Yamassee scattered in a number of villages and hamlets across the province. The non-Christian population of Guale and Mocama experienced a slight overall decrease, however, dropping from 350 in 1675 to 322 in 1681. In general, most of the individual towns noted by Arcos in 1675 were still occupied, although several new settlements had appeared in the meantime, and the overall distribution of population was somewhat distinct. The southern point of Sapelo Island was now home to a substantial new Yamassee town of some 67 adults, perhaps due to the fact that the provincial garrison was at that time located on the same island. Another new Yamassee town of 53 had appeared on the on the site of the old Mocama mission town of San Pedro, and a small group of 11 Yamassee had settled to the north between San Pedro and San Phelipe on Cumberland Island.

At the same time, there were decreases in the Yamassee populations of both St. Simons and Amelia Islands. The number of unconverted Indians on St. Simons Island had been considerably reduced, with the Colon town of San Simón dropping from 40 in 1675 to only 17 in 1681, and the Yamassee town of Ocotonico dropping similarly from 120 to 73, with these remnants of this last town apparently divided between San Simón and Guadalquini (Fuentes, 1681). On Amelia Island far to the south, four former Yamasee towns totaling 190 individuals had dropped to only 101 Yamassee living in Santa Maria, with the other three outlying towns apparently remaining abandoned. Inasmuch as the overall pagan population of the Georgia coast had only dropped by about 28 persons, however, the greater likelihood is that most of the Yamassee who left these earlier towns (a total of about 131 individuals) made up the 1681 populations of the various new settlements that had appeared since 1675 (a total of 159 individuals). The rest probably contributed to the increase in population at missions such as Guadalquini and San Phelipe, along with the results of natural population growth in both Christian and non-Christian populations.

In sum, the post-1680 era in Guale and Mocama reflected the results of a general reorganization of the population distribution along the coast. Much of this shift may have occurred as a direct result of the Chichimeco attack of 1680, with the new Yamassee towns representing yet another step in the attempt to establish a chain of more or less evenly distributed settlements. Such a move may have been the only way to prevent large-scale flight from the province, particularly considering the fact that a large part of the population had no long-term ties to the Georgia coast, having arrived only recently seeking refuge. Indeed, Captain Fuentes reported in October of 1680 that following the Chichimeco attack, the pagan town of San Simón "is almost depopulated, and I doubt that they will return due to the fear that they have developed of the Chichimecos on the two occasions that they have entered and killed many, and to return them by force would promise their flight to the woods." Just half a year later the town was inhabited by only 17 Indians, supplemented by some of the Yamassee who once inhabited the neighboring town of Ocotonico.

At about this same time the threat from the Chichimeco was rapidly fading, for the year of 1680 also witnessed the beginning of the Westo War in Carolina, during which time the Chichimeco/Westo were destroyed and driven from the Savannah River by the Carolinians themselves, the survivors taking refuge among the constituents of the nascent Lower Creek confederacy (Swanton, 1922; Crane, 1956). The Westo had become far too reckless, and their repeated attacks on the English-allied Indian groups along the Carolina coast ultimately drove the English to destroy them. Indeed, had the Chichimeco presence not been eliminated so soon after the attack on Santa Catalina by the Carolinians, the new Spanish Governor Márquez Cabrera might well have done so himself. Ultimately, the immigrant Savannah Indians, who had assisted the Carolinians against the Westo, became their replacements (lending their name to the river), but with the destruction of the Westo, the path now lay clear for English trade to the north and west (Crane, 1956).

Interestingly, during this same period, tensions surfaced between the titular leader of the old Mocama province and the immigrant Yamassee Indians living within her traditional domain. Early in 1681, the cacique of the recent Yamassee settlement at the Bar of San Pedro (on the southern end of Cumberland Island) traveled to St. Augustine, complaining to recently-installed Governor Márquez Cabrera (1681) about the tributes demanded by Merenciana, the cacica of San Juan del Puerto (and presumably the overall leader of the Mocama province). Arguing that the islands of Santa Maria and San Pedro belonged to her and her ancestors (her aunt Juana of Santa Maria inherited the position in 1665 from the powerful Clemente Bernal of San Juan), Merenciana demanded a share of the products gathered by the immigrant Yamassee, including bear fat, deerskins, acorns, and palmetto berries. In his letter of response, the governor tactfully relieved the Yamassee from this obligatory tribute, indicating that as refugees forced off their original lands, they were to be protected and treated with charity. All contributions from the Yamassee were to be considered strictly voluntary, and as pagans they were not to work in the mission fields.

As noted by Governor Márquez Cabrera (1681), the Yamassee were already contributing to the royal labor draft, and were exempt from tribute. Given that the King had granted the Indians of Spanish Florida an exemption from royal tribute due to their poverty (permitting the Florida caciques to extract tribute from their own vassals), the governor urged Merenciana to grant a similar exemption for the Yamassee immigrants. As a result of this decision, Governor Márquez Cabrera thus effectively circumvented the political power of the Mocama leadership, making the *repartimiento* labor draft (managed by the Spanish governor) the only formal expectation of the pagan Yamassee within the old Mocama province. At the same time, however, the governor granted the possibility of "voluntary" contributions to Merenciana, permitting considerable flexibility in practice.[33] Ultimately, the Yamassee presence within Mocama was only temporary, for the islands of San Pedro and Santa Maria were vacated in just over two years.

The year 1681 in Guale was also marked by other conflict, but this time between the Franciscans and the Spanish military. A running battle developed almost immediately between newly installed Governor Márquez

Cabrera and the missionaries of Guale, and the documentation which was developed as a result is voluminous (see Gannon, 1981; Bushnell, 1994). At stake was a fundamental jurisdictional struggle (indeed, one which had been simmering for years) between the Franciscans and the military government of Spanish Florida, and during the next year Guale would become a focal point for occasional clashes between the provincial Lieutenant Francisco de Fuentes and Fray Juan de Uçeda in the crowded atmosphere of San Joseph de Sapala. Tensions shifted away from the Georgia coast with the transferral of Captain Fuentes to the Lieutenancy of the western Apalachee province in mid-1682 (where the church/state struggle nevertheless raged on), however Guale and Mocama were due for a rude awakening the following year.

FLIGHT OF THE YAMASSEE

Following a 22-year retreat southward and seaward in the face of English-sponsored aggression, Guale and Mocama consisted of a narrow string of mission towns and refugee villages scattered along a 30-league stretch of the barrier island chain of southern Georgia and northern Florida. Although the number of mission towns had been cut in half, and all the mainland settlements had been relocated to the islands, the defense of Guale and Mocama was not yet assured. In fact, these mission provinces now lay wide open to another kind of enemy: pirates. The poorly defended but comparatively rich missions were ripe targets for plunder from the sea, and within the space of only 18 months, two successive raids would finish the retreat from the Georgia coast.

Although certainly unintentional, the English-sponsored campaign of land assaults launched by slave-raiding Indians from the interior of Georgia during the previous two decades left Guale and Mocama in an almost perfect distribution for sea-based attack. Not only were the mission towns and refugee settlements located on islands, but they were also strategically located at the water's edge for ease in communication and travel. What had once been a distinct advantage against the wide-ranging Chichimecos was now a liability, and it was not long before English and French pirates saw their opportunity and took it.

Late in the spring of 1683, the first blow fell in the old Mocama province. Under the leadership of the notorious French pirate Grammont (or Agramon, as the Spanish knew him), a group of French and English vessels launched a bold assault against St. Augustine itself (Wright, 1960; Bushnell, 1994). On April 30, the guard post at Matanzas to the south of the city was captured while the sentinels slept. A detachment of Spanish infantry was quickly dispatched, and the pirates were engaged, losing one vessel to the Spaniards, along with its entire crew, almost all of whom were killed by soldiers under the command of former Guale Lieutenant Francisco de Fuentes.

In need of provisions, the remaining pirates under Grammont sailed northward, passing St. Augustine on their way to the exposed mission towns in the old Mocama province. Although details are sketchy, the pirates made at least two landings, sacking and defacing both the southernmost mission town of San Juan del Puerto, and San Phelipe on Cumberland Island, the next mission town to the north (Bushnell, 1994). Among the items plundered were four mission bells, two from each mission (Barbosa, 1683). Based on subsequent events, the pirates may well have additionally assaulted the intervening Yamassee towns of Santa Maria and San Pedro. Nevertheless, whether as a response to direct attack, or simply a realization of their exposed position in the coastal mission provinces (perhaps serving to exacerbate existing difficulties with Governor Márquez Cabrera), the Yamassee fled, and within a month's time, the population of Guale and Mocama was cut in half.

Guale's provincial Lieutenant Captain Francisco de Barbosa soon embarked on a brief visitation of Guale and Mocama. Beginning at the garrison headquarters in San Joseph de Sapala on May 27 and finishing at San Juan del Puerto on June 7, Barbosa (1683) documented the dramatic effects of the Grammont raid. Although the Barbosa census recorded only the adult male population of the mission towns, a comparison of these figures with those of the Fuentes census taken only two years earlier reveals that the internal population of the remaining five missions of Guale and Mocama was virtually unchanged, indicating that few if any of the Christian Guale or Mocama inhabitants had fled the mission provinces (see table 1).

What was missing in Barbosa's 1683 census, however, was the Yamassee population of Guale and Mocama, which had been placed at some 322 adults in Fuentes's census of 1681. Whereas prior to the Grammont raid of 1683, Guale and Mocama had been home to hundreds of unconverted refugees scattered in perhaps half a dozen settlements along the Georgia and north Florida coast, in the immediate aftermath of the assault, not a single Yamassee was enumerated. The sites of two of the primary Yamassee towns were visited by Barbosa on his way southward, but no inhabitants was found in either one. San Pedro was described as "the village that the Yamazes left," and Santa Maria was noted as "a town also left by the Yamazes" (Barbosa, 1683). No other Yamassee settlement was mentioned, indicating that the Yamassee had fled as a group beyond the mission provinces. As summed up by ex-Governor Hita Salazar that May, the province of Guale was ruined, and not even half of the fugitive Indians would return (Hita Salazar, 1683).

As a part of Governor Márquez Cabrera's overview of the current state of the colony, which was sent to Spain that June along with Barbosa's census, a map of all of Spanish Florida was drawn up at this time by Ensign Alonso Solana, and his rendition of the northern coastal provinces reveals much regarding the results of the Grammont raid (figure 3). As reflected in the Barbosa census, only five mission towns with Christian Indians remained in the Guale and Mocama provinces. However, Solana did locate one pagan Indian village on St. Simons Island between Asajo and Guadalquini, undoubtedly the Colon village of San Simón, which would later merge with Guadalquini (see below).[34] Perhaps the most important piece of evidence provided by Solana, however, was his placement of a "town of pagans" in the middle of present-day Hilton Head Island.

This town was located precisely in the no-man's land between Charles Town to the north and the Guale mission province to the south, and was probably a recent development. Based on later evidence, it seems reasonable to conclude that this was a new town formed by fugitive Yamassee. Whether or not all 300 or so fugitives from Guale and Mocama had settled together on this island is unclear, but there seems little doubt that following the Grammont raid of 1683 a substantial number of Yamassees took up a position between English Carolina and Spanish Florida. The intent of this move seems to have been an attempt to shift allegiances from the Spanish to the English colonists, for the following year these same Yamassee would welcome the new Scotch colony of Stuart's Town into their midst. The Yamassee's confidence in the ability of the Spanish infantry to provide protection was severely shaken by the Grammont raid, and the decision appears to have been made to relocate closer to the English in order to fall within their sphere of protection. Although this might seem illogical considering the fact that English Carolina was a safe harbor for pirates during this period (see below), it must be remembered that many or most of the pirates who raided Mocama in 1683 were French like their leader Grammont, and their connection to Carolina was a closely guarded secret.

TABLE 1
Adult Male Population of Guale and Mocama Missions, 1681-1683

Mission Town	1681 Fuentes Census	1683 Barbosa Census
Sapala (with Santa Catalina, Satuache, and Tupiqui)	87	86
Asajo	17	21
Guadalquini	45	42
San Phelipe	28	29
San Juan	17	20

In retrospect, although only two mission towns were robbed, the Grammont raid represented a rude awakening for all of Guale and Mocama. The Yamassee refugees, recognizing how vulnerable they were in the mission provinces, chose to shift allegiances to the English, relocating to the north after a wholesale flight from Guale and Mocama. The Spanish, along with the Christian Indians living in the mission towns, came to the realization that with the population of the

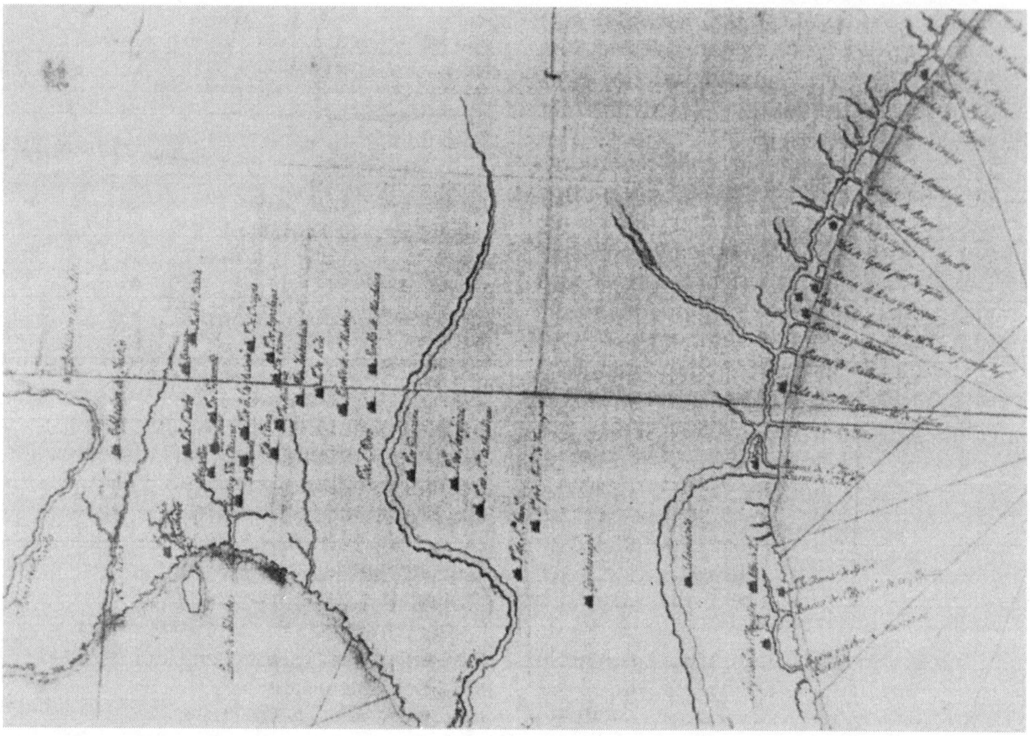

Fig. 3. Detail of the 1683 "Map of the Island of Florida," showing Christian and pagan towns in the Guale and Mocama mission provinces. The original map, located in the archive of the Servicios Geographico e Histórico del Ejército in Madrid, includes the following notation on the back: "Map of Florida, remitted by the Marquis Governor Juan Márquez Cabrera with his letter of June 28, 1683." The letter originally accompanying the map is in the Archivo General de Indias in Seville (Márquez Cabrera, 1683). North is to the top.

Transcribed toponyms. **Horizontal names along coast (*north to south*)**: Barra de Sin Pro[vecho]; Bahia de Sta Elena; Pueblo de Ynfieles; Bahia de los Bajos; Baya de Cruzes; Barra de Aguadulce; Barra de Asapo; Ysla de Sta Cathalina despobl.^{a}; Barra de Sapala; Ysla de Sapala pobl.^{n} de Xpnos; Barra de Asajo y Aspogue; Ysla de Guadalquini con dos Pob.^{es} de Xpnos y una de Ynf.^{s}; Barra de Guadalquini; Barra de Ballenas; Ysla de Sn Phelipe con Pob.^{n} de Xpnos; Barra de Sn Pedro; Barra de Sta Maria; Barra de S.^{n} Ju.^{n}; P.^{o} de Thomas de Xpnos; Barra de Sn Agustin de florida; Barra y vijia de Matanzas; Barreta. **Vertical names to east of St. Johns river (*north to south*)**: Xpnos; Salamototo; Nobre de D.^{s}; Cast.^{o} y Ciud.^{d} de Sn Agustin.

northern mission chain effectively halved following the departure of the Yamassee, the remaining population of Guale and Mocama was spread far too thin to be able to resist another attack. Immediate plans were drawn up for a rapid and massive retreat southward, and now it was only a race against time.

THE FINAL RETREAT

The Barbosa visitation of May–June 1683 accomplished more than just a census of the remaining men in the mission towns. During his stays at each town, Captain Barbosa held meetings with aboriginal leaders in order to judge their reactions to a new plan of retreat formulated by Governor Márquez Cabrera. At San Joseph de Sapala, where the towns of Sapala, Tupiqui, Santa Catalina, and Satuache were aggregated, Barbosa (1683) reported that

> having proposed that they should withdraw to three villages, one to Santa Maria and San Pedro, and another to the Island of San Juan, and another in San Pablo, to [the last of] which all responded that it was not appropriate, by having poor landings, and the herds very near, from

which they will receive damage from the livestock, and they say that they remain willing to move themselves to the places indicated, less that of San Pablo due to the incoveniences.

Although Barbosa ultimately concluded that the location of San Pablo on the southern bank of the St. Johns River was "not appropriate for any village," the results of his meeting at Sapala indicated that the four aggregated towns there were perfectly willing to relocate to the three sites of San Pedro, Santa Maria, and San Juan in accordance with the governor's plan.

Two days later in his meeting at Asajo on the northern end of St. Simons Island, Barbosa (1683) reported that "having said that they should soon pass to cultivate that which was left in Santa Maria, they responded that they have cultivated their fields in the said village of Asajo, and that they will move in the time that the rest move." To the south at Guadalquini, "the cacique and vassals remain willing to move upon harvesting their crops to the Island of San Juan, by all being of one language." At San Phelipe on Cumberland Island, the caciques responded similarly, indicating their willingness to relocate to "the Bar of San Pedro, three leagues [away]." While at San Pedro, the lieutenant further reported that "all the Indians say that there is land for one of the three villages which have to be made in the said town of San Pedro, joining that of San [Phelipe][35] and Asahoo." In the abandoned town of Santa Maria, Barbosa (1683) judged that "there are enough lands for the village of Sapala,[36] and thus they request, and all those of one language remain within [the range of] an arquebus and can aid one another." In his last meeting on San Juan, the lieutenant reported that its inhabitants "remain willing that the town of Guadalquini should move to this [town] of San Juan, by all being of one language, and they say there is enough land for everyone."

In the end, the modified plan of retreat called for the resettlement of all the northern missions in Guale and Mocama to three towns within a contracted zone only four or five leagues long (Márquez Cabrera, 1683). The four towns of San Joseph de Sapala, Santa Clara de Tupiqui, Santa Catalina de Guale, and San Diego de Satuache were to relocate far to the south, settling in the abandoned town site of Santa Maria on Amelia Island. Santo Domingo de Asajo and San Phelipe were to form a joint town on the abandoned site of San Pedro, and the two remaining Mocama towns of San Buenaventura de Guadalquini and San Juan del Puerto were to fuse at San Juan.

Over the next year, the two towns of Santa Catalina and Satuache successfully accomplished their relocation to the abandoned site of Santa Maria, where the two towns were already located at least as early as August 22, 1684 (Márquez Cabrera, 1684). No documentation has yet been discovered regarding the details of their move, but a dispute that arose among some of the remaining towns provides a glimpse of the final stages of the relocation of the rest of the towns. As described by Governor Márquez Cabrera (1684) in an investigation that resulted, the original plan described above had come into question, and some of the aboriginal leaders were now proposing an alternate location for removal.

> [T]he said natives have been in agreement to join and congregate themselves on the Island of Guadalquini, one of the next to last, distant from this presidio where they cannot be aided as instantaneously as if they settle in Santa Maria and on the Island of San Juan, and because among the said caciques, tunaques, and mandadores there are some faction leaders, like Don Joseph, a tunaque of the town of Sapala[37] and Don Lorenzo, cacique of Guadalquini, and it would be suitable that these settle as near as they can, like in San Pedro, Santa Maria, and San Juan, where at the present they voluntarily urge the settlement, having left to their execution that they should propose where it would be more comfortable and more secure.

Documenting the opinions of a number of officers in St. Augustine, who all agreed that Santa Maria and San Juan were the appropriate resettlement locations for Sapala and Guadalquini, respectively, Governor Márquez Cabrera subsequently met with a number of aboriginal leaders in order to settle the matter. At the meeting were Phelipe, the cacique of Sapala, Diego, the cacique of San Phelipe, Don Joseph, the tunaque of Tupiqui, and Xolata Xirigua, the pagan cacique of "the Colon nation," all of whom eventually agreed to follow the original plan "so that they are aided more promptly with infantry from the invasions that the enemies make due to the remote location in which they found themselves on the [islands] of Sapala and Guadalquini, in which the hours advanced to the point that no aid could be managed, as happened last year and this present year, when although [aid] was sent with all promptness, no effect was produced" (Márquez Cabrera, 1684).

Attached to the above documentation was the response of Guale's provincial Lieutenant Captain Don Juan Saturnino de Abaurrea to a letter sent by the governor following the conclusion of his investigation. This document, written in San Joseph de Sapala on September 12, provides crucial information regarding the last weeks of Guale and Mocama on the Georgia coast.

> I received the [letter] from Your Lordship, its date the twenty-second of the past [month], in which you mention what the caciques of this province determined, telling Your Lordship that they wanted to move to the Island of Santa Maria, and that of Guadalquini to San Juan, and it is certain that withdrawing from these places and being together is done in great service to God and to the King for many reasons, and in order to get a start on what Your Lordship desires so much, the good of these natives, and for the great increase that they will have in the future with the favor of God. I have determined today, on the date of this [letter], that a canoe loaded with corn and other gear should leave for Santa Maria, by this [town] being the most numerous of the rest of the towns, and by this said village not having a single vessel, I have dispatched a soldier so that he should bring me a canoe that there is in Santa Catalina, and another from San Phelipe, so that this [town] goes sending little by little as the time gives us opportunity, endeavoring to overcome some difficulties that will occur, and when this stated village has moved, that of Sahao [Asajo] will be [moved] with brevity, with respect to the people being few and the little corn that they have, if it is good. The [town] of Guadalquini will delay some time. Although the [town] of San Phelipe is not very prepared, it does not matter, by being four leagues from San Pedro, which is where they are to make a town together with those from Asajao (Saturnino de Abaurrea, 1684).

The original plan, though delayed, was still to be implemented, and Captain Saturnino focused his efforts over the next few weeks on the relocation of San Joseph de Sapala.

In the end, however, time was to run out for Saturnino. The final blow in the retreat of Guale and Mocama fell that October, when a combination of coincidences turned a failed pirate assault on St. Augustine into the death knell for the indigenous occupation of the Georgia coast. Rushing to relocate the missions to a more secure area, Guale's inhabitants were caught literally in the act of moving. Although the withdrawal would have taken place sooner or later, what happened during that next month ensured that the retreat was even more rapid and drastic than originally planned.

Unknown to the residents of Guale, that year a group of some 11 pirate ships had united off the west coast of Florida and decided to mount yet another assault on St. Augustine. A sudden storm scattered 5 of the vessels, and the remaining 6 ships—including three larger ships and three smaller vessels under the command of a pirate known to the Spanish as Thomas Jingle—decided to abandon their plan, slipping past St. Augustine to scour the northern coastlines for desperately needed supplies. On September 30, news arrived in St. Augustine that a group of 6 ships had been sighted off the coast, and that a small group had landed in a piragua at the sentinel-post called "Las Cañuelas" only 9 leagues north of St. Augustine on the coast. Although this group of 11 pirates, including the soon to be notorious crewmember Andrew Ranson (Wright, 1960; Bushnell, 1994), was quickly captured by a detachment of 33 soldiers under the future Governor of Florida Sergeant Major Pedro de Aranda y Avellaneda (Aranda y Avellaneda, 1688), reports soon surfaced of sightings even farther to the north, in Mocama and Guale.

On the evening of October 3, Aranda received word that a pair of small vessels (a sloop and a ketch) had anchored off San Juan del Puerto, and were stealing corn from the mission town. The following day the soldiers marched north to the mouth of the St. Johns River, and in the fire fight that ensued, the pirates were forced to withdraw. On the morning of the fifth, the sergeant major reported news that other pirates had landed in Guale, expressing the desire to "march to the village of Sapala, which is where they say a large ship with eighty men and eight [artillery] pieces is anchored." Later that same day, the pirate sloop at San Juan headed north toward Santa Maria. When Aranda was replaced as leader of the troops by Captain Fuentes on the eighth, he related conflicting reports, some indicating that the pirates had landed in San Pedro, and others suggesting that they had gone (Aranda y Avellaneda, 1684a, 1684b, 1684c, 1684d).[38]

The pirates had indeed entered Guale, and some would remain there for several weeks. Probably in the first days of October, the friar at Santa Maria sent a letter to Guadalquini reporting the landing north of St. Augustine, and relating that a pair of pirate ships had been seen off Santa Maria (see Document 10). At the time, Lieutenant Saturnino was in the town of Sapala attending to the final details of the relocation of the town. Most of the inhabitants of the two remaining aggregated towns of Sapala and Tupiqui had already moved to the mainland by that time with their property. With the news of the pirates, the Lieutenant ordered the missionary to retreat to the mainland with the church furnishings, leaving Saturnino with only five Spanish soldiers and eight Indian men on the island.

Soon thereafter, an Indian dispatched by the friar from the mainland reported that the inhabitants of the towns of "Asajo, the Colones, and Guadalquini" had also moved to the mainland (constituting virtually the entire population of St. Simons Island). The friar at Asajo described the reason for his retreat in a letter, saying that "he found himself on the mainland through two piraguas with enemy people having entered [Asajo], and that they had burned the church, convent, and six houses" (Saturnino de Abaurrea, 1685). Faced with only limited forces, and even those desirous of crossing to the mainland to join with the rest, Saturnino de Abaurrea withdrew from Sapala on or about the third of October, leaving what remained of the town undefended. If Captain Aranda's information on October 5 was accurate, a pirate ship soon anchored off the freshly-abandoned Sapala, sacking the mission before sailing north toward Charles Town.[39]

The events of the next weeks would ultimately cost Lieutenant Saturnino de Abaurrea his rank, and sealed the fate of the Georgia coastal mission chain. Failing to dispatch a message to Governor Márquez Cabrera following his retreat from the garrison headquarters on Sapelo Island, Saturnino de Abaurrea remained on the mainland with the rest of the refugees from Sapelo and St. Simons Island for some two weeks. During this time, a remarkable coincidence found a small sloop filled with 11 unfortunate English and Flemish passengers sailing north from Jamaica to Charles Town. Apparently robbed by the pirate Grammont during their voyage (perhaps as one of the group of 11 ships that planned the 1684 raid on St. Augustine), the little vessel sought desperately needed fresh provisions along the Georgia coast, anchoring on October 18 off the mission town of Guadalquini (Clar, 1686).

It was during this time, of course, that most of the inhabitants of the Guale and Mocama missions had sought shelter from the pirates on the mainland. Indeed, the principal cacique of San Buenaventura de Guadalquini, Don Lorenzo de Santiago, had only left his second-in-command—Santiago, the cacique of Pisocojolata—in charge of a detachment of 10 Indian men in guard of the port (Lorenzo, 1685; Santiago, 1685). By a ruse, however, Santiago was able to effect the capture of the sloop's unarmed passengers, and Thursday morning sent word to Don Lorenzo and Lieutenant Saturnino de Abaurrea regarding the prisoners. Early on Saturday morning, the lieutenant arrived in Guadalquini, and although he was advised to take the captured English vessel and prisoners back to the mainland due to their exposed position, the decision was made to remain on the island until Sunday, and Indian sentinels were posted (see Document 10).

Unfortunately, a lingering frigate under the command of the pirate Captain Jacob Everson saw the sloop anchored off the southern end of St. Simons Island early that Sunday morning, and Lieutenant Saturnino de Abaurrea was forced to abandon his prisoners and flee to the woods when the pirates landed in Guadalquini. At about this time, a detachment of eight soldiers under Ensign Bernardo de Medina was making its way northward from the Islands of Santa Maria and San Pedro in search of Lieutenant Saturnino de Abaurrea, and following Medina's arrival on the mainland the following Monday, the two arranged to meet and join forces. Joined by some 27 Indians and 10 Spanish soldiers, all armed with firearms, Saturnino de Abaurrea spent Tuesday night reconnoitering Guadalquini, where the pirates had fortified themselves inside the mission convent.

In the end, however, the Spanish force returned to the mainland, convinced that the previously abandoned mission town was not worth the risk of an assault. On Wednesday morning, October 25, 1684, the pirates completed the sack of Guadalquini, and "burned the church, the convent, and all the town" (Luna 1686). Carrying with them the captured sloop's passengers in order to sell them for the price of their rescue and passage, the pirates sailed north toward Captain Jacob's house in Charles Town (Clar, 1686; also see Document 10). Close on the heels of the pirates, Captain Francisco de Fuentes arrived that afternoon with another 30 soldiers, only to find the smoking ruins of Guadalquini. Lieutenant Saturnino de Abaurrea was subsequently replaced and prosecuted for desertion of duty (Document 10).

The pirate raid of 1684 resulted in the burning of at least Santo Domingo de Asajo and San Buenaventura de Guadalquini, and possibly the nearby Colon town of San Simón. San Phelipe's fate is unknown, but when the survivors from the other missions regrouped to the south, its inhabitants left their home on Cumberland Island behind, retreating with the rest of the refugees. Although these towns would probably have been relocated within a year even without the extra incentive, the pirate assault left them with few options. The last northern missions of Guale and Mocama had been wiped out in the space of a month, and the Georgia coastline was now abandoned by its indigenous peoples.

REGROUPING TO THE SOUTH

In the aftermath of the destruction of the Georgia coastal missions in October of 1684, the remaining inhabitants of Guale and Mocama made their last retreat from the region, regrouping far to the south and below the present-day border of Georgia. Though departing in several details, the final configuration of the remaining mission towns was largely similar to that of the plan agreed to the previous summer. In his letter to the Spanish Crown the following March 28, Governor Márquez Cabrera wrote

> I have determined, at the request of the caciques of the province of Guale, who have been aided in whatever was possible in the movement, establishment, and union of their towns, reducing themselves to three villages, one on the island of Santa Maria, another on the Island of San Juan, and the other one league from the said island on the mainland. The motive of this undertaking was that six ships of the enemy had come to invade this presidio, of which I give an account to Your Majesty with the [legal] instruments I have made about it. The three villages find themselves in the district of [fourteen][40] leagues from this presidio on good lands and with the solace of protection, from having seen themselves aided on the said occasion of the hostilities of the enemy, which they have done three times in the said province, these tasks of the move having been at the request of the caciques and *mandadores* of the said towns, and with the aggregation of one to another with their conformity in order to help themselves on the daily occasions and labors, without paying attention to those who have wished to perturb the action for the consumption of the *doctrinas* (Márquez Cabrera, 1685a).

Ultimately, Guale and Mocama would actually remain divided into five separate towns, although three of these were indeed located on the Island of Santa Maria (Amelia Island). Although the governor's account glosses over some of the problems involved with gaining the accord of the Indian leaders (and totally ignores the complete failure of the Guale garrison to protect the northern mission towns the previous fall), Márquez Cabrera did make note of the fact that there was some resistance to the move.

This resistance seems to have manifested itself in a limited degree of flight from the missions immediately following the pirate raids of 1684. Interestingly, as mentioned above, at precisely this time (early November), a group of nearly 150 Scottish colonists landed at the old site of Santa Elena to found Stuart's Town (see Document 11). The town was established very near to the Yamassee town that had been founded in mid-1683 following the Grammont raid on Guale, and an alliance followed soon thereafter between the Scots and the Yamassee under the leadership of the Indian chief "Aratomahan," or Altamaha (perhaps the leader of the 1675 Yamassee town of La Tama, located on the now-abandoned Island of Santa Maria).

Beginning early in January of 1685, however, other Yamassee, who seem to have been living in the deep interior among the Coweta and Kasihta (ancestral head-towns of the Lower Creek), began to flow into the area around Port Royal Sound, joining Altamaha next to Stuart's Town. On January 10, the Scottish leaders noted that "Yesterday some moe of the nation of the Yamassee arrived at St. Helena to settle with those of their nation formerly settled there having come from above St. Augustine" (Cardross and Dunlop, 1685). As described by the trader Caleb Westbrooke just over a month later "Since my last [letter] to you I heare newes that even amazes me. I fear it is too true that all Amercario, all the Westoe River, is come downe from the Cowetaws and Kussetaws, Yamasses that lived amongst them, a thousand or more + dayle more expected and ten cassiquas with them" (Westbrooke, 1685). Seemingly, as word spread throughout the interior of the new alliance between Altamaha and the Scottish colony of Stuart's Town, massive numbers of expatriated refugees who had been living in other areas and among other groups began to relocate, aggregating as a group in the region around Port Royal Sound.

Most important for the present discussion, among these immigrants were a number of former mission Indians, noted to be from "3 nations of the Spanish Indians that are Christians, Sapella, Soho, and Sapickay" (Westbrooke, 1685). Undoubtedly, these were fugitives from the mission towns of Sapala, Asajo, and Tupiqui. Indeed, among the Mocama Indians living late in 1685 at the new site of Guadalquini, it was known that these fugitives included "some Indians of the Colones, Yguajas,[41] and from Asajo, who are distributed and aggregated among the Yamasses, and in other forests" (see Document 9). Based on the evidence above, then, some of the former inhabitants of the missions forced to relocate after the pirate raids of 1684, including Sapala, Tupiqui, Asajo, and the Colones (from San Simón), fled from the mission provinces and joined their former Muskoghean-speaking neighbors, the Yamassee, in the interior, many of whom soon aggregated around Stuarts Town on the northern coast. Indeed, the fact that the mission town of Asajo had not been reestablished among the newly relocated Guale and Mocama towns to the south during the visitation of 1685 (nor was there a cacique or leader in attendance from Asajo) suggests that the inhabitants of Asajo, forced to flee from St. Simons Island as their town was being burned by pirates, chose not to return within the Spanish domain (although the name Asajo reappeared in two subsequent mission lists, suggesting that at least some inhabitants did return later [Ebelino de Compostela, 1689; Pueyo, 1695]).

Following the retreat from the Georgia coast, Guale and Mocama represented a transformed mission province. In December of 1685, Governor Márquez Cabrera dispatched Sergeant Major Domingo de Leturiondo on a formal visitation of the northern missions, and his account provides ample detail regarding the newly restructured province (see Document 9). Based on this documentation, along with later evidence, Guale and Mocama were after 1685 composed of five mission towns clustered between the northern end of Amelia Island and the mouth of the St. Johns River (figure 4). The three remaining towns in the province of Guale were now clustered on a single island. As later described by the Guale caciques of the towns of San Phelipe and Santa Maria in 1699, "today. . .we find ourselves destroyed and annihilated, and all the province reduced to only one hundred men divided between three villages, which are Santa Maria, San Phelipe, and Tupiqui" (Aluste and Chicasli, 1699).

On the tip of Amelia Island, at the new northern frontier of Spanish-held territory, was the town of Santa Clara de Tupiqui, severely reduced in population and without a formal cacique in 1685.[42] Tupiqui was almost certainly established at the now-abandoned site of the 1675 Yamasee town on the northern end of Lieutenant Arcos' "Island of Mocama." The fact that Tupiqui seems to have

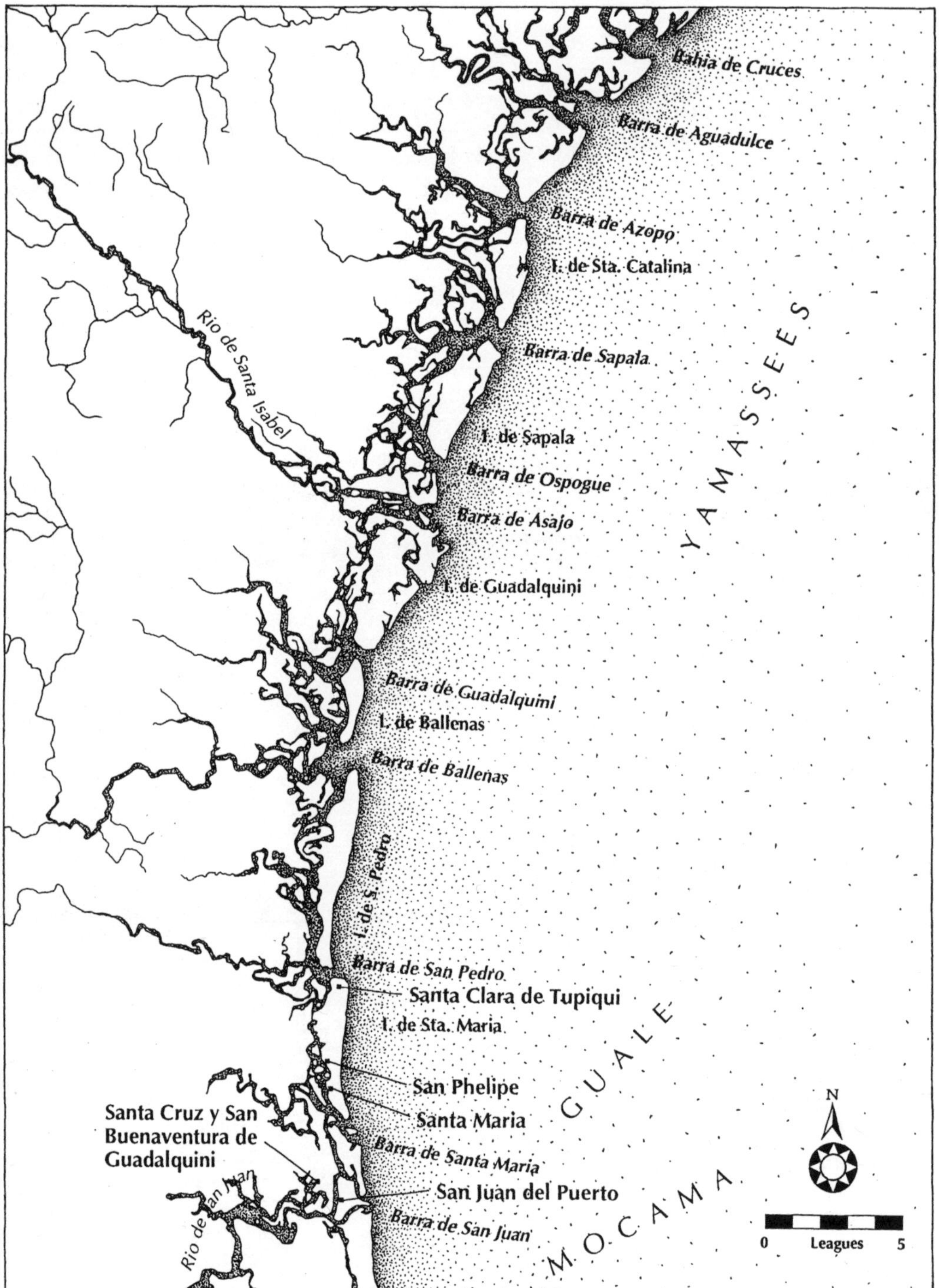

Fig. 4. Projected locations of principal Guale and Mocama missions in 1685, based on information contained in the visitation that year (Leturiondo, 1685) and in two later mission lists (Menéndez Márquez and Florencia, 1697; Dickenson, 1697).

separated temporarily from Sapala after more than 10 years together on Sapelo Island might relate to internal political difficulties which had persisted throughout the period.[43] Nearly 3 leagues to the south, the town of San Phelipe had been established on the old site of the 1675 Yamassee town of La Tama. Here lived several caciques under the general leadership of San Phelipe's cacique Lucas, all of whom may have been associated with San Phelipe's leadership since the early 17th century (see Document 9). Half a league to the south, on the old site of Mission Santa Maria, now twice-abandoned (by the Mocama and then the Yamassee), the recently relocated town of San Joseph de Sapala had joined Santa Catalina de Guale and San Diego de Satuache (present since mid-1684) to form the new administrative center and garrison headquarters of the Guale/Mocama province. The Island of Santa Maria (Amelia Island) had now become the new Guale province, with all the remaining Muskhogean-speaking towns aggregated into three settlements.

Some 6 leagues to the south, the new Mocama province consisted of two towns. San Juan del Puerto, still in its original location on Fort George Island, had now been joined by the newly established town of Santa Cruz y San Buenaventura de Guadalquini, approximately a league to the west on the northern side of the St. Johns River (inasmuch as previous scholars placed this mission far to the south, detailed arguments regarding the location of Santa Cruz y San Buenaventura are located in Appendix A). The composition of the town's leadership and inhabitants does not seem to have changed, but the name was altered upon the relocation, perhaps because Guadalquini had been founded on an abandoned site once named Santa Cruz. Guadalquini was now situated on the mainland, and although this location persisted for more than a decade, Guadalquini eventually fused with the nearby San Juan del Puerto on its island location between 1695 and 1697, complying with the wishes of the governor, "knowing clearly how endangered they are in the said village of Santa Cruz of being infested by enemies from the mainland" (Pueyo, 1695; also see Appendix A). Indeed, Guadalquini's cacique Don Lorenzo de Santiago had become the cacique of San Juan by 1701 (Zuñiga y Cerda, 1701).

During the visitation of 1685, the inhabitants of Guale and Mocama were admonished to plan carefully for the defense of the missions, because

> this province and its villages are all on islands, bars, and ports where the enemy French and English corsairs, and also the Chiscas[44] and Chuchumecos, have endeavored by sea and land to invade, assault, and sack them, achieving this on some occasions, the cause of the towns having been moved and aggregated to one another for better strength and defense, retreating to the proximity of the presidio so that they might be aided that much earlier by the infantry with greater promptness, and it is necessary that for the referred, and what could happen to them, they should remain with all care and vigilance, being with all the necessary sentinels and guards, prompt and prepared with weapons for such occasions (Leturiondo, 1685).

Detailed plans were drawn up for the protection of the province, including a rapid and effective system of communication (Document 9). Ultimately, the newly reorganized mission province of Guale and Mocama was to become a sort of last stand for the indigenous inhabitants of coastal Georgia. During the next 17 years, the missions north of St. Augustine would enjoy a period of comparative tranquility, although in the interior, the battle was only beginning.

Very soon after the nearly simultaneous establishment of Stuarts Town and the final retreat of Guale and Mocama from the Georgia coastline, the swelling body of Yamasee Indians allied to the Carolina colonists embarked on several aggressive moves that would force a rapid Spanish reprisal. In February of 1685, a group of perhaps 50 Yamassee under the leadership of Chief Altamaha descended upon the interior mission of Santa Catalina de Afuyca in the Timucua province, burning the town, killing some 18 Indian residents, and taking away 21 slaves and the furnishings of the mission church (Rodríquez Tisnado, 1685; Livingston, 1686; Crane, 1956; Bushnell, 1994). The Yamassee had entered into a contract with the Scottish colonists at Stuart's Town, who gave them 30 shotguns and cutlasses as the price of the slaves they could bring back with them. The slaves were taken to Stuart's Town, where some were sold to an Englishman from Charles Town, and the rest to an Irish ship bringing more colonists (Livingston, 1686).[45]

By the end of the following March, Scottish colonists from Stuart's Town had explored almost as far south as St. Catherines Island, "which we hear the Spainards have desarted on the report of our setling here, and we desyre this summer to vew it and tak possessione of it in his Majesties name for the behove of the lords proprietors" (Cardross and Dunlop, 1685). The Scottish proposal may have been acted upon soon after this letter, for by November of that year, Don Lorenzo Santiago, the cacique of Guadalquini, received intelligence that "all the Yamazes are settled on the islands that the Indians of Guale left, Santa Catalina and Zapala" (Gómez, 1685). Although Don Lorenzo proposed to the provincial lieutenant of Timucua that he should "go from here [Santa Fé] with fifty men to his village of Guadalquini, and thirty that he had, with the aid of canoes, and they would go in search of the Yamazes, since he knows their hideouts" (Gómez, 1685), this expedition does not seem to have taken place, since the English-allied Yamassee were not routed from this region for another year.

During the following year of 1686, Governor Márquez Cabrera took his vengeance, effectively checking the rapid encroachment of Carolina and its Yamassee allies along the Georgia coast. In August of that year, three Spanish galliots set sail from St. Augustine on a pivotal expedition to destroy Stuart's Town. Stopping at the recently established Guale refugee towns on Amelia Island for additional warriors, the vessels under Captain Alexandro Thomás de León cruised northward along the Georgia coast and made their landing on Santa Elena Island, burning the freshly abandoned Scottish colony to the ground (see Document 11). Pursuing the fugitive colonists north into accepted English territory, the Spaniards sacked several Carolina plantations, including that of the governor, discovering clear evidence of Carolina complicity in earlier pirate raids, and also a robe taken from the church at the Santa Catalina de Afuyca mission. Although a hurricane resulted in the loss of the expedition's leader and flagship, the Spanish invasion of Carolina had made its mark, successfully wiping out the Scottish frontier colony of Stuart's Town (Dunlop, 1929; Crane, 1956: 31; Bushnell, 1994; also see Document 11). A follow-up raid led by Captain Francisco de Fuentes during December of 1686 effectively dislodged the remaining Yamassee on the Georgia and lower South Carolina coast (Document 11; Bushnell, 1994).

At about the same time as the León expedition, the adventurous Carolina explorer Dr. Henry Woodward was deep in the western interior, busy laying the groundwork for trading relationships that would shape the battle for control of the Southeast for years to come. Following a first visit to the Apalachicola province the previous summer of 1685, which had prompted the dispatch of an expeditionary force under Apalachee's provincial Lieutenant Antonio Matheos, Woodward was once again among the Coweta and Kasihta during the summer of 1686, while Stuart's Town was being destroyed (Crane, 1956: 34–36). In a curious twist of fate, the closing contest for the Georgia coast would link with the coming struggle for the western interior during the return journey of the León expedition. A group of five Guale Indians returning along the coast from the invasion of Carolina crossed paths with five English traders and a pair of Uchise Indians descending the Savannah River, returning from Dr. Woodward's trading expedition along the Lower Chattahoochee River. Although the traders initially captured the Guale, the prisoners subsequently escaped and killed the Englishmen to a man (Agustín et al., 1686; Matheo, 1686).

Although Dr. Henry Woodward, returning simultaneously by a different route to Charles Town, would never return to the western interior, the groundwork was laid for Carolina expansion into the deep frontier (Crane, 1956). Over the next two decades the Spanish/English struggle for Georgia would focus on the western provinces, leaving the remnants of Guale and Mocama comparatively secure in their new settlements on Amelia Island and the mouth of the St. Johns River. The coast of Georgia had been abandoned, effectively negating the Spanish claim to much of old Guale and Mocama. In the uneasy peace that followed on the eastern frontier between Carolina and Florida, the battle raged in the west, marking the closing chapter in the struggle for Georgia. Guale and Mocama had played their role, and attention now shifted to the interior.

THE RETREAT OF GUALE AND MOCAMA IN RETROSPECT

The 1685 regrouping of Guale and Mocama along the northern coast of present-day Florida represented the culmination of a struggle that had lasted nearly a quarter of a century. What began with the first Chichimeco assault in the summer of 1661 had concluded with the disastrous pirate raid of the fall of 1684. The effective result was the depopulation of the Georgia coast, leaving old Guale and Mocama a virtually uninhabited borderland between the Spanish and the English. Once a functioning part of the colonial system of Spanish Florida, the northern mission provinces gradually retreated seaward and southward, ultimately forming a huddled cluster of villages under constant Spanish protection. Over the course of only 23 years, Guale and Mocama had shrunk from some 10 mission towns distributed across more than 40 leagues of coastline to only 5 towns within the district of 8 leagues. Only one mission, San Juan del Puerto, remained in its original location throughout this turbulent period.

The retreat of Guale and Mocama involved two related processes: relocation and aggregation (figures 5 and 6). Mission towns were often moved, frequently as a result of direct assault, from one location to another. As noted above, the overarching strategy of such relocations appears to have been the relocation of mainland towns to the more sheltered barrier islands, and the redistribution of exposed northerly towns to the south in order to maintain links in the chain of travel and communication. At the same time, once separate towns were joined together, forming aggregated towns composed of the former inhabitants of as many as four distinct missions. This process typically took the form of one or more refugee towns settling in a preexisting town.

Despite this, chiefly lineages seem to have been maintained even within these aggregated settlements, and thus although the overall population of each town had in many cases been devastated, the identity and name of then effectively defunct villages often persisted in these traditional lineages. Even the brief influx of immigrant refugees between the late 1660s and 1683 does not seem to have substantially affected the internal sociopolitical structure of Guale and Mocama. Indeed, the vast majority of Yamassee Indians who filtered into the northern mission provinces later relocated as an entire group, effectively detaching themselves from their short-lived association with the Spanish colonial system.

Based on admittedly limited documentary evidence, the processes of relocation and aggregation characterizing Guale and Mocama during this period do not seem to have resulted in an inherent homogenization of preexisting social identity. Although once-separate villages and towns had been depopulated, relocated, and aggregated, the internal sociopolitical structure of the Guale and Mocama provinces was more or less maintained within the resultant refugee settlements. Whole towns were first aggregated, then separated, then aggregated once again, suggesting that at least in the short term, the aggregation of towns did not result in the loss of former identity.

Contrary to what might be expected, the contraction and removal of Guale and Mocama from the Georgia coast did not extinguish the multiplicity of chiefly lineages reflecting the precontact social order. The visitation records of 1685, 1695, and 1701 list many aboriginal names belonging to towns that may not have existed individually for more than half a century,[46] suggesting that although by that time the inhabitants of Guale and Mocama had been reduced to only a handful of refugee settlements, much of the traditional aboriginal hierarchy remained intact (Leturiondo, 1685; Pueyo, 1695; Zuñiga y Cerda, 1701). Although the rapidity with which the settlement distribution of Guale and Mocama was transformed may have contributed to such continuity (since many aboriginal leaders lived through the entire process), the maintenance of these chiefly lineages provides a remarkable example of the

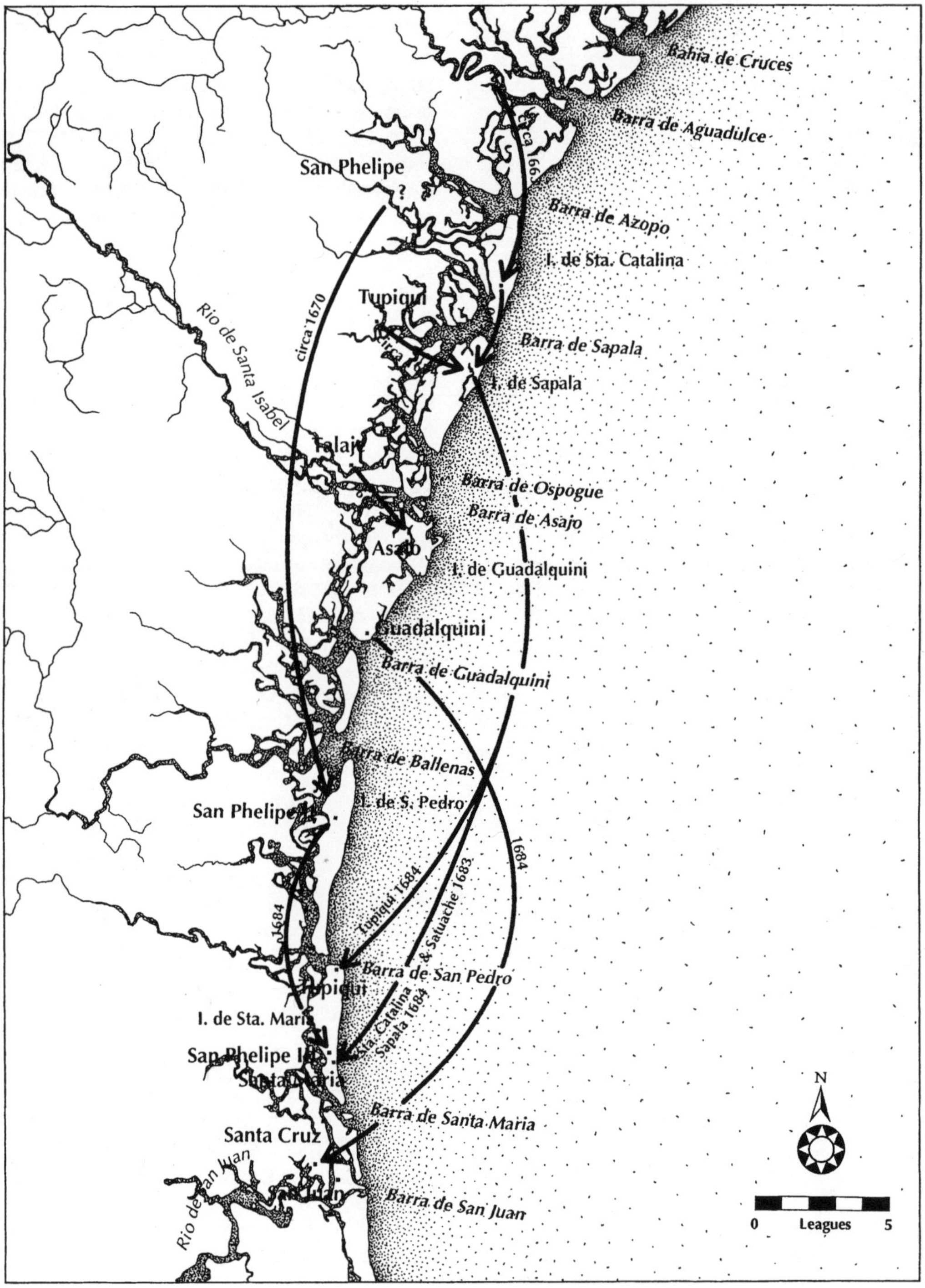

Fig. 5. Synthetic map of the retreat of principal Guale and Mocama missions between 1655 and 1685. Successive locations for individual missions correspond to table 8 (see Appendix A).

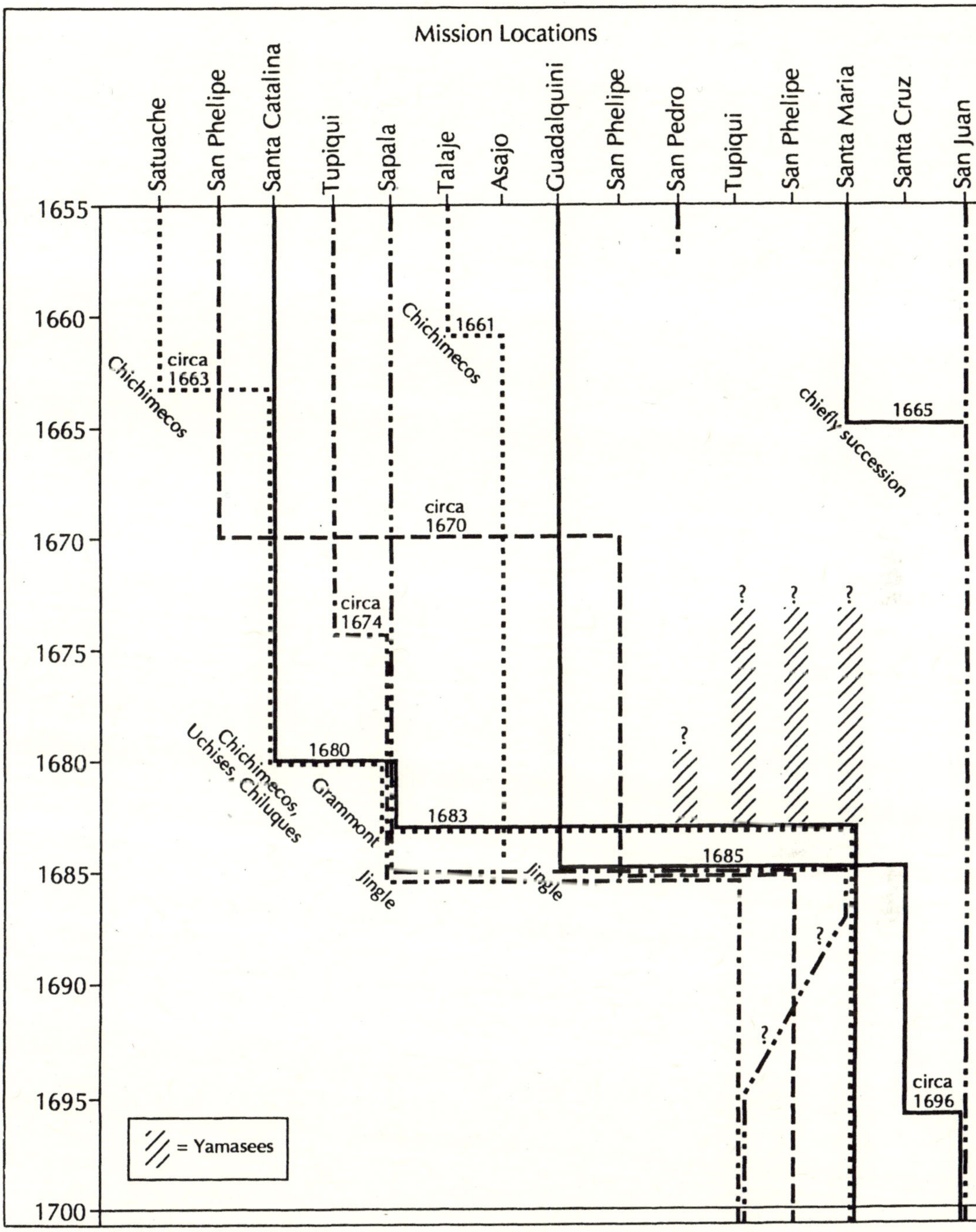

Fig. 6. Synthetic diagram of the retreat of principal Guale and Mocama missions between 1655 and 1702. Individual geographic locations are at the top; dates are on the left.

persistence of aboriginal culture in the face of the massive, and ultimately fatal, stresses of the European colonial era.

In the end, however, the regrouping of Guale and Mocama along the northern coast of Florida would only delay the inevitable. Eighteen years after that final 1684 raid on the Georgia coastal missions, the huddled towns of Guale and Mocama were subjected to one last invasion. Early in the morning on November 4, 1702, Amelia Island was overrun by English forces on their way to burn St. Augustine (Arnade, 1959; Bushnell, 1994). By nightfall, the Spanish garrison and the remaining inhabitants of the three Guale towns had retreated to San Juan del Puerto. As related by Governor Zuñiga y Cerda (1702) the following day,

> I remain besieged on all sides, while the English enemies, with Indians and blacks, have come to carry off, burn, and lay waste to 3 villages that there were on the Island of Santa Maria, the province of Guale, which are San Pedro de Tupiqui,[47] San Phelipe, and Santa Maria, the multitude of people obligating the lieutenant to retreat to the village of San Juan del Puerto, where the town of Santa Cruz is aggregated twelve leagues from this presidio.

By the end of the month, San Juan had been abandoned. Probably soon after penning his last letter to the governor from the southern bank of the St. Johns River on November 27, Captain Francisco de Fuentes, the long-time provincial lieutenant of Guale and Mocama, was himself captured by the English aggressors, eventually to die a prisoner in Charles Town.[48] The refugees of Guale and Mocama retreated to St. Augustine, where they would soon be joined by those from Apalachee and Timucua.

Following the 1702 rout, the provinces of Guale and Mocama were reduced to only two towns under the guns of the Castillo de San Marcos in St. Augustine. By 1711, Guale was a refugee village under the name of Santa Catalina de Guale, and Mocama was a single village named San Juan del Puerto (Hann, 1987). In all, only 400 inhabitants made up the total of seven settlements inhabited by the last of the mission Indians. Ironically, following the Yamassee War of 1715, these villages were augmented by an influx of pagan refugees, probably in some cases the very same Yamassee (or their descendants) who had fled to Carolina from Guale and Mocama in 1683 (Hann, 1987). Ultimately, these remaining towns would spend the last decades of their existence on the North American continent clustered around St. Augustine before the final withdrawal to Cuba in 1763.

The retreat of Guale and Mocama between 1661 and 1684 forms only one chapter in the transformation of these aboriginal societies in the context of European colonization. Nevertheless, the events of those 23 years marked the rapid acceleration of societal change among the inhabitants of these provinces, fueled primarily by the processes of retreat and aggregation in the face of English-sponsored aggression from the north. The details of these processes reveal in many cases the remarkable persistence of aboriginal sociopolitical structure under conditions of substantial depopulation, frequent relocation and aggregation, and increasing ethnic diversity. In the end, however, the tragic events of this brief era resulted in the near-complete depopulation of the Georgia coastline, effectively paving the way for the creation of the Georgia colony nearly half a century later. In broad perspective, the aboriginal societies of Guale and Mocama, already transformed within the context of the Spanish colonial system, finally became victims of a broader late 17th-century geopolitical struggle between England and Spain. Long before James Oglethorpe arrived to found Savannah in 1733, the buffer zone between Carolina and Florida had been established on the ruins of old Guale and Mocama.

NOTES

1. The 1655 list also included a reference to the mission of Santiago de Ocone, which was located on the eastern side of the Okefenokee Swamp within the jurisdiction of the Mocama town of San Pedro (Worth, 1992: 183). Though originally a distinct indigenous province, by the mid-17th century the Ocone town was largely composed of fugitive Indians from the interior Timucua province (Ruiz de Salazar Vallecilla, 1646), and was finally burned to the ground in 1656 under the direction of Governor Don Diego de Rebolledo. Although some of its inhabitants retreated to San Pedro de Mocama, most fled to the interior after 1656 (Al-

cayde de Cordoba, 1660). As a result, Mission Santiago de Ocone will not be considered in this essay.

2. The last-known reference to Mission San Pedro appeared during the 1660 *residencia* of Governor Don Diego de Rebolledo, when Captain Martín Alcayde de Cordoba (1660) made note of the 1655 destruction of Santiago de Ocone, which was "in the province of Mocama . . . withdrawn from the village of San Pedro, which is the head of the said province." At the same time Clemente Bernal was referred to as only being "the principal cacique of the village of San Juan del Puerto, province of Mocama, and its jurisdiction" (Ranjel, 1660), and upon his death in 1665, Bernal was named "principal cacique of San Juan del Puerto, and of all Mocama" (Guerra y Vega, 1665b), suggesting that Alcayde's reference to San Pedro as the provincial capital in 1660 may have been an erroneous reference to its former status. The reasons for the disappearance of San Pedro are unclear, although they may relate to a shift in chiefly succession.

3. These other caciques were Don Francisco de Ybarra (lineage unknown), Don Juan de Zapala (presumably the cacique of Mission San Joseph de Sapala), Bernabé de Aluste (based on later visitation records [see Document 9], probably the cacique of Mission San Phelipe), and Don Thomás de Yor (probably of the lineage that once led the former Guale town of Yoa).

4. In this same petition, the caciques of Guale complained about the common abuses of the *repartimiento* labor system, in which a specified number of unmarried males were drafted from each mission town during the winter to serve as field hands in the spring and summer for the Spanish soldiers in St. Augustine (relevant translations appear in Worth, 1992: 126–129). Unofficial additions to the yearly quotas were evidently common, inasmuch as soldiers typically used Indian laborers in their own fields, selling the harvest back to the royal storehouses in St. Augustine for personal profit. An examination of typical labor draft orders dating to the 1660s and 1670s (see Document 5, and the Addendum) reveals wording that effectively permitted such abuses.

5. Although it is a commonly reported fact that general Spanish colonial policy forbade the possession of firearms by Indians, ample evidence from Spanish Florida reveals that mission Indians were regularly armed with arquebuses and shotguns by the middle of the 17th century, and that these trained Indian warriors formed an important part of the aboriginal militia forces frequently employed in Florida as a direct supplement to the typically sparse complement of Spanish infantry. Although the pure quantity of firearms and munitions marshaled by English-backed slave raiders from the north typically overwhelmed the small number of antiquated weapons held by mission Indians, it is a myth that they were forced to rely only on bows and arrows.

6. This *aranzel* was probably similar to that which Governor Rebolledo posted in the provinces of Apalachee and Timucua during his visitation a year earlier (translated by Hann, 1986a).

7. Here Governor Rebolledo undoubtedly refers to the standing Indian militia in the mission provinces, primarily composed of Indian leaders and warriors (Worth, 1992: 140–147). As noted above, the governor's 1656 activation of this militia, and his subsequent treatment of the Guale warriors who arrived in St. Augustine, very nearly sparked an uprising in Guale similar to that of the Timucuan rebellion.

8. This presumably refers to the yearly *repartimiento* labor draft quota.

9. *Chacal* was a term generally employed in the Apalachee province, and referred to a secondary Indian official (Hann, 1988: 106, 401).

10. The letter was unfortunately placed in Legajo 965 of the section Contaduria, which was severely burned in the early 20th century. The original letter is heavily charred, and only portions can still be read (the right margin of all lines is missing, for example). Gaps in each line of text are indicated by [–], and missing lines at the top or bottom of each page are indicated by [— -].

11. This rendition is uncertain, inasmuch as the original Spanish text is heavily charred here. The lines in question read as follows: "andaba una nacion de grande num [–] yndios que decian eran chichumecos [–] ellos algunos yngleses con bocas [–] y este año de mil y seiscientos y sese [–] en beinte del mes de junio yc [–] trada en la probincia de Guale." The term "bocas de fuego" ("muzzles of fire") was commonly used during that period to refer to firearms. Based on the typical structure and usage of the era, the appearance of "ellos" ("them") before the reference to the Englishmen, and following the first mention of the Chichimeco, most likely means that the original passage read "andaba una nacion de grande num[ero de] yndios que decian eran chichumecos [y entre] ellos algunos yngleses con bocas [de fuego] y este año de mil y seiscientos y sese[nta y uno] en beinte del mes de junio yc[e en]trada en la probincia de Guale."

12. As I have discussed elsewhere (Worth, 1992: 68–69, 76–77), the river of Santa Ysabel was undoubtedly the modern Altamaha River, inasmuch as documentary sources dating to the period 1616–1636 place the deep interior mission of Santa Ysabel at the forks of the Altamaha, from which the river derived its 17th-century name. The location

of Mission Santo Domingo de Talaje on the banks of this river made it the first town encountered by the Chichimeco raiders, and thus a likely first target.

13. The probable location of the province of Tama (Altamaha) during the 16th and early 17th centuries was the Fall Line region of the Oconee River, perhaps centered at the Shinholser Mound site (Hudson et al., 1984; Worth, 1994). Catufa most likely refers to one of several nearby towns to the north of Tama, noted more than a century before by the chroniclers of the Hernando de Soto expedition as Ocute, Cofaqui, and Patofa/Tatofa.

14. Among the soldiers known to have participated in this expedition under Captain Juan Sánchez de Uriza are Juan Francisco de los Santos (Santos, 1672; Sánchez de Uriza, 1672), and probably also Manuel de Espinosa (Royal Cédula, 1680). As is the case with Santos, military service records often provide many little-known details regarding the various events in which soldiers participated, making a list of participants in such actions invaluable as a guide for future historical research.

15. Another distinct group of displaced Indians, the Chisca, had been preying upon the mission Indians of Timucua, Apalachee, and Guale since as early as 1618, but there is as yet no evidence that their depredations were directly linked with a slave trade to Virginia. Defeated by Spanish infantry in their Appalachian Mountain homeland during the Juan Pardo expeditions of 1566–1568 (Hudson, 1990), the Chisca seem to have maintained a "parasitic" existence along the deep western mission frontier, preying on the poorly defended Spanish mission towns (Worth, 1992: 152–155). In 1651, Governor Nicolás Ponce de León (1651a, 1651b) was prompted to name Captain Antonio de Argüelles as his Lieutenant in Guale in order to rid the province of Sisica (Chisca) Indians, who had been raiding both Guale and Timucua that year (Worth, 1992: 154).

16. At least two later military service records indicate a date of 1660 for one Chichimeco raid on Guale, although these were probably references to the 1661 raid (particularly since both of these citations were made decades after the fact, and could easily be mistranscriptions or the result of erroneous recollections). A summary of the military service of Captain Matheo Luis de Florencia indicated that in 1660, "he helped recover [*recuperar*] a village of the province of Guale, where the Chichimeco Indians had fortified themselves, until forcing them out of it, and the Governor left him as head and leader of the infantry with which he garrisoned the said province" (Florencia, 1682). Similarly, Juan Sánchez de Uriza certified in 1675 that Diego Díaz Mexia participated in the 1660 expedition when he (Sánchez de Uriza) was named "as head of the infantry that were dispatched to the province of Guale by order of Governor and Captain General Don Alonso de Aranguiz y Cotes in order to resist the invasion that the Chichimeco enemy made in those provinces." Since Sánchez de Uriza is known to have led the retaliation force sent against the Chichimeco in 1661, this last reference is almost certainly an erroneous date.

17. Governor Nicolás Ponce de León (1651b) had named Captain Antonio de Argüelles his provincial lieutenant in Guale during the Chisca raids of 1651, and in 1658 Governor Don Diego de Rebolledo named Captain Nicolás Estevez de Carmenatis as the lieutenant of Guale and Mocama in order to conduct a visitation of the provinces (Rebolledo, 1658a; Estevez de Carmenatis, 1669).

18. It should be noted here that during the last half of the 17th century, small infantry garrisons were eventually placed in all three major mission provinces. Each of these garrisons was commanded by an officer eventually given the official title of lieutenant to the governor of Florida. Lieutenant was not a military rank as such, but rather an assigned post that could be occupied by officers of many ranks, ranging from sergeant to sergeant major.

The military structure of 17th-century Spanish Florida was organized around a limited number of official posts, with accompanying royal salaries, that were occupied in succession by a much larger number of infantry soldiers based in St. Augustine (see, for example, Bushnell, 1981). The governor served as overall military commander, and under his direct command was the sergeant major of the fort, along with a handful of adjutants to the sergeant major, all of whom operated in and around the city of St. Augustine. The rest of the infantry were divided into two, and later three, companies under the command of a single captain, along with several ensigns and a sergeant. Each of these companies was divided into five squads made up of roughly 25 soldiers each, which were individually commanded by a squad leader.

As a soldier advanced from active post to active post, he gained additional rank and pay. When succeeded by others in a particular post, the individual lost the additional pay but maintained his rank, becoming what was known as a *reformado*, or officer without an active post. As the 17th century progressed, there were larger and larger numbers of these *reformados*, serving as a pool of inactive officers who were typically sent on journeys far from St. Augustine, such as to the mission provinces or even the deep interior. As a consequence, half a dozen officers may have shared the rank of sergeant major, while only one held the active post of sergeant major in the fort.

From this pool of inactive officers were selected

the infantry who were stationed in the provincial garrisons, and one of them was given the post of lieutenant, which was continually maintained in the mission provinces (and thus transferred to temporary lieutenants during journeys back to St. Augustine, etc.). A complete listing of the officers holding these posts has yet to be compiled, although many are documented.

19. These two towns were both indigenous to the southern coastal region of present-day South Carolina. The former was apparently on or near the original site of the late 16th-century Spanish colonial outpost of Santa Elena, and the second was probably the nearby town known as Ahoya at that time, visited by the Juan Pardo expeditions of 1566–1568 (Hudson, 1990).

20. The order of Guale missions listed on the 1673 labor draft (Addendum, Document 1) strongly suggests that San Phelipe was at that time located to the south of Asajo (on St. Simons), and not in its original location near Santa Catalina. The fact that Governor Guerra y Vega sent Don Nicolás Ponce de León on a formal visitation of Guale and Mocama beginning on November 22, 1670, might possibly relate to the relocation of San Phelipe at about this same time (Cendoya, 1671). Unfortunately, the 22 folios of documentation that resulted from this visitation have yet to be located.

21. A small force of Guale Indians were collected from Santa Catalina on the way northward for the failed expedition (see Document 14).

22. This officer had earlier been chosen to deliver the fateful 1656 Rebolledo order for the remission of corn and warriors from Guale, the corresponding version of which sparked the Timucuan Rebellion in the western provinces (Worth, 1992). Much later, in 1699, the two remaining aboriginal leaders of Guale, Diego Aluste (in San Phelipe) and Juan Chicasle (in Santa Maria), confirmed that "thirty years ago, more or less, finding ourselves infested by some enemy nations, we asked Don Francisco de la Guerra y de la Vega, who was governor of these provinces, that he would be served to concede us a garrison of infantry to defend us in the encounters that we had with the said enemies, and that we would aid them with the sustenance of meat or fish, firewood, cassina, and the rest that might present itself for the said infantry; and the said governor having seen our petition, he conceded it thus" (Aluste and Chicasle, 1699).

23. The lieutenant was almost certainly arranging for the settlement of one or both of the two Yamassee towns listed two years later by Pacheco's successor Pedro de Arcos (1675). This reference may thus fix the date at which the Colon town of San Simón and the other Yamassee town of Ocotonico were established on the inland side of St. Simons Island.

24. Diacun was interviewed in St. Augustine with two interpreters present: Antonio Camuñas, "interpreter of the language of Guale," and Diego, "a native of the town of Santa Catalina" (Cendoya, 1672).

25. When a group of Rickohockans were murdered at the Ocaneechee town in 1670, Lederer made particular note of the face paint of the Indian warriors, which was made from "auripigmentum," bringing to mind the 1659 Spanish reference to the newly arrived Indian warriors from the north, who were singled out as having "striped" faces.

26. The combined evidence regarding the location of this town, including its situation between the two missions noted above (see Appendix A) and its position on the 1683 Solana map, places it more or less directly on the site of General Oglethorpe's later colonial settlement associated with Fort Frederica. Indeed, this goes a long way toward explaining the adoption of the name of St. Simons for the island that had originally been known as Guadalquini. Indeed, the first English settlement was established in the old fields of the then-abandoned pagan town of San Simón.

27. Female aboriginal leaders in Guale were designated as *mica* or *cacica* (instead of *mico* or *cacique*).

28. Florida pilot Martín de Echagaray (1684) later recalled that the attackers, who came from the vicinity of Charles Town, comprised "up to 200 men, masked [*enmascarados*] and armed with their shotguns, without being able to distinguish whether they were Frenchmen or Indians." The king's *fiscal* commented that it was obvious that the culprits were Indians, since the French did not disguise themselves in battle. Echagaray may have been referring to warpaint covering the faces of the Chichimeco attackers, calling to mind the "striped" faces first mentioned in reference to the Chichimeco in 1659 (see above).

29. This officer would ultimately play an important role in the southward retreat of Guale and Mocama, and was eventually prosecuted for dereliction of duty after the final pirate raid of 1684 (see below, and Document 10).

30. The population of Mission Santa Catalina (including the attached town of Satuache) was noted to be 140 persons five years earlier (Arcos, 1675), and experienced Florida pilot Martín de Echagaray (1684) said that in 1679 he saw 60 families in "town called Santa Cathalina," just prior to the abandonment of the site. Following the 1680 raid, this number had been reduced to only 104 adult inhabitants (Fuentes, 1681; see below).

31. As will be noted on all the maps for this volume, the sound immediately north of St. Cath-

erines Island (St. Catherines Sound) was known as the Bar of Azopo during the latter half of the 17th century. It is important to note, however, that documentary evidence dating to the late 16th and early 17th century reveals that the Bar of Azopo was originally situated by the Spanish farther to the north, on the northern side of Ossabaw Island (Ossabaw Sound). The fact that the name for the original Bar of Azopo was changed to the the Bar of Aguadulce (a Spanish term for "freshwater") by the late 17th century may relate to the disappearance of the town of Azopo (presumably located on Ossabaw Island) during the colonial period.

32. This missionary, Fray Simón de Salas, had been one of the two missionaries in Sapala immediately before the raid of 1680 (Barreda, 1680). The Franciscan serving Santa Catalina at that time, Bernabé de los Angeles, disappears from the documentary record for Guale after the retreat to Sapala (not surprisingly, there was a marked turnover of friars in Guale between the period immediately before and after the Chichimeco raid).

33. The same phrasing in labor draft orders was frequently exploited by Spanish soldiers during the 17th century in collecting "voluntary" additions to the yearly drafts (Menéndez et al., 1657; also see Document 5).

34. The indication that the village of the Colon Indians remained in the mission provinces supports other evidence in suggesting that this group somehow managed to retain its original identity amidst the homogenizing effect of the Yamassee confederacy (see below). Indeed, in 1681 Francisco de Fuentes chose to specify the Colones as a distinct group, lumping the rest of the unconverted Indians living in Guale and Mocama into the broad category of Yamassee.

35. Although the original text reads "San Pedro" here, the fact that this town had been depopulated, combined with later statements (see below), indicate that the plan was to join San Phelipe and Asajo in the abandoned town of San Pedro.

36. This refers to the entire population of the four towns then aggregated in San Joseph de Sapala.

37. Don Joseph de la Cruz was in fact the *tunaque* of the town of Tupiqui, as becomes clear from later documents (and from another section of this document).

38. Copies of the original orders to both Aranda y Avellaneda (dispatched October 2) and his subsequent replacement Fuentes (dispatched October 7) are located in AGI SD 856.

39. Since the mud-packed walls of the convent and chapel were apparently burned by the Spanish during the 1686 Fuentes raid (noted by William Dunlop [1687], who viewed the ruins of the mission the following year), it seems likely that the pirates left Mission San Joseph de Sapala standing after their 1684 raid. Yamassee Indians soon reoccupied the abandoned structures (see Document 11).

40. Although the text reads *quatro* or 4, the actual distance is closer to *catorce*, or 14, suggesting that the governor erred in what he wrote.

41. Yguaja seems to have been the Timucua (and thus Mocama) term for the Guale Indians.

42. Tupiqui seems to have been governed by the *tunaque* Don Joseph de la Cruz since at least as early as mid-1684, and probably prior to 1681 (the *mica* Ana Estasia may have died soon after the 1677–1678 Argüelles visitation), indicating that the lack of a cacique was not a result of the recent pirate raid.

43. Interestingly, Phelipe, the cacique of Sapala, was in Mission Santa Clara de Tupiqui during the 1695 visitation (Pueyo, 1695), and his successor was still in Tupiqui in 1701 (Zuñiga y Cerda, 1701), suggesting that the separation of Sapala and Tupiqui in 1685 was only a short-lived condition.

44. The Chisca were apparently a dislodged Indian group from the Appalachian highlands who harassed the western mission chain during the second quarter of the 17th century, and who briefly appeared along the frontier of Guale in 1651 (Hann, 1988a; Hudson, 1990; Worth, 1992). This predatory group had little direct effect on Guale and Mocama.

45. Too late to avoid the attack on Afuyca, a Yamassee cacique named Niquisaya revealed plans for the assault to Guale's Lieutenant Alonso de Argüelles, citing his allegiance to the Spanish (Márquez Cabrera, 1685b). The exact identity of this leader is unclear, but contrary to the conclusions of many researchers (e.g. Arredondo, 1742; Bolton, 1925; Bushnell, 1994), he was not the old cacique of Santa Elena who interacted with the English in the 1660s (see note 56 in Document 11).

46. A good example of this is provided in the 1685 visitation record of the mission town of Tolomato, situated 3 leagues north of St. Augustine (Leturiondo, 1685). Although this Guale town had been destroyed during the 1597 Guale rebellion and relocated far to the south during the late 1620s, the name given in 1685 for the council house in the town of Tolomato in which the visitation was held was Otax, a name for a satellite town in the Guale province that had not appeared in documentary records since the visitations of the early 17th century (i.e., Ybarra, 1604). Christobal, the principal cacique of the town of Otax, was undoubtedly the distant heir to the leadership of that original town far to the north (see Document 9).

47. The use of the name San Pedro with the relocated town of Tupiqui undoubtedly stems from its location on the northern tip of Amelia Island, immediately south of the Bar of San Pedro.

48. Captain Fuentes's son Don Joseph later recounted regarding his father that "lastly being lieutenant in the said province of Guale, he was imprisoned by the English of San Jorje [Charles Town] on the occasion of the siege, where he died on the fifteenth of September, seventeen hundred and five" (Fuentes, 1708).

COVER LETTER OF GOVERNOR DON MANUEL DE MONTIANO, WITH INDEX TO SUPPORTING DOCUMENTATION

INTRODUCTION

The following letter and index were drawn up by Governor of Florida Don Manuel de Montiano in response to a specific request by the Spanish Crown to conduct documentary research into the historical justification of Spain's legal claims to the modern Georgia coast. The letter serves as an introduction to the bundle of documents sent to Spain, and provides a summary and limited analysis of the documents encountered in the archives of St. Augustine as a result of this royal order (with the exception of Montiano's later addendum). The index lists and briefly describes the numbered documents following the cover letter, arranged in chronological order. In the original bundle in the Archivo General de Indias, the index precedes the governor's cover letter, but for the present volume this order was reversed.

The first portion of Governor Montiano's letter constitutes a simple summary of the contents of each numbered document, occasionally referring to pertinent information on specific folios. While in this section governor Montiano departs only once from the chronological relation of enclosed documents for brief commentary, the second portion of his letter comprises a more analytical overview of the history of Spanish Florida with respect to the theme of the English usurpation of the northern provinces in modern Georgia. In this section, Governor Montiano briefly relates the discovery, exploration, and settlement of Florida during the 16th century, followed by a well-reasoned argument designed to prove that the English were latecomers to the regions north of St. Augustine. Much of this information was not mentioned in the documents enclosed with the governor's letter, and thus must have been drawn from other sources (or simply common knowledge).

Although there are occasional factual errors (such as dates of specific events), Montiano's cover letter reflects a literate examination of Spain's legal claim to the modern Georgia coast, and as such serves as a fitting introduction to the original and transcribed documents that follow. In this sense it sets the tone of the investigation which provided the impetus for this early 18th-century archival research, and frames the theme that underlies the entire collection of documents.

My Lord

In a letter dated May 26 of this year, the Governor of Havana advises me that he was ordered officially to arrange for me and the Governor of Cuba to send evidence of the instruments which there might be in the two archives, or in whichever other place, justifying the right and legitimacy which Your Majesty has to the provinces which the English occupy in these dominions [f.1, vto.] of St. Augustine. Taking action on this request, I pass to the Royal hands of Your Majesty all the original papers and evidences which, after a great fatigue and labor, could be discovered in this Archive of Government, and in the [archive] of the convent of San Francisco. Informed of the context of all of them, I must inform the sovereign intelligence of Your Royal Majesty that by the first evidence [Document 1], it is verified that in the year 1565 Your Majesty made an agreement [*asiento*] with Pedro Menéndez de Avilés about [f.2] the conquest of Florida, which is that on the reverse of folio 6 of this testimony, and that encouraging this intention, his beatitude Pope Pius the fifth wrote him the letter on the reverse of folio 28.

By the certification on folio 31, the great expenses which were made for this journey by account of the Royal Hacienda are on record, and by the review judgment on the reverse of folio 41, it is on record that Don Martín Menéndez de Avilés, successor and heir [*mayorazgo*] of [f.2, vto.] the *Adelantado* Pedro Menéndez de Avilés was commanded to be given the title of *adelantado* of the province and land of Florida, and four thousand ducats from the Royal Chests of Mexico in order to incorporate into the said estate, the [said] judgment about having asked that he be conceded all that was promised to the said *adelantado* by the agreement which was made with him about the discovery and settlement of the provinces of Florida, as is expressed in the second request [f.3] on the reverse of folio 46 and onward.[1]

By evidence number 2 [Document 2, this volume] in which one can only verify the year

1586[2] it is on record that His Catholic Majesty having called upon the *adelantado* in order to entrust him with the government of a fleet, he left one of his sons-in-law in the presidio of Santa Elena, and he died as a prisoner in Spain. The *adelantado* having died, the King sent Pedro [f.3, vto.] Menéndez Márquez to these provinces as governor with the order to rebuild the presidio of Santa Elena, and thus he did by account of the Royal Hacienda.

By evidence number 3 [Document 3, this volume] of the year 1587 it is on record that Governor Pedro Menéndez Márquez issued the title of notary public and notary of rations of the fort and city of Santa Elena to Juan Guisado. In the aforementioned fort and city of Santa Elena, the same governor issued in the cited year of 1587 to the same Juan Guisado the title of notary of the voyage which [f.4] he made to Jacán[3] by order of the King, and he issued the title of captain of the company of the fort of Santa Elena to Juan de Posada on August 19, 1588.

By evidence number 4 [Document 4, this volume] it is on record that in the Provincial Chapter of the year 1628 Father Fray Gaspar de Ribota was elected guardian of the convent of Santa Catalina de Guale, and Father Fray Pedro Bill[4] of that of San Buenaventura de Gualequini.

By evidence number 5 [Document 5, this volume], which comprises diverse orders and commissions and begins in the year of 1656, [f.4, vto.] the governmental faculty which the captain generals of this post had over the villages of the provinces of Guale and Mocama is on record, where they maintained their lieutenants with infantry, gathering Indians from them annually for the cultivation of the lands and fields of Florida.

By the notebook of original certifications of number 6 [Document 6, this volume], it is on record that in the year of 1663, the Fathers Fray Carlos de Anguiano, Fray Juan de Uzeda, Fray Gabriel Fernández, Fray Jacinto de Barreda, and Fray Juan Bauptista Campaña were the guardians of Tupiqui, Chatohache, Asaho, and Zapalo, and the president of the convent of the said Asaho, villages of the [f.5] province of Guale.

By the duplicate patent number 6 [Document 6, this volume] it is on record that in the year of 1679 the guardians of San Juan del Puerto, the village of San Phelipe, and Ubadalquini, Asaho, Sapala, and Santa Catalina de Guale were the Fathers Fray Mathias de Bohorques, Fray Gabriel Fernandez, Fray Francisco de Medina, Fray Domingo Santos, Fray Juan de Uzeda, and Fray Bernabe de los Angeles. [f.5, vto.]

By evidence number 7 [Document 7, this volume] it is on record that in the year of 1681 Captain Francisco de Fuentes was lieutenant of the governor and captain general of the province of Guale and Mocama, and in it he had settled the following villages: Tupiqui, Zapala, Satuache, Santa Cathalina, an aggregation of Yamase Indians, Asaho, Colones, Guadalquini, San Phelipe, San Pedro, Santa Maria, and San Juan del Puerto, and that Fathers Fray Simón Martínez de Salas, Fray [f.6] Domingo Santos, Fray Francisco García, Fray Juan Bauptista Campaña, and Fray Francisco de la Cruz administrated in the said villages.

By an original royal *cédula* number 8 [Document 8, this volume], it is on record that in the year of 1683 the King commanded the Governor of Florida Don Juan Márquez Cabrera take care that the English of the Bar of San Jorge[5] should not advance toward our towns of Guale and Zapala. Departing from the listing of these papers, I ought to call to the attention of the sovereign comprehension of Your Royal Majesty that [f.6, vto.] from these times on the complaints which the continuous mischief of the residents of San Jorge stirred up began to manifest themselves, until the second year of this century, in which not only did they effectively achieve their intentions, setting fire to this presidio,[6] but also ruining and destroying all our towns of the province of Guale, of which Your Majesty had been in peaceful possession from the year of 1565, when the *Adelantado* [f.7] Pedro Menéndez de Avilés conquered and settled it, and afterwards the Governor Pedro Menéndez Márquez rebuilt it.

By some original *autos* of visitation of number 9 [Document 9, this volume] it is on record that in the year of 1685 Sergeant Major Domingo de Leturiondo visited the province of Guale, and in it twenty caciques reduced to five towns, by commission of Governor Don Juan Márquez Cabrera.

By some original *autos* of number 10 [Document 10, this volume], begun the first day of January of the aforementioned year of 1685, it is on record that in the preceding year [f.7, vto.] of 1684 the English burned and sacked the town, church, and convent of Gualquini, as is expressed on the reverse of folios 1, 3, 9, 10, 12, and the reverse of folio 19 of the aforementioned autos.

By other original *autos* from the year 1686 [Document 11, this volume] the same [event] as in the preceding [autos] is on record on folio 7 in the declaration of Juan Clar, a Flemish man who found himself in company of the English when they sacked and burned Gualquini. In the declaration of Juan Liloston, a Scotsman, which is on folio 10, it is on record that two years before then he left from Scotland [f.8] with 100 men and some women and children. Two gentlemen came as their leaders, and they arrived at the port of San Jorge, and a month having passed, they moved on to settle the Island of Santa Elena, which in their language they call Buenbi. He also declares that the leaders of the Scottish who were on the said Island of Santa Elena gave thirty shotguns and cutlasses to Yamase Indians so that they would take Indian slaves for them, and with the result that they carried them 21 Christian Indians, church furnishings, and silver chalices, and some of the [f.8, vto.] Christian Indians they sold to an Englishman from San Jorge, where he took them, and some to an Irish ship which had brought people for the said Island of Santa Elena, and in the same declaration he also expresses on folio 11 that they had made a fortification of three [artillery] pieces, because they suspected that the Spaniards would go there because it was their land.

By an original royal *cédula* in number 12 [Document 12, this volume] it is on record that in the year of 1689 the Governor of Florida was ordered to investigate the circumstances and advantages [f.9] which would result from resettling the Island of Santa Catalina, of the province of Guale, abandoned by the Indians because of the invasion of the English from the town of San Jorge.

By another original royal *cédula* from 1693, number 13 [Document 13, this volume], it is on record that the aforementioned English from San Jorge had made prisoners on various occasions of some Christian Indians, and infidels of the Yguaja and Yamas languages, from the province of Guale.

By an original investigation from the year of 1726, number 14 [Document 14, this volume], in the declaration on the reverse of the first folio [f.9, vto.] of Captain Don Juan Ruíz Mexia, of the age of 82 years (who when the English introduced themselves into San Jorge was of the age of 21), it is on record that San Jorge, Santa Elena, Santa Catalina, Zapala, Guadalquini, Peraban, San Phelipe, Santa Maria, and San Juan del Puerto are towns and territories pertaining to this government, and that, [confronted] with the hostilities which they received from the English of Carolina, they came retreating back to the Island of Santa Maria, where they maintained themselves divided in three towns until the year 1702. In the declaration [f.10] of Sergeant Major Don Juan de Ayala Escobar, of the age of eighty years, which begins on folio 3, it is on record that in the year of 1683, the English were moved to settle themselves on the Bay of Santa Elena against reason and justice. In the declaration on folio 5 of Juan de Sandoval, of the age of 72 years, it is on record that as a soldier he was six [years] in garrison on the Island of Santa Catalina, which was populated with Christian Indians, and that there were another seven villages populated in the same manner, [f.10, vto.] with their religious teachers.

In the declaration on folio 6 of Adjutant Joseph Rodríguez Meléndez, of the age of eighty years, it is on record that he was in garrison in the province of Guale in the village of Santa Catalina, a population of Christian Indians, in which the lieutenant of the said provinces was always maintained.

The declaration on folio 7 of Adjutant Don Alonso Dávila Saabedra, of the age of 75 years, has some fine and very brief items of news. [f.11]

By an original certification number 15, year of 1736 [Document 15, this volume], by the Captain of Infantry Don Luis Rodrigo de Ortega, he certifies having known, held, and regarded as dominions pertaining to the Royal Crown of Your Majesty from this post toward the north the following provinces: the first, this presidio of St. Augustine; the second, the province of Mocama, which consisted of the towns of San Antonio, Salamototo, San Juan del Puerto, Santa Cruz, Pirigiligna, Guadalquini, and San Simon; the third, [f.11, vto.] the province of the Yguajas, which consisted of the village of Santa Maria, Tupiqui, Santo Domingo, San Phelipe, Asajo, Zapala, and Santa Catalina; and on the side of the mainland to the west eleven ancient villages of Christian Indians of the Yguaja nation. For all of these reasons, replete with true, firm, and solid foundations, the right of ownership which Your Majesty has to the referred provinces of Guale and Mocama up to the Island of Santa Elena, 50 leagues distant [f.12] from this post to the north, is indisputable. It is one of the first presidios of these dominions, sustained at the cost of the royal hacienda[7] of Your Majesty, and of the lives of your vassals. Finally, I must to inform the sovereign intelligence of Your Royal Majesty that all the political nations of Europe know that the first who set foot on land in the province in Florida were Juan Ponce de León, who had been Governor of the Island of San Juan de Puerto Rico; Lucas Vasquez [f.12, vto.] de Ayllón, judge of Española; Juan de Grijalba and Panfilo de Narváez, from the years of 1512, 1513, 1515 until 1520, 1521, 1524, and 1528; and that Fernando de Soto made an expedition in them in the year of 1534 with more than 1200 men,[8] and that in the year 1549, the Lord Emperor Charles the fifth sent religious of the order of San Benito so that they might instruct the Indians in the mysteries of our sacrosanct Divine Law.[9] Afterwards in the years 1565 and 1566 the *Adelantado* Pedro [f.13] Menéndez de Avilés entered through the Bar of St. Augustine in Florida in virtue of the agreement which he had made with Your Majesty, and in the region to the south, he penetrated all along its coast, and left people in the Keys, and in the mouths [of the rivers], and in the region to the north he sailed up to the province of Escamaçu, establishing two presidios, one in the very port of St. Augustine, and another on the Island of Santa Elena, 50 leagues distant from the Bar of St. Augustine toward the north, where later on he took [f.13, vto.] Fathers of the Company of Jesus in order to reduce the Indians. The *adelantado* having gone to Spain where he died, His Majesty sent Pedro Menéndez Márquez as governor of Florida, who rebuilt the presidio of Santa Elena by account of the Royal Hacienda, and made a voyage to Jacán by order of the King, and the religious of the order of San Francisco began to preach the sacred gospel in both presidios. The politicians likewise know that Carolina [f.14] is contained in the provinces of Florida, which border with Virginia, and that the English have established themselves in it [Carolina] since the year 1665, one century after these provinces were conquered by the *Adelantado* Pedro Menéndez de Avilés, whose successors had some clashes over the years with the French in Carolina itself, but never with the English. This is a truth so certain that in the year of 1663, in which the guardians [f.14, vto.] of the convents of our province of Guale gave the certifications of number 6, Don Alonso de Aranguiz y Cotis being governor of this post, they make no mention of English, but rather of Indians, expressing that they ought to have no misgivings from the Chuchumeco Indians through having sufficiently taught them a lesson on the occasion of their attack on the Christian Indians two years before, and that in the case of having similar intentions, and should they wish [f.15] to descend through the province of Escamaçu to that of Guale, it was now all populated with Yamases from Colon up to what they call Vyache Escaçu across the mainland, six, eight, four, three, two, and more days distant by road from our province of Guale, and they would find those who would impede their passage, and with great brevity would pass the news to [the province of Guale]. The settlers in those parts then were Indians, and for this those [f.15, vto.] guardians did not speak of English. And later, in the years 1683, 1685, 1686, and from then onward the English who settled in San Jorge, or Carolina, in the cited year of 1665 endeavored to invade this post, harassing the Spaniards and Christian Indians of our province of Guale by themselves and by their partisan Indians, as is verified in the *autos* numbers 9, 10, and 11, and in the investigation number 14, managing by these means to take possession of the aforementioned province of Guale illegally, where they are at the present [f.16] down to the Bar of Santa Maria, although it is in violation of that which is stipulated in the seventh chapter of the peace [treaties] arranged with the king of Great Britain in the year 1670, of which mention is made in the original royal *cédula* number 8. In this knowledge, speaking without one iota of passion, but rather with sincerity and justice, I ought to say to Your Majesty that Carolina was a province belonging to Your Majesty, but in consequence of the treaties of the year of 1670, it is now [property] of the king of [f.16, vto.] Great Britain down to the Bar of San Jorge, and from there toward the south [property] of Your Majesty.

This is all which occurs to me about the matter to inform the intelligence of Your Royal Majesty, may God grant your Catholic Royal Person many happy years for the benefit of Christianity. St. Augustine, Florida, August 15, 1739.

My Lord
Don Manuel de Montiano

[f.1]

Index to the papers which are being sent to the Court regarding justifying the dominion and ownership which His Majesty has of the provinces of the north, named Guale and Mocama, which the English have unjustly occupied.

Agreement [*asiento*] with Pedro Menéndez de Avilés for the conquest of Florida, year 1565, written in 49 folios.

A certification in testimony that comprises distinct paragraphs copied from a manuscript book found in the Archive of the Convent of San Francisco, year 1586, written in three folios [Document 2].

Testimony of three titles of notary of the fort of Santa Elena and Captain of Infantry, in two subjects, given by Governor Pedro Menéndez Márquez, year 1587, written in 5 folios [Document 3]. [f.1, vto.]

Testimony from a chapter list found in a very deteriorated [*quebrantado*] book of registry of chapters from the Archive of the Convent of San Francisco of this city, year 1628, written in 4 folios [Document 4].

A notebook of different orders and commissions for the provinces of Guale and Mocama, dispatched by different governors, which run from the year 1656 until 1680, written in 48 folios [Document 5].

Autos which comprise five original certifications from the guardians of the convents of the province of Guale, given in the year 1663, written in 5 folios [Document 6].

An original patent from the Provincial Minister Fray Jacinto de Barreda dispatched to different villages of this jurisdiction, [f.2] and among them San Juan, San Phelipe, Gualquini, Asaho, Zapala, and Santa Catalina, which are of the province of Guale, year 1679, written in two folios [Document 6].

A certification in testimony that comprises a certification given by Captain Don Francisco de Fuentes, lieutenant of the governor and captain general of the provinces of Guale and Mocama, in which he makes a relation of the villages of the said provinces, and of the people which there were in them, year 1681, written in 4 folios [Document 7].

An original royal *cédula* directing the governor of Florida to be cautious that the English who find themselves in the Bar of San Jorje do not attempt to advance themselves toward our towns of Guale and Zapala, [f.2, vto.] year of 1683, written in two folios [Document 8].

Original *autos* of the visitation of the provinces of Guale and Mocama, year of 1685, written in 21 folios [Document 9].

Original *autos* denouncing Captain Don Juan Saturnino de Albaurrea for having abandoned the province of Guale, where he was lieutenant of the governor, and retreated to the woods at the time of an attack by English enemies, year of 1685, written in 26 folios [Document 10].

Original signed *autos* about the entrance into the port of Florida of the galliots led by Captain Alexandro Thomás de León, who went to dislodge the English from the Island of Santa Elena, in which autos it is on record that the Scottish who [f.3] had settled it two years before, and the principal leaders who governed them, gave to the Yamase Indians thirty shotguns and cutlasses so that they would take them Indian slaves in price of [the weapons], and they carried 21 Christians from the province of Timucua, church furnishings, and chalices of silver, and that they turned them all over to the said principal leaders in payment for the said weapons, some of which were bought by some Englishmen from San Jorge. It is likewise on record that the said Scotsmen suspected that the Spaniards might go to dislodge them from the said Island of Santa

Elena because it was land of the Spaniards themselves, year 1686, written in 26 folios [Document 11]. [f.3, vto.]

An original royal *cédula* directing the governor of Florida to investigate the advantages which would result from resettling the Island of Santa Catalina, from which the English of San Jorge and the Chichumeco Indians had driven away the Christian Indians with their hostilities, year 1689, written in two folios [Document 12].

An original royal *cédula* directed to instruct the governor of Florida in what he should do in cases when the governors of San Jorge and their Indians should make the Christian Indians prisoners, as they had done on different occasions, year of 1693, written in two folios [Document 13].

An original signed investigation [f.4] for the purpose of ascertaining the limits and property of the provinces of Florida, year of 1726, written in 11 folios [Document 14].

An original certification given under oath by Captain Don Luis Rodrigo de Ortega, in which he lists all the villages pertaining to His Majesty in all the provinces of Florida, year 1736, written in three folios [Document 15].

St. Augustine, Florida, August 14, 1739
Don Manuel de Montiano

NOTES

1. Since the original royal *asiento* to Pedro Menéndez de Avilés, along with much of the remaining material in Document 1, had been presented elsewhere (Lyon, 1976: 213–219), this 49-folio portion of the Montiano package was not microfilmed in Seville at the same time as the rest of the material (1991).

2. This statement suggests that the date of 1586 may only refer to the date of the events related in the manuscript book found in the Franciscan Convent, and not to the date of the book itself, which was probably authored at a much later date (see the Index, and Document 2).

3. Jacán refers to the northern region later to become Virginia, and in this instance to the area of Sir Walter Raleigh's colony at Roanoke.

4. Here Governor Montiano left a blank where Francisco de Castilla was unable to transcribe the final part of this individual's surname (see Document 4).

5. San Jorge (St. George) was the Spanish name for the Charles Town (Charleston) colony established in 1670.

6. The event referred to was the assault launched against St. Augustine in 1702 by Governor James Moore of Carolina.

7. The original manuscript reads *herazio*, which is probably an error.

8. Contrary to Montiano's statement, Hernando de Soto landed in Tampa Bay in 1539, and with a force of something over 600 men.

9. Fray Luis Cancer de Barbastro led a group of Dominican friars in an unsuccessful missionary effort on the Gulf coast of Florida in 1549 (Gannon, 1965: 9–14).

DOCUMENT 2: SELECTED PARAGRAPHS OF A FRANCISCAN BOOK

INTRODUCTION

The following paragraphs were transcribed from a manuscript book of unknown origin and date that was discovered in the Franciscan convent of St. Augustine by governmental notary Francisco de Castilla in June 1739. Based on the notations in the governor's cover letter and index, along with the introductory note below, it seems likely that this volume was a compiled narrative history of Spanish Florida, written sometime between 1586 and 1739 by an unknown author (probably a Franciscan friar). Inasmuch as the Franciscan convent burned to the ground in 1599 (Hoffman, 1991), and again in 1620 "without being able to save anything" (Pesquera et al., 1621), it seems likely that the book postdates 1620. This conclusion is supported by Castillo's failure to recover any pertinent original Franciscan records dating earlier than the deteriorated 1628 chapter list transcribed as Document 4 (see below).

The book may be one written by Fray Pedro Muñoz during the mid-17th century, detailing the history of the Franciscan missions in Spanish Florida prior to that time. The volume was still located in the Franciscan archive as late as 1722, when Fray Blas Pulido cited it as the source of his review of Franciscan activity in Florida:

> All this that we have referred to is only a sample and brief summary of what the Very Reverend Father Fray Pedro Muñoz, who was provincial minister of this stated province, refers to so long and specifically in a chronicle that he wrote of all the events of this stated province. This manuscript is in this archive [of the Franciscan convent], and on account of our extreme poverty it has not been printed (Pulido, 1722).

Although the specific events and passages transcribed by Castilla below only 17 years later were not cited in the 1722 summary, Fray Muñoz's chronicle evidently began in the middle of the 16th century, making it entirely possible that Castilla's source was in fact the Muñoz chronicle. Since Pedro Muñoz arrived in Florida during the 1620s, and was stationed in both the Timucua and Apalachee provinces of Florida's interior, his description of the events of late 16th-century Florida must be considered a secondary source.

Regardless of the identity of their author, the paragraphs below appear to represent part of an historical narrative detailing some of the events of late 16th-century Spanish Florida. Unfortunately, these selections are the only extant portion of this book currently recognized. If and when the contents of the original Franciscan archive of St. Augustine are discovered, the original manuscript may still be among them.

[f.1]

Don Francisco de Castilla, general notary public of government of this presidio of St. Augustine, Florida. I certify and attest[1] to the best of my ability and duty that in a manuscript book which is maintained in the archive of this convent of San Francisco of this province of Santa Elena[2] of Florida, on folios seventeen, eighteen, twenty, and twenty-one are found the paragraphs which to the letter are of the following tenor:

> The *adelantado* placed all his diligence in the discovery of the land, whom the King called upon in order to entrust him with a powerful fleet which was prepared without knowing where it might go, and thus he left the man who was married to the elder of two daughters which he had in the presidio of [f.1, vto.] Santa Elena [Hernando de Miranda], and the other in St. Augustine [Diego de Velasco].[3]
>
> After he departed for Spain, where he died arranging the affairs of the fleet, for which reason it fell apart, many displaying great sentiment. Seeming to them that it was in his dishonor to give up a fleet because of the death of one man, and when it became known by His Majesty, they say he responded "Give me another Pedro Menéndez," so high was the esteem in which he was held, since in this absence the Indians of Santa Elena returned to their enmities, and persecuting the Castilians, they did not let them leave the fort, for which they suffered so much necessity and hunger that they abandoned the land [f.2] and joined with those in St. Augustine.[4]
>
> Both brothers-in-law being together in the presidio, he who retreated from Santa Elena [Miranda] attempted the government, seeming to him that it was owed him by being married to the elder daughter of the *adelantado*, but he who was married to the younger [Velasco] did not wish to quit, saying that that post had been entrusted to him, and for this reason he [Miranda] went away to Spain, where he was poorly received because he had abandoned [the presidio] of Santa Elena, an effect which has caused many to see what they attempted as fraudulent.
>
> After the son-in-law of the Adelantado Pedro Menéndez de [f.2, vto.] Avilés who was married to his elder daughter [Miranda] died from the sorrow of seeing himself imprisoned for the retreat which he made from Santa Elena, leaving that presidio, although the other son-in-law who was married to the younger [Velasco] was in St. Augustine, without removing the government from the family of the *adelantado*, His Majesty sent Pedro Menéndez Márquez as governor of Florida, and with the order that he should rebuild Santa Elena, as he did, all on behalf of His Majesty, for which some of the settlers settled down into positions, and others went away to other places.
>
> The year of fifteen eighty-six, Francisco [f.3] Draque scoured the coasts of the Indies with an English fleet, doing great damages in them, and arriving at St. Augustine, Florida, he seized the fort named San Juan, which was nearer to the Bar than that of today, and was not finished,[5] and burned the place and the Royal books, taking four [artillery] pieces and some money.

This agrees with the inserted paragraphs, the originals of which remain in the said book and archive to which I refer, and by verbal order of the Señor Colonel Don Manuel de Montiano, governor and captain general of this said city of Florida and its provinces, I present the above in Florida on the thirtieth of June, seventeen thirty-nine.

In true testimony,
Francisco de Castilla
Governmental Notary

NOTES

1. The phrase *doy fee y verdadero testimonio* was the standard oath given by notaries regarding the authenticity of their work, and will be translated for this volume as "I attest."

2. In 1612, Spanish Florida became the Franciscan province of Santa Elena, which also included Cuba.

3. Hernando de Miranda married Doña Catalina Menéndez de Avilés, the elder daughter of Pedro Menéndez de Avilés, and Diego de Velasco married Doña Maria Menéndez de Avilés, Pedro's younger daughter. As noted below, both Velasco and Miranda governed Santa Elena in succession, during which time Miranda deposed and imprisoned Velasco on assorted charges following the death of the *adelantado* in 1574. Miranda subsequently abandoned Santa Elena during the coastal Indian rebellion of 1576, and was himself arrested for desertion upon his return to Spain.

4. The Indians surrounding Santa Elena (including Guale to the south) rose in rebellion during the summer of 1676, resulting in the deaths of a number of Spanish officials and soldiers, including the nephew of Pedro Menéndez de Avilés. The fort was abandoned and destroyed, and its inhabitants withdrew temporarily to St. Augustine (Lyon, 1987).

5. The fort burned by Francis Drake in June 1586 was the sixth wooden fort of St. Augustine, and had been begun earlier that same year (see Connor, 1926).

DOCUMENT 3: TITLES FOR OFFICIAL POSTS AT SANTA ELENA

INTRODUCTION

The following three documents were transcribed by Royal Accountant Don Juan Menéndez Márquez from several loose copies in the first bound volume of royal *cédulas* and titles maintained in the accounting office in St. Augustine, and represent three titles for various offices associated with the city of Santa Elena during the years 1587–1588. While the text of the titles provides only limited information, these three documents were surely among the last official commissions granted for the colony of Santa Elena, which was permanently abandoned after this period. As a consequence, they provide proof of Spanish settlement as far north as modern South Carolina well into the 1580s, and thus were included in Governor Montiano's package to the Spanish crown.

Close reading of these titles reveals the standard formulaic language used for titles and commissions during the late 16th century in Florida. A comparison with orders dating roughly a century later in Document 5 reveals some differences in the Spanish structure and wording of similar documents, the most obvious of which is the 16th-century use of the *vosotros* form by Governor Menéndez Márquez in addressing his officials and soldiers. This usage lent a degree of familiarity to his orders, serving to emphasize his elevated status as governor. In the 17th century, the governors employed somewhat more formal language in addressing those under their command, whereas the *vosotros* form appeared typically only in royal *cédulas*, addressed from the king to his subjects. This shift in language seems to mirror the transition from governors who possessed a special degree of respect and position within colonial society to governors who were essentially career bureaucrats within an established governmental structure.

Notes are supplied for the first of these three orders so as to familiarize the reader with the structure of such documents (and see Document 5).

[f.1]

Title of notary of the fort of Santa Elena, for Juan Guisado, year of 1587.[1]

Pedro Menéndez Márquez, governor and captain general of these provinces of Florida for His Majesty.[2] Using the commission given to me by His Majesty, I state that I named as notary public and of rations of the city and fort of Santa Elena Alonso García de la Vera, who has been [notary] until now, and for reasons which move me to suspend him from the said office so that he cannot make use of it, and because the affairs of the service of His Majesty relative to the said office do not cease, it is suitable to provide a person who will make use of and exercise [the office], observing the above stated and the fine ability and sufficiency of speech of Juan Guisado, a soldier of this fort,[3] I name and elect you as notary public and of rations of the said fort and city of Santa Elena for as long as I choose, and you will begin to serve the said office from the day that you arrive at the said fort [f.1, vto.] and after you have notified the said Alonso García of the auto of suspension which you carry in your power, signed in my name before Torivio de Estrada, my notary,[4] and in each month during all the time that you might serve the said office of notary of rations of the said fort you will have a salary of five ducats and an ordinary ration of two and a half reales per day, which is what His Majesty orders given to the persons who serve in similar offices, which I assign you in the *situado* which His Majesty has imposed for these provinces in those of New Spain for the payment of the garrison which serves here,[5] and I command the mayor, officers, and soldiers and sailors of that fort who reside and are in it to find and hold you as notary, with voice for the said offices in the cases and affairs attached and appurtaining to it, and to guard [f.2] and make guarded all the favors, freedoms, and liberties which you ought to enjoy.[6] I order the accountant of these provinces to take the copy of this title in the royal books[7] of the accounting office of [these provinces], and [I order] the said Thorivio de Estrada to countersign it and to return the original to you in order to guard your rights,[8] and you should make use of this sign which I give you, which is like this one which has been made below,[9] in the public instruments which will pass before you as notary, which is valid and carries judicial certification apart from the stated. Signed in the city of St. Augustine on the twenty-seventh of January, fifteen eighty-seven, Pedro Menéndez Márquez. By order of the señor General, Thorivio de Estrada.[10]

Title for the said Juan Guisado, notary of the voyage which the general made to Jacán by order of His Majesty.

Pedro Menéndez Márquez, governor and captain [f.2, vto.] general for His Majesty of these provinces of Florida. I say that inasmuch as due to news which I have had, and an order from His Majesty, I am going to cruise all this coast up to the province of Jacán, which is in [Florida] and the farthest [north], to find out if the English corsair is settled in it, and for other affairs of the service of His Majesty, and for the said effect, in the frigate in which I am going to carry sailors and soldiers, provisions, and munitions, and [because] ration has to be given to the said people in the places where I will arrive, and for other things of his office where I will arrive there is need to name a notary who will make use of the said office on sea and land, and observing the above stated, and the fine ability and sufficiency of speech of Juan Guisado, notary public and of rations of this fort of San Marcos and city of Santa Elena,[11] I name and elect and command you to go with me on the said [f.3] journey and during it make use of the said office of notary in the cases attached and concerning the said office, and for the said occupation I assign you in the *situado* of these provinces five ducats per month as salary and two and a half reales as ration each day, which shall run and be counted from today forward until the said journey ends,[12] and I order all the people who might go and come with me to regard you as notary, with voice for the said office, and guard you all the honors, freedoms, and liberties which in reason of it you ought to enjoy. I order the accountant of these provinces to take the copy in the royal books of the [accounting office], and return the original to you in order to guard your rights. Signed in the city and fort of Santa Elena on the twelfth of May, fifteen eighty-seven, Pedro Menéndez Marquéz. And having arrived at the city of St. Augustine, you will turn this title over to the accountant of these provinces so that he can take the copy of it and return it to you.[13] Signed above, Pedro Menéndez Márquez. By order of the señor General, Juan Guisado.[14]

Title of captain of the company of the fort of Santa Elena for Juan de Posada.

Pedro Menéndez Márquez, governor and captain general for the King Our Lord in these provinces of Florida. Inasmuch as by a royal *cédula* I am given commission and full power to name, provide, and elect in [these provinces] all the offices and charges which are necessary and suitable to be provided, and making use of it, inasmuch as Captain Gutierre de Miranda is taking leave of the post of captain of the company of the fort of Santa Elena,[15] and has [f.4] gone from these provinces to the Kingdoms of Spain, and attentive to this, it is suitable to provide a person who will serve the said post so that there is no cessation in the affairs of the royal service, observing the above stated and the fine services and experience of speech of Captain Juan de Posada, and by it being on record that he has served seventeen years in the fleet of the *Adelantado* Pedro Menéndez, in these provinces and forts in the office of factor, and in journeys which have occurred, sending him in charge of soldiers, and in remaining in my place governing these provinces and forts in my absence, and in bringing aid of soldiers and munitions to these forts two times, one in the year of [fifteen] eighty one, and the other in the year of [fifteen] eighty six with a *cédula* from the King Our Lord in which he ordered that he do so, and that [f.4, vto.] he conduct them until turning them over to me in these forts,[16] and relation has been given regarding all the above stated, and it is hoped that you will continue, for this I name and elect you as captain of the said company of Santa Elena until the King Our Lord commands something else, and I order the remaining officers of [the company], ensigns, sergeants, squad leaders, and soldiers[17] to regard you as captain of the said company, and perform and fulfill your orders in the affairs and cases attached and appurtaining to the said office, for which I give you power and faculty as I have [received] it from the King Our Lord, and I order that you guard and have all the honors, freedoms, and liberties which in reason of the said office and services you ought to enjoy, and for [f.5] the occupation and labor which you will have with the said office, I assign you in the *situado* of these provinces two hundred ducats each year that you serve the said office,[18] and two and a half reales of ration each ordinary day, which is what the King Our Lord orders given to the persons who serve in similar offices, which salary runs and is counted from today, the date of this title, onward. I order the accountant of these provinces to take the copy of this title in the royal books and return the original in order to guard your rights, and [I order] Thorivio de Estrada, my primary governmental notary, to countersign it, who is notary in this city of St. Augustine, Florida, on the nineteenth of August, fifteen eighty-eight.[19] Pedro [f.5, vto.] Menéndez Márquez. By order of the señor General Pedro Menéndez Márquez, Thorivio de Estrada, notary.

Conforms to the copy of these titles which is found recorded in the first book of royal *cédulas* and titles which is found in the royal accounting office in my charge, in some notebooks which are loose at the first of [the *cédulas* and titles], on which their folios cannot be recognized by being poorly treated and unbound, the copy of which is well and faithfully drawn out according to how they are understood, and so that it is on record where it is suitable, by order of the señor Colonel Don Manuel de Montiano, governor and captain general of this city and its provinces. I give the present in St. Augustine, Florida on the twenty-sixth of June, seventeen thirty-nine.

Don Juan Menéndez Márquez

NOTES

1. This marginal note by Menéndez Márquez is followed by his transcription of the 16th-century order. Each order has a similar heading.
2. This initial portion of the order was located in the upper right corner of the original order, and provides the name and title of the governor issuing the order. The actual text of the order follows, with the first portion serving as an introduction to the operative sections of the order. This introduction provides the reasons for which the order was issued.
3. Here the governor names the individual to whom the order or commission is being granted, along with a brief justification of his abilities. What follows is the operative portion of the order, in which Guisado is actually named as notary. As such, this forms the core of the document.
4. The order suspending García from his former post was a separate document, to be given to him by his incoming replacement (Guisado).
5. This section assigns the appropriate salary and ration allowance to Guisado as a result of his promotion to the office of notary. Whereas the standard salary of a soldier amounted to just over two and a half ducats each month, a notary received five ducats per month, amounting to nearly double the normal salary (see Bushnell, 1981: 39 for comparison with other salaries). The ration allowance was standard for all soldiers and officers in the presidio of St. Augustine.
6. This passage in the order is directed at the remaining officials and soldiers in Santa Elena, stating that they should recognize Guisado as their notary, and afford him the proper respect.
7. The present transcription was made from the copy entered into the royal books at the time that the title was issued.
8. Here the governor inserts into the text of the original order the instructions for making an of-

ficial copy of the original for the records of St. Augustine, and notes that the original order should be given to Guisado, to whom the order is directed.

9. Although the sign referred to in the text was not copied for this transcription, contemporaneous documents bear the mark that was placed at the end of all official instruments signed by the notary in St. Augustine. This sign persisted well into the 17th century (see below).

10. This final section of the order contained the signatures of both the governor and the notary who drafted the original document.

11. Guisado was serving in this post as a result of the previous order, dated January 27, 1587 (only a few months earlier).

12. This salary was not in addition to that which Guisado earned as notary in Santa Elena, but replaced his normal salary during his absence. Presumably, another order appointed an interim notary to serve during the voyage to Jacán.

13. The Governor presumably returned to St. Augustine with the assigned soldiers and officers before the planned voyage to Jacán, during which time Guisado was instructed to permit an official copy to be made.

14. Guisado himself served as the notary for this order.

15. The military structure of Spanish Florida was established during the late 16th century, and persisted in this form throughout most of the 17th century. At the time of this order (August 1588), the infantry was organized into two companies of roughly 125 soldiers each, one being stationed at Santa Elena, and the other at St. Augustine. Although the abandonment of Santa Elena resulted in the stationing of all these soldiers in the presidio of St. Augustine, the two-company system was retained, with two acting captains of infantry at any given time.

16. The preceding relation of the services of Posada is lengthy, inasmuch as the position of acting Captain was an important post, and only to be given to those with considerable experience and merits. Posada had served as both interim governor and factor during the term of Governor Menéndez Márquez, and would ultimately drown in 1592 while serving as the official royal treasurer for Florida (see Bushnell, 1981).

17. Each company possessed an ensign and a sergeant, along with five squad seaders in charge of roughly 25 soldiers each.

18. The post of captain of infantry was an important and respected position, with a salary of more than six times that of an ordinary footsoldier (see Bushnell, 1981: 39).

19. The date of August 19, 1588, is well after the abandonment of Santa Elena in 1587. It seems likely that Posada was named captain of the infantry company formerly assigned to Santa Elena, and which still carried that name.

DOCUMENT 4: FRANCISCAN CHAPTER LIST OF 1628

INTRODUCTION

The following transcription was made by notary Don Francisco de Castilla in August 1739 from a book in the Franciscan convent of St. Augustine. The volume was a registry for Franciscan chapters—periodic meetings that were held every three years (on average) in Florida—and contained lists of those friars attending each meeting, along with their convent of origin. The list selected by Castilla was for the 1628 chapter, and thus although it does not provide a complete list of all the missions in the Franciscan province of Santa Elena in that year, the document does make note of many important Florida missions during an epoch of sparse historical documentation. In effect, the 1628 chapter list represents the only overview (if partial) of the missions of Florida between the 1616 visitation route of Fray Luís Gerónimo de Oré (1936) and the 1655 mission list (Díez de la Calle, 1655, 1659).[1]

As mentioned by Castilla in a postscript at the end of his transcription, the original document was at that time falling to pieces, suggesting that it may have been one of the only surviving volumes after the burning of St. Augustine in 1702, which reportedly resulted in the complete destruction of the Franciscan convent. Consequently, the following transcription is marred by gaps, a problem compounded by the extremely poor Latin employed by the early 17th-century Florida Franciscans. Florida was, after all, a remote frontier on the fringes of the Western world, and a colony to which few Spaniards (including Franciscan friars) ever willingly chose to be assigned.

For the present, only those portions of the text that have been translated word for word are presented below. Areas where the Latin text was unclear have been left in the original transcribed form, with notes describing the general meaning of each passage. Nevertheless, the information most important for investigators—the mission list—has been translated. However, since the Latin name for the saints associated with each mission appear only very rarely in existing historical documentation, these are presented in brackets here.

[f.1]

Don Francisco de Castilla, governmental and general notary public of this city of St. Augustine, Florida. As I best can and ought, I certify and attest that in one of the registry books of Chapter celebrations in the archive of the convent of Father San Francisco of this stated city, which the very reverend Father Fray Manuel de Beteta showed me, is found [a list] of the following tenor:

In the name of the Lord, Amen

Nurturing province Santa Elena of the [–] immaculate conception Blessed Virgin Mary [–] in the year of Our Lord sixteen twenty-eight on the true day the eighth of the month of [–] "ejuidem" Reverend Father Provincial "piafuit autoritate illi" [–] Alonso [f.1, vto.] de Montemayor for [–] Commissary General [–] "conceptiomi Veipara Virgimi civitatis" [–] and Guardian Reverend Father Fray Melchor [–] de Santa Maria.

In the nurturing convent La Concepcion [*Conceptionis*] de la Havana Reverend Father Fray Alonso Pesquera, continuing guardian.

In the vicarage and president's residence Father Fray Andrés de Santoyo [–] Divine Word Preacher Father Fray Lorenzo Martinez, "simul que notitioruz Magister continuatur."

In the nurturing convent of [f.2] Santiago [*Sancti Jacobi*] de Cuba, Father Fray Francisco Pérez, continuing guardian.

In the nurturing convent of Santa Maria [*Sancta Maria*] Angeloruz, Father Fray Diego de Allende, continuing guardian.

In the nurturing convent of San Pedro [*Sancti Petri*] Atuluteca, Father Fray Francisco de la Cruz, continuing guardian.

In the nurturing convent of Santa Catalina [*Sancta Catherina*] de Guale, Father Fray Gaspar de Ribota, guardian-elect.

In the nurturing convent of San Antonio [*Sancti Antonij*] de Enacape, Father Fray Diego de Figueroa, guardian-elect. [f.2, vto.]

In the nurturing convent of San Francisco [*Sancti Francisci*] de Potano, Father Fray Martín Prieto, continuing guardian.

In the nurturing convent of San Martín [*Sancti Martini*] de Ayacutu, Father Fray Pedro Muñoz, guardian-elect.

In the nurturing convent of San Buenaventura [*Sancti Bonaventura*] de Gualequini, Father Fray Pedro de Bill[–], guardian-elect.

In the nurturing convent of Santa Cruz [*Sancta Cruzis*] de Tarihica, Father Fray Francisco Fernández Amayuelas, continuing guardian.

In the nurturing convent of San Pedro [*Sancti Petri*] de Potohiriva, Father Fray Antonio Era[–], continuing [f.3] guardian.

In "predicatorem constituitur" Father Fray Gaspar de Ribecho "et quia ad Medelam animaruz experti medici requiruntur ideo in [–] fesores seculariuz hispanorum vivorum ac mulierum" Father Fray Juan de [–], Father Fray Antonio de San Buenaventura, Preacher and Father Fray Diego Camuñas, and [–] de Ribota, and Father Fray Francisco de la Cruz, and Father Fray Diego de Figueroa, [–] Alonso de Rea, and Father Fray Bernardo de Santa Maria.

"Secuntur Su [–]

Pro S.mo domino nostro [–] [f.3, vto.] Eclesia quilibet sacerdos du [–] pro R.mo ac Hl.mo protectore nostri orinis [–] sacerdos unam celebret missam.[2]

Pro Catholica et Regia Majestate [–] alijs que innumeni beneficijs magna que [–] orbis sustentat totam que nostrami a quolibet sacerdote missa dicatur.[3]

Pro Prelatis Generalibus nostri ordinis.[4]

Pro Gubernatore harum Provinciaruz [–] bernatione dirigat a quolibet sacerdote a celebratione caputulivique inhunc diem.[5]

[–] fatres huius Provincia qui ex hac vita disceserunti sunt quatuoi quorum [f.4] anima et omniuz fideliuz defuntoruz per misericordiaz Domini requiescant in pace Amen."[6]

This is a transcription faithfully taken from the list of the congregation which was celebrated in the convent of the Immaculate Conception of the city of St. Augustine on the eighth of January of the year of sixteen twenty-eight, and by thus being true, I, Fray Juan de Guadalupe, provincial minister, signed it with my name. Fray Juan de Guadalupe, provincial minister.[7]

Agrees with the list of congregation previously inserted according to how it was found in the referred book, to which I refer, and in virtue of the verbal order of the señor Colonel Don Manuel de Montiano, governor and captain general of this post and its provinces, I give the present in this city of St. Augustine, Florida, on the eleventh of August, seventeen thirty-nine.

In true testimony,
Francisco de Castilla
Governmental Notary

Note: In all the transcribed list of congregation one can only read what is written, and where there are lines, one cannot read anything, by the book having fallen to pieces.[8]

Signed above,
Castilla

NOTES

1. Fray Francisco Alonso de Jesús (1630) included the names of seven missions in the western interior in a 1630 request for mounts, but this listing does not include the provinces of Guale or Mocama. The Jesús list does, however, provide the names of several missions not noted on the 1628 list.
2. Here the friars are ordered to say masses for the following individuals.
3. A mass was to be said for the king of Spain.
4. A mass was to be said for the general prelate of the Franciscan Order.
5. A mass was to be said for the governor of Florida, at that time Don Luis de Rojas y Borja.
6. A final mass was to be said for four dead friars, who had presumably died recently in Florida (perhaps since the last Franciscan chapter three years earlier).
7. This final section of the 1628 chapter register was written in Spanish and signed by Fray Guadalupe.
8. In this addendum to Castilla's standard certification of his transcriptions, the notary made an important comment regarding the original document, which was "falling to pieces." Based on the distribution of lines used to indicate portions of the text that were unreadable, it seems likely that the Franciscan registry book had been badly burned, consuming the ends of the lines along the margin. This comment furthermore indicates that the above transcription is almost certainly the most that historians can ever expect from the original, even if it were eventually to be discovered.

DOCUMENT 5: ORDERS REGARDING THE PROVINCE OF GUALE

INTRODUCTION

This collection of transcribed documents spans nearly a quarter of a century, extending from 1656 until 1680, and comprises various official orders issued by the governors of Florida to assorted officers under their command. The single theme uniting all orders is the province of Guale, and within this category the subject matter ranges from the installation of aboriginal leaders in specific mission towns to military preparations for the 1680 English-sponsored assault on Guale.

The following documents provide a good overview of the content and structure of standard gubernatorial orders during the last half of the 17th century. Several types of orders are represented, but the most frequent is the yearly order issued to Guale and Mocama for the *repartimiento* labor draft. Other orders are less formalized in structure, resulting from specific and isolated events. Nevertheless, these transcriptions provide a somewhat rare glimpse of one form of internal governmental documentation that only occasionally appears outside the provincial archives of the Spanish colonies, inasmuch as such local-level orders were not routinely sent to major repositories such as the Archivo General de Indias in Seville.

Each order included within this large section is preceded by a small introduction in order to place it within a broader context, and notes are provided where deemed necessary. The Overview to this volume includes a more thorough discussion of the significance of these orders and the historical events surrounding their issuance. Not all orders below were presented chronologically in the bound volume prepared by notary Francisco de Castilla, and thus although the orders are presented here in the same sequence in which they appear in Montiano's package, notes are provided where specific orders depart from chronological sequence.

ORDER 1: REBOLLEDO TO FERNÁNDEZ DE GOYAS, APRIL 20, 1656

The first order in this collection represents a direct response to the threat of an English land assault on the city of St. Augustine following the conquest of Jamaica in 1655. Following the arrival of a royal *cédula* with instructions to ensure that St. Augustine was prepared for the expected arrival of an English fleet, Governor Don Diego de Rebolledo devised a plan to bolster the existing force of Spanish infantry with Indians from the mission provinces of Florida. This order was sent to Guale and Mocama following the dispatch of a similar order to Timucua and Apalachee.

While the order to Timucua provided the spark for the Timucuan Rebellion of 1656, the aboriginal leaders of Guale and Mocama complied with the order below, arriving in St. Augustine only to be detained for months and ultimately deprived of their firearms (see Worth, 1992: 244–246 for more in-depth discussion).

[f.1]

Order to have Captain Nicolas Fernández de Goyas go to the province of Guale to ask its principals for people to reinforce this post, year of 1656.[1]

Don Diego de Rebolledo, knight of the order of Santiago, governor and captain general of this city of St. Augustine, Florida, and its provinces for His Majesty.[2] Inasmuch as I have had news from the Field Master Don Juan Montano, governor and captain general of the city of Havana, in which he relates that the Dutch enemy is making some preparations in their armada in order to come to besiege this post and set foot in it, the news of which, and the little preparation of the people, provisions, and munitions which are to be found in [this post] for its defense,[3] force me to remain as cautious as is justified, and to make the preparations which are required, dispatching to the province of Guale to advise all of its *micos*, caciques, and principals, that they should help me with some warriors [f.1, vto.] so that when the occasion arrives, this post will find itself with some defense, for which purpose it is necessary to send a person of all satisfaction and experience,[4] and because I have complete [satisfaction] of the [experience] of Captain Nicolás Fernández de Goyas, *reformado* of this presidio,[5] who I am certain has served His Majesty in it with much satisfaction, giving a very good account of his person, and because I hope that he will continue [this service] on this [occasion], by being very much in His Royal service,[6] I order that as soon as he receives this order he should leave this presidio with the infantry that I have named for him and go to the said province of Guale, and in it assemble all the *micos*, caciques, and principals, and on behalf of His Majesty and mine tell and represent to them the need in which this post finds itself, and the great importance of helping me with all [f.2] promptness with some of the foremost and most valorous Indian warriors who would not be missed greatly in their fields, and likewise that they help me with all the Indians that know how to manage firearms, assuring them many honors and favors on the part of His Majesty and me.[7] For all that and the rest which might happen I give to the said Captain Nicolás de Goyas authority so that he may arrange everything as he sees suitable.[8] And likewise he will arrange with the missionaries, caciques, and *micos* the purchase by account of His Majesty of all the corn that they have, assuring them that it will be paid for on the first opportunity. And this task being done, and having recovered all the warriors and firearms that he can gather, he will endeavor to come to this presidio immediately, since in this consists its aid [f.2, vto.] and defense. I trust from his valor, punctuality, and care that he will attend to everything with the firmness which is customary.[9] And I order all the *micos*, caciques, and principals of all the villages through which the said captain will pass to give him all the support and aid of which he has need so that this service to His Majesty, and the successful fulfillment of this order, is done that much better.[10] Juan Moreno y Segovia, public and governmental notary, will take the copy of [this order].[11] Given in the city of St. Augustine, Florida on the twentieth of April, sixteen hundred and fifty-six, Don Diego de Rebolledo. By order of His Grace, Lorenzo Joseph de León, his secretary.[12] The copy of this order by the señor governor and captain general was taken in the governmental secretary's office at his command, of which I swear, Juan Moreno y Segobia, public and governmental notary.[13]

Agrees with the order previously inserted, according to how the copy is taken in one of the governmental books of the archive at my charge, to which I refer. And by verbal order of the señor Colonel Don Manuel de Montiano, governor and captain general of this post and its provinces, I give the present in Florida on the fifth of August, seventeen thirty-nine.[14] Between lines—Fernández—valid.[15]

In true testimony,
Francisco de Castilla
Governmental Notary[16]

ORDER 2: GUERRA Y VEGA TO ALCAYDE DE CORDOBA, JANUARY 17, 1665

The following order was issued by Governor Francisco de la Guerra y de la Vega less than a month after he was installed in office. The order stems from news that Clemente Bernal, the principal cacique of the Mocama province, had recently died, evidently without leaving an apparent heir to the office. An elderly leader, Bernal was 74 or 75 years of age upon his death, and had served as an interpreter for Governor Rebolledo nearly a decade earlier during the Timucuan Rebellion of 1656 (Bernal, 1660; also see Worth, 1992). His death seems to have left a vacuum of power in the Mocama province, and in the mission of San Juan del Puerto, which served as St. Augustine's gateway to the northern coastal provinces of Mocama and Guale.

Perhaps the most interesting facet of this order is the fact that the governor was motivated to send an experienced soldier, Captain Martín Alcayde de Cordoba,[17] to facilitate the smooth transferral of power to the legitimate heir. Although the order states that the decision should be made in conference with other Indian leaders, the repeated and insistent reference to the cacica Juana, of the more northerly mission Santa Maria, implies that Captain Alcayde was dispatched to ensure her claim to leadership. This is intriguing, considering the widely cited Spanish preference for patrilineal succession among mission Indians.

Juana Menéndez was indeed installed as cacica of San Juan, probably relocating the remaining Mocama inhabitants of Mission Santa Maria to San Juan del Puerto with her. Thirteen years later, the elderly Juana renounced her position in favor of her niece and heir, Merenciana (Argüelles, 1678; also see Document 9).

[f.3]

Order to Captain Martín Alcaide de Cordoba to go to San Juan del Puerto and invest the cacique whose right it is.

Don Francisco de la Guerra y de la Vega, governor and captain general of this city and presidio of Florida and its provinces for the King our lord. Inasmuch as I have had news that Clemente Bernal, cacique mayor of San Juan del Puerto, and of all Mocama, is dead, and that there is no person in that place to govern it, by being the principal passage for the province of Guale, and the rest of the neighboring provinces; and inasmuch as I am informed that the said caciquedom pertains to the cacica of Santa Maria, named Juana, through being the most principal of that district, and the missionary who serves there having asked me to [invest] the possession of the said caciquedom to the person who is the legitimate heir of the said Clemente Bernal; and inasmuch as it is suitable to the service of His Majesty and to the conservation of that village, and of the rest of that jurisdiction and its natives, to give them a chief to govern them, according to the custom which is maintained among them, I have held for good [effect] in this matter to send a person of all wisdom, punctuality, and experience, [f.3, vto.] and who has the familiarity of the natives, so that this case can be worked out better, and because the referred [qualities] coincide in the person of Captain Martín Alcaide de Cordoba, *reformado* of this presidio, and given advantage in it by His Majesty,[18] to whom I order that as soon as he receives this order he should leave this presidio, taking in his company Juan Baptista de la Cruz,[19] interpreter of that language, and go to the village of San Juan del Puerto, where he will inform himself from the principal Indians regarding the person who has the legitimate right by inheritance to the said caciquedom upon the death of the said Clemente Bernal; and [it] being the said cacica of Santa Maria Juana, according to what I am informed, he will give her possession in the name of His Majesty according to the custom which is maintained among them, doing the necessary requirements with the said interpreter, with regard to the government [f.4] of her towns, and the conservation of her vassals, and the public peace among them, placing before these the service of God Our Lord and that of His Majesty, which as Christians they should uphold, and as loyal vassals obey. And if the said cacica, through not being able to serve in the said village of San Juan, should name a person who will govern it, the said captain will admit him in the said government of the said village in the name of His Majesty and mine, endeavoring in all to adjust matters in a manner that the said Indians remain pleased; and having done this, he will promptly return to this presidio. And I order and command all the caciques and principals to be at the order and disposition of that which the said captain orders in what is done in this matter, on pain that they will be punished with the demonstration which the case calls for,[20] and likewise [f.4, vto.] that they give him all the relief necessary for the execution of this order. The copy of [this order] will remain in the governmental secretary's office. Given in St. Augustine, Florida on the seventeenth of January, sixteen sixty-five. Don Francisco de la Guerra y de la Vega. By command of the governor and captain general, my lord, Miguel Alonso de Ojeda, secretary.

The copy of the above order by the señor governor and captain general remains in the governmental secretary's office, and the original was turned over to the aforementioned for its execution. Of this I swear, Juan Moreno y Segobia, public and governmental notary.

Agrees with the order previously inserted, according to how the copy is taken in one of the governmental books of the archive under my charge, to which I refer. And by verbal order of the señor Colonel Don Manuel de Montiano, governor and captain general of this post and its provinces, I give the present in Florida on the fifth of August, seventeen thirty-nine.

In true testimony,
Francisco de Castilla
Governmental Notary

ORDER 3: GUERRA Y VEGA TO SANCHEZ DE ENTONADO, JANUARY 17, 1665

The order below is a copy of the yearly dispatch for the *repartimiento* labor draft, sent to Guale and Mocama in 1665 at the beginning of Governor Guerra y Vega's term.[21] In style it conforms to similar orders issued at the beginning of every year during most of the 17th century for both the northern and western mission provinces (see Worth, 1992: 121–125). The order below lacks the attached instruction seen on other orders in this section specifying the exact number of Indians to be drafted from each town, which may have been omitted by either the original 17th-century notary Juan Moreno y Segobia, or by the 18th-century copyist Francisco de Castilla. Consequently, further discussion of such orders will be presented below, preceding a complete dispatch.

[f.5]

Order to bring the field hands[22] from the provinces of Guale and Mocama, year of 1665.

Don Francisco de la Guerra y de la Vega, governor and captain general of this city, presidio, and provinces of St. Augustine, Florida, for the King our lord. Inasmuch as by dispatch of this date[23] I have sent to the provinces of Timucua and Apalachee to look for the people who are customarily brought to work for the infantry who serve His Majesty in the presidio of this city, as an indispensable thing, so that they might sustain themselves better, and so that the post will have the necessary provision; and it is suitable to make a draft from the provinces of Guale and Mocama, as has been done for time immemorial in this place, and for this draft and transport, it is suitable to send a person who is capable among the natives, so that with all wiseness he attracts and cajoles them, because I am informed that most who are in the habit of coming are pagans;[24] because I am aware of the good which Adjutant Bartolomé Sánchez de Entonado,[25] *reformado* in this presidio, has done on other occasions, I have held it for good [effect] to name him, as for the present I elect and name him, so that as soon as he receives this [order] he should leave from this city [f.5, vto.] and go to the province of Guale, where having arrived, he should in my name give its *micos*, caciques, and principals to understand the suitability to the service of His Majesty, the common good, and the conservation of this post, that they send the field hands who are requested, according to the instruction which I have commanded him to turn over,[26] assuring them all good treatment, and that I will have them paid for all their labor,[27] and in case some Indians should wish to come of their own will, outside of the quantity which are ordered, he will endeavor with the best attention which he can to conduct them to this city with the rest,[28] endeavoring to leave their *micos* and caciques pleased, doing everything with the zeal which I trust from his person; and when they are gathered, he will endeavor to leave from that province at a time which he sees he can arrive at this city on the eighth of March,[29] without permitting or making exception that they come with any cargo which is not their provision, for the importance which His Majesty, may God preserve him, [f.6] charges their good treatment.[30] And below this order I command all the caciques, *micos*, *mandadores*, and remaining principals of the towns through which the said adjutant passes to give him all the support and aid which he asks them for, without any limitation, on pain that I will command him who does the contrary to be punished in public, by thus being suitable to the service of His Majesty. The copy of this order will be taken in the governmental secretary's office, which is dispatched for this, signed by my hand, sealed with the seal of my arms, and endorsed by the undersigned secretary. Given in the city of St. Augustine, Florida on the seventeenth of January, sixteen sixty-five, Don Francisco de la Guerra y de la Vega. By order of the señor governor and captain general, my lord, Bernabé de la Trinidad, notary.

The copy of the above order [f.6, vto.] by the señor governor and captain general remains in the governmental secretary's office, and the original was turned over to the aforementioned for its execution. Of this I swear, Juan Moreno y Segobia, public and governmental notary.

Agrees with the order previously inserted, according to how the copy is taken in one of the governmental books of the archive under my charge, to which I refer. And by verbal order of the señor Colonel Don Manuel de Montiano, governor and captain general of this post and its provinces, I give the present in Florida on the fifth of August, seventeen thirty-nine.

In true testimony,
Francisco de Castilla
Governmental Notary

ORDER 4: GUERRA Y VEGA TO ARGÜELLES, MARCH 4, 1665

The order which follows evidently stems from political difficulties within the province of Guale, specifically relating to a pair of Indians who disobeyed the *mico* of Mission Santa Catalina (probably Don Alonso Menéndez). It seems doubtful whether an incident of this kind alone would motivate the caciques of Guale to ask for help from the Spanish Governor of St. Augustine, but Guerra's statement that the actions of these two Indians resulted in the "general admiration" of the rest of the Indians in Guale suggests that the caciques of Guale considered these rebels as a real threat to their power. Viewed in this light, the disobedience noted in the introduction to this order may only have been the tip of the iceberg, perhaps reflecting a deeper social unrest. The causes for this are unclear, but the fact that the caciques of Guale asked Governor Guerra for assistance reveals the degree to which aboriginal leaders depended upon Spanish legitimization and support in retaining political control over their own societies.

Interestingly, the governor seems to have arrived at the conclusion that certain unnamed female leaders had prompted the disobedience through their inability to govern effectively, and thus Captain Argüelles was instructed to replace them with more capable leaders. This might suggest some sort of political split within the leadership of Guale, with the female leaders somehow involved in a general decline of respect for the *mico* of Santa Catalina. The fact that these cacicas were mentioned first in the Governor's order (prior to any discussion of the delinquent Indians) implies that this might have been the underlying motive in the petition for Spanish military assistance. Indeed, only two years earlier Captain Argüelles was sent to Santa Catalina to investigate and correct a decline in respect for the *mico* of Guale (Aranguiz y Cotes, 1663c). The 1665 trouble may have prompted a more effective solution to the same recurring problem.

[f.7]

Order to send Captain Antonio de Argüelles to the provinces of Guale, year of 1665.

Don Francisco de la Guerra y de la Vega, governor and captain general of this city, presidio, and provinces of St. Augustine, Florida, for the King our lord. Inasmuch as the caciques of the province of Guale have come to inform me of the disobedience which two Indians displayed in the village of Santa Catharina with its *mico* and lord, and the destruction[31] which they did with their evil conduct, and going to the village of San Phelipe, doing things which have caused in all that province general admiration among its natives, since they have obligated its principals to come and give me notice; and because a case of so much consequence demands a brief and effective remedy, I have determined to send a person who will arrange and adjust it; and it is suitable that this [person] is of the experience, capacity, and sufficiency which are required in similar cases; and attentive that all the necessary [qualities] coincide in the [person] of Captain Antonio [f.7, vto.] de Argüelles,[32] who is a *reformado* in the presidio of this city, and [attentive] to the good that on other occasions of similar consequence he has given entire satisfaction, leaving all those provinces in tranquil peace, I have deemed it appropriate to name him, as for the present I elect and name him, to whom I order that as soon as he receives this [order] he leave from this city with the infantry which I have commanded to be indicated and go to the province of Guale, where having arrived, he will endeavor to inform himself of what happened, and being [informed] about everything with clarity and distinction, if it is suitable, he will place in possession of the cacique-dom the heir or those deserving, because they have informed me that the women who are governing are not sufficient, and that these [women] have caused the disturbance, endeavoring with all [f.8] wisdom to adjust this matter of so much consequence, and to capture the delinquents who cause similar disturbances, and imprisoning them; and to bring them to this city so that I can order them punished as indicated by the reports which he brings me; and if he finds other discord to adjust in all those provinces, I give him complete faculty to arrange, adjust, settle, and conform them according to what he sees suitable, and I trust in his person, and in that which both Majesties have in his service. And I order and command the *micos*, caciques, *mandadores*, and remaining principals of all that province to give him all the support and aid which is necessary for the better fulfillment of this order, on pain that I will order anyone who does the contrary to be punished with demonstration, by thus being suitable to the service of His Majesty [f.8, vto.] and to the universal peace of all those provinces. And in order to expedite this order, Juan Moreno y Segobia, governmental notary, will take the copy, since I ordered it dispatched signed by my hand, sealed with the seal of my arms, and endorsed by the undersigned secretary. Given in the city of St. Augustine, Florida, on the fourth of March, sixteen sixty-five. Don Francisco de la Guerra y de la Vega. By order of the governor and captain general, my lord, Bernavé de la Trinidad, secretary.

The copy of the above order by the señor governor and captain general remains in the governmental secretary's office of this province, and I turned over the original to the aforementioned for its execution. To this I swear, Juan Moreno y Segobia, public and governmental notary.

Agrees with the order previously inserted, according to how the copy is taken in one of the governmental books of the archive under my charge, to which I refer. And by verbal order of the señor Colonel Don Manuel de Montiano, governor and captain general of this post and its provinces, I present the above in Florida on the fifth of August, seventeen thirty-nine.

In true testimony,
Francisco de Castilla
Governmental Notary

ORDER 5: GUERRA Y VEGA TO SÁNCHEZ DE ENTONADO, JANUARY 10, 1665

The fifth transcribed document (folios 9 and 10 of this notebook) is a nearly identical copy of the third order, with the sole exception of the date of issue, which appears here as January 10, 1665 (instead of January 17). This was undoubtedly taken from a separate copy of the same yearly order.

ORDER 6: GUERRA Y VEGA TO ALVAREZ, FEBRUARY 1, 1666

The following order represents a complete *repartimiento* labor draft order, including both the order and attached instruction. Yearly dispatches of this kind formed the backbone of the labor system supporting the garrison town of St. Augustine, and while very few copies of these orders are extant, similar orders were drafted every year throughout the 17th century. Replete with formulaic official jargon, these orders contain data regarding the relative population of each mission town, and as such can supply important glimpses into the changing demographic profiles of the mission provinces during crucial years in their history.

Unfortunately, however, few of these orders have been located, comprising only a fraction of the potential data available. The present Castilla transcriptions are the only known series of full copies of such orders, spanning the years 1665–1669, with only the last four containing the attached instruction with the important draft enumeration. As such, they provide a sense of both the regularities and variations in the yearly draft orders, hinting at the potential value of a full set (which remains in the lost governmental archive of St. Augustine).

[f.11]

Order to bring Indians from the provinces of Guale and Mocama for cultivation, year of 1666.

Don Francisco de la Guerra y de la Vega, governor and captain general of this city of St. Augustine, Florida, and its provinces for the King our lord. Inasmuch as by dispatch of this past twenty-fifth of January I have sent to the provinces of Timucua and Apalachee to look for the people who are customarily brought to work for the infantry who serve His Majesty in the presidio of this city, as an indispensable thing, so that they might sustain themselves better, and so that the post will have the necessary provision; and it is suitable to make a draft from the provinces of Guale and Mocama, as has been done for time immemorial in this place, and for this draft and transport, it is suitable to send a person who is capable among the natives, so that he brings them wisely; and because I am informed that most who are in the habit of coming are pagans; because I am well-informed of the good which [f.11, vto.] Adjutant Alonso de Alvarez, *reformado* in this presidio, has done on other occasions, I have deemed it advisable to name him, as for the present I elect and name him, so that as soon as he receives this [order] he should leave this city and go to the province of Guale, where having arrived, he should in my name give its *micos*, caciques, and principals to understand the suitability to the service of His Majesty, the common good, and the conservation of this post, that they send the field hands who are requested, according to the instruction which I have commanded him to turn over, assuring them all good treatment, and that I will have them paid for all their labor, and in case some Indians should wish to come of their own will, outside of the quantity which are ordered, he will endeavor with the best attention which he can to conduct them to this city with the [f.12] rest, endeavoring to leave their *micos* and caciques pleased, doing everything with the zeal which I expect from his person; and when they are recovered, he will endeavor to leave from those provinces at a time which he sees he can arrive at this city on the eighth of March, without permitting or making exception that they come burdened, only with their provision, for the importance which His Majesty (God guard) charges their good treatment. And below this order I command all the *micos*, caciques, *mandadores*, and remaining principals of the towns through which the said Adjutant Alonso Alvarez passes to give him all the support and aid which he asks them for, without any limitation, on pain that I will command anyone who does the contrary to be punished with [f.12, vto.] demonstration, by thus being suitable to the service of His Majesty. The copy of this order will be taken in the governmental secretary's office, which is dispatched for this, signed by my hand, sealed with the seal of my arms, and endorsed by the undersigned, my secretary. Given in the city of St. Augustine, Florida, on the first day of February, sixteen sixty-six, Don Francisco de la Guerra y de la Vega. By order of the governor and captain general, my lord, Miguel Alonso Ojeda, secretary.

The copy of the above order by the señor governor and captain general remains in the governmental secretary's office by his order, and [f.13] the original was turned over to the aforementioned for its execution. Of this I swear, Juan Moreno y Segobia, public and governmental notary.

Instruction and order which is to be observed in the draft of the Indians who are going to be brought from the province of Guale for the cultivation of the fields of this city and presidio this present year of sixteen sixty-six,[33] which is in the following form and manner:

> Firstly, from the village of Guadalquini, five Indians.
> From the villages of Santa Catharina and Satoache, eight Indians.
> From the village of Sapala, four Indians.
> From the village of Tupiqui, four Indians. [f.13, vto.]
> From the village of San Phelipe, four.[34]

Which in all are twenty-five Indians, and it is consistent with this reckoning if it is suitable to draft more people. He will see the disposition which there is in each one of the villages, according to the people they have, altering the quantities if it is suitable, bringing a count and copy of the people who go, and how many from each village, so that with the same [count] they can return to their villages upon finishing the cultivation.[35] And likewise he will give the Yamase caciques who find themselves in that province[36] to understand the great necessity which there is of people in order to cultivate the said fields, and by being suitable to the service of His Majesty, I order them [f.14] to give as many Indians of their nation as they can for the said effect, assuring them on my behalf good treatment, and that I will have them paid for their labor. And in everything he will act and comply in conformity with what I expect from his person, adjusting everything to this instruction. Given in the city of St. Augustine, Florida, on the first of February, sixteen sixty-six, Don Francisco de la Guerra y de la Vega. By order of the governor and captain general, my lord, Miguel Alonso de Ojeda, secretary.

As is on record and appears from the said instruction, with which it was corrected, and the copy of it was taken together with the order which was dispatched for this effect. I swear, Juan Moreno y Segobia, public and governmental notary.

Agrees with the order previously inserted, according to how the copy is taken [f.14, vto.] in one of the governmental books of the archive under my charge, to which I refer. And by verbal order of the señor Colonel Don Manuel de Montiano, governor and captain general of this post and its provinces, I give the present in Florida on the fifth of August, seventeen thirty-nine. Between lines—*micos*—valid.

> In true testimony,
> Francisco de Castilla
> Governmental Notary

ORDER 7: GUERRA Y VEGA TO ARGÜELLES, AUGUST 18, 1667

The following order is of particular importance for understanding the final years of the Guale province, inasmuch as it relates directly to the processes of flight and assimilation that were the hallmark of Guale's history after 1661. Following the initial wave of raids by the Chichimeco Indians in 1661 (see Overview), the Guale province began the step-by-step process of retreat to the south, beginning with the northernmost mission of Chatuache in the mid-1660s. While the relocation and aggregation of mission towns during the next 20 years is better understood, less well known are the details of the arrival and assimilation of various unconverted Indian groups from the regions north and west of Guale.

By the early 1680s, Guale was home to an aboriginal population of both Christian and pagan Indians, coexisting in roughly equal numbers (see Document 7). In the following order, however, the beginnings of this process are recorded, for in the summer of 1667, refugees from two northerly Indian villages—Santa Elena and Abaya—petitioned successfully for the allotment of lands to form new towns within the province of Guale (see Overview). At that time, Governor Guerra y Vega sent Captain Alonso de Argüelles to Guale with instructions to assign lands to the new arrivals. One intriguing facet of this process is the successful integration of immigrant refugees within territories pertaining to the caciques of Guale. Although there is no evidence for the manner in which Captain Argüelles managed to win the approval of these indigenous caciques, the increasing immigrant population of Guale during the next decades attests to the success of the measures employed.

Interestingly, the names of these two towns do not appear in later records for the province of Guale. Unless Argüelles's efforts were unsuccessful, the inhabitants of Santa Elena and Abaya may have been considered part of the group of Indians referred to as Yamassee, their names merging with later designations under the more general name. This possibility is explored in depth in the Overview.

[f.15]

Order to assign lands in the province of Guale to the caciques of Santa Elena, year of 1667.

Don Francisco de la Guerra y de la Vega, governor and captain general in this city and presidio of St. Augustine, Florida, and its provinces for His Majesty. Inasmuch as I have had notice that some pagan caciques with their vassals and families from the towns of Santa Elena and Abaja[37] have retreated to the town of Santa Catharina de Guale, fleeing from the Chichimecos who made war on them, and that today they find themselves without having one settlement [*población*], nor land assigned to be able to make one, and by it being very suitable to shelter them and give lands to the said caciques, so that they might form a town and make their fields, by having come to ask for aid, and having rendered obedience [f.15, vto.] to His Majesty, and since by having communication with the Catholic Indians of the said province of Guale some of the said pagans could reduce themselves to our sacred Catholic faith, and because it is necessary that, in order to assign them lands and locations to the said pagan caciques in order to form a town and make their fields without harm to the natives of the said province of Guale, a person of full satisfaction and experience, and who has the familiarity of the lands and locations of the said province of Guale, should go to it, and because the said qualities coincide in the [person] of Captain Alonso de Argüelles, *reformado* in this [f.16] presidio, I have held it for good [effect] to name him, as for the present I elect and name him for the said effect, to whom I order and command that as soon as he receives the present [order] he should go to the said province of Guale with the infantry which I have ordered assigned to him, and having arrived at [the province], he should see and identify the locations and lands which can be given to the said pagan caciques of Santa Elena and Abaya so that they might form towns with their vassals and make their fields, acting in everything with all prudence and attention, as I expect he will do, and in case [f.16, vto.] some accident should happen, he will act in everything as the situation dictates, in such a way that it is achieved that the said Indians remain settled in the said province of Guale, and that the lands which are thus given and assigned to the said pagan caciques be with the approval of the caciques of the said province of Guale, and not in harm to them or their vassals. For all the above stated and what is attached or left unsettled, I give him ample and entire faculty, by it being suitable to the service of both Majesties to shelter the said caciques and their vassals, [f.17] and to give them all the aid that they ask for, and by His Majesty having ordered and charged by different *cédulas* that they be given all attention and good treatment. The copy of this order will be taken in the governmental secretary's office of this province, which for this [effect] I ordered dispatched signed by my hand, sealed with the seal of my arms, and endorsed by the undersigned my secretary. Given in the city of St. Augustine, provinces of Florida, on the eighteenth of August, sixteen sixty-seven, Don Francisco de la Guerra [f.17, vto.] y de la Vega. By order of the governor and captain general, my lord, Miguel Alonso de Ojeda, secretary.

The copy of this order by the señor governor and captain general remains in the governmental secretary's office, and the original was turned over to the aforementioned for its execution. I swear, Juan Moreno y Segobia, public and governmental notary.

Agrees with the order previously inserted, according to how the copy is taken in one of the governmental books of the archive at my charge, to which I refer. And by verbal order of the señor Colonel Don Manuel de Montiano, governor and captain general of this post and its provinces, I give the present [f.18] in Florida on the fifth of August, seventeen thirty-nine.

In true testimony,
Francisco de Castilla
Governmental Notary

ORDER 8: GUERRA Y VEGA TO ARGÜELLES, APRIL 22, 1668

The order below was issued for two purposes, each to be carried out during the same expedition by Captain Argüelles to Guale. Initially, Argüelles was to assist in the transferral of power to a new *mico* in the mission village of Sapala, which was without a leader following the death of the previous *mico* (possibly Don Juan de Zapala, who signed the 1657 petition against Governor Rebolledo [Menéndez et al., 1657]). The impetus for this action seems to lie in the fact that the two most elderly caciques, to whom belonged the position, were considered too old or sick to govern effectively, and thus Governor Guerra y Vega seems to have decided to take preemptive action in order to prevent any future problems in leadership (potentially resulting from an internal power struggle). Argüelles was instructed to emplace the oldest cacique who was capable of governing, even though he might not be the legitimate candidate according to aboriginal custom. At the same time, the order provided Captain Argüelles with the authority to settle any other political disputes in Guale or Mocama.

Beyond this initial order, Argüelles was given a second charge: the replacement of fugitive Yamassee laborers who had left St. Augustine in the middle of their assigned labors in the fields, leaving the crops in danger of failure. Interestingly, the earlier labor draft order for that year, issued in January, had departed from the normal structure with a warning against just such flight (see Order 9), suggesting that trouble with fugitives had been experienced during the 1667 draft, and possibly earlier (see Order 11). The threat of severe punishment for both the fugitives and the caciques who permitted them to return may well have provided a strong motivation for the Yamassee caciques to comply with this order.

[f.19]

Commission to Captain Antonio de Argüelles so that he emplaces the cacique to govern the town of Zapala in the province of Guale, year of 1668.

Don Francisco de la Guerra y de la Vega, governor and captain general in this city and presidio of St. Augustine, Florida, and its provinces for His Majesty. Inasmuch as I have had notice that the *mico* of the town of Zapala in the province of Guale died without leaving a legitimate heir, and because according to the custom of that province, it is the turn of the most elderly caciques of the said town to govern it, and I have been informed that today the two [caciques] who there are find themselves unable to do so, considering their great age and other infirmities, for which cause the Indians of the said [f.19, vto.] town find themselves with great discord, from which it has resulted that many of them have fled, and in order to avoid greater damages, and what could proliferate, I have determined that in the said town of Zapala a person who is capable and meritous should be named to govern them as did the *mico* who died, and for this effect I name Captain Antonio de Argüelles, who is [captain] for His Majesty of one of the companies in the garrison of this post, to whom I order and command that as soon as he receives the present [order] he should leave this city and go to the province of Guale, and having arrived, he will endeavor, with all compassion and attention, to arrange the discords which [f.20] there might be among its Indians, and install a person to govern them, and this [person] should be one of the three most elderly caciques, the one who is most capable for the said government, although he might be the youngest, and supposing that none of the three caciques is appropriate, he will install in the said post another person from the said town, the one who is most suitable,[38] and he will perform all the remaining ceremonies which are customary in similar cases, requiring and admonishing all the caciques, principals, and remaining Indians of the said town that they should have and hold him as their [f.20, vto.] governor, and obey and respect him, as they did with the *mico* who died, until such time as I order something else, and in all the rest which might happen in this particular [case], he will act as the situation dictates, for all of which I give him authority and commission in form [of law], and likewise I give it so that in case there are whatever other dissensions in the said province of Guale, or in that of Mocama, he can adjust and arrange them, endeavoring that all might remain with all peace and tranquility, for the much that His Majesty (God preserve him) charges the good treatment [f.21] of the natives of these provinces. And the said Captain Antonio de Argüelles will give the Yamase caciques, pagans who find themselves in the said province of Guale, and in that of Mocama, to understand by the best way he can, how a quantity of Indians of the said nation have fled from the fields of this presidio, leaving them abandoned, for which cause today some of the fields are found impossible to cultivate, from which follows grave damage in harm to this presidio, and to the infantry who serve His Majesty in it, and attending to this particular [case], and to the common good and conservation of this post, the said Captain Antonio [f.21, vto.] de Argüelles will make the said caciques give him another quantity of Indians, as many as those who have fled of those who came for the cultivation of the said fields, and he will assure them on my part that I will have them treated well, and paid for their labor punctually. And I order and command all the *micos*, caciques, principals, and remaining Indians of the towns through which the said Captain Antonio de Argüelles passes to give him all the support and aid which he asks of them, thus being suitable to the service of His Majesty. And the copy of this order will be taken in the governmental secretary's office [f.22] of these provinces, which for the said purpose I ordered it dispatched signed by my hand, sealed with the seal of my arms, and endorsed by the undersigned, my secretary. Given in the city of St. Augustine, Florida, on the twenty-second of April, sixteen sixty-eight, Don Francisco de la Guerra y de la Vega. By order of the governor and captain general, my lord, Miguel Alonso de Ojeda, secretary.

The copy of this order by the señor governor and captain general remains in the governmental secretary's office, and the original was turned over to the aforementioned for its execution. Of this I swear, Juan Moreno y Segobia, public and governmental notary.

Agrees with the order previously inserted, according to how the copy appears in one of the books in the archive [f.22, vto.] of government at my charge, to which I refer. And by virtue of that commanded verbally by the señor Colonel Don Manuel de Montiano, governor and captain general of this post and its provinces, I give the present in Florida on the eleventh of August, seventeen thirty-nine.

In true testimony,
Francisco de Castilla
Governmental Notary

ORDER 9: GUERRA Y VEGA TO DOMÍNGUEZ, JANUARY 21, 1668

The following order is the 1668 *repartimiento* labor draft, erroneously copied by 18th-century notary Francisco de Castilla before the 1667 order (Order 11). It is nearly identical to those for 1665, 1666, and 1667, with the exception that Governor Guerra y Vega added a very explicit statement regarding fugitives from the labors in St. Augustine, threatening to condemn those who absented themselves without permission to forced labor in the royal constructions (essentially as slaves). The caciques were likewise threatened with public punishment if they permitted fugitives to reenter their villages. Interestingly, the 1669 order (Order 10, below) omitted this additional passage, suggesting that it was a one-time occurrence during the term of Governor Guerra y Vega. As noted above, this threat does not seem to have dissuaded a number of Yamassee Indians from leaving the fields in April of 1668 (Order 8).

[f.23]

Commission to Ensign Juan Domínguez so that he sends Indians to cultivate the fields, drafting them from the provinces of Guale and Mocama, year of 1668.[39]

Don Francisco de la Guerra y de la Vega, governor and captain general of this city and presidio of St. Augustine, Florida, and its provinces for His Majesty. Inasmuch as I have sent to the provinces of Timucua, Apalachee, and that of Ybineyuti [to look for] the people which are customarily brought for the labor of the infantry who serve His Majesty in the presidio of this city, as an indispensable thing, so that they might sustain themselves better, and so that the post will have the necessary provision; and it is suitable to make a draft from the provinces of Guale and Mocama, as has been done for time immemorial in this place, and for this draft and transport, it is suitable to send a person who is [f.23, vto.] capable among the natives, so that with all wisdom he brings them; and because I am informed that most who are in the habit of coming are pagans, and because I am well-informed of the good which Ensign Juan Domínguez, *reformado* in this presidio, has done on other occasions, I have deemed it advisable to name him, as for the present I elect and name him, so that as soon as he receives this [order] he should leave from this city and go to the province of Guale, where having arrived, he should in my name give to understand to its *micos*, caciques, and principals the suitability to the service of His Majesty, the common good, and the conservation of this post, [f.24] that they send the field hands who are requested, according to the instruction which I have commanded him to turn over, assuring them all good treatment, and that I will have them paid for all their labor, advising and admonishing the caciques of each village of those which give Indians for the said cultivation, requiring them on their part that those who come to this presidio and are distributed among the persons to whom they fall should not, as they are in the habit of doing, absent themselves nor return to their villages without finishing the cultivation, because I will condemn those who flee to the royal [f.24, vto.] constructions as forced laborers,[40] and I will order the caciques who admit them [to their villages] in the stated manner to be punished, being aware of the flight which the above [Indians] made. And in case some Indians should wish to come of their own will, beyond the quantity which are ordered, he will endeavor with the best attention that he can to conduct them to this city with the rest, endeavoring to leave their *micos* and caciques pleased, doing everything with the zeal which I expect from his person; and when they are gathered, he will leave from the said province and arrive at this city on the coming twenty-fourth of February, [f.25] without permitting or making exception that they come burdened, only with their provision, for the importance which His Majesty (God preserve him) charges their good treatment. And below this order I command all the *micos*, caciques, *mandadores*, and remaining principals of the towns through which the above stated passes to give him all the support and aid which he asks them for, on pain that I will command that anyone who does the contrary be punished in public, by thus being suitable to the service of His Majesty. The copy of this order will be taken in the governmental secretary's office [f.25, vto.] of these provinces, which I ordered dispatched for this, signed by my hand, sealed with the seal of my arms, and endorsed by the undersigned, my secretary. Given in the city of St. Augustine, Florida, on the twenty-first of January, sixteen sixty-eight, Don Francisco de la Guerra y de la Vega. By order of the governor and captain general, my lord, Miguel Alonso Ojeda, secretary.

The copy of the above order by the señor governor and captain general was taken in the governmental secretary's office of these provinces by his order, and I turned over the original to the [f.26] aforementioned for its execution. Of this I swear, Juan Moreno y Segobia, governmental notary.

Agrees with the order previously inserted, the original of which remains according to how the copy appears in one of the books in the archive of government at my charge, to which I refer. And by verbal order of the señor Colonel Don Manuel de Montiano, governor and captain general of this post and its provinces, I give the present in Florida on the eleventh of August, seventeen thirty-nine.

In true testimony,
Francisco de Castilla
Governmental Notary

[f.27]

Instruction and order which is to be observed in the draft of the Indians which Ensign Juan Dominguez, *reformado* in this presidio, is going to bring from the province of Guale for the cultivation of the fields of this city and presidio this present year, which is in the following form:

Firstly, from the village of Guadalquini, five Indians.
From the villages of Santa Catharina and Satuache, eight Indians.
From the village of Sapala, four Indians.
From the village of Tupiqui, four Indians.
From the village of San Phelipe, four.

Which in all are twenty-five Indians, and it conforms with this reckoning if it is suitable to draft more people. He will see the disposition which there is [f.27, vto.] in each one of the villages, according to the people they have, altering the quantities if it is suitable, bringing a count and copy of the people who go, and how many from each village, so that with the same [count] they can return to their villages upon finishing the cultivation. And likewise he will give the Yamase caciques who find themselves in those provinces to understand the great necessity which there is of people in order to cultivate the said fields, and by being suitable to the service of His Majesty, I order them to give as many Indians of their nation as they can for the said purpose, assuring them on my part good [f.28] treatment, and that I will have them paid for their labor. And in all he will do and fulfill according to what I expect from his person, adjusting all to this instruction. Given in the city of St. Augustine, Florida, on the twenty-first of January, sixteen sixty-eight, Don Francisco de la Guerra y de la Vega. By order of the governor and captain general, my lord, Miguel Alonso de Ojeda, secretary.

The copy of this instruction remains in the governmental secretary's office. Of this I swear, Juan Moreno y Segobia, governmental notary.

Agrees with the memorial previously inserted, according to how the copy appears in consequence [f.28, vto.] of the preceding order, to which I refer. And in virtue of the same order, I give the present in Florida on the fifth of August, seventeen thirty-nine.

In true testimony,
Francisco de Castilla
Governmental Notary

ORDER 10: GUERRA Y VEGA TO AISPIOLEA, JANUARY 16, 1669

Below is the last of the present series of yearly labor draft orders to Guale and Mocama issued during the term of Governor Guerra y Vega. In structure and wording it is largely identical to the rest, but the 1669 order marks a small departure from the three previous drafts in the enumeration of Indian laborers listed for the draft, as will be discussed below.

[f.29]

Order that Adjutant Francisco de Aizpiolea goes to the province of Guale to bring Indians for the cultivation, drafting from each town the number which are provided in the instruction, year of 1669.

Don Francisco de la Guerra y de la Vega, governor and captain general of this city of St. Augustine, Florida, and its provinces for the King our lord. Inasmuch as today I have dispatched to the provinces of Timucua and Apalachee to look for the people who are customarily brought for the labor of the infantry who serve His Majesty in this presidio, as an indispensable thing, so that they might sustain themselves better, and so that the post will have the necessary provision; and it is suitable to make a draft from the provinces of Guale and Mocama, as has been done for time immemorial in this place, and for this draft and transport, it is suitable to send a person who is capable among the [f.29, vto.] natives, so that he brings them wisely; and because I am informed that most who are in the habit of coming are pagans; and because I am well-informed of the person of Adjutant Francisco de Aispiolea, I have deemed it advisable to name him, as for the present I elect and name him, so that as soon as he receives this [order] he should leave from this city and go to the province of Guale, where having arrived, he should in my name give to understand to its *micos*, caciques, and principals the suitability to the service of His Majesty, the common good, and the conservation of this post, that they remit the field hands who are requested, according to the instruction which I have commanded him to turn over, assuring them all good treatment, [f.30] and that I will have them paid for all their labor, and in case some Indians should wish to come of their own will, outside of the quantity which are ordered, he will endeavor with the best attention which he can to conduct them to this city with the rest, endeavoring to leave their *micos* and caciques pleased, doing everything with the zeal which I expect from his person; and when they are recovered, he will endeavor to leave from those provinces at a time which he sees he can arrive at this city on the coming twenty-second of February, without permitting or making exception that they come burdened, only with their provision, for the importance which His Majesty (God preserve him) charges their good treatment. And below this order I command all the *micos*, caciques, *mandadores*, and remaining [f.30, vto.] principals of the towns through which the said Adjutant Francisco de Aispiolea passes to give him all the support and aid which he asks them for, without any limitation, on pain that I will command that anyone who does the contrary be punished in public, by thus being suitable to the service of His Majesty. The copy of this order will be taken in the governmental secretary's office, which is dispatched for this, signed by my hand, sealed with the seal of my arms, and endorsed by the undersigned, my secretary. Given in the city of St. Augustine, Florida on the sixteenth of January, sixteen sixty-nine, Don Francisco de la Guerra y de la Vega. By order of the governor and captain general, my lord, [f.31] Manuel de Torres y Villa Bicencio, secretary.

The copy of the above order by the señor governor and captain general remains in the governmental secretary's office by his order, and the original was turned over to the aforementioned for its execution. Of this I swear, Juan Moreno y Segobia, public and governmental notary.

Instruction and order which Adjutant Francisco de Aispiolea, *reformado* in this presidio, is to observe in the draft of the Indians from the province of Guale, conforming to the order which I have ordered him to turn over, as follows:

Firstly, from the village of Guadalquini, five Indians.
From the village of Asao, four.[41] [f.31, vto.]
From the village of Santa Catharina, four.
From the village of Satoache, four.[42]
From the village of Zapala, four Indians.
From the village of Tupiqui, four Indians.
From the village of San Phelipe, four.

And it is consistent with this reckoning if it is suitable to draft more people. He will see the disposition which there is in each one of the villages, according to the people they have, altering the quantities if it is suitable, bringing a count and copy of the people who go, and how many from each village, so that with the same [count] they can return to their villages upon finishing the cultivation. And likewise he will give the Yamase caciques who find themselves in that [f.32] province to understand the great necessity which there is of people in order to cultivate the said fields, and by being suitable to the service of His Majesty, I order them to give as many Indians of their nation as they can for the said purpose, assuring them on my part good treatment, and that I will have them paid for their labor. And in all he will do and fulfill according to what I trust from his person, adjusting all to this instruction. Given in the city of St. Augustine, Florida, on the sixteenth of January, sixteen sixty-nine, Don Francisco de la Guerra y de la Vega. By order of the governor and captain general, my lord, Manuel de Torres [f.32, vto.] y Villa Bicencio, secretary.

The copy was taken in the governmental secretary's office, I swear, Juan Moreno y Segobia, public and governmental notary.

Agrees with the order previously inserted, according to how the copy appears in one of the books of the governmental archive at my charge, to which I refer. And by verbal order of the señor Colonel Don Manuel de Montiano, governor and captain general of this post and its provinces, I give the present in Florida on the eleventh of August, seventeen thirty-nine.

In true testimony,
Francisco de Castilla
Governmental Notary

ORDER 11: GUERRA Y VEGA TO AISPIOLEA, JANUARY 10, 1667

The following order was erroneously marked 1677 in the margin by the notary Castilla, and thus was bound out of order. It should be located between the 1666 and 1668 labor drafts, and in this context the order below conforms well to the orders of those years.

[f.33]

Order to bring Indians from the provinces of Guale and Mocama for the cultivation, year of 1677.[43]

Don Francisco de la Guerra y de la Vega, governor and captain general of this city of St. Augustine, Florida, and its provinces for the King our lord. Inasmuch as today on this date I have dispatched to the provinces of Timucua and Apalachee to look for the people which are customarily brought for the labor of the infantry who serve His Majesty in this presidio, as an indispensable thing, so that they might sustain themselves better, and so that the post will have the necessary provision; and it is suitable to make a draft from the provinces of Guale and Mocama, as has been done for time immemorial in this place, and for this draft and transport, it is suitable to send [f.33, vto.] a person who is capable among the natives, so that he brings them wisely; and because I am informed that most who are in the habit of coming are pagans; and because I am well-informed of the person of Adjutant Francisco de Aispiolea, I have deemed it advisable to name him, as for the present I elect and name him, so that as soon as he receives this [order] he should leave this city and go to the province of Guale, where having arrived, he should in my name give to understand to its *micos*, caciques, and principals the suitability to the service of His Majesty, the common good, and the conservation of this post, that they remit the field hands who are requested, [f.34] according to the instruction which I have commanded him to turn over, assuring them all good treatment, and that I will have them paid for all their labor, and in case some Indians should wish to come of their own will, beyond the quantity which are ordered, he will endeavor with the best attention which he can to conduct them to this city with the rest, endeavoring to leave their *micos* and caciques pleased, doing everything with the zeal which I expect from his person; and when they are gathered, he will endeavor to leave from those provinces at a time which he sees he can arrive at this city on the coming twentieth of February, without permitting or making [f.34, vto.] exception that they come burdened, only with their provision, for the importance which His Majesty (may God preserve him) charges their good treatment. And below this order I command all the *micos*, caciques, *mandadores*, and remaining principals of the towns through which the said Adjutant Francisco de Aispiolea passes to give him all the support and aid which he asks them for, without any limitation, on pain that I will command he who does the contrary to be punished in public, this being suitable to the service of His Majesty. The copy of this order will be taken in the governmental secretary's office, which is dispatched for this, signed by my hand, sealed [f.35] with the seal of my arms, and endorsed by the undersigned, my secretary. Given in the city of St. Augustine, Florida, on the tenth of January, sixteen sixty-seven, Don

Francisco de la Guerra y de la Vega. By order of the governor and captain general, my lord, Miguel Alonso de Ojeda, secretary.

Instruction which was given to the aforementioned in the order above.

Instruction and order which Adjutant Francisco de Aispiolea, *reformado* in this presidio, is to observe in the draft of the Indians from the province of Guale, conforming to the order which I have ordered him to turn over, is as follows:

> Firstly, from the village of Guadalquini, [f.35, vto.] five Indians.
> From the villages of Santa Catharina and Sathoache, eight Indians.
> From the village of Zapala, four.
> From the village of Tupiqui, four.
> From the village of San Phelipe, another four Indians.

And it conforms with this reckoning if it is suitable to draft more people. He will see the disposition which there is in each one of the villages, according to the people they have, altering the quantities if it is suitable, bringing a count and copy of the people who go, and how many from each village, so that with the same [count] they can return to their villages upon finishing the cultivation. And likewise he will give the Yamase caciques who find themselves in that province to understand the great necessity [f.36] which there is of people in order to cultivate the said fields, and by it being suitable to the service of His Majesty, I order them to give as many Indians of their nation as they can for the said purpose, assuring them on my part good treatment, and that I will have them paid for their labor. And in all he will do and fulfill according to what I expect from his person, adjusting all to this instruction. Given in the city of St. Augustine, Florida, on the tenth of January, sixteen sixty-seven, Don Francisco de la Guerra y de la Vega. By order of the governor and captain general, my lord, Miguel de Ojeda, secretary.

Agrees with the order previously inserted, according to how the copy appears in one of the governmental books of the archive at my charge, to which I refer. [f.36, vto.] And by verbal order of the señor Colonel Don Manuel de Montiano, governor and captain general of this post and its provinces, I give the present in Florida on the fifth of August, seventeen thirty-nine.

In true testimony,
Francisco de Castilla
Governmental Notary

ORDER 12: HITA SALAZAR TO FUENTES, OCTOBER 11, 1679

The following six gubernatorial orders date some 10 years after the previous set of orders by Governor Guerra y Vega. The following order dates to October of 1679, several months prior to the disastrous raids on Guadalquini and Santa Catalina. At that time, Governor Hita Salazar had received word from his lieutenant in the province of Guale, Captain Don Francisco de Cigarroa, that on the fifth of September, 5 Englishmen had arrived in the northernmost mission of Santa Catalina de Guale in a boat, reporting that they were fugitives from Charleston (San Jorje), and that 20 more had left with them. The following order dispatched Captain Francisco de Fuentes to Guale in order to investigate the situation and bring the Englishmen back to St. Augustine for questioning.

[f.37]

Order to Captain Francisco de Fuentes to go to Santa Catalina to join with the Lieutenant of the province of Guale, year of 1679.

Don Pablo de Hita Salazar, governor and captain general of these provinces, city, and presidio of St. Augustine, Florida, for His Majesty. Inasmuch as Captain Don Francisco de Zigarroa, my lieutenant in the province of Guale, advises me in a letter dated the twenty-seventh of the current [month] that on the fifth of the same [month],[44] five Englishmen arrived at that location with a launch from the population of San Jorje, and that having examined them, they said that they were coming as fugitives due to the bad treatment they received, and that another twenty had likewise left in their company, not knowing the [direction?] that they had taken, and because it is suitable [f.37, vto.] to conduct them to this presidio, in order to find out with greater certitude their design, and so that there are more reinforcements of people on that frontier, and in case the twenty they spoke of arrive, and if there are other developments which could happen, for the present I order Captain Francisco de Fuentes, *reformado* in this presidio, that as soon as he receives this my order, he should go to the village of Santa Catharina with the infantry that are assigned, and having arrived, between himself and my lieutenant they will confer and discuss all that seems to them to be to the better success of the service of His

Majesty, and having done this task, the said Captain Francisco de Fuentes will come with the five Englishmen to this presidio,[45] and if it seems [suitable] to him to leave some infantry [f.38] of that which he takes at his charge, he will leave them to the said Captain Don Francisco de Zigarroa, who will give me news of all the developments which happen, with the punctuality which is required, so that I can determine what is most suitable to the royal service. Take the copy of [this order] in the governmental secretary's office of these provinces, which for this [purpose] I ordered dispatched signed by my hand, and endorsed by the undersigned, my secretary. In St. Augustine, Florida, on the eleventh of October, sixteen seventy-nine, Pablo de Hita Salazar. By order of the señor governor and captain general, my lord, Thomás Sánchez de la Bandera.

In everything the expedient will be taken [f.38, vto.] which is most suitable to the service of His Majesty, and Captain Francisco de Fuentes will take that which remains and come with the Englishmen.

Agrees with its original, which was turned over to the aforementioned. I swear, Alonso Solana, public and governmental notary.

Agrees with the order previously inserted, according to how the copy appears in one of the governmental books in the archive at my charge, to which I refer. And by verbal order of the señor Colonel Don Manuel de Montiano, governor and captain general of this post and its provinces, I give the present in Florida on the fifth of August, seventeen thirty-nine.

In true testimony,
Francisco de Castilla
Governmental Notary

ORDER 13: HITA SALAZAR TO ESTEBEDES DE CARMENATIS, MAY 23, 1680

The following order was issued within a week of Order 15 (see below), and relates to the planned counterattack against the raiders on Guadalquini and Santa Catalina. As noted in Order 17, Captain Nicolás Estebedes de Carmenatis was to be sent by land with troops to reinforce Captain Juan Saturnino de Abaurrea and Captain Fuentes, the Guale lieutenant, in the village of Sapala. There he was instructed to remain at the command of the lieutenant in any future actions.

[f.39]

Order so that Captain Nicolás Estebedes de Carmenatis passes to the province of Guale to join with its lieutenant, year of 1680.

Don Pablo de Hita Salazar, governor and captain general of this city, presidio, and provinces of St. Augustine, Florida, for His Majesty. For the present I order Captain Nicolás Estebedes de Carmenatis that as soon as he receives this my order, he should go with all speed to the province of Guale with the infantry that are assigned to him, to the town of Sapala, or the place where Captain Francisco de Fuentes, my lieutenant, *justicia mayor*, and captain at war in the said province happens to be, where having arrived, he will turn over to him the said infantry which is in his charge, and he will be under his command in all which [f.39, vto.] happens in the service of His Majesty and in the defense against the enemies who find themselves entrenched in the place of Cofunufo,[46] or any other place in the said province, endeavoring to give his opinion and conference in all that which they will find to be most suitable to the service of God and of the King, and to the conservation of these provinces, which is thus suitable to the service of His Majesty. Given in St. Augustine, Florida, on the twenty-third of May, sixteen eighty, Pablo de Hita Salazar. And take the copy of this my order in the governmental secretary's office of these provinces. Paraph. By order of the governor and captain general, my lord, Francisco López de Mediano, his secretary.

Agrees with its original, which was turned over to the contained for its execution. I swear, Alonso Solana, public and governmental notary.

Agrees with the order previously inserted, according to how the copy is taken in one of the governmental books in the archive at my charge, to which I refer. And by verbal order of the señor Colonel Don Manuel de Montiano, governor and captain general of this post and its provinces, I give the present in Florida on the fifth of August, seventeen thirty-nine.

In true testimony,
Francisco de Castilla
Governmental Notary

ORDER 14: HITA SALAZAR TO FUENTES, JUNE 18, 1680

The following order was sent to Captain Fuentes, the lieutenant of the province of Guale, in an effort to convince the Indians of Mission Santa Catalina to return to their homes and live there as they did before the raids the previous spring (see Order 15 below). The tone of the order reveals the perceived strategic importance of Santa Catalina, as the former northern frontier outpost, and emphasizes the degree to which the Spanish garrison in Guale was dependent upon Indian support. Without a mission village to provide food and shelter, the Spanish infantrymen were effectively unable to resettle St. Catherines Island.

[f.41]

Order to the lieutenant of Santa Catharina, province of Guale, year of 1680.

Don Pablo de Hita Salazar, governor and captain general of this city, presidio, and provinces of St. Augustine, Florida, for His Majesty. Inasmuch as on the occasion of the entrance which the enemy Chuchumeca, Uchises, and Chiluques[47] made in Santa Catharina, province of Guale, making the native Indians of the said town retreat to that of Sapala, together with my lieutenant and the infantry which he had there in garrison, as the head of the said province, and considering the little protection and need that they will have to attend to their fields, which are today being lost, in the town of Santa Catharina through lack of cultivation and physical presence, especially when this precedes greater damage [f.41, vto.] as a result of the said island remaining depopulated, with which the enemies will find more security and sustenance, occupying it for their safety, for the present I order Captain Francisco de Fuentes, my lieutenant, *justicia mayor*, and captain at war in the said province, that as soon as he receives this my order, he should convoke and bring together the Indians, caciques, and principals of the said town of Santa Catharina and impress upon them how important it is that they go to their houses and fields, advising that this will not be the most trivial annoyance for them, but that they should live with tranquility, and particularly that they should not consent nor make an exception that they go to the woods for cassina, except when paying them, or when they wish to go for themselves voluntarily, and [f.42] other exercises which relate to the sustenance of the infantry, without having priority over their own satisfaction.[48] And he will give me news of what is done in virtue of this order with all brevity, in order to emplace the remedy which is suitable to the service of His Majesty, and in case of not being able to determine anything in the execution of this my order, the cacique and principals of the said town of Santa Catharina will come to my presence so that, having heard them judicially, I may provide [a remedy].[49] And the copy of this my order will be taken in the governmental secretary's office of these provinces. Given in the city of St. Augustine, Florida, on the eighteenth of June, sixteen eighty, [f.42, vto.] Pablo de Hita Salazar. By order of the governor and captain general, my lord, Francisco López de Medrano, his secretary.

Agrees with its original, which was remitted to the aforementioned. I swear, Alonso Solana, public and governmental notary.

Agrees with the order previously inserted, according to how the copy appears in one of the governmental books in the archive at my charge, to which I refer. And by verbal order of the señor Colonel Don Manuel de Montiano, governor and captain general of this post and its provinces, I give the present in Florida on the fifth of August, seventeen thirty-nine.

In true testimony,
Francisco de Castilla
Governmental Notary

ORDER 15: HITA SALAZAR TO GÓMEZ, MAY 17, 1680

The following order represents the first in a series of five orders copied by Francisco de Castilla relative to the 1680 Chichimeco assault on Guale (see Overview). Inasmuch as these orders were issued in rapid succession, and related to a single set of circumstances, it is possible to gain some understanding of the preparations and responses enacted that year in defense of the Guale missions. In this sense, the documents below add depth to our comprehension of the abandonment of Mission Santa Catalina de Guale, and the rapid retreat southward which resulted. The orders are not arranged in precise chronological sequence, and thus a better understanding is possible if the orders are read in the following sequence, beginning with that below: Orders 15, 13, 17, 14, 16.

The following order provided for the collection and transport of a substantial number of weapons, including firearms and bows and arrows, from St. Augustine to Guale. Captain Juan Saturnino de Abaurrea had already been sent with reinforcements for Guale's lieutenant Francisco de Fuentes, and Sergeant Gómez was evidently sent with supplies for the forces already in Guale. These supplies were sent over land, and were to be used in the planned expedition against the English-sponsored raiders who had prompted the evacuation of Mission Santa Catalina. Interestingly, the order commands all native residents of St. Augustine to be at the disposal of Sergeant Manuel Gómez in any way he might request, serving to underline the perceived urgency of the situation.

Within the order is explicit permission for Sergeant Gómez to use the weapons if necessary during the voyage, and an additional note regarding posting sentinels and guards, indicating that there was fear of a surprise attack on the road. The overall tone of the order suggests that Governor Hita Salazar felt that the entire northern mission chain was subject to attack, and that Spanish control of Guale was slipping.

[f.43]

Order that Adjutant Manuel Gómez should go to the province of Guale, year of 1680.

Don Pablo de Hita Salazar, governor and captain general of this city, presidio, and provinces of St. Augustine, Florida, for His Majesty. Inasmuch as I have news of the invasion which the enemy Chuchumecos have made in two places in the province of Guale, and it is very possible that they are undertaking [an invasion] in other places in these provinces, and due to the importance of preparations, arrangements, and vigilance, I order Adjutant Manuel Gómez, whom I have stationed in the province of Timucua,[50] and who at the present finds himself in this city, that as soon as he receives this my order, he should depart for the said province with the munitions which are turned over to him, which he will make use of if an urgent occasion should happen, with the necessary moderation., account., and reason., due to the importance of their conservation, and if he does not employ them, he will hold them with the necessary caution and security. And I order and command all the Spaniards who are not from outside these provinces, of whatever quality and condition they might be, to attend to the share and task which the said Manuel Gómez will assign them, and to be at his orders, obeying them like my very own, written or spoken. And likewise [I order] the caciques, principals, and *mandadores*, to attend in the same conformity which he orders them, giving and assisting with what is necessary, attending to the proper defense if an enemy encounter should happen. And likewise, I order the said Manuel Gómez that he again observes and executes the order and instruction which I have given him before this on the twenty-sixth of February of this year,[51] in the points and matters which he finds as law, he should execute and understand them with the honesty which the affair offers, which is thus suitable to the service of His Majesty. And take the copy of this order in the governmental secretary's office of these provinces. Given in the city of St. Augustine, Florida, on the seventeenth of May, sixteen eighty. And likewise he will see to it that there are guard corps, night watches, and sentinels, as I have ordered, and that the firearms and bows and arrows are all in good condition and prepared, which is thus suitable for the best security. Pablo de Hita Salazar. By order of the governor and captain general, my lord, Francisco López de Medrano, his secretary.

Agrees with its original, which was remitted to the aforementioned. I swear, Alonso Solana, public and governmental notary.

Agrees with the order previously inserted, according to how the copy appears in one of the governmental books in the archive at my charge, to which I refer. And by verbal order of the señor Colonel Don Manuel de Montiano, governor and captain general of this post and its provinces, I present the above in Florida on the fifth of August, seventeen thirty-nine.

In true testimony,
Francisco de Castilla
Governmental Notary

ORDER 16: HITA SALAZAR TO LEÓN
July 22, 1680

The order below is the last in the series of five relative to the English-backed raids of 1680, and represents yet another effort to find a solution for the defense of Guale. Considering the earlier raids on Guadalquini and Santa Catalina, Governor Hita Salazar decided that outside consultation was needed, and thus ordered five Indian caciques from the province of Timucua to come to St. Augustine to meet with him. This seems an unprecedented step, inasmuch as the governor was not only asking for advice from inferior officers in the Spanish militia, but also from Indian caciques from an interior mission province. Nevertheless, this may only have been a preamble to a planned request for assistance in the defense of Guale, with Governor Hita Salazar endeavoring to avoid the kind of trouble that erupted in 1656 when the previous caciques of Timucua were drafted for military service (Worth, 1992). In that instance, the ill-advised activation of the standing Indian militia had indirectly resulted in large-scale rebellion, during which several Spanish soldiers and their servants and slaves were murdered.

[f.45]

Order to Captain Lorenzo Joseph de León about Santa Cathalina and Gualquini, year of 1680.

> Don Pablo de Hita Salazar, governor and captain general of this city, presidio, and provinces of St. Augustine, Florida, for His Majesty. Inasmuch as the enemy Chuchumecos, Uchises, and Chiluques, with the instigation of Englishmen, invaded the island of Santa Catharina in the province of Guale, and that of Guadalquini, and the Chuchumecos did some killings, and in order to have an effect on such outrages which have happened on other occasions, it is very suitable to arrange to search out these enemies in the places which they inhabit, casting them out of [these places], or that they reduce themselves to amity and tranquility, what we ought to desire for the [f.45, vto.] propagation of the sacred gospel, and the tranquility of human life, as a result of what has appeared, is to bring together the natives of these provinces, the persons who occupy the most exemplary military posts, and some caciques,[52] in order to discuss it and determine what is most suitable to the achievement of the aforementioned. For the present I order Captain Lorenzo Joseph de León that as soon as he receives this my order, he should go to the province of Timucua and bring Sergeant Major Don Thomás de Medina, cacique of Santa Fé, Captain Lucas, cacique of Santa Catharina, and the caciques of San Matheo, the [cacique] of San Pedro, and Machava,[53] so that if one of the aforementioned refuses to come due to the expense of time,[54] he will nevertheless obligate them to come to my presence, so that together we will confer regarding what ought to be done for the better success of service to both Majesties, and for the tranquility of these provinces, and the solace of its natives, which is thus suitable to [the service] of His Majesty. And the copy of this my order will be taken in the governmental secretary's office of these provinces. Given in the city of St. Augustine, Florida, on the twenty-second of July, sixteen eighty, Pablo de Hita Salazar. By order of the governor and captain general, my lord, Francisco López de Medrano, his secretary.
>
> Agrees with its original, which was turned over to the aforementioned for its execution. I swear, Alonso Solana, public and governmental notary.

Agrees with the order previously inserted, according to how the copy appears in one of the governmental books in the archive at my charge, to which I refer. And by verbal order of the señor Colonel Don Manuel de Montiano, governor and captain general of this post and its provinces, I give the present in Florida on the fifth of August, seventeen thirty-nine.

In true testimony,
Francisco de Castilla
Governmental Notary

ORDER 17: HITA SALAZAR TO RIBERA, MAY 26, 1680

The following order was issued three days after Governor Hita Salazar's meeting regarding the raids on Guadalquini and Santa Catalina which occurred only weeks previously (see Overview). It represents part of an attempt on the part of Governor Hita Salazar to strike back at the English-sponsored Indians who had forced the abandonment of Santa Catalina. A plan was devised to send soldiers and munitions by both sea and land, and to assemble a force of Spanish infantry at the village of Sapala, where the refugees from Santa Catalina had fled (including the current lieutenant of Guale, Captain Francisco de Fuentes, and soldiers already dispatched under Captains Juan Saturnino de Abaurrea and Nicolás Estebedes de Carmenatis). The order below provided for the dispatch of the ship stationed in St. Augustine for official business, in which both soldiers and equipment were to be carried to Sapalá. Within the order are explicit instructions that Captain Fuentes was to remain in charge of all operations in Guale.

[f.47]

Order so that Captain Don Enrique passes to the Bar of Sapala in the vessel of this presidio to join with the lieutenant of the province of Guale, year of 1680.

Don Pablo de Hita Salazar, governor and captain general of this city, presidio, and provinces of St. Augustine, Florida, for His Majesty. Inasmuch as in virtue of the news which I had from Captain Francisco de Fuentes, my lieutenant in the province of Guale, of enemies having invaded the island of Santa Catharina in the said province, a post of great importance for the security and risk of the said province, and of this presidio, and due to the meeting which I had on the twenty-third of this month and year,[55] from which it seemed to be very suitable to dislodge the enemy from that place, for which the aid which seemed [suitable] was sent, and the vessel of this presidio remained so that it might go to the Bar of Sapala, or that [place] in which my said lieutenant is to be found, so that with its arrival and the aid which I have sent with Captains Don Juan Saturnino and Nicolás de Carmenatis,[56] the best manner of dislodging the enemy could be prepared, and for the passage of the said vessel, it is suitable to send a person of satisfaction and experience, and because I have this from Captain Don Enrique de Ribera, who is [captain] of the artillery of this presidio, I order that as soon as he receives this my order, he embark in the said vessel with the mariners and soldiers, equipment, and munitions which will be turned over to him, so that he makes the voyage to the said Bar of Sapala, or to the place where the said Captain Francisco de Fuentes finds himself, which he will endeavor to discover with all security, and with the disposition which the time and occasion might offer him, in order to enter and turn over what he carries at his charge to him [Fuentes], so that having conferred regarding what should be done, he arranges and places in execution whatever is necessary for the success of the occasion, and the said Captain Don Enrique should be at the orders of my said lieutenant, and in the conformity which I have given order for, without offering any difficulty or retort, before conferring and determining, executing what is most suitable, observing the instruction which will be given him with this [order].[57] And I order and command all the infantry and mariners and the rest who go in the said vessel to obey the said Captain Don Enrique, and guard the orders he gives in writing or word of mouth, which is thus suitable to the service of His Majesty. The copy of this my order will be taken in the governmental secretary's office of these provinces. Given in the city of St. Augustine, Florida, on the twenty-sixth of May, sixteen eighty, Pablo de Hita Salazar. By order of the governor and captain general, my lord, Francisco López de Medrano, his secretary.

As is on record from its original, which was turned over to the aforementioned for its execution. I swear, Alonso Solana, public and governmental notary.

Agrees with the order previously inserted, according to how the copy appears in one of the governmental books in the archive at my charge, to which I refer. And by verbal order of the señor Colonel Don Manuel de Montiano, governor and captain general of this post and its provinces, I give the present in Florida on the fifth of August, seventeen thirty-nine.

In true testimony,
Francisco de Castilla
Governmental Notary

NOTES

1. This passage is a summary of the order to follow written by the 18th-century notary Francisco de Castilla. Although the original was placed in the left margin of Castilla's transcription of the 17th-century order, the summary will be placed at the head of the text for this translation.

2. The preceding passage identifies the name of the individual (in this case the governor of Florida) issuing the order. While Castilla copied this portion of the document at the head of the text, on the original order this would have appeared in the upper right corner of the initial folio, with the text of the order separated below.

3. The preceding portion of the text describes the circumstances that prompted the issuance of the order.

4. The preceding passage summarizes the action which the Governor is about to take with the order.

5. The term *reformado* refers to an officer without command, or an individual who holds an officer's rank, but who is not currently fulfilling the duties of that post. Such officers were typically given the standard pay of a normal soldier, but could be activated for special duties when the need arose. Although the garrison in the city of St. Augustine possessed a relatively small number of ac-

tive-duty posts, there were generally a large number of *reformados* available for service outside of the city, particularly on expeditions to the mission provinces, or among the Indians of the deep frontier.

6. This passage provides a brief justification for the election of the named officer for the task contained in the order, including some mention of past services.

7. The preceding section describes the actions which the named officer is instructed to take, and thus constitutes the core of the order being issued.

8. This passage constitutes the bestowal of authority on the named officer, and thus provides written justification for his actions. The phrasing of this sentence provides some leeway for independent action on the part of the officer, permitting him to perform duties not specifically outlined in the written order, but nonetheless within its bounds.

9. The preceding section includes any additional instructions or duties, and describes the completion of the task contained in the order.

10. This portion of the order was commonly attached below the primary order to the named officer on expeditions into the mission provinces, and represents a direct command to the Indian leaders to provide any assistance that might be deemed necessary by the officer during the execution of the order. Many of the common abuses of the mission Indians could be justified in the field by this passage, such as the drafting of burden bearers or the seizure of food or other supplies.

11. Within the original order were these instructions to make a copy for the permanent records of the governmental archive of St. Augustine. Since the original was given to the officer executing the command (and retained for his own records, or for use in proving military service), this instruction provided for the duplicate copy that the notary Francisco de Castilla transcribed in 1739, from which this translation derives.

12. The place and date of issuance were placed at the end of the text of the order, and the Governor's signature followed below. The secretary or notary who penned the original order signed as well.

13. This final passage in the transcription of this order represents the certification by the notary who actually made the copy of the original order and turned over the original to the officer named within.

14. This section is the certification by the 18th-century notary Francisco de Castilla that the indented transcription above is a faithful copy of the transcription that he located in the governmental archive of St. Augustine. The books to which Castilla refers were undoubtedly the bound volumes containing copies of all the orders issued by each governor of Florida during his term. Unfortunately, the original books that Castilla used have not been located by modern researchers.

15. The last line of this portion of the transcription represents the standard format for validating any corrections or insertions made by the notary who copied the previous document. In this instance, Castilla accidentally omitted "Fernández" from the name of Captain Nicolás Fernández de Goyas, but later discovered his error and wrote the correction between the lines of his transcription. In order to certify the changes he had made himself, and to assure that no further changes could be made to his transcription by other persons, the name was written between the words "Between lines ———— valid." Had there been other changes, these would have been listed as well. As will be seen on several of the orders that follow, this was a common feature of Spanish documents.

16. Below the certification by Castilla is the standardized wrap-up of documents written or copied by notaries, in which the notary swears to the faithfulness of his work and signs below. The phrase *En testimonio de verdad* is generally written in broad, flowery script, framing an official symbol used by the notary. The signature, often quite elaborate, and with a paraph, appears at the end of the document.

17. Captain Martín Alcayde de Cordoba was a 58-year-old soldier with substantial experience among the Indians of the mission provinces. He served as the lieutenant of the Apalachee province in 1652 (Horruytiner, 1652), and was lieutenant of the Timucua province between 1658 and 1660 (Rebolledo, 1658b). Alcayde de Cordoba had visited Mocama at least once; probably during 1656 he was dispatched to recover fugitive Indians from the destroyed town of Santiago de Ocone (on the modern Okefenokee Swamp), within the jurisdiction of the Mocama province (Alcayde, 1660; Worth, 1992).

18. A soldier who had been "advantaged", or *aventajado*, had successfully petitioned the Spanish Crown for a supplement to his normal pay in reward for exceptional service.

19. Juan Bauptista de la Cruz was a 34-year-old soldier who served as an interpreter of the Timucuan language during much of the late 17th century, including extensive service during the pacification of the Timucuan Rebellion of 1656 (Worth, 1992). He was also known by the name Nayo, and thus might possibly have been an Indian himself (Cruz, 1660).

20. This passage contains the standard statement ordering all the Indian leaders to provide assistance to the officer named in the order, but in addition includes the direct threat of public pun-

ishment. Depending on the severity of the case, such punishments could have included public mutilation and execution, not an uncommon practice in 17th-century Europe.

21. This order was issued on the same date as that above, and thus the two soldiers probably accompanied each other on separate missions to Guale.

22. The Spanish term *gente de cava* refers to male Indians drafted for service in the agricultural fields in and around St. Augustine, ostensibly belonging to the Spanish crown as a source of food for the Spanish garrison. In practice, abuses to this system developed, and the use of these field hands in privately-owned fields for individual profit was common.

23. Orders for the yearly labor draft were generally dispatched in late January or early February. One was sent to the northerly provinces of Guale and Mocama, and another two were sent to the western provinces of Timucua and Apalachee (see Worth, 1992: 122).

24. This note may refer to the influx of non-Christian Yamassee Indians into the Guale province, a process which seems to have begun during the early 1660s (see Overview).

25. Sánchez de Entonado was a 31-year-old soldier with experience among the Indians, including service during the Timucuan Rebellion of 1656 (serving as a squad leader at that time).

26. The instruction that originally accompanied this order was not transcribed here, but undoubtedly resembled that sent with the 1666 labor draft (see below).

27. The required wages for an Indian laborer in St. Augustine was one *real* per day, or slightly more than the daily wage of a Spanish infantryman. Inasmuch as Spanish currency did not circulate among the mission Indians, however, laborers were paid in cheap trade goods, such as cloth, iron tools, and beads.

28. This statement effectively opened the door for some of the abuses of the labor system, for it granted permission to bring more Indian laborers than were requested in the written instruction, provided they came of their own volition. Considering the potential forms of subtle coercion, however, Spanish officers would have found it easy to draft more Indians than the requested amount, as the repeated complaints of these very Indians affirm (see Overview).

29. The specified arrival date varied from year to year, but generally occurred during late February or early March, just before the first crops were planted in St. Augustine.

30. The prohibition on burden bearing was a long-standing but frequently abused rule in Spanish Florida. Indians were commonly used as bearers for a variety of purposes, ranging from carrying personal equipment and supplies for individual soldiers to serving as cargo carriers on private Spanish trading expeditions.

31. The term used here is *desmantelo,* which literally refers to dismantling, but which in this case probably refers to a loss of prestige or power of the *mico* of Santa Catharina.

32. Captain Antonio de Argüelles was a 45-year-old soldier with substantial experience in the mission provinces, and particularly those of Guale and Mocama. Serving as *capitan reformado*, or inactive, since 1650, he had been dispatched on many occasions for duty in the interior, including a trip to mission Santa Catalina in January of 1663, relating to the lack of proper respect among the Indians for the its *mico* (Argüelles, 1663c). Indeed, this earlier incident might have been directly related to this order of 1665.

33. This instruction was presumably attached to the official order to Adjutant Alvarez, and provided the specific details of the yearly labor draft from Guale and Mocama, including the precise numbers of Indians to be selected from each village. This portion of the order was theoretically to be shown to the Indian caciques of Guale, but this practice was not always observed (see Overview).

34. The enumeration of laborers to be drafted from each village represents perhaps the most important section of these yearly orders, for in these figures lies a rough estimate of the relative population of each town. In this list, the villages of Santa Catalina and Satuache are combined due to their recent aggregation after the Chichimeco raids of the early 1660s (see Document 6, and the Overview).

35. Following the precise listing of the number of Indian laborers to be drafted from each village is a disclaimer, indicating that more Indians can be brought if the Spanish officer delivering the order decides so (provided that a revised list is drawn up in order to keep track of the number of laborers who actually come to St. Augustine). This option seems to have been exercised liberally (Worth, 1992: 127; also see Overview).

36. This is the earliest documented reference to the request for Yamassee Indians in the yearly *repartimiento* labor draft for Guale and Mocama, although it is possible that they appeared in earlier drafts (such as that of 1665, for which the instruction portion is missing). Based on the friars' letters in Document 6, the Yamassee had been living in the region to the north of Guale since soon after the disastrous Chichimeco raids of 1661 (see below).

37. The first of these two names is the familiar village of Santa Elena (on modern Parris Island,

South Carolina), which had remained devoid of regular Spanish presence since 1588. The second name, spelled Abaja (or Abaya later in the order) is unfamiliar, but may be the town of Ahoya visited by Juan Pardo during his second expedition from Santa Elena in 1567–1568. This town was some two days' walk from Santa Elena, and was located on or near the mainland (Hudson, 1990).

38. The replacement installed by Argüelles may have been Phelipe, who was cacique of Sapala in 1677 (Argüelles, 1678), and who remained cacique until at least 1695 (Document 9; Pueyo, 1695).

39. The 1667 labor-draft order by Governor Guerra y Vega was incorrectly dated 1677 in the margin by Castilla, and was thus placed out of order in this bound notebook. It appears as Order 11 below.

40. Indians who were condemned to perform royal labor as *forzados*, or forced laborers, were essentially transformed into imprisoned slaves and assigned to the most onerous tasks associated with the construction and maintenance of fortifications or other public works in the city of St. Augustine. In many cases, such a punishment was a death sentence for the Indians, who died from overwork, malnutrition, or disease.

41. This is the first time that the village of Asao appears on the *repartimiento* labor-draft orders presented here. This might suggest that Asao had received an influx of new population, or perhaps that a previous exemption from the labor draft had expired (see Overview).

42. Unlike the instructions dating to 1666–1668, this enumeration lists Santa Catalina and Satuache separately, with four Indians to be supplied by each. Although the total number is identical to that requested from the two villages when listed together (eight), the present enumeration reveals that laborers were drafted in equal numbers from the population of each village.

43. Although notary Francisco de Castilla erroneously copied the date as 1677 in this marginal note, the actual date appears as 1667 in the text of both the order and instruction. Furthermore, Governor Guerra y Vega was not in office in 1677.

44. This undoubtedly refers to September 1679, since the order was dispatched on October 11.

45. These five Englishmen were interrogated in St. Augustine on October 25, where their names were given by the Spanish scribe as John Hash (age 22), Thomas Jibe (age 23), Daniel Tornelo (age 23), Juan Val (age 21), and Eduardo David (age 21). This testimony appears in Governor Hita Salazar's March 6, 1680 submission to the King, located in AGI SD 839.

46. During the late 16th and early 17th centuries, Cofunufo was the name for the Bar between St. Catherines Island and Ossabaw Island, now known as St. Catherines Sound. Later that same year, however, Fuentes described the location of Cofunufo as being a defensible position only one league north of mission Santa Catalina, at the same time referring to modern St. Cathernines sound as the Bar of Azopo (as it appeared on a later Spanish map). Governor Hita Salazar must have had reports that the English-sponsored Indians were entrenched in the site of Cofunufo (see Overview).

47. The three groups of Indians noted here included not only the Chichimeco, or Westo, who are known to have served as slave raiders acting with direct English backing and supply during the late 1670s, but also the Uchise (a name eventually associated with the Lower Creek confederacy) and the Chiluque, apparently situated at Santa Elena at this time, and probably not identical with the Cherokee (see Overview).

48. The preceding passage makes it clear that returning to Mission Santa Catalina would not be an easy task, and that precautions would be necessary in order to insure the safety of its residents. Interestingly, the only item singled out is the collection of cassina leaves for the "black drink," which was prohibited unless the Indians doing so were paid, or chose to do so of their own volition. In all activities, Captain Fuentes was instructed to give precedence to the wishes of the Indians over the desires of the garrison of infantry living in the town.

49. Here Governor Hita Salazar makes it clear that if Fuentes was unable to convince the Indians to return to Santa Catalina, its caciques were to come to St. Augustine for an audience with the Governor.

50. Sergent Manuel Gómez was a 47-year-old soldier with substantial experience in the province of Timucua who had been named lieutenant of that province in February 1680.

51. This date refers to the original commission as lieutenant of Timucua, issued on February 26, 1680.

52. The Indian militia was formally established as early as the late 1640s, with aboriginal caciques and leaders serving as ranked officers.

53. Don Thomás de Medina, the cacique of mission Santa Fé de Toloco, was undoubtedly the principal leader of the entire Timucua province at that time, and thus occupied the highest rank in the Spanish militia system—sergeant major (second only to the governor). Lucas, the cacique of Santa Catalina (and former cacique of Ajoica prior to its fusion with Santa Catalina in the mid-1670s), also in Timucua, was probably a secondary leader in Timucua political structure, and thus occupied the post of captain. The remaining caciques of

three missions in the Yustaga region of the Timucua mission province may have held only inferior ranks in the Indian militia.

54. This passage presumably refers to the cultivation of the fields in Timucua.

55. Probably refers to a meeting on April 23, 1680.

56. The order dispatching Captain Nicolás Estebedes de Carmenatis to Guale, dated the 23rd of May, apears above as Order 13.

57. The preceding passage makes it clear that Captain Ribera was outranked by Captain Fuentes (the provincial lieutenant) in Guale, and that all decisions were subject to his approval.

DOCUMENT 6: ORIGINAL FRANCISCAN DOCUMENTS

INTRODUCTION

The following pair of documents, lumped by the notary Francisco de Castilla under a single heading, date to 1663 and 1679–80, respectively, and comprise original manuscript documents taken by Castilla from the Franciscan Archive of St. Augustine in 1739. As in the case of Document 4 (transcribed by Castilla), these original manuscripts are in considerably poorer condition than those drawn from the Governmental Archive of St. Augustine, although the text is almost completely intact. Inasmuch as the original Franciscan Archive remains lost to modern researchers, these documents provide a privileged glimpse of some of the internal documentation of the Franciscan province of Santa Elena. Each piece will be preceded with a short introduction.

The first document in this section comprises five letters, each on a single folio, written by the Franciscan friars stationed in Guale in early April, 1663 (see table 2). They were drafted at the order of Governor Alonso de Aranguiz y Cotes, who on March 24, 1663, dispatched Captain Antonio de Argüelles to the Guale province in order to investigate the suitability of placing a garrison of infantry to protect against further attacks by the Chichimeco (Aranguiz y Cotes 1663a). The original order stated that Argüelles was to consult with the Indian leaders of Guale, who were to provide not only an overview of the current state of the province (and any news of the Chichimeco), but also their opinion regarding the placement of soldiers in garrison.

At the same time, Argüelles was instructed to have "each one of the missionaries of the said province to give their opinion apart, in writing, signed with their names" regarding the same matter (Aranguiz y Cotes 1663a). Although no other record of this expedition than a copy of the original order has been located previously by modern researchers, the original handwritten letters by the friars of Guale were included within notary Francisco de Castilla's 1739 report to Governor Montiano. The five letters were drafted over the course of a week, beginning on April sixth in Santa Clara de Tupiqui, on the seventh in San Diego de Chatoache, on the eighth in San Phelipe de Alave, on the tenth in San Joseph de Sapala, and on the fourteenth in Santo Domingo de Asajo. Although this probably represents the actual visitation route of Captain Argüelles, the letters may instead have been sent to a central location from the outlying missions. As described in greater detail in the Overview, the content of these letters provides considerable information regarding the years immediately following the Chichimeco assault of 1661, and in addition reveals the recent arrival of Yamassee refugees in the Escamaçu province to the north of Guale. In this sense, the following document sheds further light on a little-known period in the history of Guale.

Jesus, Mary, Joseph[1]

Original certifications from the guardians of the convents of the province of Guale, given in the year of 1663, in which time the English had not yet usurped the province of Escamaçu, also called San Jorge, or Carolina.

The certifications are from the year 1663.

TABLE 2
Guale Province in 1663

Mission	Friar
San Diego de Chatohache	Juan de Uçeda, president
San Phelipe de Alave	[Gabriel Fernández, April 8, 1663]
Santa Catalina de Guale	Carlos de Anguiano, guardian
Tupiqui	[Carlos de Anguiano, April 6, 1663]
San Joseph de Sapala	Jacinto de Barreda
Santo Domingo de Asajo	Gabriel Fernández, guardian
	Juan Baptista Campaña, president

[f.1]

I, Fray Carlos de Anguiano, preacher to the natives, customary definitor of this Sacred Province of Santa Elena of Florida, and guardian of the convent of Santa Catalina de Guale, say that, Captain Antonio de Argüelles, *reformado* of the presidio of St. Augustine, having come by order of señor Don Alonso de Aranguiz y Cotis, knight of the Order of Santiago, governor and captain general of these provinces for His Majesty, to find out and inquire into the state of, or tell what is to be found in this province of Guale with regard the Chichimeco Indians, who assaulted it two years ago now, and likewise to take the opinion of the missionaries, *micos*, and caciques of the said province if it would be suitable or not to place infantry in garrison in it; with regard to the Chichimeco Indians, today at present there are (thanks to God) no new developments, suspicions, or fears, nor has there been anything with foundation or truth during the last two years relative to coming or descending to the said province, but rather many signs of the contrary, because of the bad treatment which the natives made them, according to some information which has come down on some occasions, in which they left the location where they lived when they descended to this said province of Guale,[2] and went away very much farther to the mouth of another river which one can only descend through it to the province of Cofitachique, or to that of Escamaçu, distant from this [province] of Guale.[3] With regard to what is my opinion of placing infantry in garrison or not, [f.1, vto.] I find that, through the experience which I have of more than twenty-four years, it is not suitable to do so, and that having them, or placing infantry, would be at minimum to finish off and lose this stated province of Guale, through not counting more than six villages,[4] and of these, those which have the most Christian Indians have twenty and twenty-two Indians, beyond the fact that in case the Chichimecos should wish to descend through the province of Escamaçu to this [province] of Guale, today it is all settled from Colon to what they call the Uyache Eslaçu[5] across the mainland by Yamasis, six, eight, four, three, two, and more days distant by road from these provinces, with which I swear vigorously they will first find resistance which will impede their passage, and with much brevity [bring] news to this province. This is my opinion and no other, and what I feel, and if I felt another thing I would say so, because I love my life and that of my children whom I administer as much as everyone, and I would not want to place them in danger. In Topiqui[6] on the sixth of April of the year 1663.

Fray Carlos de Anguiano

8 shirts
6 collars
3 others
5 armed
22[7]

[f.2]

I, Fray Juan de Uçeda, president of this convent of San Diego de Chatohache, certify that, as there are no news of Chichimecos, nor at the present have I known anything of foundation, but rather that they are in the lands of the Yamasis on account of their sowing,[8] and these news I had on March 24 by some

Yamasi Indians who told me this, and thus I swear that they are all quiet and calm, as I see at present, and by being true I sign in this convent on April 7, 1663.

Fray Juan de Uçeda

[f.3]

I, Fray Gabriel Fernández, preacher and guardian of the convent of Santo Domingo de Asajo, say that Captain Antonio de Argüelles having come to this province of Guale with order and power of señor Don Alonso Aranguiz y Cotes, knight of the habit of Santiago, governor and captain general of these provinces for His Majesty, in order to find out and look at the state in which this province finds itself at the present with the Chichimeco Indians who descended to it now two years ago, and likewise to take the opinion of the missionaries, *micos,* and caciques of the said province if it would be suitable or not to place a garrison of soldiers in it, my opinion is that it is not suitable that they be placed for now, by not having news of such Indians, nor even less do I presume that they could come, through finding themselves very distant and badly treated from the earlier fight, according to some news which we have had, and that having infantry in this province, according to the paucity of the Indians and their misery, which even in order to sow their fields and kill a deer from month to month for the fathers who administer them they do not have time, opportunity, nor persons to command that they attend to them, it would be cause so that [f.3, vto.] the infantry, with the aid and service of their persons, would make an even greater war than the worst which the enemy (if they come) could make upon them, and this is my opinion, through what I have found and understood at the present relative to this question and inquiry which he came to make. With regard to if they will come or not, only God knows, and only he will be able to assure it, and as true I sign it in this convent of San Phelipe de Alave[9] on April 8, 1663.

Fray Gabriel Fernandez

[f.4]

I, Fray Jacinto de Barreda, say that inasmuch as Captain Antonio de Argüelles has come to this province of Guale by order of señor Don Alonso de Aranguis y Cotes, governor and captain General of these provinces of Florida for His Majesty in order to inform himself and inquire of the missionaries who serve in the said province, and likewise from the *micos* and caciques, if there are or if they have some suspicion that the Chichimecos have design or determination to descend to this province to make war, and if it is suitable that there be infantry in the said province, I say that not only are there no such news that the enemy has such a determination, nor have I had [such news] in the two years since they retreated from this province, but rather very much to the contrary, on account of the great loss of people which they had, including the times that the Indians of this province fought with them, killing some of the principal leaders, as well as seventy Indians having drowned in a vessel which they made from the boards from the church and convent of Talaje,[10] when the current of the Bar of Ospoque drew them out to sea, and all drowned in view of everyone, with no small sentiment from the enemy through among the said people those of most valor, and many more who, in their retreat and flight died of hunger on the road. By these and other news that I have that the enemy does not have such intention to descend to this province, but rather they have retreated to a more concealed place, I say that it is not suitable that there be infantry in this province, because in having them there would follow much damage and the total destruction of the said province on account of the few people which there are in each town, and they are so annihilated and perishing, and this is what it seems to me according to God, and no other thing. [f.4, vto.] Furthermore, if some *mico* or cacique[11] should ask for infantry for himself, for his particular interests, not being of common consent of all the *micos* that the said *mico* or town should be obligated to sustain the infantry, it seems to me that it is not just that perhaps someone for his particular expediency and likes, without attending to the common good of these poor natives, should wish to ask for infantry without having need, for if there were [need], I and all the religious would ask for it; and thus it will not be just that for the preference of merely one and for no other thing should the remaining towns be damned or disturbed, and this is my opinion. Signed in this convent of San Joseph de Sapala on April 10, 1663.

Fray Jacinto de Barreda

[f.5]

I, Fray Juan Bauptista Campaña, president of this convent of Santo Domingo de Asajo, say[12] that, Captain Antonio de Argüelles, *reformado* of the presidio of St. Augustine, having come with order of the señor Don Alonso de Aranguiz y Cotes, knight of the Order of Santiago, governor and captain general of these provinces for His Majesty, to find out and inquire about the state in which this province of Guale finds itself with the Chichimeco Indians, which two years ago now they assaulted, and likewise to take the opinion of the missionaries, *micos*, and caciques of the said province if it would be suitable to place infantry in garrison in it, with regard to the Chichimeco Indians, today at present there are no new developments, suspicion, or any fear, nor has there been anything of foundation, or true, in two years regarding coming to descend to the said province, rather many news to the contrary, due to the bad treatment which the natives made them, according to some news which have descended on some occasions, for which they left the place where they were living when they descended to this said province of Guale and went much farther away to the mouth of another river by which one can only descend to the province of Cofitachiqui, or to that of Escamaçu, distant from these [provinces] of Guale. With regard to what my opinion is about placing infantry [f.5, vto.] in garrison, I find that by the twelve years of experience which I have it is not suitable that there should be [infantry], and that having or placing the said infantry would at least result in terminating and losing this said province of Guale, by not counting more than six villages, and all those that have more Christian Indians are twenty or twenty-two Indians, beyond the fact that in case the Chichimecos should wish to descend through the province of Escamaçu to this [province] of Guale, it is today all settled from Colon down to what they call Uyache Eslaçu across the mainland by Yamasis, six, eight, and more days distant by road from this province, with which I swear they must find first resistence, and those who would impede the passage and with much brevity [bring] the news to this province, and this is my opinion, and no other, and what I feel, and if I felt another thing I would say so. In Açajo on April 14, 1663.

Fray Juan Bauptista Campaña

I left a copy these certifications written on eight folios.[13] Florida, August 11, 1739.

Castilla

The second document in this section is a patent, or legal register, and comprises an official letter directed to all the Franciscan missionaries in Florida by the Provincial Minister Fray Jacinto de Barreda. The letter, written on December 21, 1679, in the Apalachee mission of San Francisco de Ocone, served to inform the friars of the death of the oldest friar in Florida at that time, Fray Sebastian Martínez, and instructed each friar to perform a specified number of masses for the soul of the respected elder friar. While the text of the letter contains no ethnographic information regarding Florida Indians, at its side was placed a list of the missions then present in Florida, to be used as a routing guide for the transferral of the letter. Furthermore, and most importantly, each friar signed his name on the back of the letter, indicating when and where the order was complied with.

The resulting document provides a complete list of not only all the Franciscan missions in Florida at that time, but also which friar was stationed at each mission. Beyond this, the dates of each signature provide a rough idea of rapid-travel time between each mission, and the order in which each was encountered on a complete visitation circuit beginning in Ocone (see table 3). Coincidentally, the letter wound its way northward into the Guale province by mid-January of 1680, providing the last known list of missions and friars prior to the destruction of Mission

TABLE 3
Barreda Mission List of 1679-1680

Mission	Date	Friar
Ocony/Oconi	December 23	Juan de Villalua
Ychotafu/Ychutafu	December 23	Juan Arias
Tomoly/San Martín de Tomoli	December 23	Marcelo de San Joseph
La Tama	December 23	Juan Sugol [?]
San Luis	December 24	Antonio de la Cruz
Chactos/San Carlos	December 24	Juan Mercado
Izcanbi/Izcabi	December 25	Domingo Gadura Ysassi
Bacuqua/San Antonio de Bacuqua	December 25	Miguel Martorell
Pataly/San Pedro y San Pablo de Patale	December 25	Francisco Blanco
Ocuia/San Joseph de Ocuya	December 26	Francisco de San Joseph
Asipalaga/San Juan de Aspolai	December 26	Miguel de Zalverde
Aiubaly		[no friar]
Evitachuco/San Lorenço de Ivitachuco	December 26	Bartolomé de Ayala
Asile		[no friar]
San Mateo	December 27	Marcos de Soto
Machaba/Santa Helena	December 27	Francisco de Roxas
San Pedro	December 28	Antonio de la Concepción
San Juan de Guacara	December 29	Feliciano López
Tarijica/Tarihica	December 29	Juan Guerrero
Ajuica/Santa Catalina	December 30	Toribio de Barreda
Santa Fé	December 31	Pedro Fernández Maladino
San Francisco	January 2	Joseph Bamba
Salamototo/Salomototo	January 5	Francisco Pérez
Nombre de Dios	January 7	Alonso del Moral
St. Augustine	January 7	Martín de Alacano
Tolomato	January 8	Juan Baptista Campaña
San Juan/San Juan del Puerto	January 10	Martín de Bohorques
San Felipe/San Phelipe	January 13	Gabriel Fernández
Obalaquiny/Ubadalquini	January 16	Francisco de Medina
Asao	January 16	Domingo Santos
Sapala/San Joseph de Sapala	January 17	Juan de Uzeda Simon de Salas
Santa Catalina/Santa Catalina de Guale	January 18	Bernabé de los Angeles

Santa Catalina by English-sponsored Indian warriors only three months later.

Year of 1679 Number 6, Duplicated[14]

Fray Jacinto de Barreda[15] of the Order of Friars Minor of the Regular Observance of Our Sacred Father San Francisco, preacher and provincial minister of this sacred province of Santa Elena of Florida, the island of Cuba, and the nuns of Santa Clara of the city of Havana,[16] to all the missionaries of the provinces of Apalache, Timucua, and Guale, health and peace in Our Lord Jesus Christ.

We[17] make known to all your reverend fathers how Our Lord was pleased to take for himself to the eternal rest the Very Reverend Father Fray Sebastian Martínez, eldest perpetual father of this our province,[18] on the sixteenth of this current month, after having suffered two years in bed with extremely intense pains, with which the Lord granted [rest] to him, who with unspeakable patience, strength, and forbearance, with divine will, supported and suffered for divine love, after having received, as a faithful Christian and true son of Our Seraphic Father San Francisco, all the sacraments of our sacred mother Church, having lived all the time of his life in the upright observance (as is well-known) of what he promised in his profession to God, Our Lord, and to Our Father San Francisco, of which only the consolation remains for us, through the much that this our province can lament his absence, by having been such a father and firm column to it, as an extremely zealous man of the observance of our evangelical order; for as much,

By the tenor of the present, signed by our hand, sealed with the main seal of our office, and endorsed by him who at present performs the office of secretery, we order all you very reverend fathers for sacred obedience to attend to the customary aid in this our province for each one of the missionaries who die, since it is such a just debt to attend to our deceased brothers with our sacrifices, each one of your reverend fathers saying the ten masses for the spirit of the said deceased reverend father, which this our sacred province has ordered and determined, and the Our Fathers[19] which the lay brothers are obligated to say, and because in the last breaths of his life, with humble spirit and enraptured in the love of God, he asked us with tears that we do him the charity of ordering all the missionaries that when they say the masses for his soul, at the end of each one they say "Praised be the Blessed Sacrament"[20] five times, applying to him the indulgence which is conceded to the above stated. I request and charge this to your reverend fathers whenever you can that you do so in the love of God, and this our patent will pass from convent to convent, according to the order in the margin, with the brevity possible, and from the last it will be remitted to us so that its fulfillment is on record to us.[21] Given in our convent of Our Father San Francisco de Oconi on December 21, 1679.

Fray Jacinto de Barreda
Provincial Minister [seal[22]]

By order of his Reverend Paternity,
Rodrigo de la Barreda
Vice Secretary

[routing list[23]]

Ocony	Pataly	San Pedro	Nombre de Dios	San Felipe	and from there to my presence
Ychotafu	Ocuia	San Juan de Guacara	St. Augustine	Obalaquiny	
Tomoly	Asipalaga	Tarijica	Tolomato	Asao	
La Tama	Aiubaly	Ajuica	San Juan	Sapala	
San Luis	Evitachuco	Santa Fé		Santa Catalina	
Chactos	Asile	San Francisco			
Izcanbi	San Mateo	Salamototo			
Bacuqua	Machaba				

Read and obeyed in this [doctrina] of Oconi, today, December 23, 1679.

Fray Juan de Villalua[24]

Read and obeyed in this [doctrina] of Ychutafu, today, December 23, 1679.

Fray Juan Arias

Read and obeyed in this [doctrina] of señor San Martín de Tomoli on December 23, 1679.

Fray Marzelo de San Joseph

Read and obeyed in this [doctrina] of La Tama on December 23, 1679.

Fray Juan Sugol [?]

Read and obeyed on December 24 in this [doctrina] of San Luis.

Fray Antonio de la Cruz

Read and obeyed in this [convent] of San Carlos on December 24, 1679.

Fray Juan Mercado

Read and obeyed in this [doctrina] of Izcabi on December 25, 1679.

Fray Domingo Gadura Ysassi

Read and obeyed in this [convent] of San Antonio de Bacuqua on December 25, 1679.

Fray Miguel Martorell

Read and obeyed in this [convent] of San Pedro y San Pablo de Patale on December 25.

Fray Francisco Blanco

Read and obeyed in this [doctrina] of San Joseph de Ocuya on December 26, 1679.

Fray Francisco de San Joseph

Read and obeyed in this [doctrina] of San Juan de Aspolai, today, December 26, 1679.

Fray Miguel de Zalverde

Read and obeyed in this [doctrina] of San Lorenço de Ivitachuco on December 26, 1679.

Fray Bartolomé de Ayala

Read and obeyed in this [convent] of San Matheo on December 27, 1679.

Fray Marcos de Soto

Read and obeyed in this [doctrina] of Santa Helena on December 27, 1679.

Fray Francisco de Roxas

Read and obeyed in this [convent] of San Pedro on [December] 28, 1679.

Fray Antonio de la Concepción

Read and obeyed in this [convent] of San Juan de Guacara on December 29, 1679.

Fray Feliciano López

Read and obeyed in this [convent] of Tarihica on December 29, 1679.

Fray Juan Guerrero

Read and obeyed in this [convent] of Santa Catalina on December 30, 1679.

Fray Toribio de Barreda

Read and obeyed in this [doctrina] of Santa Fé on December 31, 1679.

Fray Pedro Fernández Maladino

Read, obeyed, said the masses, San Francisco on the second of [January] of 1680.

Fray Joseph Bamba

Read and obeyed in this [convent] of Salomototo, January 5, 1680.

Fray Francisco Pérez

Read and obeyed in this [convent] of Nombre de Dios on January 7, 1680.

Fray Alonso del Moral

Read and obeyed in this [convent] of Our Father of the city of St. Augustine on January 7, 1680.

Fray Martín de Alacano

Read and obeyed in this convent of Tolomato on January 8, 1680.

Fray Juan Baptista Campaña

1.[25] Read and obeyed in this [convent] of San Juan del Puerto on January 10, 1680.

Fray Martín de Bohorques

2. Fulfilled on January 2, and obeyed on [January] 13, 1680 in this [convent] of San Phelipe.

Fray Gabriel Fernández

3. Read and obeyed in this [convent] of Ubadalquini on January 16, 1680.

Fray Francisco de Medina

4. Fulfilled on January 4, and obeyed on the 16th of the said month, year of 1680.

Fray Domingo Santos[26]

5. Read and obeyed in this doctrina of San Joseph de Sapala on the seventeenth of January, 1680.

Fray Juan de Uzeda
Fray Simon de Salas

6. Read and obeyed in this [convent] of Santa Catalina de Guale on January 18, 1680.

Fray Bernabé de los Angeles

Note[27]

The villages of San Juan del Puerto, San Phelipe, Gualquini, Asao, which is where Fray Domingo Santos was, Sapala, and Santa Catalina are of the province of Guale, and run numbered from 1 to 6.

That Asao is where Fray Domingo Santos was [stationed] is on record from the testimony from the year 1681 in the certification of Captain Fuentes.

I left a copy written on seven folios.[28] Florida, August 6, 1739.

Castilla

NOTES

1. This folio was drafted by Castilla to serve as a cover page for the original 17th-century documents that follow. The letters "J.M.J.," or Jesus, Mary, Joseph, appear below the symbol of a cross. These were common headings to Spanish documents, although more commonly the cross served as the only heading.

2. While the precise location from which the Chichimeco launched their assault in 1661 is not known, their route of attack, the Río de Santa Ysabel (the modern Altamaha) suggests that they were at that time staying in the interior coastal plain of southern Georgia, perhaps in the vicinity of the earlier Mission Santa Ysabel de Utinahica at the forks of the Altamaha River.

3. This passage is somewhat ambiguous, but inasmuch as the 1674 location of the Chichimeco, or Westo, Indians was along the lower Savannah River, Fray Anguiano (and Fray Campaña below) may have been describing this location. The Savannah does indeed descend to the region of the Escamaçu province along the lower South Carolina coast, but the province of Cofitachequi had apparently been located along a more northerly river drainage (the Wateree), and deeper into the interior during the late 16th century (see Hudson et al., 1984; Hudson, 1990). The friars here may have been referring to the location of the Chichimeco directly between Guale and Cofitachequi.

4. These six villages presumably included Satuache, San Phelipe, Santa Catalina, Tupiqui, Sapala, and Asajo (see table 2).

5. Neither of these aboriginal names can be located on the landscape with any degree of precision, but other contemporaneous evidence suggests that Uyache Eslaçu was the same as Huyache, described as five leagues from Guale, probably referring to the province and not the village (Aranguiz y Cotes, 1662b). In this case, the location might be some 13 miles north of Satuache (the northernmost frontier of Guale), perhaps near the mouth of the modern Savannah River. The location of Colon was probably somewhat northward, along the southern coast of South Carolina, and well within the Escamaçu province. The inhabitants of Colon ultimately were to play a role in the history of Guale into the 1680s.

6. Though guardian (and probably resident) of Mission Santa Catalina, Fray Anguiano signed the letter in Tupiqui, perhaps there only temporarily.

7. These marginal notes appear below the main text of Fray Anguiano's letter. Their significance is unknown, although the coincidence of the total 22 with Anguiano's mention of the maximum population of Christians in each Guale village suggests it may be related. They seem to relate to articles of clothing.

8. This passage indicates that the Chichimeco were in the process of planting their fields during that spring, and were thus considered less of a threat.

9. Like Fray Anguiano above, Fray Fernández signed this letter in a different mission than that of his normal station (at Asajo).

10. The Chichimeco evidently dismantled the church and convent of mission Santo Domingo de Talaje after their attack of June, 1661 (when Talaje was abandoned). The fact that the vessel which they constructed from the planks was drawn out to sea at the Bar of Ospogue (Doboy Sound) suggests that this was an attempt to cross from the mainland at the mouth of the Altamaha River to Sapelo Island, presumably to direct an assault on Mission San Joseph de Sapala (see Overview).

11. This passage suggests that Fray Barreda expected (or knew) that one or more Indian leaders were in favor of the proposed garrison; with this statement, the friar may have hoped to overrule the opinion of any dissenting cacique.

12. The text of Fray Campaña's letter is substantially similar to that of Fray Anguiano's dated seven days earlier, suggesting that it was largely copied.

13. The 18th-century notary Castilla indicated here that he transcribed a copy of the preceding letters, written on eight folios, prior to extracting the original. In this manner, although the original had been removed from the Franciscan archive, a transcription of its contents was preserved there for future reference.

14. These notes were placed by the notary Castilla at the head of this original 17th-century document as an introduction. The term "Duplicated" may refer to the fact that Castilla made a copy before extracting the original.

15. Fray Jacinto de Barreda had been in Florida at least since 1663, when he was stationed at the Guale mission of San Joseph de Sapala (see the previous letters in Document 6). The exact date of his arrival is unknown, inamuch as his name does not appear on any of the official Franciscan registers of friars sent to Florida from Spain during the 17th century.

16. The Franciscan province of Santa Elena included not only Florida, but also Cuba. The nuns of Santa Clara represent the female branch of the Franciscan order.

17. Fray Barreda's use of the first person plural in referring to himself presumably stems from the fact that he represented the Franciscan Order (as the provincial minister of the province of Santa Elena).

18. Fray Sebastian Martínez, originally from the Franciscan convent in Medina de Rioseco (in the northwestern region of the Valladolid province, Spain), sailed from Seville in June of 1631 (Geiger, 1940; Arenas Frutos, 1991). Fixing the date of his death on December 16, 1679, Fray Martínez served as a missionary in Florida roughly 48 years.

19. The Lord's Prayer, or *Padre Nuestro*, was to be repeated by the lay brothers, members of the Franciscan order who were not priests and who thus could not say mass or administer sacraments (generally acting as servants for the friars).

20. *Alavado sea el Santissimo Sacramento* was the phrase to be repeated after each mass.

21. This portion of the letter provides instructions for the passage of the patent throughout all three mission provinces of Florida, indicating the order in which it should be passed, and that it should move as rapidly as possible before being remitted again to Fray Barreda (probably at the Franciscan convent in St. Augustine). This was indeed accomplished, inasmuch as the patent seems to have passed between missions several leagues apart in only a single day.

22. A wax seal was originally placed at the bottom center of this letter, between the signatures of Barreda and his secretery. The seal itself no longer remains (it may have been removed during the letter's original journey, inasmuch as it partially overlapped the letter's text), but it was probably an official seal of the Franciscan province of Santa Elena, almost certainly showing a traditional representation of the life of Saint Helen.

23. The list below was copied along the left margin of the letter above, and represents a routing list, including all the missions in Florida at that time, and the order in which the letter was to be passed from mission to mission.

24. This portion of the Barreda patent comprises the written acknowledgments of compliance by all the Franciscans in Florida missions. Each friar penned a small note on the inside of the folded page, generally indicating the place and date of compliance, and personally signed the note. In most cases these notes were ordered from top to bottom on the page, with three columns on each page. In cases where the notes had been placed out of order, the date in each permits reconstruction of the actual order of travel (as presented here).

25. The numbers beside these last six missions were placed there in 1739 by the notary Castilla in order to draw attention to those of the Guale and Mocama province (see his marginal note below).

26. Fray Santos was the only friar who failed to record his location, but the 18th-century notary Castilla provided evidence below that this was the mission of Asao.

27. The following marginal note was added on the original 17th-century document by Castilla, indicating the relevant part of the document and providing evidence for the name of the mission where Fray Santos was stationed.

28. Castilla noted here that he had made a transcript of the preceding document on seven folios prior to removing the original.

DOCUMENT 7: 1681 CENSUS OF GUALE AND MOCAMA

INTRODUCTION

The following document is notary Castilla's 1739 transcription of an original census compiled by the lieutenant of the provinces of Guale and Mocama in June of 1681. By order of then-governor Don Juan Márquez Cabrera, Captain Francisco de Fuentes composed a certification detailing the exact number of Indians in each aboriginal village within Guale and Mocama, including information on the relative locations of each village. This census represents one of the most detailed synthetic descriptions of the Guale/Mocama region which is currently known, and as such is an important source for understanding not only the locations of Indian villages within these provinces, but also the demographic profile of Guale and Mocama during the last years before the final Spanish retreat southward. The locational information is exceptional, particularly since Fuentes provided not only the distances between villages, but also specific notes such as whether or not specific villages were on the same island, and where. Perhaps even more important, the comprehensive census provided by Fuentes gives a relatively clear picture of the adult population of each village.

Based on a detailed examination of the numbers and the wording of each listing, it seems likely that the census was compiled with specific reference to the needs of the *repartimiento* labor system of Spanish Florida. Four figures are listed for the Christian mission villages: the total number of males over the age of 12, the number of caciques and principals within that number, the number of those men who were married, and the remaining number of unmarried women over the age of 12. The first three figures surely relate to the labor draft, for the first figure presents the total male work force, and the second two figures modify the first figure with reference to two categories of males who were legally exempt from the labor draft: leaders and married men (Bushnell, 1981, 1989; Worth, 1992). The last figure represents the remaining unmarried females in each village.

Inasmuch as the wording of the census is somewhat ambiguous, it is difficult to extrapolate the precise number of individuals being described in each count. Female leaders (cacicas), who were certainly present, were evidently not listed separately in this census, probably because as women they were not even considered for the labor draft. The number of male caciques and the number of married men do not always amount to the total of the first overall figure, and in one case (Tupiqui), the combined total exceeds the total number of men listed for the village. This suggests that the reckoning for the number of married males was independent of the number of caciques and principals, making it possible to simply subtract the number of married men from the total number of men to find the number of unmarried men (with perhaps some of each category being caciques and principals). Then it is a simple matter to calculate the number of married women, and add to this the fourth number of unmarried women given at the end of the listing in order to arrive at the total number of adult females.

Despite these difficulties, however, one can arrive at an accurate count of the total male and female adult population of each Christian mission village, and within these figures the number of male leaders, and the number of married couples (see also the Barbosa census of 1683 mentioned in the Overview). For the pagan villages, however, only two figures are typically provided: the number of males and the number of females. The number of married couples is not specified, inasmuch as the Catholic church did not recognize marriages apart from the Christian ritual. The fact that the number of males is always larger than that of females (in many cases substantially so) is difficult to explain, although it is possible that Fuentes only counted the number of unmarried women. Nevertheless, it is also possible that these figures include each adult, whether male or female, in which case the pagan towns might be argued to possess a remarkably skewed demographic profile, with the larger number of males somehow reflecting their immigrant status and the state of war in this region.

Table 4 presents the original figures as related by Captain Fuentes, but no totals are provided due to the degree of uncertainty noted above. Table 5 provides a hypothetical interpretation of those figures, with the calculated totals for each category (leaving out the number of male leaders). The implications of these results are explored in the Overview. The groupings of these villages by island are based on Fuentes's text, using both physical descriptions and distances in order to derive the locations of each village (also discussed in the Overview).

TABLE 4
1681 Fuentes Census of Guale and Mocama

	All Men	(Caciques/ Principals	Married)	Single Wom-en
Island of Sapalá and Tupiqui				
Tupiqui	23	(6	19)	6
Sapalá	15	(5	10)	9
Satuache	21	(3	18)	8
Santa Catalina	30	(6	21)	8
Yamazes	44	(3	–)	23
Island of [Asajo]				
Asajo	17	(4	13)	9
Colones	9	(–	–)	8
Yamazes	50	(–	–)	23
Guadalquini	45	(13	28)	14
Island of [San Phelipe and San Pedro]				
San Phelipe	28	(6	23)	20
Yamazes	11	(–	–)	??
San Pedro	36	(–	–)	17
Island of [Santa Maria]				
Santa Maria	72	(–	–)	29
Island of [San Juan del Puerto]				
San Juan del Puerto	17	(–	14)	6

[f.1]

Here is on record the villages which the provinces of Guale and Mocama had in this year of 1681.

Don Francisco de Castilla, notary public of government and war in this city of St. Augustine, Florida. To the best of my ability, I certify and swear faithfulness and true testimony that in a certified copy of *autos*, which is found filed in the archive of the convent of San Francisco of this province of Santa Elena, authorized by Ensign Don Alonso Solana, who was public and governmental notary of this presidio, on the twenty-second of September of the past year of sixteen eighty-three, pursued between parties,[1] on the one [side] the Reverend Father Blas de Robles, provincial minister of the said province, and on the other [side] Captain Don Francisco de Zigarroa, protector of Indians[2] in the court of Sergeant Major Don Juan Márquez Cabrera, who in that time was governor and captain general of this post and its provinces, is found presented a certification given by Captain Don Francisco de Fuentes, lieutenant of the governor and captain general for the provinces of Guale and Mocama, its date in the village of Tupiqui, of the said province of Guale, on the fourth of June, sixteen eighty-one, [f.1, vto.] the tenor of which is to the letter the following:

Certification[3]

In the village of Sapalà, of the province of Gualè,[4] on the fourth of June, sixteen eighty-one, I, Captain Francisco de Fuentes, lieutenant of the governor and captain general in this said province of Gualè and Mocama, by title and commission of the señor Governor and Captian General Don Juan Márquez Cabrera, say that in fulfillment of a command and order by His Grace, in which he orders me to send an enumeration [*nomina*] of the people and distances of the villages, and for its fulfillment, for that which I have done, I do so in the following manner:

Tupiqui

In this village and island of Sapalà and Tupiqui, frontier of the enemy English, Chichumecos, Ohiluques, Chalaques,[5] and other nations, the said village of Tupiqui has in population twenty-three men, [f.2] six of them caciques and principals, nineteen married couples, and six women more.

Sapalà

The said village of Sapalà has fifteen men, five of them caciques and principals, ten married couples, and nine women more.

Satuache

The village of Santa Cathalina and Satuache, which are aggregated here due to the invasion which the enemy Chichumeco made the past year, the said village of Satuache has in population twenty-one men, three of them caciques and principals, eighteen married couples, and eight women more.

Santa Catalina

The said village of Santa Catalina has thirty men, six caciques and principals, twenty-one married couples, and eight women more. Father Fray Simón Martínez de Sala serves as *doctrinero* of these four villages.

Aggregation of Yamace Indians

On the point of this island, at two leagues of distance to the south, are aggregated [f.2, vto.] three pagan Yamaze caciques with forty-one men and twenty-three women.

TABLE 5
Adult Population of Guale and Mocama, 1681

	Male		Female		
	Married	Single	Married	Single	Total
Sapelo Island					
Tupiqui	19	4	19	6	48
Sapalá	10	5	10	9	34
Satuache	18	3	18	8	47
Santa Catalina	21	7	21	8	57
Yamazes	—	44	—	23	67
St. Simons Island					
Asajo	13	4	13	9	39
Colones	—	9	—	8	17
Yamazes	—	50	—	23	73
Guadalquini	28	17	28	14	87
Cumberland Island					
San Phelipe	23	5	23	20	71
Yamazes	—	?	—	?	11
San Pedro	—	36	—	17	53
Amelia Island					
Santa Maria	—	72	—	29	101
Fort George Island					
San Juan del Puerto	14	3	14	6	37

Asajó or Asaó[6]

From six to seven leagues of distance, [having] embarked in the direction of the south–southwest, is the village and Bar of Asajó. It has in population sixteen men, four of them caciques and principals, thirteen married couples, and nine women more. Father Fray Domingo Santos serves as *doctrinero.*

Colones

In the village and midpoint [*mediania*] of the said village and island is the village of the pagan Colones, its population nine men and eight women, and aggregated to this nation and to Guadalquini fifty pagan Yamaze Indian men and twenty-three women.

Guadalquini

On the southern point of this said island, at a distance of three leagues, is the village and Bar of Guadalquini, of the Mocama [f.3] nation. It has in population forty-five men, thirteen of them caciques, twenty-eight married couples, and fourteen women more. Father Fray Francisco García is *doctrinero* of the said village.

San Phelipe

At at distance of eight leagues to the south is the village of San Phelipe, in population twenty-eight men, six of them caciques, twenty-three married couples, and twenty women more. The Reverend Father Fray Juan Baptista Campaña is *doctrinero* of the said village. At two leagues of distance on the said island of San Phelipe are aggregated eleven pagan Yamazes.

San Pedro

At a distance of three to four leagues to the south is the Bar and village of San Pedro, of pagan Llamazes,[7] up to thirty-six men and seventeen women.

Santa Maria

At a distance of four leagues to the southwest is the village and Bar of Santa Maria, of pagan Llamazes, the population seventy-two [f.3, vto.] men and twenty-nine women.

San Juan del Puerto

From six to seven leagues to the south is the village and bar of San Juan del Puerto, of the Mocama nation. It has in population seventeen

> men, fourteen of them married, and six women more. Father Fray Francisco de la Cruz is *doctrinero* of the said village. All the referred Indians are those of twelve years and older[8] who are in the said eight villages of Christians, and five religious in them, and the said four villages of pagans, where enter the large part of elderly invalids,[9] without leaving out one, and through being true at the present, in the village of Tupiqui, on the fourth of June, sixteen eighty-one, Francisco de Fuentes.[10]

Agrees with the certification previously inserted [f.4] which remains in the referred *autos*, to which I refer. And in virtue of a verbal order by the señor Colonel Don Manuel de Montiano, governor and captain general of this city and its provinces, I give the present in Florida on the first of July, seventeen thirty-nine. Stained[11]—Tupiqui—between lines—a—the—all valid.

In true testimony,
Francisco de Castilla
Governmental Notary

NOTES

1. An *auto entre partes* was a judicial action initiated by some sort of dispute between parties, and thus the document referred to here formed only part of a larger volume of documentation generated by the process. The fact that this particular case involved a dispute between the Franciscan provincial minister for Florida and the official protector of Indians, appointed by the governor, might make the details of this documentation quite interesting, particularly considering the fact that a detailed census and description of the entire mission provinces of Guale and Mocama was generated during the case.

2. The post of protector of the Indians was designed to provide legal defense for the Indians in the Spanish colonies, but although such a post was obligatory in theory, Florida had no official protector throughout much of the 17th century. The attempt to reestablish this post during the term of Governor Márquez Cabrera (Bushnell, 1981: 111–112) might have resulted in the *autos* cited here.

3. Following this marginal note by Castilla is the beginning of Fuentes's 17th-century text.

4. Both of these names were written by Castilla (presumably copying directly from Fuentes's original manuscript) with slashes over the final vowel. The significance of this is unknown (although it might relate to the aboriginal pronunciation of these names).

5. This list of English-allied Indians demonstrates that the Chiluques (here mistranscribed by Castilla as Ohiluques) of Santa Elena were considered distinct from the Chalaques, or Cherokee (see Overview).

6. In this document, these two names were written by Castilla (and thus presumably Fuentes) with an accent over the final vowel in each instance, suggesting that the last syllable was stressed in pronouncing this name in the Guale language (instead of the middle syllable). Indeed, this might also explain the alternate spellings used by the Spanish for this Guale name, since the name Asaó might tend to be pronounced with an aspiration before the final syllable, resulting in Asajó.

7. This alternate spelling for Yamassee was used by Fuentes here and in the following entry.

8. Here Fuentes states that the census includes only those individuals of the age of 12 or more. No younger children were included in the reckoning.

9. This passage is somewhat vague, but probably refers to the large number of elderly invalids who live in the pagan villages, perhaps explaining the substantial number of males in these towns.

10. Here ends the transcription of the certification by Captain Fuentes. Following this is notary Castilla's standard certification and signature.

11. In addition to the standard form of notation for corrections added between lines by the notary (discussed previously), here Castilla made note of the fact that in his transcription, the name Tupiqui was slightly blurred by ink staining, and thus he placed a clear copy of the nearly illegible name here at the end of the transcription.

DOCUMENT 8: ROYAL CEDULA TO GOVERNOR MARQUEZ CABRERA, 1683

INTRODUCTION

The following document is an original royal *cédula*, or a letter of instruction, from the King of Spain to the governor of Florida Don Juan Márquez Cabrera. Dated October 26, 1683, in the royal palace of Buen Retiro near Madrid, the *cédula* provides an official answer to an earlier letter by Governor Márquez Cabrera (dated more than two years earlier), and sets official state policy regarding the English colonists at Charles Town (San Jorge) and the province of Guale. The document itself was personally signed by King Charles II of Spain, and included the paraphs of the Council of the Indies.

The contents are self-explanatory, but it should be noted that this *cédula* represented an important decision on the part of the Spanish crown, and established a diplomatic policy that was to play a significant role in the abandonment of the provinces of Guale and Mocama. The key to the Spanish strategy lay in the attempt to adhere to the letter and the spirit of the treaty established with Great Britain in 1670, not providing any excuse for the English to charge the Spanish with a direct violation. Unfortunately, the English assaults on Guale were typically only indirect (using Indians or pirates with secret support in Carolina), leaving Governor Márquez Cabrera with few excuses for direct responses (but see Document 11 regarding the raid on Stuarts Town, and the Overview).

Year of 1683, Number 8[1]

The King

Don Juan Márquez Cabrera, my governor and captain general of the provinces of Florida. In this [letter] of June 14, 1681, you refer to the news that the [governor] of Havana notified you about the intention which the English had of invading that post, with which motive you moved on to discuss what seemed to you should be done with the population which this nation [England] has on the Bar of San Jorje, and each day it continues growing, being able through its nearness to seize the province of Guale, and the town of Zapala.[2] Seen in my Junta de Guerra of the Indies, having present what I have ordered to your predecessors in dispatches dated June 20, 1671, and January 23, 1675,[3] and what is stipulated by the seventh chapter of the peace treaties made with the King of Great Britain the year of 1670, that the dominion, propriety, and possession of all the lands which they had and posessed then in whichever part of America should be left suject to them, and [the Junta] having consulted me about everything, I have resolved to charge and order you (as I am doing) that with respect to being so appropriate religiously to obey the provisions of the peace treaties, you will observe what is relevant with great punctuality, keeping watch that the English who find themselves on the Bar of San Jorge do not endeavor to advance with greater population toward our towns of Guale and Çapala, because in such a case it would not be an infraction of the treaty to oppose them or invade them,[4] and you will also pay strict attention and care to conserve all good relations with them, since they should understand how much the maintenance [of the treaty] is desired and endeavored on my part, since by this means, it gives more justification of the reason for what might have to be done if they fail to do that which is stipulated, and you will give me account of everything which happens. From Buen Retiro, October 26, 1683.

I, the King

By order of the King Our Lord,
Don Francisco de Salazar

The Council[5]

[paraph] [paraph] [paraph] [paraph] [paraph]

To the Governor of Florida about the manner in which he should behave with the English of the population of San Jorje.

Registered.[6]

[f.2, vto.]

I made a copy of this royal *cédula* which remains archived in the office of government at my charge. Florida, August 4, 1739.

Castilla[7]

NOTES

1. This filing note was added by the notary Francisco de Castilla on the original 17th-century document.

2. By the date of the noted letter from Governor Márquez Cabrera, Mission Santa Catalina had been abandoned (May 1680), and the town of Sapala was the northern frontier of Spanish holdings in North America.

3. This is a reference to two previous royal *cédulas* relating to this subject.

4. When this clause was specifically violated with the 1684 foundation of a Scottish colony near the abandoned 16th-century Spanish town of Santa Elena, Governor Márquez Cabrera did indeed sponsor the invasion of the new intrusion (see Document 11).

5. The members of the Council of the Indies provided their rubrics at the bottom of the *cédula*.

6. The note here at the foot of the page certified that a copy had been taken in Spain of this royal *cédula*, the original of which was sent to Florida (and ultimately extracted by Castilla for Governor Montiano's package to Spain).

7. Castilla evidently transcribed a copy of this original *cédula* before removing it for dispatch to Spain in Governor Montiano's 1739 package.

DOCUMENT 9: 1685 VISITATION OF GUALE AND MOCAMA

INTRODUCTION

In theory, every new governor in Spanish Florida of the 17th century was required to make an official inspection tour, or visitation, of all the mission provinces under his jurisdiction. While this rule might have resulted in an official visitation (with accompanying documentation) every six years, in practice such visitations were far more scattered, and only rarely conducted by the governor himself. Nevertheless, as the Florida colonial system developed, and particularly during the last half of the 17th century, governors routinely appointed an officer under their command to conduct visitations of the mission provinces, often dividing the western chain (Apalache and Timucua) and the northern chain (Guale and Mocama) between two individuals.

Visitations were conducted with the express purpose of providing an opportunity for the airing of grievances by Indians living in the mission provinces against both Spaniards and fellow Indians alike. In this manner, excesses committed by provincial lieutenants and the soldiers in their garrisons, and even by individual Indian caciques, were to be related to the official visitor, who would either provide a solution or relate the grievance to the governor himself. Although under normal conditions the provincial lieutenant served as the local judiciary authority, during a visitation his position was temporarily suspended in favor of the visiting officer, who could then act independently of the lieutenant. In this way the Indians would theoretically feel free to lodge complaints against the lieutenant himself, who could be investigated or even arrested by the visiting officer.

In practice, official visitations also served as an opportunity to lay down regulations and give specific instructions relating to the general management and government of the mission provinces by aboriginal leaders. Visiting officers often left a list of orders posted in the council house of each village, generally following the termination of the visit.[1]

During the course of the official visitation of each mission town, a notary busily transcribed all the business being conducted in the council house, recording sometimes the names of aboriginal leaders, along with the various statements and complaints made by them. In this manner, a substantial amount of information with ethnographic value was documented during each visitation, and the transcripts of these proceedings are remarkably useful for anthropologists and historians. Perhaps one of the most important features of such visitations is the fact that each separate town within a mission province was individually visited, lending a level of detail not normally present within historical documentation. In this sense, visitations provide an important window into the internal composition and function of each mission town.

The set of documents below represents one of the few original visitation records for the mission provinces of Guale and Mocama that are known to have survived to the present day. Indeed, following three visitations during the first decade of the 17th century, only three others predating the final destruction of Guale and Mocama in 1702 (Argüelles in 1677–1678, Pueyo in 1695,[2] and Zuñiga y Cerda in 1701) have been located previously. The present visitation falls neatly between the first two, and precisely during the most turbulent years of the history of Guale and Mocama. More specifically, the Leturiondo visitation of 1685 occurred just a year after the final removal of Guale and Mocama missions south of the modern Georgia border, the penultimate stage in the retreat toward St. Augustine. In this sense, then, the following documents are quite informative regarding the details and impact of the process of migration.

The original visitation record included the entire visitation of 1685, including all the mission provinces of Florida, starting with Apalachee, proceeding through Timucua, and ultimately concluding with Guale and Mocama. This bound notebook included some 113 folios of handwritten text, with only the last 20 being devoted to the visitation of Guale and Mocama. As can be seen on the final folio of the present extract, the 92 folios preceding those below must have contained a great deal of information regarding those provinces. Unfortunately, the 18th-century notary Francisco de Castilla decided to cut the original notebook apart, selecting only the portions dealing with Guale and Mocama for his purposes. While modern researchers are indeed fortunate that he did even this, one can only wonder what the Apalachee and Timucua visitations contained.

Autos of visitation of the provinces of Guale and Mocama, comprising the caciques of the northern part reduced to our sacred Catholic faith, year of 1685.[3]

In the village of Santa Cruz

Lorenzo Santiago, cacique of Santa Cruz.
Marcos, cacique of Utista.
Santiago, cacique of Pisocojolata.
Manuel, cacique of Zamomo.
Clara, cacica of Utinajica.
Francisca, cacica of Hapofaye.

In the village of Santa Maria

Maria, cacica of Santa Catalina.
Juan Chicasle, cacique of Santa Maria.
Phelipe, cacique of Sapalá.
Elena, cacica of Satuache.

In the village of San Phelipe

Lucas, cacique of San Phelipe.
Diego, cacique of Aleste.
Benito, cacique of Talapo.
Antonio, cacique of Ospogue.
Marcos, cacique of Fascule.

Tupiqui

Don Joseph de la Cruz, *tunaque* of Tupiqui.

In San Juan del Puerto

Juan Luis, cacique of San Juan del Puerto.
Alonso, cacique of Santa Lucia.
Clemente, cacique of Hebalaza.
Domingo, cacique of Chololo.

[f.93][4]

The Captain and Sergeant Major Don Juan Márquez Cabrera, governor and captain general of the city of St. Augustine, Florida, and its provinces for His Majesty:

Inasmuch as Sergeant Major Domingo de Leturiondo, whom I have named as commissary visitor of the provinces of Apalache and Timucua finds himself now on the return journey from visiting the said provinces,[5] and it is advisable because of the satisfaction and confidence which I have in his person that he go to the provinces of Guale and Mocama to visit the towns of Santa Maria, Santa Cruz, San Pedro, and San Juan; therefore, aware of the zeal with which he attends to the royal service of His Majesty, for the present in his royal name I elect and name him as commissary visitor of the said provinces of Guale and Mocama, so that as such he should visit the said towns, placing them in order and social regulation, keeping in everything to my instruction which he carried, which for all that he performs and sets in motion in the said visitation, I give him ample and sufficient commission, as I have from His Majesty, and all the permanent residents and inhabitants, caciques and *mandadores*, and the rest of the native Indians should regard him as commissary visitor, and observe all the honors, favors, privileges, freedoms, and liberties which ought to be well and completely observed on account of the said charge. And the accountant of the royal hacienda will take the copy of this dispatch in the books of the royal contaduria, for which

> I commanded the present to be dispatched, signed by my hand, sealed with the seal of my arms, and endorsed by the undersigned public and governmental notary. Given in the city of St. Augustine, Florida, on the eighteenth of the month of November, sixteen eighty-five, Don Juan Márquez Cabrera. By order of the señor governor and captain general, Alonso Solana, public and governmental notary.[6]

Agrees with the original title, to which I refer, and by order of the señor Sergeant Major Domingo de Leturiondo, judge visitor general [f.93, vto.] of these provinces of Apalache, Timucua, and Guale, I transcribed this copy in order to place it in this visitation as its head, finding themselves present at this transcription as witnesses in attendance Squad Leader Antonio del Pino and Diego Camuñas, who signed. The said squad leader did not sign because he did not know how. To all the above I, the notary, swear. Signed in the village of Santa Cruz de Buenaventura on the twenty-first of the month of December, sixteen eighty-five.

Bernardo Nieto de Carvajal
Named Notary

Diego Camuñas

[f.94]

Auto[7]

In the village of Santa Cruz de San Buenaventura in the province of Guale and Mocama on the twenty-first of the month of December, sixteen eighty-five, His Grace the señor Sergeant Major Domingo de Leturiondo, maintained with advantage by His Majesty in the presidio of St. Augustine, Florida, judge visitor general of the provinces of Apalache, Timucua, and Guale. By titles and commission of the señor Captain and Sergeant Major Don Juan Márquez Cabrera, governor and captain general of the city and presidio of St. Augustine, Florida, and its provinces for His Majesty, before me, notary, and the witnesses in attendance who will be declared later, said that inasmuch as His Grace having visited the said provinces of Apalache and Timucua, he found in the town of San Diego de Salamototo the title of visitor of this province of Guale and Mocama, dispatched by the said señor governor, and in order to fulfill this which is ordered by him, it is necessary that it be made known to Captain Alonso de Argüelles, lieutenant of this province, that in virtue of [this title], rendering the obedience which is ordered, he should cease in the government and political and military command so that His Grace, the said señor visitor might proceed to deal with the said visitation,[8] and that I, the present notary, by virtue of the title which His Grace dispatched in order to act in the preceding visitations, should proceed and continue in conformance with this,[9] together with the witnesses in attendance for greater justification, and he named as interpreters for this visitation Diego Camuñas and Santiago, an Indian native of this province, and the said Bartholomé, who served in the [province] of Timucua, so that he might speak in this said village and that of San Juan, by being of the language of Mocama, and this *auto* was made known to them to them, so that they should respect it and swear to perform the said office well and faithfully, and the present notary should extract a copy of the said original title and place it as the head of this visitation so that it might be on record for all time. And for this his *auto*, he thus provided, commanded, and signed, being present as witnesses in attendance Squad Leader [f.94, vto.] Antonio del Pino and Diego Camuñas, who signed it, and the said squad leader did not sign, not knowing how to, and to everything I, the notary, swear.

Domingo de Leturiondo

Diego Camuñas

Before me,
Bernardo Nieto de Carvajal
Named Notary

Notification of the Suspension of the Lieutenant[10]

In the said village of San Buenaventura on the said day the twenty-first of December, sixteen eighty-five, I, the notary, in the presence of the witnesses in attendance stated before, notified and made the preceding *auto* known to Captain Alonso de Argüelles, lieutenant of this province, and showed him the original title of visitor of it dispatched by the señor Governor Don Juan Márquez Cabrera to Sergeant Major Domingo de Leturiondo, and having seen, heard, and understood it, [f.95] he said that he would obey, and that in regard to what is ordered by the said auto, he surrendered himself to be suspended from the post and lieutenancy which he exercises in order not to make use of it in any manner. And so that it is on record he signed it together with the said Diego Camuñas as witness in attendance. The said squad leader did not sign it, not knowing how to. To all of the above I, the notary, swear.

Alonso de Argüelles

Diego Camuñas

Before me,
Bernardo Nieto de Carvajal
Named Notary

Notification, Acceptance, and Oath of the Interpreters[11]

Then in continuance His Grace Sergant Major Domingo de Leturiondo, judge [f.95, vto.] visitor general of these provinces of Guale and Mocama, before me, the notary, and Squad Leader Antonio del Pino, witness in attendance, received the oath before God and a sign of the cross, in legal form, of Diego Camuñas, Santiago, and Bartolomé,[12] interpreters contained in the preceding *auto*, and the above stated did so, and aware of this, they said that they were accepting and accepted the charge of such interpreters, and will make use of their office faithfully and legally to all of their true knowledge and understanding, aware of the said oath, and His Grace signed together with the said Diego Camuñas. The rest did not sign, nor did the said squad leader, not knowing how to. To all the above I, the notary, swear.

Domingo de Leturiondo

Diego Camuñas

Before me,
Bernardo Nieto de Carvajal
Named Notary

[f.96]

General Auto *of the Visitation of Guale*[13]

In the village of Santa Cruz y San Buenaventura, of the language of Mocama, in the province of Guale, on the twenty-first of the month of December, sixteen eighty-five, His Grace the señor Captain and Sergeant Major Domingo de Leturiondo, maintained with advantage by His Majesty in the presidio of St. Augustine, Florida, judge visitor general of all the provinces of Apalache, Timucua, and Guale, by titles of the señor Captain and Sergeant Major Don Juan Márquez Cabrera, governor and captain general of the said city of St. Augustine, Florida, and its provinces for His Majesty, said that in order to begin and fulfill the visitation of this province of Guale and Mocama which is committed to His Grace by the said señor governor, it is necessary that in each village what His Grace is arranging in this auto be made known to its residents and natives. Therefore, fulfilling everything, and beginning this visitation, he commanded that all the caciques, *micos*, *tunaques*, *hinijas*, *mandadores*, *elesaches*, heirs, *aleiguidas*, and the rest of the principals,[14] men and women, occupants and inhabitants, residents and natives of the said towns, and those who find themselves in them in transit, gather in the council houses [*bujios principales*] of their villages so that in the said meetings, by means of the named interpreters, it might be made known to them, and that they be given to understand, the commission which His Grace has, and how in virtue of it, Captain Alonso de Argüelles is suspended and deprived of his post and lieutenancy for the time that His Grace resides in this province and while its visitation lasts so that all the soldiers of this garrison, and the remaining *micos*, *tunaques*, [f.96, vto.] and the rest of the residents and natives may freely speak against the said [lieutenant], and against the remaining lieutenants and soldiers who have been and at the present are in this garrison, what they have to say, giving the accusations, complaints, and grievances which they have of them, placing before them the demands which they might have about whatever debts which they owe them, so that in everything

His Grace might guard their rights and justice, and if they might have to ask for anything against persons of another authority [*fuero*] and jurisdiction they should do so before their superiors and ministers whom it may concern, as and when it suits them,[15] having it understood that regarding all the complaints and grievances that they might represent against the past and present lieutenants and soldiers, about whichever disturbances and charges with the usurpation of goods which have been made at the hand of such lieutenants, and by the caciques, *micos*, and *tunaques* toward their vassals, all their complaints and grievances will be heard and redressed, giving to each one what was his; and if the vassals obey their superiors, fulfilling their duty and obeying what they command and order them with punctuality, in lawful and just matters, as they ought and are obligated; and if, regarding their caciquedoms, posts, and inheritances, they have some disagreement with regard to the possession of them, they should ask for whatever occurs to them in this regard, and also the differences and adjustments which they have between themselves about all types of cases, so that they might be heard and justice might be maintained for him who might have it. With regard to the fact that in this province there could have been committed some crimes and excesses and other public and scandalous sins which concern and could concern the public vindication and also the particular satisfaction of the damages of the natives, for which remedy His Grace admonishes and requires that they state to his exempt person everything they might know in this regard which is subject to royal jurisdiction, about what he charged them following the conventions, and those who might be found out to know of some of these crimes and not declare them will be punished, as persons who conceal such crimes, being cause and motive that the suitable remedy is not emplaced, inasmuch as this is suitable to the service of God, Our Lord, and the good of the souls, and of their villages, provided that no one states maliciously what he does not know due to some enmity or enemy which he has.[16] Likewise, His Grace, the said señor visitor, attending to the fact that this province and its villages are all on islands, bars, and ports where the enemy French and English corsairs, and also the Chiscas and Chuchumecos, have endeavored by sea and land to invade, assault, and sack them, achieving this on some occasions,[17] the cause of towns having been moved and aggregated one to another for greater strength and defense, retreating to the proximity of the presidio so that they might be aided that much earlier by the infantry with greater promptness, and it is necessary that for the aforementioned, and what could happen to them, they should remain with all care and vigilance, remaining with all the necessary sentinels and guards, prompt and prepared with weapons for such occasions, for which His Grace orders that in all these villages each Indian should have fifty arrows when least prepared in his quiver for the invasions which could happen unexpectedly, and the shotgunners [*escopeteros*] and arquebusiers [*arcabuceros*] that there are [should be prepared] with the necessary munitions and with their weapons ready and well-conditioned.[18] Likewise they should have sufficient canoes in each village for transport and commerce, and also in order to give news and pass the letters, provisions, and munitions which might be necessary to be remitted in whatever occasion which might happen, endeavoring in case some [occasion] of enemies should happen to put the said canoes in a secure place where the said enemy might not make use of them, and where they might serve to be able to give news with all security without being noticed, so that in this manner, and by helping each other, having a force, they will be able to attempt and succeed in carrying out some ambushes, searching out the most convenient places, and where all the damage which is possible might be done to the said enemies with the least risk, obeying the orders which are given them by the lieutenant of this province at that time, who will help them with his person and with the infantry that he can. Regarding the referred, if the said caciques, *micos*, and *tunaques* should have something to represent to His Grace at present, they should do so, and he will hear them about this, and help in that which is possible. And likewise in each village they are to cultivate the field [*savana*] which they call the community field, which they should understand is not of the King or the Church, nor of the convent,[19] because it is and has to be and shall be called the community field, inasmuch as it is to be commonly worked and cultivated by everyone, and its distribution and disbursement is to be among the poor, orphans, and needy widows who find it impossible to work due to infirmity, old age, and other accidents which render them unable to cultivate; and also the amount which some soldiers who go and come in the service of the King make use of is to come from this field, giving them freely, if it is their will, something for their sustenance, and in order to make provisions if it should occur to leave in search of the enemy outside of this province, and for the general expense of the council houses [f.98] and the purchase of some axes for their service; and if something is left over in the future when the crops are harvested, they may be used to aid and help, if it is their will, and if it is necessary, in the purchase of some ornament for their church, and the rest to be distributed among the poor who do not have the means to be able to cultivate, gathering at the time of the harvest what they are to give. There is to be a good count and copy of all of this, which is suitable to have, taking all care, and being advised that what might be necessary for the sowing and cultivation of the said field the next year should be assured before everything else. There is not to be anyone who meddles in investigating, finding out, or inquiring what is spent of the gathered fruits, but they are to have the obligation of giving account to the lieutenant who might be of these provinces each year of what they reap, and of the form and manner in which it is spent, so that he might see if they observe or not the manner in which its distribution is arranged, because there has been notice that at the hand of caciques, *micos*, and *tunaques*, they give what they wish to their relatives to whom they are partial and friends of theirs, and to remedy this, there are to be two keys for the corncrib [*garita*] in which [the fruits] of the said field are locked. The principal cacique or *mico* of each village is to hold one [key], and a principal of each town is to have another distinct [key], and this [principal] is to be he whoever the lieutenant names, so that in this manner the said corncrib is not to be opened without common consent between both of them, thus being how the guards of the said keys are to be distinct from one another.[20] His Grace likewise has had notice that some Indians in this province heal with ancient usage, using orations, superstitions, chants, and false rites, and it is necessary to avoid similar abuses for the damage which it causes to their souls, therefore to remedy this His Grace commands and charges the caciques, *micos*, and principals [f.98, vto.] that in no way should they permit any of their vassals to heal with the said superstitions, but rather that they should only make use of the medicinal herbs which have virtue, without any abuse, with the penalty that, knowing that they are accomplices in this, they will be castigated with grave punishments. His Grace, the said señor visitor, likewise commanded that in all of the towns of this province where a friar might serve, they should cultivate his field, according to custom, for the servants [*pequatas*[21]] who assist him in the service of the church, and that everyone should have the veneration, respect, and reverence which they ought to have for the religious ministers of Our Father San Francisco, obeying him in everything as their spiritual father, assuring that all the vassals attend mass on the days of their obligation without missing one, nor should the young people miss going to the Christian instruction every day, morning and evening, attending with all punctuality and care, and likewise that there is imitation of the ordenances which the Indians of Peru and New Spain observe and keep, having in their house some images, or at least crosses at the entrances of their houses and the head of their beds, with the greatest decency that they can, reciting some prayers when they go to bed and when they awake so that their children, seeing this practice, will continue exhorting virtue, since they ought to do it thus as Christians, showing signs of good faith and zeal, and they should attend to the service of God, Our Lord. Likewise, they should raise the pigs [ganado de cerda] that they can, and hens [*gallinas*],[22] assisting with what they can in the cultivation of corn and beans and other legumes in use, not failing to hunt and fish, so that in this manner they continue helping in the sustenance and clothing. In view [f.99] of the visitation which he makes, His Grace will leave the orders which seem to him to be appropriate for the good rule and government of their towns and vassals, which they will observe, fulfill, and execute quickly and punctually, since from their observation will result the good government, peace and tranquility, and security and defense of their towns, and the regulation of all of them. This *auto*, with the points which are expressed, will be given to understand with all clarity and specification to the said caciques, *micos*, *tunaques*, and principals, and the rest of the residents and natives, so that by virtue of them they might say whatever occurs to them, as they are ordered, in order to resolve everything according to how His Grace might see as suitable to the good administration of royal justice, and for this his *auto* he thus provided, commanded, and signed, being present as witnesses in attendance Squad Leader Antonio del Pino and Diego Camuñas. The said squad leader did not sign, not knowing how to, and to everything, I, the notary, swear.

Domingo de Leturiondo

Diego Camuñas

Before me,
Bernardo Nieto de Carvajal
Named Notary

[f.99, vto.]

Meeting in Santa Cruz[23]

In the village of Santa Cruz y San Buenaventura, on the twenty-first of the month of December, sixteen-eighty five, His Grace the señor Sergeant Major Domingo de Leturiondo, judge visitor general of this province of Guale and Mocama, before me, the notary, and the witnesses in attendance who will be declared below, commanded to gather in the council house of this village: Lorenço Santiago, principal cacique of this village, and captain of its people;[24] Marcos, cacique of Utista; Santiago, cacique of Pisocojolata;[25] Manuel, cacique of Samomo; Clara, cacica of Utinajica;[26] Francisca, cacica of Napofaie; and other principals, residents, and natives of this village, and by means of Bartolomé de la Cruz, interpreter of the Mocama language, he gave them to understand and read the General *Auto* of Visitation, dated on today's date, and having heard and understood it, they said that they will respond whatever might occur to them and what they might have to ask, and not one of them signed, not knowing how to. I, the notary, signed it in the presence of Squad Leader Antonio del Pino, Diego Camuñas, and Juan Martín, who did not sign, except for the said Diego Camuñas, who signed. To everything, I, the notary, swear.

Diego Camuñas

Before me,
Bernardo Nieto de Carvajal
Named Notary

[f.100]

Visitation in Santa Cruz de San Buenaventura[27]

In the village of Santa Cruz de San Buenaventura, of the Mocama language, on the twenty-second of the month of December, sixteen eighty-five, His Grace the señor Sergeant Major Domingo de Leturiondo, judge visitor general of this province of Guale and Mocama, all those contained in the preceding meeting being together in the council house of this village in the form of visitation, and before me, the notary, and the witnesses in attendance who will be declared later on, and by means of the said interpreter Bartolome, Captain[28] Lorenço Santiago, principal cacique of this village, in the name of all the remaining caciques and principals, said that the first thing that occurs to them to say is to ask His Grace for permission to be able to aggregate to their lands some Indians of the Colones, Yguajas, and from Asajo[29] who are distributed and aggregated among the Yamases, and in other forests, by the said [Indians] having sent two messages, the first with a pagan Indian, and the second with a Christian Indian named Lorenço, a native of Guadalquini, in which they ask and supplicate the said cacique Lorenço to give them some lands, and that they want to come to live near to them, and that the said cacique Lorenço had the intention of going to St. Augustine to propose the aforementioned to the señor Governor Don Juan Márquez Cabrera, and to ask for the said permission, but since now His Grace has come, and comes as he has indicated in his name to hear them in everything, they ask him to concede to them this permission, which the said cacique Lorenço, having it, will go to encourage them and attract them, through being many Christians, and of the language of Guale.[30] His Grace, having heard and understood the aforementioned, and considering that the principal goal which is aimed for is that all the Christian Indians who walk as brigands through the woods and who are aggregated in other villages of Yamases should continue aggregating themselves, and that all the pagans who can be attracted should be obtained, he conceded the said permission, and advised the said cacique [f.100] that firstly, and above all things, he should see and penetrate, endeavoring to find out if the goal with which they ask for these lands is good, and that it not be that they come with intention of making some vexation to this village and fleeing another time, because one might presume something about this case, to which the said cacique said that he would endeavor to find this out, and beyond this, he would be with caution for what could result, and that in virtue of the permission which His Grace has given him, he will go to see them in order to tell them how he has now arranged giving them the said lands, so that they might go about arranging for their arrival, because according to what they sent to tell him, they will not be ready until a year from now. And likewise the said cacique Lorenço said that he has heard the way and manner which His Grace provides in case some weapon of the enemy should be fired, and that he will do as he commands and expresses, but that he has only one thing to state, and it is that the arquebusiers and shotgunners are commanded to remain with the necessary munitions, and with their weapons prepared, and that there are some which could serve as great relief on occasion, but they do not have powder or balls, nor do they find themselves in a position to buy them, although they would like to, and they have represented this to the lieutenant of this province, and he has said that when the occasion arrives, he would supply them with what he could of munitions, and they find that this reply is the same as nothing, because if the enemy should come at midnight, as they might, or during the dawn watch, and even if it were during the day that they should come and assault them, how would the lieutenant, being more than six leagues distant from this village,[31] aid them with munitions, or even with people, because even if he should send them, and come himself, it will already be too late. On account of this, he implores His Grace, the said señor visitor, that he ask His Lordship on his behalf, and on behalf of this entire village, to aid them with some powder and balls, to which His Grace, the said señor visitor said that he [f.101] would represent it thus to the said señor governor, but that in case he should concede this and send some munitions, he must understand that they are to be distributed by the mark of the said cacique Lorenço, so that, giving them to familiar persons, they would not dispense or waste them on something other than the occasion [of enemies] happening, in which he is to take all caution, registering to whom [the munitions] might be given every eight days in order to see if they have them in their possession,[32] and that thus he commands that he should do, given the case that some [munitions] are remitted to them, to which the said cacique said that he was content, and that their dispensation and conservation would be at his charge, and that regarding the fifty arrows, and remaining with the necessary watches and guards, and sufficient canoes, he will have all care in that, and from today onward he will encourage this, since now he knows that success and news of everything results from being on guard. As to the community field, they will do what they are commanded in its distribution and regulation, and they will serve and respect the father who serves them as they have done up to now and ought to do, and they will assure that everyone attends mass, and the young people attend to their instruction with all punctuality and care, and that they will cultivate and hunt and do all the rest that they are commanded through recognizing that they are the interested party in this, and with regard to having crosses in their houses, they will have them with all decency and reverence, praying like Christians in order to give their children a good example and instruction. With regard to avoiding public and scandalous sins, and relating if there have been any, for his part he does not know that there are any about this particular [point] to be able to represent or advise His Grace, and that he will avoid for his part what he can, punishing the crime in the manner it deserves. As to curing with ancient customs using the ceremonies and [f.101, vto.] rituals which are expressed, he does not know that there is anyone in his village who makes use of similar superstitions, only that they cure themselves with herbs which they have found to be virtuous and healthy, but without any abuse, because they do not have or know other cures.[33] Nevertheless, if it should come to his notice that one of his vassals makes use of those deceptions [*embustes*],[34] he will order them punished severely, because he recognizes that it is against the law of God, which as Christians they profess and ought to observe. As to observing and commanding his vassals to observe the orders which His Grace says [the visitor] is to leave them for the government of their villages, he will place particular care in this and its observation, with which His Grace declared the visitation of this town concluded, and he advised them that of all the rest which might occur to them and which they have to ask for, they should do so in the interim that His Grace serves in this province, and that he will hear them wherever they might find him, and His Grace signed it together with Diego Camuñas, a witness in attendance with the Squad Leader Antonio del Pino, who did not sign, not knowing how to.

Domingo de Leturiondo

Diego Camuñas

Before me,
Bernardo Nieto de Carvajal
Named Notary

[f.102]

Meeting in the Village of Santa Maria

In the village of Santa Maria, of the language of Guale, where the towns of Santa Cathalina, San Joseph de Sapala, and San Diego de Satuache, of the same language, are aggregated, on the twenty-second of the month of December, sixteen eighty-five, His Grace, the señor Sergeant Major Domingo de Leturiondo, judge visitor general of this province of Guale and Mocama, commanded to gather in the council house of this village all the *reformados* and soldiers of this garrison; and Maria, cacica of Santa Cathalina;[35] and Juan Chicasle, governor and cacique of the said village;[36] Phelipe, cacique of San Joseph de Sapala;[37] and Elena, cacica of San Diego de Satuache,[38] and all the remaining principals, *hinijas,* heirs, *mandadores,* residents, and natives, and before me, the notary, and the witnesses in attendance who will be declared below, and by means of Diego Camuñas and Santiago, named interpreters, he read to them and gave them to understand the General *Auto* of Visitation signed for these provinces in the village of Santa Cruz, and having heard and understood it, they said that they will respond whatever might occur to them and what they might have to ask for, and the witnesses in attendance signed, who were Ignacio de Ycasante, Juan de Monçon, and Luis de Granada, soldiers of this garrison.[39]

Juan de Monzon

Ignacio de Ycasa

Luis de Granada

Before me,
Bernardo Nieto de Carvajal
Named Notary

[f.102, vto.]

Visitation of the Village of Santa Maria

In the village of Santa Maria, of the language of Guale, on the twenty-fourth of the month of December, sixteen eighty-five, His Grace the señor Sergeant Major Domingo de Leturiondo, judge visitor general of this province of Guale and Mocama, all those contained in the preceding meeting being together and congregated in the council house of this village in form of visitation, and by means of the interpreters Diego Camuñas and Santiago, and before me, the notary, and the previously stated witnesses in attendance, having signed in the said meeting, the cacique Juan Chicasle, governor in the name of everyone, and Juan Hinija, as principal, appeared and said that the first thing that it occurred to them to say is that when this province was in its good government, development, and conservation, before the English enemy invaded it, as has happened in years past, they governed themselves differently than now, each village helping the others with regard to the aid of the infantry who served in the garrison on Santa Cathalina and Sapala, such as each village giving each week the deer, firewood, shellfish, jars [ollas], bowls [caçuelas], pitchers [*jarros*],[40] and cassina, which although it is not an obligation, they now recognize that they ought to do it because they are serving them and guarding their neighboring villages in whatever defense and resistance in case the enemy attempts to invade the villages of this province, and that they cannot sustain themselves with only what the King gives them as ration, and that now they alone are with this charge and pension, with the remaining villages in no way helping them in anything, being able, if they wished it, to send each week one cup [*taçalo*] of cassina, some deer, and each month a pitcher, a jar, and a bowl for the service of the said infantry, to which His Grace told them regarding what they had represented that he will give an order to the lieutenant that he should act according to and how His Grace orders about this particular [case], and he will indicate it to all the caciques and *tunaques* in each village in the visitation which he makes to them so that they understand it. And likewise the said principal cacique and *hinija* said that, feeling sorry to see the infantry with the discomfort in which they find themselves living in the hut where when it rains they are all soaked, by [the hut] being poorly treated, and they are unable to guard [f.103] with as much fitness, and that thus if it seems [suitable] to His Grace that they build a house of palm so that the said infantry might inhabit it, roomy and sufficient so that they are with some comfort,[41] they will put [the plan] in execution, but only that to do so reduces the provisions in order to feed the people who are to labor in working the palm and cutting the wood and building [the house], to which His Grace replied that it seems very good to him that they should have the intention that they say, but that with regard to the food, he did not know in what form it could be adjusted, if it were not making use of the community field, making a distribution among all the villages so that each one might give enough for the quantity which is its share, and that they should consider if they would have enough for this so that some would remain for the sowing and cultivation of the said field, and what seems to them to be necessary for the total expense for food, at which they said that with regard to giving the corn from the community field, they will not express doubt, but that they have always been paid for what they have given in food for similar tasks by providing them some axes and hoes, and by buying them new if some were necessary, until it equals what they spent in giving it,[42] and that in this way they have no doubt that they will be given the corn which it costs, through all the villages having it, and it being little what they will each have to give, and that up to thirty arrobas[43] will be necessary, for which His Grace said that about this point he would leave to the lieutenant the form and manner with which the distribution is to be made, and the form of the dispensation, so that [the project] would have the outcome and good success that they desire. They likewise said that regarding the couriers, canoes, and good disposition of the sentinels, they do what the lieutenant orders them, and will take care that each one has the fifty arrows prepared as is commanded, but that regarding the munitions, they do not have any, because they do not find any to buy, and thus if the occasion should happen, those [firearms] which can shoot will be very few if he does not aid them, and [f.103, vto.] it could be that in the interim some enemy assault could happen, and they might find themselves without having anything to be able to use the firearms that they have, to which the said señor visitor said that he would speak about this to the señor governor, and he will see the form that he gives so that they might have some defense and remit some munitions to the lieutenant, because although he would like to give them some of those that he has, they are so few that there are not sufficient even for the infantry, and that thus if they come, the said lieutenant will distribute them with his count and copy so that they might have them always in their possession. They likewise said that regarding what is commanded relating to the community field, they will do according to and consistent with what has been explained and given for them to understand, and with the orders that are left for them, and in what relates to the field of the father, and always having respect, they have always had it, and have assisted with everything that is necessary. They likewise said that it has not come to their notice anything relative to public sins which they could relate, but if they find out about any, they will emplace the necessary remedy. Neither do they know that anyone in their town cures according to ancient custom using false ceremonies, prayers, and rituals, but rather with herbs of virtue, but nevertheless, they will take all care in finding out if one of their vassals makes use of similar rituals in order to punish them. As to having crosses in their houses, they will observe it as they are ordered, and regarding raising pigs and hens, along with the rest of the cultivation and fishing of their usage and custom, they will do so and continue as they have done up to now, with which His Grace, after having arranged and composed extrajudicially some minor matters which were offered, pronounced the visitation [f.104] in this said village concluded, and His Grace signed it. The said caciques and principals did not sign, not knowing how to. The previously stated witnesses in attendance who signed in the previous meeting signed below.

Domingo de Leturiondo

Ygnacio de Ycasa

Juan de Monzon

Luis de Granada

Before me,
Bernardo Nieto de Carvajal
Named Notary

Meeting in San Phelipe

In the village of San Phelipe, on the Island where the village of Santa Maria is,[44] of the language of Guale, on the twenty-fourth of the month of December, sixteen eighty-five, His Grace the señor Sergeant Major Domingo de Leturiondo, judge visitor general of this province [f.104, vto.] of Guale and Mocama, commanded to meet in the council house of this village Lucas, its principal cacique;[45] Diego de Santiago, cacique of Aleste;[46] Benito Carmenatis, cacique of Talapo;[47] Antonio, cacique of Ospogue;[48] and Marcos, cacique of Fasque; and all the remaining principals, residents, and natives of the said village, and before me, the notary, and the witnesses in attendance who will be declared below, and by means of the named interpreters, they were read and given to understand the general *auto* of the visitation signed in the village of Santa Cruz, and having heard and understood it, they said that they would respond with what occurred to them to say. They did not sign because they did not know how. One of the witnesses in attendance, who were Diego Camuñas and Squad Leader Antonio del Pino, signed. To all this I, the notary, swear.

Diego Camuñas

Before me,
Bernardo Nieto de Carvajal
Named Notary

[f.105]

Visitation of San Phelipe

In the village of San Phelipe on the twenty-fifth of the month of December, sixteen eighty-five, His Grace the señor Sergeant Major Domingo de Leturiondo, judge visitor general of this province of Guale and Mocama, all those mentioned in the preceding meeting being together in the council house of this village, and before me, the notary, and the witnesses in attendance aforementioned in the said meeting, and by means of the named interpreters, the cacique Lucas said in voice and in name of the rest of the caciques and principals that they do not have one complaint against the lieutenants or soldiers who are [there] at the present or who have been in the past, and that in what His Grace commands relative to the canoes, and that each Indian should have fifty arrows, they will do as they are ordered, and they will have the watches necessary for the news of enemies which could happen, but that regarding powder and munitions, they do not have anywhere to get them, unless the señor governor concedes to give them some so that they are prepared. To this His Grace said that about this same point he is charged by the remaining villages to speak and implore the señor governor to aid them with some [munitions] so that they might have that with which to defend themselves, and that he will also do so in common for this village and the rest so that all remain in the same form. And the said cacique said that regarding the community field, understanding the form and manner to cultivate it, they will do and comply with everything he orders them, and that relative to the field of the father, and holding him in all veneration and reverence, they will do according to how they have done up to now, and as they are ordered, and they will make all their vassals and young people [f.105, vto.] who miss one day attend mass and instruction with great punctuality. Relative to the healers and public sins, they do not know that there are any in their town of which they can relate, but that they will take all care and punish those who are found to be accomplices in the said crimes, and regarding having crosses at the heads of their beds, and praying in order to give a good example to their children, from today on they will do so with the greatest reverence that they can, as likewise they will raise [livestock] and cultivate, each one as he can, and will attend to the fishing and hunts, since this is useful and advantageous to them. His Grace, seeing that they did not have anything else to represent, pronounced the visitation of this town concluded, and signed it together with one of the witnesses in attendance, who were Squad Leader Antonio del Pino and Diego Camuñas, who also signed as interpreter.

Domingo de Leturiondo

Diego Camuñas

Before me,
Bernardo Nieto de Carvajal
Named Notary

[f.106]

Auto

In the village of San Phelipe, on the twenty-fifty of the month of December, sixteen eighty-five, His Grace the señor Sergeant Major Domingo de Leturiondo, judge visitor general of the provinces of Guale and Mocama, said that inasmuch as in the village of Tupiqui there is no cacique, nor [scarcely] any people, and because its inhabitants are few, and in order not to detain His Grace, for the great importance of the brevity of this visitation, His Grace commands that word be sent to the *tunaque* of the said village so that he will come with his people to the village of Santa Maria, where they will be able to state if they might have anything to say, and they will be given to understand the general *auto* of the visitation, aware of being three leagues distant from the said village,[49] and for this his auto he thus provided and signed together with one of the witnesses in attendance, who were Squad Leader Antonio del Pino and Diego Camuñas.

Domingo de Leturiondo

Diego Camuñas

Before me,
Bernardo Nieto de Carvajal
Named Notary

[f.106, vto.]

Visitation and Meeting of the Principals and People of Tupiqui

In the village and Island of Santa Maria, on the twenty-sixth day of the month of December, sixteen eighty-five, His Grace Sergeant Major Domingo de Leturiondo, judge visitor general of the province of Guale and Mocama, said that inasmuch as in virtue of the preceding *auto* there have arrived at this village of Santa Maria today, the day of the date above, Sergeant Major[50] Don Joseph de la Cruz, principal *tunaque* of the town of Tupiqui; Alonso Espinosa, *tunaque*; Bernabé Espinosa, *elesache*;[51] Pedro Muñoz, *aleyguita*; and Juan Chisca, *aleiyguita*; and other principal Indians and residents of the said village, and that all are together in the council house, where before me, the notary, and the witnesses in attendance who will be declared later on, and by means of the named interpreters, they were read and given to understand the general *auto* of the visitation signed in Santa Cruz, and having heard and understood it, they said that they do not have any general complaint to present about the lieutenants who have been and at the present are [there], nor against the soldiers, by not having been subjected to any disturbance, and only in particular[52] did the said *tunaque* Don Joseph de la Cruz say that he places a demand and [f.107] complains, representing a grievance against Captain Francisco Barbosa, who was lieutenant of this province, and referring to the case, he said that at the time and when the said [Barbosa] was lieutenant,[53] trade goods [*resgates*] came from the presidio so that they might be traded for corn for the King,[54] and that he traded two hundred forty arrobas,[55] and he knows that there were that many because he was counting and making an inquiry of to where, to whom, and how much he traded to each Indian. Within this quantity entered a portion of fifty-nine arrobas[56] which one particular individual gave alone in trade, and having all the said corn together, the said Captain Francisco Barvosa asked the said *tunaque* to loan him his corncrib [*garita*] in order to store the corn, and he vacated it and loaned it, as states Ensign Bernardo de Medina, who is present and who found himself in the said corncrib at the time of the deposit. The said ensign also found himself present when they took it out in order to ship it, and thus at the entrance and receipt of the corn and also at its removal and delivery, there was not one difference to compare, as says the said ensign, who compared it, and at least the delivery came well, nor is there a count which the said captain had. This having occurred, and the corn having been carried to St. Augustine, the said Captain Francisco Barbosa came and told the said *tunaque* that there [in St. Augustine] the said fifty-nine arrobas referred to above had been missing, even though the first which entered in the corncrib were those [59 arrobas], and the said [f.107, vto.] *tunaque* reprimanding him about this, and by asking him how could he say that that quantity was lacking, being thus that through being so considerable, and he having a count and copy of what he had delivered, he did not deposit less, nor did [the lieutenant] say that they were lacking at the time of the delivery? The said Lieutenant Barbosa not paying attention to all this, he took as much corn as the said *tunaque* had in his house, down to the seed which he had to sow, which all amounted to twenty-two arrobas.[57] This having occurred, Adjutant Gabriel Salguero returned when he came to this province as lieutenant[58] and said that that corn was his, and that thus he [the *tunaque*] should pay him what he had in his power, which were twenty-three arrobas. The said *tunaque* seeing that he was lieutenant, he said that he would do so and that it would occur. He obligated him to come to this village of Santa Maria and look for the said twenty-three arrobas and give them to him, nevertheless he also reprimanded him with the same as to Captain Francisco Barbosa. In a few days Nicolás, the fife, came and said that he was going for his fourteen arrobas of corn on what remained of the account of the fifty-nine which he had failed to deliver when Captain Barbosa traded for the King's corn, which he has not given him. When the said *tunaque* was in St. Augustine, he was ready to tell this to the señor governor, but he did not do so, believing that he would not believe him, or that he would get angry for his having come to him with this annoyance, but now he asks that he be paid the twenty-two arrobas which the said Captain Francisco de Barbosa carried off, and the twenty three which were taken by Adjutant Gabriel [f.108] Salguero, who, as they were lieutenants, obligated him to pay by force with no more reason than to say that they were missing. To this His Grace, the said señor visitor, seeing that his complaint was just, commanded that it be placed in this visitation, so that it might be compared with the count and copy which there should be in the Royal Contaduría about the said barter, and so that the señor governor might arrange what he finds to be justice about it. And the said *tunaque*, in name of all the rest of his principals, said that he had heard and understood everything contained in the said general *auto*, which he would observe and fulfill as he ought and is obligated by law as a Christian and vassal of our King and Lord, whom God preserve a thousand years, along with whatever else he should be ordered by the lieutenants who might be of this province, and the orders which His Grace leaves in it. Not one signed because of not knowing how to. His Grace, the said señor visitor signed it, being present the witnesses in attendance Squad Leader Antonio del Pino, Francisco Ansures, and Diego Camuñas, who signed it, and the rest did not sign, not knowing how to.

Domingo de Leturiondo

Diego Camuñas

Before me,
Bernardo Nieto de Carvajal
Named Notary

[f.108, vto.]

Meeting in San Juan del Puerto

In the village of San Juan del Puerto, Island and language of Mocama, on the twenty-seventh of the month of December, sixteen eighty-five, His Grace the señor Sergeant Major Domingo de Leturiondo, judge visitor general of the provinces of Guale and Mocama, commanded to gather in the council house of this village Juan Luis, principal cacique; Merenciana, cacica of this said village,[59] his wife; Alonso, cacique of Santa Lucia; Clemente, cacique of Nebalasa; and Domingo, cacique of Chololo; and all the remaining principals and natives inhabitants and residents of this village, and before me, the notary, and the witnesses in attendance which will be declared later on, and by means of Bartholomé, interpreter mentioned in the visitation of Timucua and Santa Cruz, they were read and given to understand the general *auto* of visitation signed on the twenty-first of the current [month], and having heard and understood it, they said that they will say and state what occurs to them. They did not sign, not knowing how to. One of the witnesses in attendance, who were Squad Leader Antonio del Pino and Diego Camuñas, signed. Of everything I swear.

Diego Camuñas

Before me,
Bernardo Nieto de Carvajal
Named Notary

[f.109]

Visitation in San Juan del Puerto

In the village of San Juan del Puerto, of the Mocama language, on the twenty-ninth of the month of December, sixteen eighty-five, His Grace the señor Sergeant Major Domingo de Leturiondo, judge visitor general of the province of Guale and Mocama, all those mentioned in the preceding meeting being together in the council house of this village in the manner of a visitation, and before me, the notary, and the witnesses in attendance aforementioned in the said meeting, and by means of Bartholomé, interpreter of this language, the said Juan Luis, principal cacique, said in name of the rest of the caciques and principals that what occurs to him to state to His Grace is that more than two years ago they made a piragua of good capacity in order to have it in this village for the passage and traverse of the Bar, and ever since they made it it has been in Santa Maria, where the lieutenants have on rare occasions have made use of it, and that thus they implore His Grace to command that they turn over the said canoe, because without it they experience much hardship, and cannot cast themselves into the Bar to cross every time due to the bad weather, but rather with much risk, and with it they will be able to go more securely, and likewise that they should be aided with some nails in order to reinforce the canoes of the crossing, by being very poorly treated, and by not having the means to be able to buy them, and also they used to be given them before now, which for a long time has not been done. To this His Grace the said señor visitor told them that regarding the canoe, upon making a [journey?] [f.109, vto.] which has to be made with other canoes from Santa Maria to bring some Christian and pagan Indians who have remained on Santa Cathalina and Sapala, from the towns which were there when they moved,[60] it will then be brought to them, and that for this, and also so that it is not taken from them except in a very urgent occasion, he will give an order to the lieutenant of this province. With regard to the nails, he will represent it to the señor governor so that His Lordship sees what has to be done about the case, and the said cacique said that regarding what relates to the general *auto* of visitation, about what he says that they should remain with caution, and the necessary guards, and that each Indian should have fifty arrows prepared, they will have everything taken care of, as also in being ready with the canoes for the crossing and traverse of the Bar, but that the firearms which they have are of no use to them because they lack powder and munitions. As to avoiding public and scandalous sins, they do not have notice from their vassals that they cure with rituals and ceremonies, but he will take all care to inquire and find out if they make use of similar abuses, in order to punish them, and that regarding the community field, they will do as they are ordered in everything, and also with the father, cultivating [his field] and caring for him in what he has need of as they have up to now, having great respect [for him]. With regard to having crosses in their houses, he will charge this to his vassals so that they should have them with all decency, and pray some orations, and that he will take all care that they attend mass every day, and to the Christian instruction, and that they will raise the hens and pigs, and cultivate everything that they customarily have, and will fish and hunt as they do for their sustenance, and His Grace pronounced the visitation of this village concluded and signed it together with one of the witnesses in attendance, who were Squad Leader Antonio del Pino and Diego Camuñas.

Domingo de Leturiondo

Diego Camuñas

Before me,
Bernardo Nieto de Carvajal
Named Notary

Auto *and Orders for Guale and Mocama*[61]

In the village of San Juan del Puerto, language of Mocama, on the twenty-ninth of the month of December, sixteen eighty-five, His Grace the señor Sergeant Major Domingo de Leturiondo, judge visitor general of the provinces of Guale and Mocama, before me, the notary, and the witnesses in attendance who will be declared below, said that inasmuch as he has made the visitation of all the villages of this province of Mocama and Guale, and it is necessary that for its good rule and government he orders and commands that the clauses and conditions which will be expressed below should be observed, which are suitable and necessary by having recognized it to be so by the said visitation, and which are the following:

1. Firstly, that no person should burden Indians with any load without paying them for their work.

2. Also, that in all the villages of this province they should always have the canoes of the passage prepared in order to pass along the news if something happens unexpectedly, and also in order to transport some soldier, provisions, or anything else which might happen, and in particular, this care is to be taken with the crossing of the Bar of San Juan del Puerto. And he who is presently lieutenant of this province, and those who might be so in the future, are ordered not to retain the canoe of the said port of San Juan in the village and Island of Santa Maria, due to the fact that it is needed there, with the penalty that at his own account and risk will be the damages and delays in the service to His Majesty, and the risks to the natives, which result from [the canoe] not being there at the time so that it might serve for what could happen regarding some news or invasion by enemies.

3. Also, that each Indian should have fifty arrows prepared in his quiver for an invasion which could happen unexpectedly, and the shotgunners and arquebusiers with their weapons prepared; and this precaution and that of the canoes is entrusted to the lieutenant so that they are not left undone, registering the villages and passing an inspection of the weapons every three months.

4. Also, that the villages of Tupiqui, San Phelipe, and Santa Cruz should help and aid with cassina, firewood, and other things which the lieutenant has pointed out to the village of Santa Maria, by being where the infantry lives, and because they have a greater burden and allowance than in [f.111] any other village, and the same is to be understood with the other hut[62] regarding the obligation, like the rest of the villages, and the distribution of what each village thus has to give and at what times. This is to be left at the charge of the lieutenant, and what remains settled about this is always to be observed from now on.

5. Also, that all the Indians of this province of Mocama and Guale should have crosses in their houses with the greatest decency possible, and that they should attend mass on the days of their obligation without missing one, and the young people should attend their instruction, and this is entrusted to the caciques.

6. Also, that they have to cultivate the community field, and its dispensation is to be among the poor, orphans, and needy widows, and other common needs of the village, and what is gathered is to be locked in a corn crib, of which the principal cacique or *mico*

of each village is to have one key, and a principal another key, which they may not open without the lieutenant, to whom they have to give an account of the dispensation of the said field.

7. Also, that no cacique, *mico*, *tunaque*, or any other principal may be punished without first giving an account to the señor governor so that he determines what he finds to be suitable about the case, and that each cacique, *mico*, or *tunaque* should be left to act and command what relates to him by reason of his leadership, and that in no manner should they meddle in the royal jurisdiction.

8. Also, that the natives should not be forbidden to dance their dances in set style when they wish except during Lent, and they should not be permitted to dance prohibited dances, punishing those who contravene, and also those who are found out to heal with abuses and superstitions, chants, and false rites.

9. Also, if of their own will they wish to give something to eat to the soldiers who go and come in the service of His Majesty, they [the soldiers] may receive this, and not in any other manner, and in all the council houses of this province the Royal Arms should be placed.

10. Also, that they should not make changes in or alter the prices which today are in set form, but rather that they should continue as up to now relative to fruits of the land,[63] and that neither the lieutenants nor caciques consent that there be Apalachee Indians, married or single, in all this stated province.

His Grace commands that all the above stated ten conditions and [–] be copied to the letter so that [–] Captain Alonso de Argüelles, so that as lieutenant of this province, he commands they be fulfilled and executed, and that a copy be taken for each council house and village, affixing it in it, so that they are informed of what they have to observe [f.111, vto.] and execute, as His Grace commands to the lieutenant that he observes them and has them observed and fulfilled, since in their fulfillment will result the good rule and government of its towns, and the security and defense of all of them. For this his *auto* he thus provided, commanded, and signed together with one of the witnesses in attendance, who were Squad Leader Antonio del Pino and Diego Camuñas.

Domingo de Leturiondo

Diego Camuñas

Before me,
Bernardo Nieto de Carvajal
Named Notary

Auto[64]

In the village of San Juan del Puerto, language of Mocama, on the twenty-ninth of the month of December, sixteen eighty-five, His Grace the señor Sergeant Major Domingo de Leturiondo, judge visitor general of the provinces of Guale and Mocama, said that inasmuch as he has made the visitation [f.112] of all the villages of this stated province, and has arranged and ordered what is to be observed and maintained in it, and that in all its villages there has not resulted one charge against Captain Alonso de Argüelles, lieutenant of the governor and captain at arms of the said province, it is necessary to return him to the post, usage, and exercise as such lieutenant, as he was before; therefore, in name of His Majesty, whom God preserve a thousand years, he was returning and returned him to the continuation and prosecution of his office and lieutenancy, so that in virtue of the title which he has he should make use of it as he made use of and exercised it before; and he was giving and gave the thanks and was approving and approved him as a good soldier and judge for having acted with all justification and rectitude, in both political and military affairs, and he commands that a dispatch in this form be sent about the aforementioned, and for this he thus provided, commanded, and signed together with one of the witnesses in attendance, who were Squad Leader Antonio del Pino and Diego Camuñas.

Domingo de Leturiondo

Diego Camuñas

Before me,
Bernardo Nieto de Carvajal
Named Notary

[f.112, vto.]

Auto, *Visitation, and Orders of Tholomato*[65]

In the village of Nuestra Señora de Guadalupe y Tholomato, on the thirtieth of the month of December, sixteen eighty-five, His Grace the señor Sergeant Major Domingo de Leturiondo, maintained with advantage by His Majesty in the presidio of St. Augustine, Florida, comissary judge visitor general of all the provinces of Apalachee, Timucua, and Guale, said that regardless of the fact that this village is two leagues from the presidio, where for whatever matter which occurs to them they can have recourse to the señor governor, it is necessary to gather the people who find themselves in it and see if at the present there is anything which occurs to them about which he can effect a remedy, and in order to give them to understand some points of the general *auto* of visitation. For [this purpose] there met in the council house of the town of Otax[66] its principal cacique Christobal and all the remaining men and women, its natives and residents, and being together, by means of Diego Camuñas, the interpreter, and before me, the notary, and the witnesses in attendance, they were read and given to understand the most essential points of the said general *auto,* and the said principal cacique and residents said that they did not have anything at present to be able to represent to His Grace, and that regarding what they are commanded in the *auto* which has been given them to understand, they will comply without leaving out anything. His Grace, the said señor visitor, said that so that they might observe, fulfill, and execute it even better, and know what they are to observe, the orders are to be placed here which are most suitable for its good government, which are the following:

1. Firstly, that the community field is cultivated with all care, and its fruits are to be locked in a corncrib which is to have two keys, one to be held by the cacique Christobal, and another by a principal, who is to be the *mandador* Xinija Baltasar,[67] whom His Grace names so that the said corncrib is not opened without common consent between them; and the proceeds from the said field are to be dispensed [f.113] according to how they are ordered by the señor Governor Don Juan Márquez Cabrera to the said cacique Christobal in the title which he has from His Lordship, among the poor, orphans, and widows, and for other common needs of the town, and a count and copy of everything is to be kept of what is taken and spent, so that it might be given to the said señor governor when he asks for it.

2. Also, they are all to have crosses in their houses, and must attend mass on the days of their obligation, and the young people to the Christian doctrine, and this remains under the charge of the said cacique Christobal.

3. Also, they are to remain cautious day and night in case some soldier who comes with some news, or in the service of the King, should happen to cross [the channel], for the great importance of this, and for this they are to have the canoes for the crossing prepared, and this remains under the charge of the said cacique Christobal.

4. Also, each of the Indians of this village should have fifty arrows prepared in his quiver, and the shotgunners and arquebusiers should have the necessary munitions for the occasion which could happen unexpectedly.

5. Also, if something should happen which the said cacique Christobal is unable to remedy, they will take recourse to the señor governor, who will hear them and preserve justice as he has done up to now.

His Grace commands that a copy of all the said conditions be taken in order to place and fix them in the council house, and that they be given to understand them by the said interpreter so that in everything they are observed, fulfilled, and executed by everyone, as they are expressed, and for this his *auto* of visitation he thus provided, commanded, and signed together with one of the witnesses in attendance, who were Squad Leader Antonio del Pino and Diego Camuñas. The rest did not sign, not knowing how to. Scratched out = cacique Domingo = not valid = between lines = *mandador* Hinija Baltasar [–]

Domingo de Leturiondo

Diego Camuñas

Before me,
[Bernardo Nieto de Carvajal]
[Named Notary]

[f.113, vto.]

Auto[68]

In the village of Nuestra Señora de Guadalupe de Tholomato on the thirtieth of the month of December, sixteen eighty-five, His Grace, the señor Sergeant Major Domingo de Leturiondo, maintained with advantage by His Majesty in the presidio of St. Augustine, Florida, judge visitor general of the provinces of Guale and Mocama, before me, the notary, and the witnesses in attendance who will be declared later on, said that inasmuch as His Grace has finished, concluded, and terminated the visitations of Apalachee, Timucua, Mocama, and Guale, and it is necessary to make a delivery of them and other autos and documents made during the time of his visitation so that His Lordship the señor Governor Don Juan Márquez Cabrera, to whom they are to be delivered, finds himself informed about the visitations in which some cases and points arrive still pending, in which it is necessary that the said señor governor intervene in order to conclude their resolution, about the propositions and entreaties which the natives of these provinces have made, and that the first is that of San Luis de Thalimali, which is on folio 42 and following, about making the house of the King at the request of the natives;[69] the visitation of Santa Cathalina, which is on folio 74 and following, about the tasks of the village, and that they should be aided for their development;[70] the visitation of San Diego de Salamototo, which is on folio 87 and following, about some lands and fields that they ask for which Ventura González has occupied; the visitations of Santa Cruz; Santa Maria; San Phelipe; Tupiqui; and San Juan which begin from folio 100 up to 110, about different points, requests, and circumstances; and likewise His Grace commands that the general *autos* of visitation be placed by folio and number so that His Lordship the señor governor might see the form and disposition [–] had in giving them to understand what [–] they have to observe and maintain.[71]

NOTES

1. The 1657 visitation of Apalachee by Governor Rebolledo was an exception to this practice, inasmuch as he seems do have composed the regulatory code to be posted at each mission prior to the beginning of the official visitation (Hann, 1986a).

2. Full translations of these first two visitations have recently been published by John Hann (1993).

3. This page forms a title page for the 1685 visitation of Guale and Mocama, and was drafted by 18th-century notary Francisco de Castilla in order to serve as a cover for the original folios which he cut out of a bound notebook dating to 1685. The names which follow were extracted by Castilla from the original text, and thus are in some cases spelled differently than the original (perhaps due to errors in paleographic transcription).

4. Here begins the 17th-century visitation record, starting on folio 93 of the original bound notebook including in addition the visitations of Apalachee and Timucua. Serving as the cover sheet for the visitation of Guale and Mocama, this initial folio was drafted after the *auto* that follows on folio 94, inasmuch as a copy of the original commission to Sergeant Major Leturiondo was ordered to be made and attached to the front of the visitation record within the text of the second auto (see below).

5. A letter from the provincial Lieutenant of Timucua Manuel Gómez to Governor Márquez Cabrera dated November 12, 1685, reveals, among other things, that Sergeant Major Domingo de Leturiondo had sent him a letter from Apalachee instructing him to meet him in the border mission of Asile "in order to come with him making the visitation" of the Timucua province (Gómez, 1685). Only six days later the governor dispatched the official title of visitor of the provinces of Guale and Mocama, which Leturiondo encountered in Salamototo.

6. The preceding order was dispatched by Governor Márquez Cabrera in late November, while Leturiondo was concluding his visitation of Apalachee and Timucua. The Sergeant Major would eventually receive it in the village of Salamototo, from which point he apparently proceeded directly to Guale and Mocama (see the *auto* that follows).

7. This document initiates the process of visitation for the provinces of Guale and Mocama, setting forth the background for the visitation, the various participants in the process, and the order to attach the original commission as visitor to the front of the record.

8. As a standard feature of any official visitation, the acting lieutenant governor within the province was suspended from his post during the visitation in order to permit free and open airing of all grievances against him or the soldiers under his command, and to give the visiting officer power to act independently of the resident lieutenant. The lieutenant's post was reinstated at the end of the visitation, presuming no substantial charges had been lodged against him.

9. This passage indicates that Bernardo Nieto de Carvajal served as notary for all the visitations carried out by Leturiondo that year.

10. The following section provides an official record of the suspension of the provincial lieutenant of Guale and Mocama, Captain Alonso de Argüelles, and records his acceptance and signature.

11. The section below names the interpreters to be employed during the visitation of Guale and Mocama, and records their oath of accurate translation, along with a signature (when possible).

12. Diego Camuñas was a 55-year-old soldier who had served as a Guale interpreter on other occasions. The 1678 service record of Diego Camuñas reveals that he began to serve as a soldier in Florida on November 10, 1655, and was officially instated as "*atequi* [interpreter] of the language of Guale" by Governor Manuel de Cendoya (Menéndez Márquez, 1678). Santiago was noted to be a native Guale Indian, and he and Camuñas served together as interpreters of the Guale language for the 1685 visitation. Bartolome de la Cruz (see below) seems to have been an Indian who served as interpreter during the visitation of the Timucua province, and who thus served in the same capacity for villages of the Mocama language.

13. The following document constitutes the core of the visitation process, inasmuch as its text was read in the council house of each village visited, setting forth the purpose and scope of the visitation. Although the general *auto* provided an opportunity for the Indian residents to lodge complaints or make requests, a large section was devoted to general instructions and orders on the part of the Spaniards, to which the Indians were instructed to respond.

14. This full listing of the titles political office holders in Guale and Mocama provinces includes an assortment of names in the Guale, Mocama, and even Spanish languages. Beyond the caciques or *micos*, the titular leaders, were listed the principals, specifically the *tunaques*, *hinijas*, *mandadores* (a Spanish-derived term, meaning "commanders"), *elesaches*, *herederos* ("heir" in Spanish), and *aleiguidas*. All but one of the names commonly appear in other documents relating to Guale and Mocama, but *elesache* is virtually unknown beyond this visitation. It is undoubtedly equivalent to the term *ibissache* noted by Hann (1987: 15) as a lower-ranking principal Indian. As noted below relative to the visitation of Tupiqui, *elesache* probably signifies "heir."

15. This passage indicates that grievances against members of a separate authority (such as the church, or specifically the Franciscan Order) should be dealt with in a different format. Leturiondo's visit centered primarily on military affairs.

16. Here ends the first part of the general *auto* of the visitation, in which Leturiondo ordered the airing of all grievances against lieutenants, soldiers, or Indian leaders. Following this is the even longer section relating the instructions and orders that he will be giving them at the end of the visitation.

17. Only a year earlier, the pirate raids of September–October 1684 had resulted in the destruction of at least two missions, and the final retreat south of the modern Georgia border (see Document 10, and the Overview). Earlier raids by English-backed Indians in 1680, and by French and English pirates in 1683, had caused considerable damage in Guale and Mocama.

18. Although rarely discussed in the secondary literature, mission Indians had been armed with Spanish firearms since the middle of the 17th century. Despite official Spanish policy forbidding such practices, the Guale Indians owned and used firearms at least as early as 1656 (Worth, 1992: 244–246, 252). In all probability only a few such weapons were in the hands of Indian leaders and warriors in the Spanish militia system, and were only rarely of service (due principally to the lack of gunpowder and shot).

19. This passage explicitly states that the community field referred to was not to be used for the upkeep of the resident friar (whose field would be discussed below), nor was it royal property, but rather was to be maintained by and distributed among the Indians of each village.

20. The system described above was designed to ensure that no individual Indian cacique would be able to open the stores of corn grown in the community field alone, but rather only in the presence of another leading Indian to be selected by the provincial lieutenant (and thus probably an ally or friend of the lieutenant). Evidently some caciques were in the habit of using the corn for their own purposes, such as for gifts to close family and friends.

21. The term *pequata* was Timucuan (or in this case in the Mocama dialect) for servant (Granberry, 1993), and undoubtedly referred to the Indian assistants who aided the friar in maintaining

the church and convent, and in preparations for religious functions.

22. Pig remains have been recovered from the pre-1680 site of Santa Catalina de Guale, confirming that at least some domestic European animals were raised in the province of Guale (Reitz, 1991).

23. The formal visitation process at each mission village involved two stages, the first of which involved a preliminary meeting, or *junta*, of the official visitor with the Indian leaders and residents who were to be present at the visitation the following day. During the first meeting, the Indians were read the general *auto* of the visitation, and indicated that they would relate whatever they felt was necessary to the visitor. It is in this portion of each visitation that the names of all the principal caciques or other leaders were listed, providing evidence as to the social makeup of the mission town.

24. Lorenzo Santiago was still governor of Mission Santa Cruz de Guadalquini in 1695, and had become overall leader of Mocama after the fusion of Santa Cruz with San Juan del Puerto by 1701 (Pueyo, 1695; Zuñiga y Cerda, 1701).

25. This was almost certainly the cacique Santiago left in command of Guadalquini by Lorenzo during the pirate raids of 1684 (see Document 10).

26. This is the last known reference to Utinahica, an early 17th-century interior mission located near the forks of the Altamaha River between 1616 and 1636 (Worth 1992: 76). The inhabitants of this Timucuan-speaking town presumably aggregated to Guadalquini prior to the 1655 mission list, since Santa Isabel de Utinahica was not mentioned at that time (Díez de la Calle, 1659).

27. The visitation itself occurred a day or two following the preliminary meeting, during which all the previously listed individuals met to listen to the response of the Indians to the points raised in the general *auto* of the visitation. In general, one cacique spoke for the rest during the proceedings, presumably having conferred during the previous evening with the rest of the leaders regarding what was to be stated.

28. The military rank listed here related to the established aboriginal militia system, in which Indian leaders were given honorific titles and posts within the Spanish militia structure.

29. As discussed further in the Overview, these Indians seem to have been scattered remnants of the inhabitants of St. Simons Island (other than Guadalquini, which moved to Santa Cruz), which had been overrun by English pirates in late October 1684. The mission of Asajo was the only one not to aggregate just north of St. Augustine with the rest of the Guale and Mocama missions following this attack, and some are known to have moved north to the Scottish colony at Santa Elena. Yguaja seems to have been the Timucua (or Mocama) term for Guale. The Colones were the former pagan inhabitants of the town of San Simón, an immediate neighbor of the old Guadalquini Mission. In 1695, Pantaleon, the cacique of Colon, was listed in Mission Santa Cruz de Guadalquini, suggesting that Lorenzo's 1685 attempt was successful.

30. Asajo was a former Guale mission, and the Colones seem to have been Muskhogean speakers as well (see Overview).

31. Mission Santa Cruz y San Buenaventura de Guadalquini had been recently founded far to the south of the original location of San Buenaventura de Guadalquini on the southern tip of St. Simons Island. The location of this mission has long been presumed to be some 3 leagues north of St. Augustine, and 6 south of San Juan del Puerto, placing it very near the mission of Tolomato. The cacique Lorenzo's statement here suggests instead that Santa Cruz was 6 leagues south of Santa Maria, where the garrison was then headquartered. This would potentially place Santa Cruz slightly inland from the mouth of the St. Johns River, directly west of San Juan del Puerto. The fact that Leturiondo proceeded from Salamototo on the middle St. Johns River to Santa Cruz, and then to Santa Maria and San Phelipe, prior to heading south along the coast to San Juan and Tolomato, seems to bear out this conclusion (see Appendix A).

32. Although Leturiondo suggests here that an inspection of the weapons and munitions should be made every eight days, he eventually ordered that this be done only every three months (see below).

33. This passage is particularly intriguing, inasmuch as it indicates that although converted Christian Indians in Florida missions were forbidden to practice traditional pagan rituals associated with the use of medicinal herbs, their use in curing was not universally banned. While the Spaniards did concern themselves with eradicating non-Christian beliefs and rituals, they evidently recognized the practical utility of Indian medicines.

34. The term *embustes* may instead refer to trinkets or charms of little value, and in this instance might refer to items used as magical aids in curing, perhaps similar to the feathers and arrows described by Fray Francisco Pareja in 1613 as part of the curing ritual among the Timucuan-speaking Indians at Mission San Juan del Puerto (Milanich and Sturtevant, 1972: 32, 42).

35. Maria remained cacica of Santa Catalina in both the 1695 and 1701 visitations of Guale (Pueyo, 1695; Zuñiga y Cerda, 1701).

36. Juan Chicasle was apparently the acting leader of the newly aggregated mission town of Santa Maria, although the cacica of Santa Catalina, Maria, was listed first. This was also the case in both the 1695 and 1701 visitations at Santa Maria (Pueyo, 1695; Zuñiga y Cerda, 1701). Inasmuch as each of the component towns which had aggregated to form Santa Maria are listed separately, and since Santa Maria had evidently been abandoned prior to the 1684 arrival of the immigrant Guale towns by the Yamassee Indians who had lived there during the previous decades, it is difficult to interpret Chicasle's sociopolitical origin.

37. Phelipe was listed as the cacique of Sapala in 1677 (Argüelles, 1678), and remained so through 1695, although at that time he apparently resided in Santa Clara de Tupiqui on the northern end of Amelia Island (Pueyo, 1695). In 1701, Phelipe's successor Benito was still situated in Tupiqui (Zuñiga y Cerda, 1701), suggesting that the association between Sapala and Tupiqui did indeed persist after the abandonment of the Georgia coast (even though Phelipe was listed here in Mission Santa Maria).

38. Elena is probably the same Elena who was installed as the cacica of Faslica at the request of the caciques of Satuache during the visitation of Mission Santa Catalina in 1677 (Argüelles, 1678). The association between the chiefly lineages of Faslica and Satuache seems to have persisted, since Diego, the cacique of Fuslique/Fuslico, was listed in Santa Catalina's new location at Mission Santa Maria in both 1695 and 1701. The name Satuache was conspicuously absent from these same visitation lists, strongly implying that Diego was Elena's successor (Pueyo, 1695; Zuñiga y Cerda, 1701).

39. These witnesses signed during the two visitations held at Santa Maria (see Tupiqui below) because they were members of the resident garrison of infantry under Captain Argüelles' command.

40. The three items mentioned here—ollas, *caçuelas*, *jarros*—refer to three separate types of ceramic vessels, all of which might have been found within the range of Precolumbian aboriginal pottery forms used among the Guale (see Hally (1986) for a discussion of prehistoric Lamaroid vessel forms and functions). The olla, or jar, was a large, deep vessel presumably used for cooking or storage. The *caçuela* was a shallow bowl with an incurvate rim, used for both cooking and serving. The *jarro*, or pitcher, refers to a vessel designed for storing and pouring liquids. Although these may well have been of Indian design, it is also possible that this passage refers to ceramics made by Indians in Spanish shapes, known as Colono wares by modern archaeologists.

41. As was customary for visitors passing through Indian towns in 17th-century Florida, the soldiers living in garrison at Santa Maria in 1695 were evidently living in the village council house [*buhio*], perhaps because the village had only recently been settled after the abandonment of Sapala (the old headquarters) in October of 1684. Given that such public structures typically possessed a large open space in the roof (that of Santa Maria was described by Dickenson in 1697 as having a 20-foot opening), it could not have been very comfortable during rainstorms. For this reason the Indians proposed constructing a new thatched house specifically for housing the resident soldiers.

42. The system being described seems to have involved the voluntary donation of corn by each village in order to accomplish some project for the Spaniards, with the expectation of reimbursement in the form of iron tools of equal value.

43. One *arroba* equals approximately 25 pounds of corn, making this amount roughly 750 pounds of corn.

44. San Phelipe was situated only half a league to the north of Santa Maria at that time.

45. By 1695, Alonso, Lucas's successor to the caciquedom of San Phelipe , had apparently been reduced in status below Diego, the cacique of Aluste (Pueyo, 1695). In 1701, Aluste's cacique Diego González was the only cacique principal listed for the town of San Phelipe (Zuñiga y Cerda, 1701). This association between the chiefly lineages of San Phelipe de Alave and Aluste during the late 17th century suggests that the original Mission San Phelipe was part of a cluster of villages associated with the important northern Guale town of Aluste, which was mentioned frequently during the late 1500s and early 1600s.

46. As noted above, although Aluste's cacique Diego de Santiago was in 1685 listed as subordinate to Lucas, the cacique of the town of San Phelipe, by 1695, Diego Aluste was the principal governor of the town (Pueyo, 1695). Six years later, Diego González (possibly the same individual) was listed as the cacique of Aluste and the overall cacique of Mission San Phelipe (Zuñiga y Cerda, 1701).

47. Benito remained cacique of Talapo (written as Taljapu and Tarapu) through the 1695 and 1701 visitations of Mission San Phelipe (Pueyo, 1695; Zuñiga y Cerda, 1701).

48. Ten years later, Antonio was listed as the cacique of Juzpo, but Francisco was subsequently installed as the cacique of Azpogue (Pueyo, 1695). In 1701, Francisco was listed as the cacique of Jospo (Zuñiga y Cerda, 1701), suggesting strongly that Ospogue and Ospo referred to the same chiefly lineage.

49. The village of Tupiqui was located 3 leagues to the north of San Phelipe, on the northern tip of

modern Amelia Island. As such, Tupiqui was the northern frontier of the Guale and Mocama province.

50. Although not a full-fledged cacique, Don Joseph's militia rank was higher than the only other Indian leader listed as holding a military rank in Guale and Mocama (Lorenzo, the principal cacique of Santa Cruz, was a captain).

51. Bernabé was listed 10 years later as the *mico* of Mission Santa Clara de Tupiqui, suggesting that his earlier title of *elesache* might have been the Guale term for heir (Pueyo, 1695). This seems even more likely in view of the fact that during the same 1695 visitation, Benito, the future cacique of Sapala (Zuñiga y Cerda, 1701), was listed as an *ybissache* living in Tupiqui along with Sapala's long-time cacique Phelipe.

52. Don Joseph's complaint was a personal one, and was thus denoted as "particular," as opposed to "general" complaints lodged by Indian leaders in the name of entire communities.

53. Captain Francisco de Barbosa was lieutenant of Guale between late 1682 and early 1684.

54. An example of the items used as trade goods during this period is provided by an entry in the Contaduría (accounting records) of St. Augustine during 1685 (AGI Contaduría 965):

> By the book under the charge of the treasurer, about what is delivered and received in the [–] warehouses, in order to provide a relation from it, it is on record that a charge was made on the 17th of April of 1685 of the following:
>
> Firstly, sixty-seven knives.
> Two and a half varas of *jerguetta* [fabric].
> Four and a half masses of beads.
> Twenty-nine and a half varas of *fresa* [fabric].
> And nineteen island bedspreads [*covertores ysleños*].
>
> All of which is on record as having been received by Fr[–] Anzures, a soldier of the garrison of Guale, who delivered them in the name of Captain [Alonso] de Argüelles, its lieutenant . . . and on the tenth of December of the said year it is on record that a charge was made of twenty-four hoes, [–] axes, and thirty adzes [*achuelas*], as received by Gabriel Salguero who was the lieutenant of the province, to which he returned.

Interestingly, Gabriel Salguero's return to Guale in mid-December of 1685 immediately preceded the visitation of Tupiqui, and the complaint against him (see below).

55. This amount roughly equals 6000 pounds of corn.

56. Fifty-nine arrobas amounts to nearly 1500 pounds of corn.

57. Roughly 550 pounds of corn.

58. Salguero replaced Captain Don Juan de Saturnino as lieutenant of Guale and Mocama following the disastrous pirate raids of October 1684, which led to Saturnino's criminal prosecution for negligence (see Document 10).

59. Merenciana had been installed as cacica of San Juan when her aunt Juana Menéndez stepped down in 1678 (Argüelles, 1678). Although she seems to have been the highest-ranking leader in San Juan as late as 1681 (Márquez Cabrera, 1681), by 1685 her husband Juan Luis was listed as principal cacique, and spoke for the rest during the visitation (see below).

60. These were almost certainly Yamassee Indians, who had recently relocated to these two abandoned Guale islands (see Overview).

61. This final section of the official visitation of Guale and Mocama provinces presented a list of 10 orders for the provinces, a copy of which was to be posted in each council house.

62. Referring to the proposed house to be built for the residence of the Spanish garrison.

63. The passage following this first part of number 10 was added after the concluding material below, and between the lines, suggesting that it was only an afterthought. The ends of the lines are deteriorated, and thus the passage actually refers to prohibiting *Yndios ap. . .inos casados ni solteros*, the missing portion of which was most probably *apalachinos*.

64. The following *auto* officially reinstated Captain Argüelles as lieutenant of Guale and Mocama, commending him for his exemplary work (particularly as not one charge had been leveled at him during the visitation).

65. This section of the visitation record was more of an addendum, for Leturiondo conducted a sort of impromptu visitation of the mission of Tolomato, located only 3 leagues north of St. Augustine. The following *auto* compressed the meeting, visitation, and order sections for Tolomato.

66. The fact that Tolomato's council house was identified as that of Otax strongly suggests a correlation between the two. The appearance of a cacique of Otax (in the absence of any contemporaneous reference to Tolomato) during the early 17th century may imply that Otax was the name for the chiefly lineage of the town of Tolomato following the Guale rebellion of 1597 and the death of Tolomato's rebel leaders several years later (see Jones, 1978). When Tolomato was relocated in the late 1620s, the lineage of Otax was probably also transferred to the south.

67. The notary Bernardo Nieto de Carvajal originally wrote "the cacique Domingo" in this space, but this was later crossed out and replaced by the "*mandador* Xinija Baltasar" (see Nieto's validation at the foot of this document). Domingo

was undoubtedly unwilling or unable to serve, or was later determined to be a relative of the principal cacique Christobal (as had been prohibited earlier in the general *auto* of the visitation).

68. The final portion of the 1685 Leturiondo visitation represents a sort of summary and explicitly served to draw the governor's attention to those folios in the visitation record that contained unfinished business which he would need to attend to. Coincidentally, it also provides some hint of the nature of the material contained in the previous 92 folios relating to Apalachee and Timucua provinces, left behind by 18th-century notary Francisco de Castilla.

69. This brief mention seems to refer to the construction of a structure for the Spanish at San Luis, the provincial garrison headquarters (see Hann, 1988b).

70. The Timucuan mission Santa Catalina de Ahoica had been largely destroyed in a Yamassee raid during February of 1685, and the visitation in November or December most likely centered on reconstruction or relocation.

71. Here ends folio 113 of the Leturiondo visitation of 1685. The content of the final entry suggests that only one folio more (folio 114) may have been left behind by Castilla, perhaps due to deterioration (folio 113 is in poor shape).

DOCUMENT 10: A CRIMINAL CASE AGAINST THE LIEUTENANT OF GUALE, 1685

INTRODUCTION

The months of September and October of 1684 witnessed the final enemy raid on the provinces of Guale and Mocama on the Georgia coast. Following the violent destruction of at least two of the remaining four missions north of the St. Marys River, the entire northern mission chain was withdrawn to Amelia Island and southward. Until the discovery of the following document, this final blow to Guale and Mocama remained effectively unknown to modern researchers. Although the text that follows is largely self-explanatory, and the event is treated in greater detail in the Overview to this volume, a few brief comments here serve to place the criminal case in context.

The events treated in this trial happened in late September and October of 1684, some two to three months prior to the testimony and judicial action taken here. The following documents detail Governor Don Juan Márquez Cabrera's successful criminal prosecution of his former provincial lieutenant in Guale, Captain Don Juan Saturnino de Abaurrea, a 31-year-old officer with considerable previous experience in the province of Guale (including two stints as lieutenant of the Guale garrison). During the eventful raid led by the pirate known to the Spanish as Thomas Jingle, in which an aborted attempt to sack St. Augustine resulted in an assortment of landings and raids by scattered pirate vessels along the Atlantic coastline north of St. Augustine (see Wright [1960] for a discussion of the early stages of this event), Lieutenant Saturnino de Abaurrea apparently abandoned his post at Sapala, retreating to the mainland, only to appear once again in a botched attempt to take charge of a boatload of unfortunate prisoners captured by the Indians of Guadalquini.

Inasmuch as Saturnino de Abaurrea's reputed negligence resulted in the burning of at least two mission towns (admittedly already in the process of relocating to the south), Governor Márquez Cabrera gathered witnesses following the New Year for an official investigation. As will be seen below, the testimony was damning, and Lieutenant Saturnino de Abaurrea paid heavily for his decisions that fall. Ultimately, however, the criminal proceedings that follow provide a remarkable glimpse into the final days of Spanish control on the modern Georgia coast, and set the stage for the last retreat southward.

The structure of the following documents reflects the Spanish legal norms for a criminal case during the late 17th century. The first document is the *auto* that describes the reasons for the investigation, which is immediately followed by the individual testimony of various witnesses called for the case. It is important to realize that this initial stage of the case was not preceded by an official charge against the accused, who was not even present during the proceedings. Only after all the appropriate testimony had been gathered was the accused officially informed and, presuming there was sufficient evidence for a charge, imprisoned. The accused was then referred to as the prisoner (as opposed to a witness), and his testimony was taken as a confession (as opposed to a declaration).

Following all this, provided that there was still sufficient evidence to pursue the case, the prisoner was then declared guilty and charged with the crime. The next stage of the case involved calling all the previous witnesses in order to affirm and ratify their original declarations (and to add to or modify the written version of their oral testimony), and during this time the prisoner was given the opportunity to construct whatever defense he wished on his behalf (in this case a written letter of defense). This defense seems to have been aimed primarily at mitigating the sentence, inasmuch as the guilt had already been established by the judge (in this case the governor).

Number 10[1]

Year of 1685

Criminal *autos* against Captain Don Juan Saturnino de Abaurrea for having abandoned the province of Guale when he was lieutenant of the governor, and retreating to the woods during the time of an attack by English enemies.

Florida Year of 1685

Criminal[2]

Against Captain Don Juan Saturnino, who was lieutenant of the province of Guale, about having retreated to the mainland as soon as he had notice that enemies were coming to the said province.

Judge
Captain and Sergeant Major
Don Juan Márquez Cabrera,
Governor and Captain General of the provinces of Florida.

Notary
Alonso Solana.

[f.1]

Auto, *Head of Prosecution Against Don Juan Saturnino*[3]

In the city of St. Augustine, Florida, on the first day of the month of January, sixteen eighty five, Captain and Sergeant Major Don Juan Márquez Cabrera, governor and captain general of this stated city and its provinces for His Majesty, said that inasmuch as on the occasion that the English enemies came to this coast to the north with six vessels which placed people on land in the province of Guale and sacked, robbed, and burned some towns of the said province, Captain Don Juan Saturnino Abaurrea, lieutenant of the governor and captain general, was withdrawn from it on the mainland throughout, without His Grace having notice in this presidio where the said lieutenant found himself, by failing to send any news of the designs of the enemies until, with the occasion of the cacique of Guadalquini, named Don Lorenzo, having ten Englishmen prisoners who had entered in his said town with a boat with topsails on the pretext of peace, by saying that they came lacking provisions, the said cacique sent news to the said lieutenant of having in his said town the ten prisoners, that he came to [the town] so carelessly and inattentively that, having been able to place them in a safe and secure place, after he reached the said prisoners he let other enemies who entered by the Bar of the said Hoadalquini[4] take them away without having remedied [the situation] nor having offered the least resistance, impediment, nor any defense, although he had occasion and time to be able to do so, the said lieutenant rather having fled to the woods with the soldiers and Indians with whom he found himself, and although later the same [f.1, vto.] day the support of thirteen[5] soldiers and rations arrived, he did not decide to assault [the town] with the rest of the people whom he found himself in charge of, [and the enemies] burned the town, church, and convent of the said Oadalquini, having found himself with nearly forty firearms. And so that the aforementioned be investigated and punished in the service of the King, Our Lord, therefore he commanded to make this the beginning of the prosecution, and that by its tenor the persons who might know of the case be examined, so that it should serve as lesson and punishment to the said [lieutenant], and to others as an example, and for this his *auto* he provided, ordered, and signed.

Juan Márquez Cabrera

Before me,
Alonso Solana
Public and Governmental Notary

Declaration of Ensign Felipe de Santiago[6]

In the city of St. Augustine, Florida, on the first day of the month of January, sixteen eighty-five, the señor Captain and Sergeant Major [f.2] Don Juan Márquez Cabrera, governor and captain general of this stated city and its provinces for His Majesty, commanded to appear before him Ensign Felipe de Santiago, *reformado* of this presidio, who before me, the notary, was sworn in before God and a sign of the cross, in legal form, and having signed, aware of it, he promised to tell the truth, and being questioned in the tenor of the *auto* which is the head of this case, said and declared the following: that being in the company of Captain Don Juan de Saturnino Abaurrca in garrison in the presidio of Guale, being in the town of Sapala, head of the province, the said captain had notice that the enemy had arrived upon this Bar with six vessels, and had placed people on the beach of San Matheo,[7] by a letter which the father *doctrinero* of the Island of Santa Maria[8] wrote to the father *doctrinero* of the town of Guadalquine,[9] with which as soon as he had this news, the said Lieutenant gathered the people who had remained and tried to cross to the mainland, to which this witness told him that he should send a soldier or person to find out about the state of this presidio, and at the end of eighteen days, the lieutenant and this witness and two soldiers determined to return to the said town of Guadalquini, through Lorenzo, cacique of the said town of Guadarquine, having advised him of the entrance of a sloop [*balandra*[10]] with ten men and a woman, whom he had as [f.2, vto.] prisoners, and having arrived Saturday in the morning at the said town of Guadalquini and seen the said sloop and prisoners, this witness said to the said lieutenant "Señor captain, what are we doing here? We should try to put this vessel and these prisoners in a safe place," in the presence of the missionary of the said doctrina and town, who, supporting what this witness had said, said to the said lieutenant "Señor captain, here it is not safe today," to which the said captain responded that he did not have vessels to be able to do so [relocate the prisoners], finding himself at the present with only one canoe, nor enough people here to be able to put them in a secure place. The following day, at dawn, a frigate [*fragata*[11]] of enemies entered through the Bar, and when it was noticed it was already anchored, the sentinels of the Indians having advised before how two piraguas were entering through the Bar, with which suddenly the said lieutenant and the rest of the people retreated to the woods and from there returned to the mainland, where on Tuesday they were found by Ensign Bernardo de Medina, who had come with thirteen soldiers and munitions,[12] and up to thirty-eight men joined and crossed again to the said town of Guadalquini, this witness having remained on the mainland because of being sick in the eyes, this witness having represented this to the said lieutenant on the [f.3] occasion. Being in the said town of Sapala,[13] having notice that the enemy was going in piraguas in the direction of the said town, this witness told [the lieutenant] that it would be good to come forth to receive them at the village of the Colones, thirteen leagues distant,[14] and in that instant, the weapon of a vigil sounded, and the said lieutenant wishing to proceed with the voyage, this witness told him "Señor captain, if we are going to look for the enemy, here we have them. Look after your credit; the worse blade to be had has to be me,"[15] with which he disembarked, and remained in the said post two days, and crossed to the mainland, in which interval the enemy landed in the town of Asajo and burned it, without the said lieutenant having had notice of it, by finding himself on the mainland. Regarding what happened when the enemy took away the vessel and prisoners, he does not know, because he remained sick on the mainland as he has said. Regarding what he was asked about how the lieutenant found himself without munitions, His

Grace the said señor Governor having turned over to this witness a jar [*botijuela*[16]] of ten pounds of fine powder and one hundred ninety-six balls so that he should give them to the said lieutenant in order to have them in reserve with the rest of the munitions which there were there, he said [f.3, vto.] that about eight days [before] the occasions with the enemy, he arrived at the said town of Sapala and turned them over to the said lieutenant, and that what he has said and declared is the truth and what he knows, aware of the oath which he has signed, in which he affirms and ratifies, and that he is of the age of thirty-seven years, and signed it together with His Grace the said señor governor. Underlined—that—not valid—stained—that—valid.

Felipe Santiago

Juan Márquez Cabrera

Before me,
Alonso Solana
Public and Governmental Notary

Declaration of Ensign Bernardo de Medina

In the city of St. Augustine, Florida, on the fourth of January, sixteen eighty-five, His Grace the said señor governor and captain general, for the said investigation, commanded to appear before him Ensign Bernardo de Medina, *reformado* of this presidio, who, before me, the notary, was sworn in before God and a sign of the [f.4] cross, in legal form, and having signed it, aware of it, he promised to tell the truth, and being read the *auto* which is at the head of this case, in its tenor he said that he knows, by Captain Don Juan Saturnino having said so, that having arrived one Saturday in the morning at the town of Guadalquini, due to news which he had from the cacique Don Lorenzo of the said town, of having there ten English prisoners and a woman who had entered in a sloop on the pretext that they were perishing,[17] the entire day passed without [the lieutenant] having commanded to put them in a safe place by crossing them to the mainland, having been able to do so by having time for it before a ship [*navio*] arrived the following day, Sunday, in the morning; and that, leaving the prisoners in the council house of the said town, they [the pirates] set them free by likewise being enemies, of their nation, without the said lieutenant on his part offering any resistance. And this witness having arrived on Monday night on the mainland with aid of eight soldiers where he found Ensign Felipe de Santiago, questioning him about what happened in Guadalquini, the said ensign referred likewise [f.4, vto.] what he has said above, and that Lieutenant Don Juan Saturnino had retreated in the woods of the Island of Guadalquini, and this witness sent to advise him with two Indians how he was on the mainland with eight men whom His Grace the said señor governor sent as aid, and that he should look after what had to be arranged. The said lieutenant having come to where this witness was, he resolved to cross to the said Island of Guadalquini Tuesday night, where they arrived with up to nearly fifty firearms between Spaniards and Indians in view of the town, where the enemies still were. Having dispatched two spies at night in order to certify if there were many people, as they said, he recognized it to be thus, and the said lieutenant being resolved to assault them, this witness found out that the cacique Don Lorenzo of the said town said that he did not wish to fight, so that they might not kill the people, and that he did not have anything left to lose or guard there, because he already had the [f.5] women and young people, and all their furnishings [*trastos*] and corn, and that if he lost his Indians he would lose everything, for which reason the said lieutenant did not resolve [to assault] the enemies, all of which was said to [this witness] by the said cacique Don Lorenzo and Juan de Peñalosa, a soldier of this presidio who also went as aid with this witness. And he knows, by being a sentinel in the watchtower of San Juan when the señor sergeant major of this post withdrew from the province of Guale, and he left him there and had gone as aid as soon as the enemies came to the post of Las Cañuelas, where they had the intention of disembarking the people on land in order to come to invade this post,[18] that the said lieutenant was always on the mainland, deserting the town of Sapala, where his post was, because of having news of enemies cruising those coasts, and that what he has said and declared is the truth, and what he knows, aware of the oath which he has signed, in which he affirms and ratifies, and he declares himself to be of the age of more than forty years, and signed it [f.5, vto.] together with His Grace, the señor governor.

Bernardo de Medina

Juan Márquez Cabrera

Before me,
Alonso Solana
Public and Governmental Notary

Declaration of Juan de Peñalosa

In the city of St. Augustine, Florida, on the said day, month, and year, His Grace the said señor governor and captain general, for the said investigation, made appear before him Juan de Peñalosa, a soldier of this presidio, who, before me, the notary, was sworn in before God and a sign of the cross, in legal form, and having signed it, aware of this, he promised to say the truth, and being questioned as to the text of the said *auto*, according to its tenor, he said that he left in company of Ensign Bernardo de Medina from the Island of Santa Maria and San Pedro in order to pass to the towns [f.6] of Guale, as he carried an order to do so, where they came across Simón de los Reyes in the town of San Phelipe,[19] who told them that there was no more enemy than a sloop which had entered the town of Guadalquini, and that the Indians of the said town of Guadalquini had made those who came in it [the sloop] prisoners, and had turned them over to Captain Don Juan de Saturnino, lieutenant of the said province, with the vessel, and the said lieutenant remained in the said town. He proceeded on his journey with the said Ensign Bernardo de Medina in search of the said lieutenant, and the following night, arriving near the said town, a canoe passed in front of [the canoe] in which the said ensign and this witness were going, and advised them that the enemy was in the said town with a large ship.[20] They determined to go to the mainland, from which the said ensign dispatched a canoe in search of the said lieutenant, who was on the Island of Guadalquini, and having met on the mainland, they determined to cross again to the said island in search of the enemy with forty men between Spaniards and Indians, and having arrived at a little more than one musket shot from the said town, the said lieutenant [f.6, vto.] sent four Indian archers to reconnoiter the said town, and upon returning, the said Indians said that there were many people, and that they did not wish to lose their lives, and then the said lieutenant determined to return with all the people to the mainland, and what he has said and declared is the truth and what he knows, aware of the oath which he has signed, in which he affirms and ratifies, and he is of the age of fifty-four years. He did not sign, not knowing how to. His Grace the said señor governor signed it.

Juan Márquez Cabrera

Before me,
Alonso Solana
Public and Governmental Notary

Declaration of Lorenzo,
Cacique of Guadalquini

In the city of St. Augustine, Florida, on the seventh of January, sixteen eighty-five, the señor Captain and Sergeant Major Don Juan [f.7] Márquez Cabrera, governor and captain general of this stated city and its provinces for His Majesty, commanded to appear before him Lorenzo, cacique of the town of Guadalquini,[21] who, by means of Juan Bautista,[22] a mariner who performed the office of interpreter, aware of the necessary oath that he made according to law to make use of the said charge, before me, the notary, and by means of the said interpreter, he was sworn in before God and a sign of the cross, in legal form, and having done so, and given him to understand the solemnity and gravity of the oath, he promised to tell the truth, and being questioned according to the tenor of the said auto, he said that being in his town of Guadalquini, the father missionary told him that he should cross to the mainland,[23] as he did, entrusting the guard of the Bar and town to Santiago, a cacique, until he returned, and in this interim a sloop entered with ten Englishmen and anchored next to the said town, and placed three men on land, another three remaining in the boat [*bote*], and the said cacique Santiago came forth with two Indians and imprisoned the three Englishmen, and the others returned with the boat to the said sloop. The said Santiago sent to call upon this witness, giving him an account of what happened, and having come and seen the said sloop anchored, he told one of the Englishmen that he should come forth to the beach [f.7, vto.] and call to those who were in the said sloop [saying] that he would give them quarter, and then they came, and he determined to take them to the council house, placing guards on them. Thursday afternoon he dispatched to the mainland to look for Lieutenant Don Juan de Saturnino, giving him account of what had happened, and the following Saturday, early in the morning, the said lieutenant arrived where this witness found himself with the prisoners and vessel, and he turned them over and said that he should put them in a safe place, sending them to this presidio, and that he should put the vessl in a secure place, and that he would take it to the mainland to hide it. The said lieutenant said that he was tired, and also an order would come to him from this presidio to send them, to which this witness said look, he was not sure, because vessels could pass and see [the sloop] anchored,[24] to which [the lieutenant] said again that he was tired. Then this witness told the said lieutenant how his people found themselves with few provisions, by having withdrawn to the woods, and the said lieutenant responded [f.8] that he should leave him six men in order to make a guard for the said prisoners along with four soldiers that he had, and this witness left him eight men with four firearms [*bocas de fuego*] and four archers, with provisions for everyone. Having gone to the mainland with the rest of the people, preparing provisions to carry to the town for the people and prisoners on Sunday morning. Being [ready] to put himself on the journey at about nine in the morning on the said day, he heard a shot from an [artillery] piece, upon which, having remitted provisions with twelve persons whom he had in front, they arrived in view of the town, where they saw a ship, and next to it the said sloop. Withdrawing another time to where this witness was, seeing what had happened, he sent a small canoe with two men in search of the said lieutenant, with the order that if they found him they should give him those provisions and return to advise him of the place where he [the lieutenant] remained. And the said two men having found the said lieutenant on the Point of Olaya, a quarter league distant from the said town,[25] with the four soldiers and two Indians, by the others having remained hidden in the woods seeing what happened, [f.8, vto.] the said lieutenant, having received the provisions, sent a canoe with one soldier and the said two Indians in search of this witness, so that he should send a canoe in which the said lieutenant might cross to the mainland. This witness being [ready] to send a canoe so that he might withdraw, Ensign Bernardo de Medina arrived in a [canoe] with eight soldiers, whereupon this witness, seeing the reinforcements, named twenty-five well-armed men of his people, and with the said ensign and soldiers, he crossed in search of the said lieutenant. Having found him on the said Point of Olaya, they determined to go to the said town of Guadalquini, and having arrived about one musket shot distant from the said town, they made a halt, and the said lieutenant dispatched three Indians early that morning, who walked around the town without noticing or seeing anyone, and they only saw the ship beached on dry [land] at the landing [*embarcadero*], about half an arquebus shot [distant],[26] and they returned to give this news to the said lieutenant. He said that they should wait until it was day, and at dawn he sent another two Indians, who saw a quantity of people at the landing and town, and the said two Indians having [f.9] returned with this news, the said lieutenant spoke with Ensign Bartolomé Pérez, and this witness said that they would send [word] to hide the three canoes in which they had crossed, and in this interim the said lieutenant determined to cross to the mainland, which they did, where they found out from an Indian who remained hidden that after crossing to the mainland they had burned the town and church, and the vessels were gone by the time that Captain Francisco de Fuentes arrived at the said town with thirty soldiers whom he took at his charge,[27] dispatching a canoe to the mainland to advise the said lieutenant how he had arrived there, with which the said lieutenant embarked in a canoe with the rest of the soldiers whom he had. And what he has said and declared is the truth and what he knows, aware of the oath that he has made, in which he affirms and ratifies, and that he is of the age of forty years, a little more or less. He did not sign, not knowing how to. His Grace the señor governor signed it.

Juan Márquez Cabrera

Before me,
Alonso Solana
Public and Governmental Notary

[f.9, vto]

Declaration of Santiago

In St. Augustine, Florida, on the said day, month, and year, His Grace the said señor governor and captain general, for the said declarations, commanded to appear before him Santiago, cacique of the said town of Guadalquini, who, before me, the notary, and by means of the said Juan Bautista, the interpreter, was sworn in before God and a sign of the cross, in legal form, and having done so, and given him to understand the gravity and solemnity of the oath, he promised to speak the truth, and being read the said *auto*, according to its tenor he said that the cacique Lorenzo having left him as guard of the town of Guadalquini with ten men so that he might watch the Bar and port of the said town, one morning he saw a sloop enter it, and having anchored, six Englishmen came to land in the rowboat, and upon three landing, this witness imprisoned them, and the said boat returned aboard [to the sloop]. This witness sent to advise the said cacique Lorenzo, and having come and turned his town over to him, he made a prisoner come forth to the beach and call to the boat, offering them good quarter, as a result of which came the seven Englishmen who remained in the said sloop, which soon remained high and dry with the low tide. They took the said prisoners, which in all were ten and an English woman, to the council house, and afterward the said cacique sent word to the mainland to advise the Lieutenant Don Juan de Saturnino of what had happened. He came Saturday early in the morning, and [this witness] saw that the said cacique Lorenzo turned the said prisoners and vessel over to the said lieutenant. And after that, about what happened regarding the ship which entered having taken them away, he knows nothing because he was on the mainland until the large ship entered, when he crossed with the said cacique and the soldiers to look for the said lieutenant, whom they found on the Point of Olaia, and they came near the town, from which they dispatched two Indians in the early morning to see where the enemy was. Having returned, and sent other Indians as soon as the day dawned, [this witness] saw that the said lieutenant withdrew along with the rest of the soldiers and Indians, who were about forty persons. Afterward, he found out that Captain Francisco de Fuentes had arrived at the said town with the people whom he led, having found it burned and sacked, and what he has said and declared is the truth and what he knows, aware of the oath [f.10, vto.] which he has made, in which he affirms and ratifies, and he is of the age of thirty years. He did not sign, not knowing how to. His Grace, the said señor governor, signed it.

Juan Márquez Cabrera

Before me,
Alonso Solana
Public and Governmental Notary

[f.11]

Declaration of José Hortio

In the city of St. Augustine, Florida, on the eighth of January, sixteen eighty-five, the señor Captain and Sergeant Major Don Juan Márquez Cabrera, for the said investigation, made appear before him Joseph Hortio, native of the town of Guadalquini, who, by means of Juan Bautista, interpreter, he was sworn in before God and a sign of the cross, in legal form, and having done so, aware of it, he promised to speak the truth, and being questioned according to the tenor of the *auto* which is at the head of this case, to its tenor he said and declared the following: that one Saturday in the morning Lorenzo, cacique of the said town of Guadalquini, turned over seven men so that they might remain in the company of Captain Don Juan de Saturnino, lieutenant of the said province, to guard ten prisoners from a sloop in which they had captured them, and in order to attend to the sentinels of the Bar of the said town, while the said cacique went to the mainland for provisions, and that the following Sunday at dawn this witness came and told the said lieutenant that a launch was entering through the bar, and the said lieutenant came forth [f.11, vto.] from the council house with this witness and Ensign Felipe de Santiago and went to the point of the Bar, one arquebus shot distant from the said town, and not seeing anything, the said lieutenant said that it was a lie, since they did not see it. This witness and the Indian on watch who had seen the launch responded that it must have come to take soundings of the Bar, and gone back in search of the ship, whereupon [the officers] said again that it was a lie and returned to the council house. At the end of a short time, this witness returned and told the said lieutenant that there was a ship which was entering with a launch and a piragua, and then everyone came forth to the landing and saw that it was anchoring, and the lieutenant said "Let's go to San Simón," a place two leagues distant from the said town,[28] to which the said Ensign Felipe de Santiago responded "What is to happen with these prisoners?", and the said lieutenant responded "It's too late," and they went away, leaving the prisoners in the council house. This witness remained with two Indians in order to see what the enemy was doing, and saw that when [the ship] anchored, it fired an [artillery] piece toward the town, and then the pilot of the said sloop came forth from among the [f.12] prisoners to the marina, and with a cloth, and shouting, he called them, and the launch came and took him aboard. The launch and piragua returned at once and disembarked people on land and carried the rest of the prisoners and the sloop aboard, and they began sacking what there was in the houses, and at the end of three days, the set fire to the church and the said town and embarked and went away. On the afternoon of the day they went away, Captain Francisco de Fuentes arrived, and seeing what had happened, he sent word to advise the said lieutenant on the mainland, and then he crossed with the people he had, and what he has said and declared is the truth and what he knows, aware of the oath which he has made, in which he affirms and ratifies, and he is of the age of forty-six years. He did not sign, not knowing how to. His Grace the said señor governor signed it.

Juan Márquez Cabrera

Before me,
Alonso Solana
Public and Governmental Notary

[f.12, vto.]

Auto *to take the Confession of the Prisoner*[29]

In the city of St. Augustine, Florida, on the ninth of January, sixteen eighty-five, the señor Captain and Sergeant Major Don Juan Márquez Cabrera, governor and captain general of this stated city and its provinces for His Majesty, having seen these *autos* and investigation which from the office of Royal Justice have been fulminated against Captain Don Juan de Saturnino Abaurrea for having failed to put the English prisoners and sloop which entered in the port of Guadalquini in a safe place, and for his neglect in the defense, protection, and safekeeping of the towns of the province of Guale, which was in his charge and care as its lieutenant of the governor and captain general, retreating to the woods of the mainland, His Grace told Adjutant Joseph de Beganbre to bring him imprisoned to this royal fort, and that his confession be taken according to the tenor of the beginning of this prosecution, and for this his *auto* he thus provided, commanded, and signed.

Juan Márquez Cabrera

Before me,
Alonso Solana
Public and Governmental Notary

[f.13]

Confession of the Prisoner

In the city of St. Augustine, Florida, on the ninth of January, sixteen eighty-five, the señor Captain and Sergeant Major Don Juan Márquez Cabrera, governor and captain general of this stated city and its provinces for His Majesty, ordered to appear before him Captain Don Juan de Saturnino Abaurea, who was lieutenant of the province of Guale, imprisoned for this process, for the purpose of taking his confession, and, before me, the notary, he was sworn in before God and a sign of the cross, in legal form, and having signed it, aware of it, he promised to tell the truth. The following questions and cross-examinations were made to him: he was questioned how, having the command of lieutenant of the province of Guale at his charge, he left the defense of the said province and crossed to the mainland, and having been able to put a sloop of Englishmen which entered in the town of Guadalquini in a safe place, he let another vessel of the said Englishmen which entered in the port of the said town carry them away, without taking any measures to secure them. He said that, being in the town of Sapala with five Spaniards and eight Indians, by being [in the process of] moving to Santa Maria,[30] he had [f.13, vto.] news by a letter which the missionary of the said Island of Santa Maria wrote to the missionary of the town of Guadalquini about two ships having been seen on the said Island of Santa Maria, and that likewise they said that the enemy had placed the people from six ships on the Beach of San Matheo, a cannon shot from this presidio, in order to take the presidio. With this news, he saw the Indians that he had were somewhat fearful, with which this confessant told them that they should embark the canoes with all the church furnishings and cross with the missionary to the mainland, remaining in his company up to eight Indians armed with firearms and bows, and in this time an Indian arrived at the council house and told this confessant that the towns of [?] Asajo, the Colones, and Guadalquini[31] had gone to the mainland, as he found out by letter from the Father of the said town of Sapala, who was on the mainland, and that they were not there willingly, but rather in order to be there with the Spaniards, having their wives and children on the mainland. [f.14] At this time, he had another letter from the Father of Asajo, in which he gave account that he found himself on the mainland because two piraguas with enemy people had entered, and that they had burned the church, convent, and six houses, upon which, seeing this, and likewise that the Spaniards and Indians said to him "What are we doing here?", he endeavored to cross to the mainland, where he remained until he got news how the Indians who were in the town of Guadalquini had captured a sloop with eleven persons which entered in that Bar. Having crossed with this news and arrived Saturday early in the morning, and the said sloop and eleven prisoners having been turned over to him, he found it not to be the right time to be able to take them to the mainland, it being high tide, and seeing that it was changing, he awaited the next high tide, which would be at about four in the afternoon.[32] Beginning to take them [to the mainland], Ensign Felipe de Santiago returned at the end of three-quarters of an hour and told this confessant that the missionary had said that the cacique Lorenzo had said that that was not the [appropriate hour], and that in the morning he would be there [f.14, vto.] with the canoes. With this, [this confessant] placed three Indians as sentinels, one in the mouth of the Bar and the other two at the landing and anchorage. Before dawn, as the day arrived, the Indian came from the Bar and told this confessant how a piragua was arriving at that port, and with this news he came forth with the said Ensign Felipe de Santiago to find out about it, and not finding the Indian who gave him the news, he left the said ensign in a shed [*baraca*[33]] and passed onward. Seeing that the Indian was missing, he returned to where the said ensign was, and the two of them went up to the post of the sentinel, and not having seen anything, he returned to the council house. In a little while another Indian arrived and told this confessant how there was a ship which was entering in the landing, and having come forth with the said Indian to the shore [*marina*], he saw the ship a little more or less than one musket shot from the landing, with which he sent the Indian to the council house to tell them to kill the Englishmen. When this confessant arrived at the said council house, he was already tired, and seeing that they had not done it, and that the soldiers said that neither the Indians nor they had wished to do so, they retreated to the Point of Olaia until they came to look for him at the end of two days, [f.15] giving him news that Ensign Bernardo de Medina had arrived there as reinforcements with six soldiers, with which he crossed to the mainland and returned to the Island of Guadalquini with twenty-seven armed Indians and ten soldiers. Having arrived within a musket shot from the town, he sent three Indians ahead to see what there was of the enemy, and having returned and said how they had been in the council house and had not seen one candle, nor heard a sound of people, and that the sloop was at the stern of the ship, and that this was before daybreak, with a clear moon.[34] Although he wanted to go with the people to the council house and town, they told him that the enemy might be lying in ambush where he wished to go, and might kill them, as a result of which he postponed his entrance until it was daylight and he saw where the enemy was. As soon as it was daylight, although he wanted to go to the village, the Indians told him that they did not have more than one charge of powder,[35] and His Grace, the said señor governor, asking this confessant what he had done with the jar [botija] with eleven pounds of powder, and the hundred and ninety-six balls that the said Ensign Felipe de Santiago had brought him only a few days before, in addition to what his predecessor turned over to him, he said that it had been left on the mainland [f.15, vto.] where he had withdrawn, and that through the interpreters [*atequies*] the Indians said that they did not want to fight, the spies having come and said how the enemy was in the church and convent. He endeavored to retreat or traverse to the mainland, where he remained until Captain Francisco de Fuentes arrived with the infantry and vessels that were going in search of the enemy, and then he crossed again to the said town of Guadalquini, where he found it burned. The said Captain Francisco de Fuentes returning to this presidio, this confessant returned to the mainland until he was replaced by Adjutant Grabiel Salguero,[36] and what he has said and declared is the truth and what happened, aware of the oath which he has signed, in which he affirms and ratifies, and he is of the age of thirty-one years, a little more or less, and he signed it together with His Grace the said señor governor.

Juan Saturnino de Abaurrea

Juan Marquez Cabrera

Before me,
Alonso Solana
Public and Governmental Notary

[f.16]

Declaration of Guilt and Charge[37]

In the city of St. Augustine, Florida, on the tenth of January, sixteen eighty-five, the señor Captain and Sergeant Major Don Juan Márquez Cabrera, governor and captain general of this stated city and its provinces for His Majesty, having seen these *autos* and the guilt that emerges from them against Captain Don Juan de Saturnino Abaurrea, *reformado* of this presidio, and who was lieutenant of the province of Guale, about not having fulfilled the obligation of his office, said that he was pronouncing and did pronounce him guilty and charged with everything that emerges against him from the *autos,* so that within the limit of six days he should prove and dispute in his favor whatever suits him, with all charges of publication, conclusion, and citation for the sentence, and within the same limit the witnesses should ratify the summary [of their testimony], and for this his *auto* His Grace thus provided, commanded, and signed.

Juan Márquez Cabrera

Before me,
Alonso Solana
Public and Governmental Notary

[f.16, vto.]

In the city of St. Augustine, Florida, on the tenth of January, sixteen eighty-five, I, the notary, notified and made this *auto* on the other side [of this folio] known, as is contained in it, to Captain Don Juan de Saturnino Abaurrea, a prisoner in the royal fort of this presidio, in person. He heard and understood. To this I swear.

Alonso Solana
Public and Governmental Notary

[f.19]

In the city of St. Augustine, Florida, on the tenth of January, sixteen eighty-five, the señor Captain and Sergeant Major Don Juan Márquez Cabrera, governor and captain general of this stated city and its provinces for His Majesty, commanded to appear before him Lorenzo, cacique of the town of Guadalquini, for the purpose of ratifying[38] a statement and declaration which he made in the summary of this case on the [seventh[39]] of this present month before His Grace, for which, before me, the notary, he was sworn before God and a sign of the cross, in legal form, and having done so, aware of it, he promised to speak the truth, and the said witness being read his statement and declaration word for word, he said that he said all that is written in it, according to and as is contained in it, and it only occurs to him to add, having reflected upon his memory, that at the time and when the aid of the eight soldiers arrived, the said Captain Don Juan de Saturnino, who was lieutenant, arrived at the same time, by him having sent two Indians to the mainland, where this witness was, to call upon him. Having said in the preceding declaration that the said lieutenant had arrived after the aid of the eight soldiers was an error of this witness, and that all that is written in his said declaration and in this one is the truth, [f.17, vto.] it having happened thus, aware of the oath that he has made, in which he affirms and ratifies, and being necessary, he states it again. He did not sign, not knowing how to. His Grace, the said señor governor, made a paraph.

Juan Márquez Cabrera

Before me,
Alonso Solana
Public and Governmental Notary

In St. Augustine, Florida, on the said day, month, and year, His Grace the said señor governor and captain general commanded to appear before him Santiago, cacique of the town of Guadalquini, for the purpose of ratifying a statement and declaration which he made in the summary of this case on the seventh of this present month and year before His Grace and me, the notary, [f.18] for which, by means of the said Juan Bautista, the interpreter, he was sworn in before God and a sign of the cross, in legal form, and having done so, aware of it, he promised to speak the truth, and being read his said declaration word for word, and given to understand it by the said interpreter, he said that all that is written in it is certain and true, as is contained in it, and being necessary, he says it again, by being the truth, aware of the oath which he has made, in which he affirms and ratifies. He did not sign, not knowing how to. His Grace, the said señor governor, made his rubric.

Juan Márquez Cabrera

Before me,
Alonso Solana
Public and Governmental Notary

[f.18, vto.]

Another

In St. Augustine, Florida, on the said day, month, and year, His Mercy the said señor governor and captain general commanded to appear before him Joseph Hortis, native of the town of Guadalquini, for the purpose of ratifying a statement and declaration which he made before His Grace in the summary of this case, for which before me, the notary, and by means of the said interpreter, he was sworn in before God and a sign of the cross, in legal form, and having done so, aware of it, he promised to say the truth, and being read his said declaration word for word, and given to understand it by the said interpreter, he said that he said and declared all that is written in it according to and how is contained in it, and being necessary he says it again, by being the truth, aware of the oath which he has made, in which he affirms and ratifies. He did not sign, not knowing how to. His Grace, the said señor governor, made a rubric.

Juan Márquez Cabrera

Before me,
Alonso Solana
Public and Governmental Notary

[f.19]

Another, of Phelipe de Santiago

In the city of St. Augustine, Florida, on the fourteenth of January of sixteen eighty-five, the señor Captain and Sergeant Major Don Juan Márquez Cabrera, governor and captain general of this stated city and its provinces for His Majesty, commanded to appear before him Ensign Felipe de Santiago for the purpose of ratifying a statement and declaration which he made before His Grace in the summary of this case on the first day of this present month and year, for which, before me, the notary, he was sworn in before God and a sign of the cross, in legal form, and having done so, aware of it, he promised to tell the truth, and being read his said declaration word for word, he said that all that is written in it is certain and true, and this witness said it as is contained in it, and furthermore, being necessary, he says it again, by being the truth, aware of the oath which he has signed, in which he affirms and ratifies, and he signed it together with His Grace the said señor governor, who made his paraph.

Felipe de Santiago

Juan Márquez Cabrera

Before me,
Alonso Solana
Public and Governmental Notary

[f.19, vto.]

Ratification of Juan de Peñalossa

In the city of St. Augustine, Florida, on the fourteenth of the month of January of sixteen eighty-five, His Grace the said señor governor and captain general commanded to appear before him Juan de Peñalossa, a soldier of this presidio, for the purpose of ratifying a statement and declaration which he made before His Grace in the summary of this case, for which, before me, the notary, he was sworn in before God and a sign of the cross, in legal form, and having done so, aware of it, he promised to tell the truth, and being read his said declaration word for word, which is in folios five and six of the *autos*, he said that he said and declared thus all that is written in it, by being the truth, and being necessary, he says it again, and in it he affirms and ratifies, aware of the oath which he has made, and he did not sign, not knowing how to. His Grace signed it.

Juan Márquez Cabrera

Before me,
Alonso Solana
Public and Governmental Notary

[f.20]

Ratification of Ensign Bernardo de Medina

In the city of St. Augustine, Florida on the fourteenth of the month of January of sixteen eighty-five, the said señor governor and captain general commanded to appear before him Ensign Bernardo de Medina, *reformado* of this presidio, for the purpose of ratifying a statement and declaration which he made in the summary of this case on the fourth of this present month before His Grace and me, the notary, for which he was sworn in before God and a sign of the cross, in legal form, and having done so, he promised to speak the truth, and being read his said declaration word for word, he said that all which he has said and declared in his said declaration he said as is written in it, and in it he affirms and ratifies, by being the truth, and furthermore he says it again, aware of the oath which he has made, in which he affirms and ratifies. He declared himself to be of the stated [age], and he signed it together with His Grace the said señor governor and captain general.

Bernardo de Medina

Juan Márquez Cabrera

Before me,
Alonso Solana
Public and Governmental Notary

[f.21]

Captain Don Juan Saturnino de Abaurrea, *reformado* of this presidio, and a prisoner in the royal fort, as is most suitable to my rights, I appear before Your Lordship in the most proper form for which there is occasion in my favor[40] in the criminal case which, in the office of royal justice, has been brought against me about having failed in the defense, guard, and custody of the province of Guale, where I found myself as lieutenant at the time that the enemy infested it with the entrance in its villages, and also about not having put in a safe place the prisoners and sloop which entered at peace, and who were imprisoned in the town of Obadalquini, from which a charge results against me by the declarations of the summary, which appears by the *autos* of the said case by means of my being notified by the *auto* of guilt and charge for having failed the obligations at my charge, which I obtained, conceding me the limit of six consecutive days for my rebuttal, conforming to which, according to the tenor and context of the said general and subsequent *autos*, I say that as is on record by my confession, at the time and when I had notice that six vessels found themselves upon this port, and that two of them had placed people on land at the port of Santa Maria, I found myself with a scant number of soldiers in the town of Sapala, capital [*cavezera*] of the said province, and the site of its presidio,[41] attending to the removal of the said [town], the large part of [the people] of which found themselves on the mainland with their property, fearful since the preceding enemy,[42] and this without canoes in which to be able to descend to scour the province and give news of the designs or movements of the enemy, or for the opposition, resistance, and defense, due to those which I could have used being away, as will be on record from what Captain Francisco de Fuentes carried to the village of Santa Maria at the time that he found himself there, loaded with the utensils [*trastos* [43]] of the natives of the said town who were moving themselves, and some mediocre [canoes] which were to be found on the mainland for the needs of the women and men who found themselves withdrawn. Having had notice of the said enemy having entered the town of Asajo, one day's journey from the said [town],[44] suspecting that they might obtain notice of the few people with which I found myself, like those who were serving [f.21, vto.] on the said mainland, finding myself with not one defense, and not having more than up to eight Indians, and these, together with the said infantry insisting that we should not await the enemy in the said town, but rather that we should cross to the mainland to join with the remaining people and defend ourselves as we could, in which consideration, not finding myself with sufficient forces for the defense, I ordered that they should embark the ornaments and property of the church, and with them and the people with whom I found myself I crossed to the mainland for the expressed reasons and grounds, where I remained until the missionary of Asajo gave me news of a sloop with eleven persons having entered in the village of Obadalquini, at which notice I immediately placed myself on the journey, where I encountered news from the cacique of Obadalquini of a sloop with the said eleven persons having entered in that port at peace in order to reinforce themselves with provisions and equip themselves with what was necessary. I arrived at the said town on Saturday at dawn, where I found the said prisoners and sloop, which the said cacique turned over to me, and having the said sloop in custody at the landing in the said [town], considering its little security, by being located in the mouth of a Bar, and the enemy on those coasts being able to discover it while passing, I determined to secure it, sending it to the mainland, for which effect I named Ensign Felipe de Santiago, with the necessary equipment and three of the said prisoners, who said they were Christians, so that they might assist in taking the said sloop, and likewise to leave them secured in the place where the people of the said village found themselves withdrawn. When I imagined that the said ensign was on his way, he returned at the end of three quarters of an hour and told me that he could not take [the sloop] by not being [high] tide now, and that the said cacique had told him that if they took it, they could not arrive at a time when the missionary of the said doctrina, who was going on the same occasion, could say mass, and thus he should leave it off, and on the next day he would return for him. The said cacique having already gone to the mainland with the equipment with which to be able to withdraw [the sloop], he remained prepared for the following day [f.22], by not having been able to do more, as I express. I having been with all vigilance in guarding the said prisoners and in that of the said sloop, and in the watch of the Bar, early in the morning on Sunday, finding myself in the council house of the said village, one of the sentinels of the Bar advised me that a launch was entering, at which notice I went to the said Bar, taking in my company the said Ensign Felipe de Santiago, and by actions which I took, I could not discover anything, and at the end of a long time that I was occupied in this, I returned to the said council house not having found out anything new, and then at dawn one of the sentinels informed me that a vessel was entering through the Bar of the said port, at which I came forth to the landing with all speed, and at the time I arrived, the said vessel anchored, and recognizing it to be certain that they would place people on land next, without giving me occasion to be able to free the said sloop, by being close to it, and likewise to the said prisoners, I sent the order to the soldiers and Indians who found themselves in the said council house that they should kill the said prisoners, now that they could not be saved due to the shortness of time which the case promised, in which supposition, returning to the council house, I found that they had not complied with the said order to kill them, by the said soldiers and Indians saying that they did not wish to do so, at which, seeing that I could not place it in execution, nor withdraw them either, I left them and retreated with the people that I had to the Point of Olaya, on the said Island, where I remained until at the end of two days notice arrived that Ensign Bernardo de Medina had arrived on the mainland with six soldiers. Having crossed and joined with the said [ensign], I returned to the said Island with twenty-seven armed Indians and ten soldiers, and setting out for the said town, I arrived in view of it at the dawn watch [*quarto de el alba*[45]] and sent three spies to reconnoiter whether the said enemy was to be found in it, and upon returning they said that there was no sign of them, and that the said sloop was there, and that they had it secured at the stern of the said ship. Seeing that the day was coming, I wanting to pass to the said town, the people that I took told me [f.22, vto.] that I should not do so, because they might be waiting in ambush, as they were sleeping in the open, and by cutting us off, something bad could happen to us. Considering this, I detained myself until the daylight, and to see the position of the said enemy. Setting out, the said Indians who carried firearms told me that they did not have more than one charge of powder with which to fire, and the spies likewise having brought notice how the enemies found themselves fortified behind the wall of the convent, and that they did not wish to fight because they had nothing to defend but their lives, and as the village gave them nothing, they should burn it when they had secured their wives, children, and posessions, for which reason, I, not being able to get them to follow me, I retreated in consideration of the fact that without the help of the said Indians, I could not do any damage to the said enemy when they found themselves having made a fort in a place which is [a fort] in itself, because the infantry were no more than ten men, and with those, and one can imagine the effect I could have made, and even more finding myself without munitions, because although it is true that I had them in the said presidio [of Sapala], not preparing for the contingency, I did not take more than that necessary for the infantry who accompanied me, being credible what the said Ensign Felipe de Santiago declares, that finding me in the said presidio, he urged me to come forth to encounter the enemy at the town of Asajo, as he expresses in his declaration with other reasons, when he will not prove or assure [?] not having withdrawn the said sloop and three prisoners when I ordered him to, for which reason it was not secured, nor could I have done more in this case than to order it, when it was necessary for me to keep custody of the remaining prisoners until having a reply from Your Lordship regarding the resolution which was to be taken, and what was to be done with them, because although it is true that it was unavoidable after seeing the said vessel not to kill the said prisoners, it was not without the understanding that it ought not be done, but rather being obligated from not being able to free them, because in reason I should not have done so when they had entered in the said port under the assurance of the peace which they obtained with us, passing in transit on their voyage and finding themselves without any sustenance or equipment with which to be able to proceed, as is manifest, and being seen and recognized not to be bringing even one offensive or defensive weapon, not necessarily being, when it was not clear to me, that they were enemies in the protection of those who found themselves on those coasts, in which presumption I gave notice of the form which was to be observed, without being the master nor having action to perform anything, in understanding that the resolution which had to be was for me to order that they be given sustenance and the rest of what they needed for the prosecution of their journey, as I have seen done in this presidio, and has been done in the present time with those who have entered in transit to relieve themselves. Bearing this in mind, being the time of all these occurrences, the guilt should not be attributed to me for the contingencies of one day, and for that which was not my responsibility, when there was not time to determine or perform anything else, because now that the preceding—not being able to have freed the said sloop for the lack of the tide, equipment, and the rest of the reasons—had happened, in the last instance of the entrance of the said ship [*bajel*] in the same form, there was an even greater impossibility, since it was anchored in the same place, and being so near one could not set fire to it or perform any other action, and consequently afterwards, having advanced to the said convent where the said enemies found themselves fortified, due to their strength and force of people, as well as finding myself with only ten soldiers, because the twenty-seven Indians were now divided, and I could not expect any help, since as is on record from the declarations of the summary, my statement has been confirmed that they told me they did not wish to fight when they did not have anything to defend but their lives, and they did not wish to risk them, what results against me in the declaration of the said Ensign Felipe de Santiago not being nor needing to be of any harm to me when it is not compatible that [a person] subject to such reasons should advance against a superior [enemy] when there were no grounds to do so, if everyone urged me not to await the enemy in the said presidio [of Sapala], if I passed to the mainland from which I did not leave for the said province due to the lack of canoes and the scarcity of infantry, because the natives are of no help when they all find themselves withdrawn in the woods, and if it is not the fervor of the infantry, they were not going to accompany me, because to defend and go to the rescue of as many ports as there are in the said province, it is necessary to have enough people and time to do so, and when I lack one and another [of these things], it is not admirable to address the formal point of what happened, for all of which, in attention to all of the verifications and foundations alleged and expressed on my behalf, and all the rest which could have been favored me by the unobserved and unexpected occurrence of the entrance of the said ship and freeing of the said prisoners in the time as short as that of one day in which everything happened, and also by the unfavorable declarations not being able to do me harm, by being from [opposing] sides, consisting in the same lack, being precisely for his own defense to charge me with his defects by means of imploring and being aided by all the favor of the law which I have or could have in my favor.

I ask and implore that Your Lordship be pleased to substantiate and determine this case with the attention which is merited by the impossibility which I found myself of being able to attend to the movements of the enemy in the said province, by being in the process of attending to the removal of the town of Sapala, and finding myself due to this reason without a canoe with which to do so or a force of people to put up a defense or secure the prisoners and sloop in the shortness of the time and in the opportunity which I lacked to withdraw the said sloop with the contingent, unforseen, and unexpected case of the entrance of the said ship, and also with the infantry not having fulfilled nor observed the order which I gave to kill them, finding myself obliged to do so [withdraw], and lacking any other remedy, and in the same manner not having advanced to the said enemy through my having lacked the said Indians, like all the rest of the reasons expressed and alleged, admitting in part that if I deserve some punishment [it is for] the retreat and departure which I had to achieve, since to the letter of my obligations, the said demonstration seems to be enough, as consequently to attend to the harm which resulted upon me from the pressure in which I found myself due to my needs; upon doing so [the above] with the attention which I hope, Your Lordship will be able to act with the justification which I need, which is what is suitable and done in my favor.

Juan Saturnino de Abaurrea

Since this petition was presented, place it with the *autos* and bring them so as to see and provide justice.

The señor Captain and Sergeant Major Don

Juan Márquez Cabrera, governor and captain general of this city and presidio of St. Augustine, Florida, and its provinces for His Majesty, provided this,[46] and made his paraph on it on the fifteenth of January, sixteen eighty-five.

Before me,
Alonso Solana
Public and Governmental Notary

[f.25]

In the lawsuit and criminal case in the office of Royal justice [–] against Captain Don Juan Saturnino Abaurrea, who was lieutenant of the governor and captain general of the provinces of Guale, about his oversight, carelessness, and negligence in the protection, custody, and defense of the towns of the said province, and also in putting in a safe and secure place the sloop and eleven prisoners who entered in the town of Obadalquini on the pretext of lacking provisions, having seen the *autos* and the rest, it is suitable that I find, heedful of the *autos* and merits of the case, that I ought to condemn and do condemn the said Captain Don Juan Saturnino Abaurrea to having his post as soldier, which he has in the entries and royal books, removed, and that for the time of ten years he shall not be able to obtain an office or honorific post in these provinces,[47] bearing in mind what is on record in the said case about having been careless and negligent in not having defended the towns of the said province of Guale, and about having been able to place the said sloop and eleven prisoners in a safe and secure place on the mainland as soon as he arrived at the said Island of Guadalquini, for which I order and command the principal accountant of the Royal Hacienda to remove the post of soldier of the said Captain Don Juan Saturnino and place the certification of having done so at the bottom of the page of this sentence,[48] and [I order] the lieutenant of the royal fort to set him free by virtue of it, and place this my sentence [f.25, vto.] definitively, judging the pronouncement thus, and I sign, with costs.

Juan Márquez Cabrera

The sentence above was given and pronounced by the señor Captain and Sergeant Major Don Juan Márquez Cabrera, governor and captain general of this city and presidio of St. Augustine, Florida, and its provinces for His Majesty, making a public audience[49] today, the day of the date, January seventeenth, sixteen eighty-five. Witnesses Sergeant Bernardo Nieto de Carval and Diego Poldenava, residents in this said city.

Before me,
Alonso Solana
Public and Governmental Notary

The post of soldier remains annotated in virtue of this sentence against the aforementioned [Saturnino de Abaurrea], with a note of it in the register of his account and station. St. Augustine, January 17, 1685.

Don Francisco de Zigarroa

In St. Augustine, Florida, on the seventeenth of [f.26] January, sixteen eighty-five, I, the notary, notified and made known in person the sentence on the previous folio, as is contained in it, to Captain Don Juan de Saturnino Abaurrea, a prisoner in the royal fort of this presidio, who heard and understood it, being witnesses Ensign Sebastian López, Ensign Francisco Aldeco, and Squad Leader Francisco de Pedrosa, and many other infantrymen who found themselves present.

Alonso Solana
Public and Governmental Notary

In St. Augustine, Florida, on the said day, month, and year, I, the said notary, made the said sentence known in person to Captain Francisco de Fuentes, lieutenant of the said royal fort, who heard and understood it. I swear,

Alonso Solana
Public and Governmental Notary

A copy of this sentence and the remaining actions which follow was taken on the second of May, 1689.[50]

[paraph]

I received ten pesos and six reales in fees from this case from the señor judge and mine.

Solana

I left a copy of these *autos* written on sixty folios. Florida, the sixth of August, seventeen thirty-nine.

Castilla[51]

NOTES

1. This cover sheet was drafted by the 18th-century notary Francisco de Castilla as an introduction to the original *autos* dating to 1685, which he had taken directly from the Governmental Archive of St. Augustine in 1739.

2. This folio served as the original 17th-century cover sheet for the *autos* compiled in this case. The heading "Criminal" refers to the nature of the case being tried, and following this is a brief description of the charges and a notation regarding the judge and notary employed for the trial.

3. This section serves as the introduction to the trial that follows and describes the specific allegations being made against the defendant. This *auto* was then read to each of the called witnesses, who then responded to this summary.

4. Recognizing that the notary Alonso Solana was recording oral testimony, he does not seem to have settled upon a uniform spelling of the Indian name Guadalquini until reaching the third folio of the case, well into the testimony of the first witness. Solana spelled the name no fewer than five ways (Guadalquini, Hoadalquini, Oadalquini, Guadalquine, Guadarquine) before deciding upon the first. This serves to reinforce the fact that Indian names were recorded phonetically by Spanish notaries, and thus are often spelled differently from document to document.

5. Other evidence indicates that this number was actually only eight (confirmed by their leader in his testimony below). The fact that this number corresponds to the declaration of the first witness, Ensign Felipe de Santiago, suggests that Santiago was the principal source for Márquez Cabrera's initial accusations.

6. Here begins the testimony of witnesses called for the case against Captain Saturnino de Abaurrea. In most cases, each declaration raised specific points that required verification by separate witnesses, many of whom were then called for testimony. In this case, declarations were ultimately taken from six witnesses prior to the confession of the prisoner himself.

7. The initial landing took place to the north of St. Augustine, just south of the mouth of the modern St. Johns River, on September 30, 1684.

8. The Guale missions of Santa Catalina and Satuache had already completed their move to Santa Maria, a village site previously abandoned by the pagan Yamassee who inhabited it during the 1670s and early 1680s (see Overview). The identity of the friar is unclear from the documentary sources. It might have been Fray Simón de Salas, who ultimately resettled with the inhabitants of Santa Catalina, Satuache, and Sapala in mission Santa Maria (although Salas may have been the friar who was still at Sapala during the pirate raid of October 1684).

9. The friar stationed at San Buenaventura de Guadalquini during the pirate assault of 1684 was Fray Pedro de Luna (Luna, 1686), who had been stationed there at least once before nearly a decade earlier (Arcos, 1675).

10. A *balandra* was a small sailing vessel with two masts, primarily used along the coastlines.

11. The *fragata* was a substantially larger vessel, with as many as three masts, and a more sizable crew complement and armament.

12. Ensign Medina's party had been dispatched northward from an earlier encounter with the pirates at mission San Juan del Puerto (see Medina's testimony below).

13. Here Santiago backtracks in his testimony, relating events that occurred prior to the preceding testimony.

14. Other documents locate this village (also known as San Simón) in the immediate vicinity of modern Fort Frederica on St. Simons Island. The 13-league distance cited by Santiago corresponds well to the actual distance of travel by canoe (using the winding channels of the Intracoastal Waterway), and not to the straight-line distance between Sapala and the village of the Colones.

15. The original manuscript reads "Señor Cappitan, si bamos a buscar el enemigo aqui le tenemos uste mira por su credito que el peor cuchillo que a de tener e de ser yo." The last portion of this quote is difficult to interpret, and if the last words were retranscribed as "deserto," the passage might easily translate as "Look after your credit, since the worst cut to be had is desertion."

16. The term *botijuela* is the diminutive form of *botija*, which is a rounded earthen jar with a short, narrow neck. This almost certainly corresponds to what archaeologists refer to as the olive jar, fragments of which are common elements in Spanish missions of this era.

17. Based on the testimony of one of the sloop's crew, a Flemish sailor named Juan Clar (see Document 11 below), it seems evident that the members of this group were victims of unfortunate timing, since their innocent landing at Guadalquini as a stopover on the way to the northern English colonies occurred during the unrelated pirate raids of October 1684. Not only were they captured and held by the Indians of Guadalquini as a result, but they were also subsequently taken aboard Captain Jacob Everson's pirate frigate for ransom in Charles Town.

18. The preceding passage refers to an earlier encounter with the pirates, in which Sergeant Major Pedro de Aranda y Avellaneda was dispatched to the lookout post called Las Cañuelas (meaning "the canebrakes," situated along the shore be-

tween San Juan del Puerto and St. Augustine), where 11 pirates who had put ashore looking for supplies were captured (Wright, 1960). Following an exchange of fire at the mouth of the St. Johns River to the north, at least two groups of Spanish infantry (under Captain Fuentes and Ensign Medina) marched north in pursuit of the raiders (see Overview).

19. San Phelipe was located on modern Cumberland Island, some 3 leagues north of the abandoned Yamassee village at San Pedro.

20. This encounter probably occurred in or just south of modern St. Simons Sound, as Peñalosa's canoe approached Guadalquini Mission on the southern end of St. Simons Island.

21. Don Lorenzo de Santiago was the 40-year old principal cacique of San Buenaventura de Guadalquini, whose testimony appears later in this court record. This important Mocama leader would ultimately ascend to the top leadership position in the last remaining aggregate Mocama mission of San Juan del Puerto, following its fusion with Guadalquini's population between 1695 and 1697 (see the Overview, and the visitation of Santa Cruz y San Buenaventura in Document 9).

22. This may have been the Timucuan language interpreter Juan Bauptista de la Cruz, who had served in that same function during the pacification of the Timucuan Rebellion of 1656 (Worth, 1992), and who would have been some 54 years old in 1685.

23. Fray Luna was presumably responding to the news he had received from Santa Maria that pirates were headed in their direction.

24. Given the location of Mission San Buenaventura de Guadalquini on the southern tip of St. Simons Island, probably at the modern lighthouse, the cacique Lorenzo was correct in saying that any ship passing across St. Simons Sound (then the Bar of Guadalquini) would be able to spot the sloop anchored next to the mission.

25. Presuming that the mission of Guadalquini was indeed located at or near the modern St. Simons lighthouse, the Point of Olaya may have been the point of land just west of this location, closest to Jekyll Island, and facing the southwest. Contrarily, it might also have been the point of land to the east of Mission Guadalquini, where Oglethorpe's 18th-century Delegal's fort was later situated (now eroded into the sea).

26. The pirate frigate was undoubtedly resting just off the shore of the Guadalquini boat landing due to low tide that night.

27. Captain Fuentes, the acting lieutenant of the Castillo de San Marcos in St. Augustine, had chased the pirates up the Florida and Georgia coasts beginning after the skirmish at Mission San Juan del Puerto (see Overview).

28. San Simón was a village of the pagan Colones, evidently located at or very near modern Fort Frederica to the north.

29. The following *auto* provides for the arrest of Captain Saturnino de Abaurrea based on the preceding testimony, and orders that his own statement, termed a confession, be taken.

30. As discussed in greater detail in the Overview, the pirate attack of October 1684 caught Lieutenant Saturnino de Abaurrea in the middle of relocating the remaining missions of Guale southward. San Joseph de Sapala, the former garrison headquarters of Guale, had already been largely depopulated, with its inhabitants waiting on the mainland for the final evacuation.

31. These three towns constituted the entire Indian population of St. Simons Island.

32. Lieutenant Saturnino de Abaurrea must have realized that with the tide already going out, there was not enough time before low tide to be able to sail the sloop to the sheltered mainland location (the shallow channels of the marshes would have beached the craft), forcing him to await the next high tide, late in the afternoon.

33. Although it can refer simply to a hut, the term *barraca* probably designated a type of storage shed, perhaps alongside the canoe landing. The usage of this term is unique here, contrasting with the common designation of *buhio* during this era for both domestic and public structures (see discussion by Hann, 1991a: 386).

34. The full moon during the month of October 1684 occurred on Sunday, October 22. This information, along with other contextual clues from this and other documentary sources, assists in fixing the date of these events during the weekend of October 21–22, 1684. Saturnino de Abaurrea's Indian scouts were sent out the following Tuesday night, just two days after the full moon.

35. Saturnino de Abaurrea's preceding statement seems to have surprised Governor Márquez Cabrera, prompting the direct question that follows immediately in the text. In Saturnino de Abaurrea's later written defense, he elaborated upon this point.

36. Captain Saturnino de Abaurrea appears to have stayed on the mainland with the remaining refugees from the missions disrupted by the pirate raid until Governor Márquez Cabrera had him recalled, replacing him as provincial lieutenant with Adjutant Salguero. This action undoubtedly resulted from rumors of Saturnino de Abaurrea's inaction during the crisis, probably reported principally by Ensign Felipe de Santiago, who must have returned with Fuentes due to his illness.

37. This auto formally charged Captain Saturnino de Abaurrea with guilt in the crimes described previously, and provided for his notifi-

cation in the prison of the Castillo. He was then given six days to prepare whatever kind of defense he wished, during which time all the previous witnesses were recalled for ratification of their statements.

38. Following the declaration of guilt, each witness who had previously testified was recalled in order to legally ratify his statement. This step presumably gave each witness the opportunity to alter or recant his testimony (in this case only the cacique Lorenzo modified his earlier statement).

39. The notary Solana left a blank space here, but never filled it in with the correct date.

40. The following document was handwritten by Captain Saturnino de Abaurrea in his prison cell at the Castillo de San Marcos in St. Augustine, and it served as his last opportunity to disculpate himself of the charges brought against him by the governor, or at least to ameliorate his punishment. While some of the material within his defense repeated his earlier verbal confession, more details were provided on specific points, and a plea was made to the governor to consider various mitigating circumstances.

41. This passage refers to the fact that the provincial garrison was located in the mission of Sapala at that time (and had been since the retreat from Santa Catalina in May 1680).

42. Early in the summer of 1683, the notorious French pirate known as Agramon had descended upon Guale, sacking missions San Juan and San Phelipe (see Bushnell 1994, and the Overview).

43. The term *trastos* refers to domestic items such as furniture or utensils (such as pots).

44. Asajo was the nearest mission south of Sapala, located some 6–7 leagues away. The mission of Sapala was the next likely target for the pirates heading northward.

45. The *quarto de él alba* is a military reference to the last quarter of the night watch preceding sunrise. The sun set on the preceding Tuesday evening just before 7 p.m., with dawn arriving on Wednesday, October 25, at just after 7 a.m., placing Saturnino de Abaurrea's arrival perhaps around 3 a.m. in the morning.

46. Solana certified here that Governor Márquez Cabrera had written the above note after receiving Saturnino de Abaurrea's letter of defense.

47. The sentence handed down by Governor Márquez Cabrera against Captain Saturnino de Abaurrea amounted to a dishonorable discharge for the space of 10 years, during which time he was effectively cut off without royal pay, and without any possibility for advancement (or even participation) in the military structure of St. Augustine. Nevertheless, this decision seems to have been reversed by Governor Márquez Cabrera's successor, since in 1701, Royal Accountant Juan de Pueyo certified that although Saturnino de Abaurrea's post was erased on January 17, 1685, he was reinstated on May 10, 1687 as a result of another *auto* (Pueyo, 1701). More than a decade after his trial, Saturnino de Abaurrea was once again listed as a captain in St. Augustine, requesting a future post for his minor son (Saturnino de Abaurrea, 1696).

48. The requested certification, along with various others, appears below.

49. The sentence was read publicly, perhaps in the plaza of the Castillo, or in the town of St. Augustine itself.

50. The identity of this individual, and the reason for which this copy was made, is not currently known.

51. The notary Castilla here left his obligatory note stating that he left a transcription archived in St. Augustine.

DOCUMENT 11: THE SPANISH INVASION OF CAROLINA, 1686

INTRODUCTION

In August of 1686, Governor Don Juan Márquez Cabrera sponsored a retaliatory strike against the English colony of Carolina, venturing to within 10 leagues of Charles Town itself in an attempt to rid the northern coast of enemy presence (see Hortelano, 1686; Juan, 1686; Moore et al., 1686; Márquez Cabrera, 1687; Quiroga y Losada, 1687; Torre, 1687; Barios, 1688; Dunlop, 1688; Penate, 1688; San Payo 1688; Crane, 1956; Bushnell, 1994; and below). The raid followed three years of nearly constant English-supported assaults on Spanish Florida, including the Grammont pirate raid of 1683, the Jingle pirate raid of 1684, the Yamassee invasion of Timucua in 1685, and yet another pirate raid by Grammont in 1686. Furthermore, the Scottish colony of Stuart's Town, illegally established in late 1684 on Santa Elena Island within Spanish territory, had remained a constant source of irritation for Governor Márquez Cabrera over the past year and a half, and the expedition was specifically directed to extirpate the invaders from their island home.

In response to a direct request for aid by Governor Márquez Cabrera, the Governor of Havana dispatched two galliots,[1] including *El Rosario*, led by Captain Alejandro Thomás de León, an experienced pirate hunter in the coastal guard of the Indies, and another, *Nuestra Señora de Regla*, based in Havana under the command of Pedro Hortelano. In St. Augustine, these two vessels were outfitted for the expedition and joined by a third galliot that had been taken from the pirate Grammont during his last raid. Manned by volunteers without official posts in Florida (including at least one slave), the presidio's galliot was sent north under León's overall command on a mission to push the Carolina frontier back within its legal bounds.[2] Stopping by the newly aggregated refugee towns of the former Guale and Mocama provinces on modern Amelia Island during early August, León convinced a number of Guale Indians to join the expedition, promising them that "whatever they might be able to take in pillage would be theirs" beyond the profits from any silver or black slaves, to be divided evenly among the members of the expedition (Agustín et al., 1686).

Arriving on August 17 to find Stuart's Town freshly deserted, the expedition captured a hapless Scottish boy before putting the settlement to the torch, and pushed northward three days later in pursuit of the fleeing colonists. Now navigating within the recognized bounds of Carolina, León's three galliots made landfall again on Edisto Island before August 24, plundering several English plantations, including those of Governor Joseph Morton and his secretary Paul Grimball. Capturing 2 young indentured servants and 11 black slaves, the Spanish corsairs proceeded to sack the plantations, carrying off silver and other goods, including the spoils of recent English raids on Campeche and the Timucuan mission of Santa Catalina.

Following its early success, the León raid was destined for disaster, for on August 26, the unexpected arrival of a hurricane with unfortunate timing nearly destroyed the tiny fleet. *El Rosario*, the flagship (*capitana*), was caught in a wave that lifted it from the water, wrecking the galliot on land in a muddy swamp. Among the dead was Captain León himself, along with the imprisoned brother-in-law of Governor Morton. Two of León's crew—a mulatto slave owned by Captain Antonio de Argüelles and an Indian named Pedro—took advantage of the confusion and fled on foot toward the north, eventually providing intelligence reports to advancing English forces. After removing several weapons and a chest with León's personal papers, Pedro Hortelano set fire to the ruined galliot. After cutting new masts for the remaining two vessels, the corsairs abandoned their Guale Indian companions on shore and limped back toward St. Augustine. In yet another example of remarkable timing, four of these Indians and an escaped Guale Indian from Charles Town stumbled across the path of a party of Carolina traders returning from the deep interior province of Apalachicola. Initially imprisoned by the Englishmen, the Guale Indians freed themelves and killed their captors to a man, commandeering their boat loaded with pelts and guns to join up with the corsairs on Amelia Island.

Seizing the Indians' prize upon their return to Guale and burning their captured boat, León's lieutenant led the two remaining galliots to St. Augustine, initiating a formal visitation of the returning vessels and the interrogation of their prisoners. This documentation follows, preceded by a preliminary *auto* that predated the expedition itself. Interestingly, there is currently no evidence that a copy of the following document was forwarded to Spain. The contents of the testimony from the three prisoners was indeed damning for the Carolina colony, effectively proving their complicity in pirate raids that had been officially outlawed by the English government. Nevertheless, the evidence contained in the following documents was obtained in an unauthorized and illegal extension of the original plan by Governor Márquez Cabrera, and thus was effectively useless as a major diplomatic bargaining tool.

The details of the raid and the controversy that initially followed the return of the galliots are revealed in the text below, with numerous explanatory notes. Text from related Spanish and English accounts is provided in order to supplement the accounts translated in full here. Unlike other documents in this volume, however, these translations are followed by a postscript in order to trace some of the related events that immediately followed (as these events are only touched upon in the Overview).

Florida, Number 11[3]
Year of 1686

Autos made about the entrance into the port of the galliots, of which Captain Alexandro Thomás de León, deceased, was leader, and the expulsion of the inhabitants of Santa Elena, of the English nation.

By the señor Captain and Sergeant Major Don Juan Márquez Cabrera, Governor and Captain General of this city and presidio of Florida and its provinces for His Majesty.
Notary
Adjutant Alonso Solana

[f.1]

Auto

In the city of St. Augustine, Florida, on the fifth of the month of August, sixteen eighty-six, the señor Captain and Sergeant Major Don Juan Márquez Cabrera, governor and captain general of this stated city and its provinces for His Majesty. His Grace said that inasmuch as he has seen that the English and French enemies have come to invade this presidio on three occasions, in the years sixteen eighty-three, sixteen eighty-four, and this present year of sixteen-eighty six,[4] when [this presidio] found itself lacking people and munitions, and without having provisions, it was urgent to contact the governors of Havana so that in everything possible they might send aid of people as well as provisions and munitions, because this presidio and provinces see themselves exposed to experience the damages and hostilities by land and sea which the said enemies have made in other parts and places of these Indies, and the señores governors having done so in a meeting which they held about this with the general of galleons and the governor and royal officials of that city, seeing that it was important to make all effort for the said aid, and to secure the said presidio and provinces, they determined [f.1, vto.] to send Captain Alexandro Thomás de León, who is [captain] of the piraguas and coastal guard of these Indies, so that, adding the [galliot] that was taken from the Monsieur de Agramont on these coasts to the two galliots which he brought under his command in order to go in his convoy, the said Captain Alexandro Thomás should traverse and clean these coasts of enemies, following and pursuing the said enemies in all the places, islands, and inlets where he might find them, inflicting upon them all possible hostilities, and driving them away from these coasts in such a manner that His Majesty is served, giving fulfillment to his royal *cédulas*. In this regard, it is necessary to equip the said galliot with whatever is necessary so that it navigates and follows the said Captain Alexandro with the voluntary people without posts who might wish to go forth from this presidio.[5] He therefore ordered and commanded that the royal officials of this presidio meet in order to contrive the means and form in which to outfit the said galliot and arrange whatever is most suitable to royal service and for the security and protection of these provinces, and so that His Grace might resolve [f.2] what is thus suitable,[6] and for this he provided, commanded, and signed.

Juan Márquez Cabrera

Before me,
Alonso Solana
Public and Governmental Notary

The copy of this *auto* was taken in the contaduría of these provinces.

Francisco de Zigarroa

[f.3]

Auto[7]

In the city of St. Augustine, Florida, on the nineteenth of the month of September, sixteen eighty-six, the señor Captain and Sergeant Major Don Juan Márquez Cabrera, governor and captain general of this stated city and its provinces for His Majesty, said that inasmuch as there just entered [in this port] two galliots under the command of Captain Alexandro Thomás de León, coastal guard of the city of Havana and the rest of the ports of the Indies, which went to dislodge the English enemies from the Bar and Island of Santa Elena, and to clean these coasts of the said pirates, and because they report having lost the *capitana* of the said galliots, and of the said Captain Alexandro and other soldiers having perished after having entered in Santa Elena, and it is suitable to investigate and inquire into the cause or shipwrecks which there were, and likewise that [the galliots] be visited and registered by the royal officials of these royal coffers in case they bring some spoils or anything of value, since the said sack should be approved according to how His Majesty has arranged, and in the interim that the said visitation is made, guards [f.3, vto.] should be placed, and a copy of everything should be made in order to make a report to His Majesty and the señores of His Royal and Supreme Council of the Indies, and for this he provided, commanded, and signed.

Juan Márquez Cabrera

Before me,
Alonso Solana
Public and Governmental Notary

The copy of this *auto* was taken in the Contaduría of these provinces.

Thomás Menéndez Márquez

[f.4]

Visitation of the Galliots

In the city of St. Augustine, Florida, on the nineteenth of the month of September, sixteen eighty-six, the señores Captains Don Thomás Menéndez Márquez, accountant for His Majesty, and Francisco de la Rocha, treasurer and quartermaster, official judges of the Royal Hacienda and Coffer of these provinces, in fulfillment of the *auto* provided today the aforementioned day by the señor Captain and Sergeant Major Don Juan Márquez Cabrera, governor and captain general of this stated city and its provinces for His Majesty, in which he commands that the two piraguas which have entered in this port be visited by Their Graces, and in its fulfillment they went to make a visitation of them, which came from the city of Havana in aid to this presidio, sent by the señores governors of that city, of which Captain Alejandro Thomás de León was principal leader, and Their Graces having made appear before them Pedro Hortelano and Joseph Juan, leaders of the said piraguas,[8] they said that the said Alejandro Thomas de León had died. Before me, the notary, the said Pedro Hortelano and Joseph Juan were sworn in before God and a sign of the cross, in legal form, and having done so, aware of it, they promised to tell the truth, and being questioned about which port they came from, which coasts they have traveled through, in which towns they had been, what prisoners they had taken on the voyage, and of what quality and condition, they said that the said piraguas having left from this port [f.4, vto.] under the command of the said Alejandro Thomás, they went to the province of Guale, and traversing the northern coast, they entered the Island of Santa Elena, where they found a town, deserted and abandoned by its people, and in it they found only a young English boy, because the rest of the English had gone to the woods, and on the said island they found a boat.[9] Following them onward two days on the road they entered a port which seemed to be ten leagues distant, a little more or less, from the [port] of San Jorje, where they found two plantations [*estancias de labranza*],[10] and in one of them they found three black women and eight black men who they found out were owned by the governor of San Jorje,[11] who owned one of the said plantations, and in this said port they found another small boat, an English woman, and an English lad,[12] where they also found a large candlestick of silver with an inscription all around its base which says "These candlesticks were given as alms to the Sancto Christo de San Román by Captain Sebastián Sánchez in the year of sixteen seventy-six,"[13] and likewise an old chasuble of silk which tends toward orange in color.[14] Wanting to return that night that they set sail, a storm struck them and the *capitana* of the said piraguas was lost, and the said Captain Alejandro Thomás, their principal leader, perished.[15] All of this Pedro Ortelano and Joseph Juan thus declared and manifested, aware of the oath that they have made, [f.5] in which they affirm, and they did not sign, not knowing how to, with which Their Graces finished performing the said visitation and commanded me, the notary, to deliver the original together with the rest of the *autos* to His Grace the said señor governor and captain general so that it is on record for His Grace, and Their Graces signed it, of which I, the notary, swear.

Thomás Menéndez Márquez

Francisco de la Rocha

Before me,
Alonso Solana
Public and Governmental Notary

Auto

In the city of St. Augustine, Florida, on the twenty-third of the month of September, sixteen eighty-six, the señor Captain and Sergeant Major Don Juan Márquez Cabrera, governor and captain general of this stated city and its provinces for His Majesty, having seen these *autos* and visitation made by the royal officials of the galliots that were under the command of Captain Alexandro Thomás de León, [f.5, vto.] principal leader, now deceased, and the declarations of Pedro Ortelano and Joseph Juan, their leaders, His Grace said that with respect to it being on record by the said declarations that they bring two English lads and a woman, and it is suitable that their declaration be taken[16] in order to find out and inquire about the designs and intentions of the enemies, and if they have made some alliances or confederations against this presidio or whichever post or presidio of the royal crown which ought to be advised so that it might remain with the preparation which is required, therefore he was commanding and commanded that the adjutant of the guard should bring and summon them before His Grace so that their declaration is received, for which His Grace named Carlos Robson and Ricardo de la Cruz, of the English nation, as atiquies[17] so that they should serve as interpreters in order to speak the Castilian language, and they accept and swear to do this well and faithfully, and for this [auto] he provided, signed, and commanded that the declaration of a Flemish man who was in the town of San Jorje a short time ago should be received.

Juan Márquez Cabrera

Before me,
Alonso Solana
Public and Governmental Notary

[f.6]

Declaration of Juan Clar

In the city of St. Augustine, Florida, on the twenty-third of the month of September, sixteen eighty-six, the señor Captain and Sergeant Major Don Juan Márquez Cabrera, governor and captain general of this stated city and its provinces for His Majesty, commanded to appear before him Juan Clar, who said he was named thus, of the Flemish nation, native of Ostende,[18] who, being Catholic, was sworn in before God and a sign of the cross before me, the notary, in legal form, and having done so, aware of it, he promised to tell the truth, and being questioned according to the tenor of the *auto* on the folio before this one, and with the rest of the necessary questions, he said and declared the following: that two years ago, a little more or less, having embarked in London in order to come as a sailor on a ship [*nabio*] to the port of Jamaica, and the owner having sold the said ship, he embarked in a ketch [*queche*[19]] in order to come to the port of San Jorje, and from there to go to New Holland in order to pass to Flanders, and coming in prosecution of his voyage with another ten persons, and one woman, they lacked [f.6, vto.] provisions by having been met by Monsieur de Agramon, a French corsair, and arriving in the said catch at the coasts of these provinces in one of the ports of Guale,[20] they debarked on land, and some Indians came forth to receive them with their weapons, and seeing that they did not fight, they took them to the houses of the King[21] and gave them something to eat, and the said Indians said that they could not leave there until the lieutenant came, and having come and been there three days,[22] the said lieutenant told this witness that he should go to the vessel in order to take it to the other side, and this witness and two companions being in the process of doing so, having weighed one anchor, one of them advised that a frigate was entering through the port, and the three of them threw themselves into the boat [*bote*] in order to come to land, as they did although they shot some shotguns at them from the said frigate.[23] Arriving at the royal house, they only found the eight English persons, their companions, and asking about the said lieutenant and the Spaniards and Indians, they responded that they had fled to the woods, and in this time the said frigate placed people on land in a [f.7] canoe, and those who debarked on land told them that they would not do them harm, asking them about the people of the town. They responded that they had fled, with which the rest of the people aboard came and loaded the corn that they found there, which was up to one hundred and fifty quintales in his opinion.[24] They were there three days, and at the end of them they burned the church and the houses and embarked again, and upon leaving from the port, the said frigate ran aground, and as they were carrying few people, they helped themselves with the said sloop [*balandra*], and with some effort they left. On the voyage, the captain of the said frigate, who was named Chacopal,[25] told them how he came from the said sea to St. Augustine with another six vessels, and that things had gone poorly, and that the year before in the sack of Vera Cruz it had gone well for them, since they had left much wealth in San Jorje, and with his share, the said Captain Chachopal had built in the said town of San Jorje a white house on the bank of the great river, with its port, and having arrived at San Jorje, this witness saw it. In the time of three weeks that they were there, they prepared the said captain with people and provisions, placing twenty more men, and in the said time of the three [f.7, vto.] weeks, one vessel of the seven which had come to seize this presidio entered, because they found the other five in the said port of San Jorje, where they had entered before them and were equipping in order to leave again. This witness embarked in a sloop in order to return to Jamaica, and the said sloop left him in Siguate,[26] where he remained working about eight months for the food of the passage, and in this time Captain Alejandro Thomás de León went with two piraguas, and the people of the said Siguate having fled, this witness came forth to turn himself over to the Spaniards, and since then he has served with the said Captain Alejandro, until he came as aid from Havana to this presidio and they went privateering toward the north, where the said Captain Alejandro lost his galliot and his life.

He was questioned if in the time that he was in San Jorje he saw and communicated with some Spanish prisoners or slaves from Vera Cruz or Campeche, and he said that on the occasion that he says he went to San Jorje, he saw that the corsairs who he has said sold there a Spaniard for thirty quintales[27] of corn due to all the time that the said Spaniard did not pay his value, and he heard it [f.8] said that there were many slaves from the sack of Vera Cruz in the interior,[28] and this witness was in the town of San Jorje very little time and did not see more.

He was questioned if he knows or has heard it said that when the said seven vessels came to take this presidio, they left from San Jorje or were helped and incited by its governor, and he said that he only knows that the said corsair Captains Cahopal and Thomas Jingle[29] have their houses and haciendas there, and careen their vessels and go there to take on provisions.

He was questioned if in the said time that he was in the said town of San Jorje he had heard it said that vessels were to leave in order to return to this presidio, or to sack other ports of the Indies, and he said that as he was going as a passenger, they tried to sell him for the passage from this province to San Jorje, and for having freed him from among the Spaniards,[30] and thus they had to sell him, as they did for the price of forty pesos, which were given for [f.8, vto.] this witness by a Frenchman who is a resident and married in New Holland, in the province of Niviorca [New York], and is known by this witness, and that in Flanders this witness had aided the said Frenchman with seven pesos, and owing to him he did not remain sold in the said town of San Jorje, and for this occasion he did not travel or have time to leave from the port, on account of which he had no communication with, nor wished to have any, the said town of San Jorje, through having seen likewise that on the said occasion of the said vessels, they had sold for four years[31] another Spanish prisoner who is named Blas, and they likewise wanted to sell another Spaniard named Christobal whom [this witness] found in the city of Havana, where he has seen that he is a barber, and that not having found anyone who would buy him, the Captain of one of the corsair ships, whose name he does not remember, embarked again, and returning to Jamaica to make a voyage, he mistrusted its governor, and he dropped him off on the coast of Havana,[32] and what he has said and declared is the truth and what he knows, aware of the oath which he has made, in which he affirms and ratifies, and he is of the age of twenty-seven years, and signed it together with His Grace the said señor governor.

[unreadable]

Juan Márquez Cabrera

Before me,
Alonso Solana
Public and Governmental Notary

[f.9]

Notification, Acceptance, and Oath

In St. Augustine, Florida, on the twenty-third of September, sixteen eighty-six, I, the notary, notified and made known the commission made in the persons of Carlos Robson and Ricardo de la Cruz for the purpose contained in the *auto* on the folio before this one, who, having read and understood it, said that they were accepting and accepted the charge of such interpreters, and swore before God and a sign of the cross, in legal form, to do so faithfully and legally, to their faithful knowledge and understanding, and the said Carlos Robson signed it, to which I, the notary, swear.

Carlos Robson

Before me,
Alonso Solana
Public and Governmental Notary

Declaration of Catalina, English

In the stated city on the said day, month, and year stated above of the twenty-third of September, sixteen eighty-six, His Grace the señor Captain and Sergeant Major Don Juan Márquez Cabrera, governor and captain general [f.9, vto.] of this stated city and its provinces for His Majesty, commanded to appear before him Cathalina Havena, a Protestant, native of the province of Lincosno in the kingdom of Old England, who said her name thus and that she is native of the said kingdom, and who was sworn in, aware of her law, and required to tell the truth through the said interpreters Carlos Robson and Ricardo de la Cruz, and she promised to tell the truth, and the following questions and cross-examinations were asked of her: How long ago did she come from England? She said that it was twelve years ago that they brought her, a deceived girl, to Providence, where they sold her,[33] and that she remained there until two years ago when the Spaniards depopulated it,[34] and she came with her owner to San Jorje and was there about eight days, and her owner having sold her, they brought her to the Island of Santa Elena with other existing [?] English to a plantation [*plantaje*] of her owner, master Gombre,[35] where the Spaniards captured her.

She was asked if she has known that it is said in San Jorje that they are going to come to this presidio in order to take it, and if there are in that place of the said San Jorje clothes, ships, or prisoners from the ports of the Spaniards. She said that she only knows, by having heard it said, that in San Jorje there are some blacks and slaves from when they sacked Vera Cruz and Campeche, which were brought to San Jorje by some corsair ships to sell, but she has not seen them, having always been on the said plantation, and she does not know anything else about what the question refers to, and this is the truth and what she knows, and she is of the age of nineteen years. She did not sign, not knowing how to. His Grace and one of the said interpreters signed it.

Carlos Robson

Juan Márquez Cabrera

Before me,
Alonso Solana
Public and Governmental Notary

[f.10]

Declaration of Juan, Scottish

Then in continuation there appeared present before His Grace the said señor Governor and Captain General Juan Liloston,[36] who said his name thus, and who is native of the city of Edinburgo [Edinburgh], capital of the kingdom of Scotland, and one of the Protestants aforementioned in the said visitation, who, through the said interpreters, was sworn in before God and his law, aware of which, he promised to tell the truth, of whom were asked the following questions and cross-examinations:

He was questioned when he came from his land, and in how many vessels, and what people came in them, and what port was the first land where they arrived,[37] and he said that it was two years ago that he left from Scotland in a ship with one hundred men with some women and children, and two gentlemen came as their leaders, and they arrived at the port of San Jorje and were there about one month, and then they passed on to settle the Island of Santa Elena, which they call in their language Vuenbi, and he has been there this time.[38] One of the gentlemen of the two leaders is mayor and justice of San Jorje,[39] and in this time another gentleman from San Jorje has come to visit them one or two times.

He was asked whether they knew about it in San Jorje, or did the leaders of Santa Elena know, when the Yamases invaded the province of Timucua and carried off its Indians and burned a village and killed some people, and that in order to do it they gave them the weapons and munitions. He said that the said leaders of the Scottish who are on the said Island of Santa Elena, as he has said, gave up to thirty shotguns [*escopeta*s] and cutlasses [*alfanjes*] to the said Yamases so that they might take them as the price for the said Indian slaves, and that they came and [f.10, vto.] carried up to twenty-one Christian persons from the said province of Timucua, and likewise carried church furnishings and some chalices of silver, and they delivered them to the said leaders as payment for the said weapons, and [this witness] saw an Englishman come from San Jorje to buy some of the said Christian Indians and took them to the said town of San Jorje, but he does not know how many went, and they sold the rest of them to an Irish ship that came six months after having established the town with more people for the same town, and those that [the ship] left in it would be up to one hundred persons.[40]

He was asked whether he knows that in San Jorje there are slaves and property from the sack of Vera Cruz or Campeche. He said that the times that this witness had gone from Santa Elena to the said town of San Jorje, he saw some slaves of Spaniards pass, but he does not know what ships brought them.

He was asked whether he had heard it said that in San Jorje they had wanted to or would like to come to make war with this presidio. He said that he has heard it said in the said town of San Jorje that there are some persons who are to come to win St. Augustine, Florida, but he does not know when or how.

He was asked whether he knows or has heard it said in the said towns of Santa Elena or San Jorje if there are some corsairs in order to come to this presidio or other Spanish presidios [f.11] of the Indies. He said that he knows no more than only that the Monsiur de Agramon arrived at the port of Santa Elena two months and a half ago in his opinion with two vessels and put the launch on land with eleven men, and they gave him provisions, and then he went away, and he does not know what route he took nor to what place he went.[41]

He was questioned about what fortification they have made on the said Island of Santa Elena, and how many [artillery] pieces it has. He said that [there is] a fortification of three [artillery] pieces,[42] because they had suspicion that the Spaniards might go there, by being their lands, and this is what he knows, aware of the oath which he has made, and that regarding what he has been questioned about if they expect more people to settle the Island of Santa Catalina and others, he said that every day they are awaiting more people for the said Island of Santa Elena, but that he does not know if it is in order to settle other islands,[43] and that this is the truth, and he knows no other thing more than what he has declared, and he signed it, and is of the age of seventeen years. His Grace and the said interpreter Carlos Robson signed it.

John Livingston

Carlos Robson

Juan Márquez Cabrera

Before me,
Alonso Solana
Public and Governmental Notary

[f.11, vto.]

In St. Augustine, Florida, on the said day, month, and year, His Grace the said señor governor and captain general, for the said declarations, commanded to appear before him Samuel Yanque, who said his name thus, and who is of the English nation, native of Old England, and of Protestant law, who, by means of the said interpreters, was sworn in before God and his law, and having done so, aware of it, he promised to tell the truth, to whom the following questions were made.

He was asked from what port he left from England, in what ship, what captain and people came in it, and to which port in the Indies did he come. He said that he left from London four years ago in a ship for San Jorje with the governor who is at present, who is called José Morton, who has been Governor for a year and a half and had governed before when he went to England and left here some country haciendas of his,[44] and this witness was in one of them until the piraguas captured him and brought him to this city.

He was asked whether in that time he has gone sometimes to San Jorje. He said that in the said four [f.12] years he had served in the said haciendas by having been sold for twelve years in servitude,[45] and that in this time he has not gone to San Jorje more than one time, which was two and a half months ago.

He was asked whether in that time that he went, or in another time, he has heard it said or seen that some corsairs have entered or left from San Jorje, and if he has heard it said that they came to take this post or wanted to take it. He said that three years ago he heard it said that one or two ships had left, and that they said they came to take and sack St. Augustine, and that when they returned from the said voyage they said that they had taken it, and that they were there some time until they spent what they took.[46] In the said time that he went to San Jorje, he heard the people of the place say that they wanted to come to take St. Augustine like they had done another time, and he also heard this said in the house of the Governor by his servants, and that the vessels which were to leave for this were to join with others in a place, but [this witness] does not know where. In the said time of the two months and a half, he heard it said that the Monsur [Monsieur] de Agramon had arrived at that port, and went away later, but he does not know if they gave him provisions or not.[47] [f.12, vto.]

He was asked whether some Englishmen have come forth through the interior for this province in order to discover lands. He said that one year ago, a little more or less, Captain Enrique left from San Jorje with ten Englishmen with an order from the governor to discover lands towards this province, but he does not know if he has returned.[48]

He was asked whether he knows if he who governs the town of Scotsmen which is on Santa Elena, an island which belongs to the Spaniards, is subject to the governor of San Jorje, or if they have communication and business with them. He said that he only knows that if something is necessary, the governor of Santa Elena sends to San Jorje for it, and that he does not know anything else about this question. He has come to understand that the said governor of San Jorje is afraid to receive letters that he is awaiting from his King, but he does not know for what occasion, nor does he know anything else to be able to declare, aware of the oath which he has made, in which he affirms and ratifies according to his law, and he is of the age [f.13] of twenty years. He did not sign by not knowing how. His Grace the said señor governor and one of the said interpreters signed it.

Carlos Robson

Juan Márquez Cabrera

Before me,
Alonso Solana
Public and Governmental Notary

Auto

In the city of St. Augustine, Florida, on the twenty-seventh of the month of September, sixteen-eighty six, the señor Captain and Sergeant Major Don Juan Márquez Cabrera, governor and captain general of this stated city and its provinces for His Majesty, said that inasmuch as it is suitable that the declaration be taken of an Indian native of the province of Guale, from the town of Santa Catalina, who was in the town of San Xorje and returned to his said province, and it is necessary [f.13, vto.] that an interpreter be named in order to find out the designs and intentions of the enemies, therefore His Grace was naming and named Alonso García, artilleryman of this presidio, skilled in the language of Guale, who is to be notified, and who should accept and swear to do so well and faithfully, to his faithful knowledge and understanding, and for this his *auto* he thus provided, commanded, and signed.

Juan Márquez Cabrera

Before me,
Alonso Solana
Public and Governmental Notary

Notification, Acceptance, and Oath

In St. Augustine, Florida, on the said day, month, and year, I, the said notary, notified and made known the *auto* above and on the other side [of this folio] to Alonso García de la Vera, who heard and understood, and said that he was accepting and accepted the commission signed in his person as such an interpreter for the examination of the Indian contained in the said *auto*, and he swore before God and a sign of the cross to do so well and faithfully, to his faithful knowledge and understanding, and he signed it, of which I swear.

Alonso García de la Vera

Before me,
Alonso Solana
Public and Governmental Notary

Declaration

In the city of St. Augustine, Florida, on the twenty-seventh of the month of September, sixteen eighty-six, the señor Captain and Sergeant Major Don Juan Márquez Cabrera, governor and captain general of this stated city and its provinces for His Majesty, in order to proceed in these declarations, commanded to appear before him Matheo, an Indian native from the town of Santa Catalina of the province of Guale, who said his name thus, and who is native of the said province, who, before me, the notary, and by means of the said interpreter Alonso García, was sworn in before God and a sign of the cross, in legal form, and having done so, aware of it, he promised to tell the truth [f.14, vto.], and the following questions were asked of him:

He was questioned why and for how much time he went away to the town of San Jorje, and he said that his said town having moved to the Island of Santa Maria, he had some [harsh] words with the wife of his cacique, and she struck this witness with a stick on the neck which laid him out on the floor, and getting up, wanting to attack her, her husband the cacique arrived and went to throw him out, and this witness feeling shamed, he attacked the cacique, and after having wanted to capture him, the elders [*ancianos*] frightened him by saying that they had to bring him before His Grace, the said señor governor, in order to put him in the *castillo* as a forced laborer. Seeing himself with these fears, he fled, leaving his wife on the said island in the town of Santa Maria, and went away, entering the interior with other countrymen [*paisanos*] of his from Santa Catalina. Seeming to him that he was not safe there, he went away to San Jorje with some Yamasis in order to spend some [f.15] time with them, and also in order to see that town of Englishmen. When he arrived there with the said Yamasis, the governor found out that he was Christian and from the province of Guale, and the said governor called this witness and asked him if he was Christian, and he responded that he was, and a vassal of the King [of Spain], but that he had fled from his cacique so that they might not hang him, as the said Yamasis would tell him, and the said governor questioned him if he had come to St. Augustine, to which he responded that he had, and [the governor] asked about the disposition of the *castillo*, and what artillery it had, and if it was finished, and how tall, and if the moat had much water, and if there were many soldiers and many people in St. Augustine, and if there were many Indians in these provinces, to which this witness responded that he had been [in St. Augustine] three or four times, and the last time he had seen that the *castillo* was finished and very tall, and that it had much artillery all around it, some higher up, and some lower, and that the moat had water, but he did not know if it was very deep, and that every afternoon he saw people and soldiers enter in order to sleep within, and that with regard to there being many soldiers, he did not understand this, but it seemed to him that there were four times one hundred, and that there were also other Spaniards who were not soldiers, and that he had not traveled through these provinces [f.15, vto.] in order to know the Indians that there were, beyond having heard it said that there were many Indians.

He was asked whether in the time that he was in the said town of San Jorje he had heard it said that they wanted to come to this presidio to take it, and saw some corsair ships enter, or if he heard it said that they had entered, and if he knows that they carried some blacks and mulattos from those of Vera Cruz or Campeche, or other goods of the Spaniards. He said that he heard some Yamasi Indians say that some English had said that when a captain who had gone to England came, then they would try to come and take this presidio, and regarding whether corsair ships have entered or left, [this witness] saw one, and those who came in it were eating and walking about on land, and the said Yamasis told this witness that those [people] said they were from the ships that traveled robbing the Spaniards on the sea, and that they had come with other ships to this presidio and had killed some people. With regard to the black and mulatto slaves of the Spaniards, [this witness] saw them work there, and they asked this witness where he was from and if he was a Christian, and he responded that he was a Christian and was from the province of Guale, of the [f.16] Spaniards, to where he would return soon, and the said slaves asked him if there were some canoes in which to be able to flee with them and come to St. Augustine, and afterwards he could not speak with them more. This witness tried to come, which he did, and upon coming for his land, he came upon the galliots which were carrying Indians of his town, and he returned with them,[49] and they went to Santa Elena, where they fought with the Yamasis, because now the English who were settled on the Island of Santa Elena had passed to another island fleeing, and being in some houses of that coast, where they had captured other blacks, a storm struck them, and the said galliots came to land and the one in which the captain was going was lost, and he died there. This witness and the rest of the Indians having heard the Spaniards who remained with the other two galliots say that they [the Indians] did not fit in the galliots, because there were many people, and that they would leave them on land and they would go across [land] to their towns, as they heard this from the said Spaniards, this witness and another five looked for a solution, and they found a war canoe, and five of them embarked,[50] and one remained on land, and [this witness] swears that he will have perished.[51] They came in [the canoe] until arriving at the mouth of a [f.16, vto.] river which seems to him, according to what he found out afterward, to descend from the provinces of Apalachecoli,[52] where five Englishmen with two Indians of the Uchise nation[53] were there in a boat [*barco*], and they captured them and tied this witness and his companions up, and placing them together, they asked them if they were Christians, and they responded yes, and they told them "Well, later on we will kill you," and they placed some skins on top of them. Seeing themselves so afflicted, and that there were four Englishmen sleeping and one awake with the two Indians, one of them, tied up as he was, came across an oyster shell[54] on the ground, and with all secrecy he cut his bonds, and thus they went giving the oyster shell to one another and untying themselves, and when they finished they got up suddenly, and with the shotguns which they had nearby and a stick, they killed four of them with blows, and the other, with two blows, went away with an Indian, whom they could not finish off nor find in the woods due to the darkness. Afterwards they returned and told the other Indian that he should call to his companion, and that they would not kill them, and the other Indian having come, they told them how those Englishmen had left from San Jorje and gone to the provinces of Apalachecoli where they had been much time, and that farther up one of their captains had gone through a narrow river to leave by another river with another Englishmen who was called Captain Enrique, and in his company went the cacique of Cabeta[55] [f.17] and a son and two nephews of Niquisaia,[56] and that the said

Niquisaia had been with the said Englishmen and helped the said Captain Enrique get through. This witness and the rest seeing what had happened, they took the shotguns and stripped the dead Englishmen and returned in the boat, in which they found one hundred twenty-six buckskins [*gamusas*], two hundred pelts of beavers and otters, and twenty skins of bears and bison [*sibolas*], and navigating now near to their towns, they caught up with the said galliots, and their leaders took the boat, the shotguns, and the rest away from them, and treated them badly, and burned the said boat because it seemed to them who knows what, and thus this witness and the rest have come to ask for justice,[57] and what he has said and declared is the truth, and what he knows, aware of the oath which he has made, in which he affirms and ratifies, and he is of the age of twenty-two years, a little more or less. He did not sign, not knowing how to. His Grace the said señor governor and the said interpreter signed it.

Alonso García de la Vera

Juan Márquez Cabrera

Before me,
Alonso Solana
Public and Governmental Notary

[f.17, vto.]

Auto[58]

In the city of St. Augustine, Florida, on the twenty-seventh of the month of September, sixteen eighty-six, the señor Captain and Sergeant Major Don Juan Márquez Cabrera, governor and captain general of this stated city and its provinces for His Majesty, having seen these autos and declarations made by the three English prisoners, and that of the Indian from Santa Catalina who came from San Jorge, and what is contained in them, His Grace said that regardless of the damage which these provinces have received and are receiving by sea and land from the town of San Jorxe, by housing and helping the corsairs, they have come to consider and be threatened they should do so [again], as is more fully on record from the news which His Grace has had, and from disturbing the provinces of Apalachicoli and Caveta, who have rendered obedience to His Majesty, sending this past year Englishmen and Yamaze Indians; and likewise in the said year sixty Yamazes of the jurisdiction of San Jorxe having entered in the province of Timucua and burned one of its towns and killed some people, and having taken twenty-one persons, including men and women, to San Jorxe, from where they embarked for other places, there remaining [f.18] there three women and one man;[59] and likewise having seized the boat [*barco*] of this presidio in the province of Guale, and having made good this seizure and bought it, making use of it for such that it came loaded with corn for the aid of this presidio in the past year of sixteen eighty-three, when the English and French enemies came to invade this post; and likewise having armed two ships [*navios*] with people and leaders for the sack of the city of Campeche, as is on record from the declaration of the Captain of the galliot which was seized in this port at the sandbar of Matanzas;[60] and likewise having had news that during the end of this past August two English captains were to come to the Island of Santa Catalina to depopulate them, and that they were bringing people in order to populate them, as is verified by what happened and the declarations made,[61] and by having populated the Island of Santa Elena and another town on the mainland with English governors subordinate to that of San Jorxe; and that for this reason the seizure made by the said galliots should be approved; and by having found in it a chasuble and some altar candlesticks of silver with the names of the person who gave them as alms to the Santo Christo de San Román, and clothing from the last sack of Campeche or from Vera Cruz, by being the wardrobe [*vestuario*] of the said lands, the said seizure made in the plantation ten leagues distant from the town of San Jorxe contravening the capitulations and royal *cédulas*; therefore, [the governor] was commanding and commanded that the royal officials ask for and get censures from the ecclesiastical judge of these provinces so that all those persons who might have taken whatever articles of silver and gold and other relevant and pertinent things of value in the said plantation ten leagues from the town of San Jorxe should present and declare them, and also the residents, occupants, and inhabitants who might have held or bought them, and for this the said royal officials should join in accord,[62] and so that the slaves and whatever other goods that might have been taken and captured from the said plantation and have ended up in the power of Pedro Hortelano, leader of the galliot *Nuestra Señora de Regla*, should be placed in deposit and secured,[63] and an inventory made so that it is on record for all time, leaving [a copy] for the said Pedro Ortelano and the [f.19] rest of his companions, and for Captian Alexandro Thomás, leader of the said galliots, who by order of the governor of Havana came as aid to this post, and to scour the northern coasts and clean them of corsairs, as he was doing when he lost his life and his galliot with the rest of the deceased [?], and an account of everything should be given to His Majesty with copies of these autos so that he might order what he wishes to do, and for this his auto he provided and signed.

Juan Márquez Cabrera

Before me,
Alonso Solana
Public and Governmental Notary

[f.19, vto.]

Accord

In the city of St. Augustine, Florida, on the twenty-eighth of the month of September, sixteen eighty-six, the señores Captain and Sergeant Major Don Juan Márquez Cabrera, governor and captain general of this stated city and its provinces for His Majesty, and the Captains Don Thomás Menéndez Márquez, accountant for His Majesty, and Francisco de la Rocha, treasurer and quartermaster, official judges of the Royal Hacienda and Coffer of these provinces, having met by virtue of the *auto* on the other side of this in the houses of the residence of His Grace the said señor governor, they were of the opinion and declared that in the interim that His Majesty might determine [the case], the said slaves should be applied to the construction of the *castillo*, where they should work, and their sustenance should be charged to the account of His Majesty, and all the remaining goods that appear to pertain to the said haciendas of San Jorxe, being held and declared, they should be deposited and secured in the same manner, and this was what Their Graces agreed to and signed, and they commanded that Pedro Ortelano, leader of the galliot, should be notified for this accord to deliver the said slaves to the lieutenant of the royal fort.[64]

Juan Márquez Cabrera

Thomás Menéndez Márquez

Francisco de la Rocha

Before me,
Alonso Solana
Public and Governmental Notary

[f.20]

Notification

In the city of St. Augustine, Florida, on the twenty-eighth of the month of September, sixteen eighty-six, I, the notary, notified and made known in person the auto and accord of His Grace the señor governor and captain general and the judges royal officials of these provinces, both that of yesterday, the twenty-seventh of the current [month], and also that of today, the said day, as is contained in them, to Pedro Ortelano, leader of the galliot *Nuestra Señora de Regla*, who understood its tenor. He said that he heard it and that [something] occurred to him to say and allege about the contents of the said *autos*, and he said this as his reply.[65] I swear,

Alonso Solana
Public and Governmental Notary

In St. Augustine, Florida, on the said day, month, and year, I, the said notary, swear and give true testimony where appropriate how Pedro Hortelano, resident in this city, leader of the galliot named *Nuestra Señora de Regla*, in fulfillment of the *auto* contained on the three folios before this one, delivered to Captain Francisco de Fuentes, lieutenant of the royal fort of this presidio, the eleven slaves contained in the said *auto*, which are eight black men [f.20, vto.] and three black women, and he took them and placed them within the royal fort, to which I swear.[66]

Alonso Solana
Public and Governmental Notary

[f.21]

Pedro Hortelano, resident in this city and presidio, the person who represents [the person] of Captain Alexandro Thomás de León, now deceased, as his lieutenant, and who he made leader of one of the privateer galliots which came from the port of Havana to this [port], in voice and name of all the soldiers and officers of the said privateer expedition, in the best way and form that by law there is cause for, and without the harm of whichever other person who might vie with me what I protest to make use of each [time] and before whom it suits me.[67] I appear before Your Lordship and say that there has been made known and notified to me an *auto* pronounced by Your Lordship in view of the proceedings that have been done officially about the seizures of eleven black slaves, two boats [*botes*], and other trifles which [?] the people brought to this port, where we find ourselves, by which *auto*, Your Lordship was pleased to command, among other things that are mentioned in it, that a delivery of all the aforementioned seized [items] should be made in order to place them in deposit until meanwhile His Majesty (may God preserve him), with view of the *autos* that are to be remitted officially, should determine and command something else, like the referred with the rest, by that said *auto*, to which I refer, according to what I have come to understand; and alleging and saying for now as is my right with reservation and protest of doing it, in the manner of each [case] that there might be cause, and that the *autos* (duly finding) should be delivered to me, and Your Lordship, in justice and right, should be served to command the suspension of the execution of the said *auto* and the remission of that which is officially carried out to His Majesty, with respect to my not having been heard in the judgment and case as I ought, by Your Lordship having proceeded solely [f.21, vto.] officially, which according to the law in this [case], as in all types of trials, the interested sides ought to be heard in them, so that the decision might be made more securely;[68] for which reason, being [an interested party] as much as I am in this case, and all the people who find themselves enlisted and in the exercise of the said privateering expedition, it will not be just, nor correct, to deprive us of the right that assists us about the propriety of the said plundering and seizure that we made against enemies, and the defense about it that we ought to have and place, to which it is alleged for more right in our favor that arranged and declared by His Majesty in his royal *cédula* of the twenty-second of February, sixteen seventy-four,[69] issued with regard to the privateering expeditions that he permits that there are and that should be armed in the Indies, since in the sixth chapter of the instruction inserted in the said royal *cédula* (that I protest to present in legal form each time it is suitable to me, and that the autos should be delivered to me), His Majesty arranges and commands that at the port where a privateering expedition might arrive with prisoners, the justices of the said ports are to find out about the causes of them solely in the first instant, and the appeals which might be interposed about it and the said causes are for the Royal Audiencias of their district and jurisdiction, and not for any other tribunal or council;[70] for which reason, with regard to that arranged by Your Lordship in the remission of the case to His Majesty, it is and results in contravention of that declared in the said royal *cédula*, as well as in notable harm to me, and to all the people of the said privateering expedition, meanwhile during the referred [remission] leaving without means the Royal Audiencia of the city of Mexico, to which belong and pertain in the second instance the cases and appeals which are interposed regarding them in this city, and to whose law and recourse we ought to be each time I, being heard in this trial and case on my part, ought to interpose some appeal of that determined and declared by Your Lordship in your *autos*; in consideration of which, and of the rest that is done or could be done in my favor and right, and in that of the said privateering expedition and its soldiers, and if it suits me more or better [f.22] to ask and allege that which is repeated and expressed here;

I ask and supplicate Your Lordship, in attention of that said and alleged in this text, that it please you to order the suspension of the execution of that determined and commanded in the said *auto*, and that the officially performed *autos* about the said reason should be delivered to us in order to say and allege about them, and in view of them to justify what is suitable to our justice and right; and of the contrary (speaking duly) I protest for myself, and in the name of all the people of the said privateering expedition, what is suitable for us to protest, and that a copy of this text as well as what Your Lordship might provide should be given to me, authorized in a certified form and manner, for the protection of our right, with respect to which I ask for the fulfillment of justice.[71] I swear in legal form and in the form which is necessary.

Pedro Hortelano

[This petition] having been presented, place it with the *autos*, and regarding what the party of Pedro Hortelano, leader of the galliot anchored in this port, asks for, that the *auto* provided on the twenty-seventh of the current [month] and the accord by His Grace and the royal officials of today, the said day, should be suspended, and that if there is cause for it, the said resolution should be remitted to the Royal Audiencia where the determination of the *autos* carried out about approving the seizure might apply, there is no cause, since an account should be given to His Grace so that he might command what serves him, by where [the seizure] was made being territory [f.22, vto.] in which seizures or other hostilities are not declared to be approved, by His Majesty having commanded the contrary by his royal *cédulas*, and by it not being on record by other [*cédulas*] or orders which the said leaders might bring from the governor of Havana, because they were sent to aid this presidio, and by His Grace having given order from this city, as is on record by it, that they should only follow the corsairs, and in particular the Monsiur de Agramont, who had been at this port and headed in the direction of those to the north, as is on record from the declarations made by reason of this, and likewise so that they should depopulate the lands of His Majesty on the Island of Santa Elena of Englishmen.[72] Therefore, His Grace ordered that the said *autos* and accord should be fulfilled and guarded, and the royal officials should pass to the execution of what is contained in them, making the inventory of the rest of the goods, and for this they should take the oath of the said leader and the rest of the persons so that under it they should declare [the goods] that they might have taken and captured in the plantations of the said town of San Jorxe, for which His Grace was giving and gave commission in sufficient form, according to and how he holds it from His Majesty, and [Pedro Hortelano] should be given a copy of this text of what was provided, and of that of yesterday, the twenty-seventh of the current [month], and the accord of today, the stated day, with that which is at the head of the *autos*, all in certified public form, attentive of not being able to give a copy of all the *autos* due to the declarations of the prisoners,[73] and in case the seizure should be pronounced as legitimate by His Majesty, the slaves should be placed in the royal fort and with good security so that they might not flee, joined by some slaves that have been brought from Havana [f.23] to be sold at this presidio as a form of exile because of their being delinquents and incorrigible,[74] and also six or seven who find themselves in the Convent of San Francisco with Andres Ranzon, a corsair and pirate on these coasts, of the English nation, on account of criminal and cruel offenses,[75] as experience demonstrates in the flight of Thomás, the mulatto slave of Captain Antonio de Argüelles, who went away to San Jorxe with an Indian, whom one ought to suspect due to his experience in these provinces.[76] The señor Captain and Sergeant Major Don Juan Márquez Cabrera, governor and captain general of this stated city and presidio of St. Augustine, Florida, and its provinces for His Majesty, provided the *auto* above, and he signed it on the twenty eighth of the month of September, sixteen eighty-six.

Juan Márquez Cabrera

Before me,
Alonso Solana
Public and Governmental Notary

In the city of St. Augustine, Florida, on the thirtieth of the month of September, sixteen eighty-six, the señores Captains [f.23, vto.] Don Thomás Menéndez Márquez, accountant for His Majesty, and Francisco de la Rocha, treasurer and quartermaster, official judges of the Royal Hacienda and Coffer of these provinces, having accepted the commission contained in the three folios with this one, which was given to Their Graces by the señor Captain and Sergeant Major Don Juan Márquez Cabrera, governor and captain general of this stated city and its provinces for His Majesty, and having sworn in legal form before God and a sign of a cross that they would make use of the said commission faithfully and legally to their full knowledge and understanding, and in its fulfillment Their Graces ordered to appear before them Pedro Ortelano, resident in this stated city, leader of the galliots that came from the city of Havana to the aid of this presidio and that went to scour these coasts to the north of this presidio, who was sworn in before God Our Lord and a sign of the cross, according to legal form, and having done so, aware of it, he promised to tell the truth, and being questioned according to the tenor of the said *auto* and commission, he said that in the declaration that he made before Their Graces, the said señores royal officials, in the visitation they made when he entered in this port, [the seizure] was the said eleven items of slaves, one candelabra of silver, an old chasuble, two boats, and beyond that a mirror, [f.24] which he newly manifests and declares, and likewise he declares and manifests a cauldron [*caldero*] of iron,[77] and that he does not know of anything other than what he has declared, and this is the truth, aware of the oath that he has made, which he affirms and ratifies, and he is of the age of thirty-seven years. He did not sign, not knowing how to. Their Graces signed it.

Thomás Menéndez Márquez

Francisco de la Rocha

Before me,
Alonso Solana
Public and Governmental Notary

[Declaration of] Cojimar

In St. Augustine, Florida, on the said day, month, and year, Their Graces for the said investigation commanded to appear before them Sergeant Sebastián de Cojimar, resident in this city, who before me, the notary, was sworn in before God and a sign of the cross, in legal form, and having done so, aware of it, he promised to tell the truth, and being questioned according to the tenor of the said *auto* he said that having left from this port in the piragua of Captain Alejandro Thomás de León, coastal guard of the city of Havana who came to this presidio by order and command of the señores governors of the said city of Havana to the aid of this post, and having arrived at it, they passed to the coasts of the north up to the plantations and towns of San Jorje, habitation of the English, and having entered four of them,[78] they only found eleven [f.24, vto.] items of slaves; a candelabra of silver, and according to what appeared on an inscription that it has on its circumference, it seems to be from the Santo Christo de San Román of the city of Campeche; a chasuble; a mirror; and a pan [*paila*] of iron; and he does not know that anything else was found in the said four plantations that he said were of the jurisdiction of San Jorje, and what he has said and declared is the truth and what he knows, aware of the oath that he has made, which he affirms and ratifies, and he is of the age of thirty-six years, and he signed it together with Their Graces.

Thomás Menéndez Márquez

Francisco de la Rocha

Sebastián Cojimar

Before me,
Alonso Solana
Public and Governmental Notary

[Declaration of] Alejandro Jorje

In St. Augustine, Florida, on the said day, month, and year, before Their Graces appeared present for the said investigation Alejandro Jorje, who before me, the notary, was sworn in before God and a sign of the cross, in legal form, and having done so, aware of it, he promised [f.25] to tell the truth, and being questioned according to the tenor of the said *auto*, he said that having gone to scour the northern coast in the piragua named *Nuestra Señora de Regla*, of which the leader was Pedro Ortelano, and this witness his lieutenant, having gone to the town of Santa Elena and passed onward from it, in a plantation they found eleven items of slaves, those whom they placed in this presidio, and he does not know to whom they pertain nor of what jurisdiction they were, because this witness did not debark on land in any of the plantations, nor does he know that anything else was found in it more than what he has declared, and this is the truth, aware of the oath that he has made, and he is of the age of thirty-eight years, and he did not sign, not knowing how to. Their Graces signed it.

Thomás Menéndez Márquez

Francisco de la Rocha

Before me,
Alonso Solana
Public and Governmental Notary

[Declaration of Diego Ruíz]

In the said city on the stated day, month, and year, before Their Graces appeared present for the said investigation Diego Ruíz, who before me, the notary, was sworn in before God and a sign of a cross, in legal form, and [f.25, vto.] having done so, aware of it, he promised to tell the truth, and being questioned according to the tenor of the stated *auto*, he said that having left from the port of Havana by order of the señores governors of it in aid of this post and to scour its coasts, they went to [the coasts], and having arrived at the town of Santa Elena, which they found already without people because of the news that they had of their coming, they passed onward in pursuit of the said people who depopulated it, of the Scottish nation, according to news they had from a boy whom they found in the said town of Santa Elena, and pursuing onward about fifteen or twenty leagues, they arrived at a plantation in which, this witness having gone on land by order of Captain Alejandro Thomás de León, they found in the said plantation eleven items of slaves, eight of them men and three of them women, whom they declared and placed in this city, and he does not know if any other thing was found in the said plantation more than what he has declared; and near the said plantation, on its coast, a small boat [*botecillo*] which they have likewise declared, and from an English boy they found in the said plantation they found out that it was of the governor of [f.26] San Jorje, and what he has said and declared is the truth and what he knows, aware of his oath, and he is of the age of thirty years, and he did not sign, not knowing how to. Their Graces signed it.

Thomás Menéndez Márquez

Francisco de la Rocha

Before me,
Alonso Solana
Public and Governmental Notary

[Declaration of Bartholomé Rodríguez]

In the said city on the said day, month, and year, before Their Graces appeared present for the said investigation Bartholomé Rodríguez, who before me, the notary, was sworn in before God and a sign of the cross, in legal form, and having done so, aware of it, he promised to tell the truth, and being questioned according to the tenor of the said *auto*, he said that having left from the city of San Christobal de la Havana in company of Captain Alejandro Thomás de León, coastal guard of the stated city and island, to scour the [coasts] of this jurisdiction and clean them of corsairs, having scoured the [coasts] of this jurisdiction to the north [f.26, vto.] and arrived at Santa Elena, a town of Scotsmen that they found deserted because of news they had of their coming, they passed onward in their pursuit, and in the jurisdiction of San Jorje, a town of Englishmen, this witness was in three plantations, those that they found deserted, and only in one of them did they find an English boy who made flight, and some plates of pewter and some old clothes of little value, and some iron tools, the number of which there were he does not know, nor in whose power they ended up,[79] and in another plantation, although this witness did not go to it, he knows that they found eleven items of slaves, which they brought and manifested in this presidio, and they found out from the prisoners that the said plantation was of the governor of San Jorje, and all that he has said and declared is the truth, aware of his oath, and he is of the age of twenty-five years. Their Graces signed it. Between lines—signed it—not valid.[80]

Thomás Menéndez Márquez

Francisco de la Rocha

Before me,
Alonso Solana
Public and Governmental Notary

I left a copy of these *autos* written on fifty-eight pages. Florida, August sixth, seventeen thirty-nine.

Castilla[81]

Postscript

Following the disputed seizure of the slaves and other booty by Governor Márquez, Pedro Hortelano refitted the galliot *Nuestra Señora de Regla* for its return to Havana. In a letter to the King the following year, the governor remarked bitterly that after returning from the León expedition, "the [galliot] from Havana was careened and outfitted in order to return to that city, because its leader, outside of not being a person in whom one can trust any duty, insisted upon returning, as he did" (Márquez Cabrera, 1686). Despite the loss of two of the three galliots, in a subsequent plan devised by Governor Márquez Cabrera and the royal officials on September 30, the remaining galliot from St. Augustine along with two war piraguas made for the occasion was armed, and 18 men from León's wrecked galliot were enlisted for six months of paid duty in Florida (Márquez Cabrera, 1686; 1688a).[82]

The free *pardos* and *morenos* (those of mixed African descent) in St. Augustine, along with several Indians and a few Spanish soldiers, were to comprise the rest of the expedition (Márquez Cabrera, 1686). The corsairs remained inactive for three months, but in December they were finally dispatched northward on a second raid (Márquez Cabrera, 1688a). In October the governor wrote to the King of his plans to recruit for this expedition some 200 Apalachee Indians armed with firearms, along with 100 from Timucua, in order to make a land assault in concert with that from the sea. Later evidence indicates that this dual attack was indeed carried out, as accounts of expenses to Indians during 1687 include a reference to thousands of pounds of corn and some 1650 pounds of salted beef (taken from Captain Joachín de Florencias cattle ranch in Apalachee) given to "three hundred fifty Timucua and Apalachee Indians who descended from the provinces of Timucua and Apalachee by order and command of the said Governor Don Juan Márquez Cabrera in order to go in the galliots and piraguas with Captain Francisco de Fuentes to the province of Santa Elena. . .and in order to return to their lands" (Reyes, 1687).[83] Accompanied by this force, the lieutenant of the *castillo* in St. Augustine, Captain Francisco de Fuentes, sailed northward in December in charge of the presidio's galliot and two war piraguas on an expedition to make a strike against the Yamassee Indians who had again settled in the abandoned zone between Florida and Carolina (Márquez Cabrera, 1686; 1688a).[84]

Fuentes certainly made another assault against Santa Elena, newly resettled by the Yamassee, during which the Indian leader Niquisaya and his son and nephew were killed (Royal *Cédula*, 1688). During his return, several further attacks seem to have occurred, including a raid near the mouth of the Savannah River. The following spring, William Dunlop journeyed south from Carolina into the abandoned lands south of Stuart's Town on a reconnaissance mission, and viewed a bluff on the south bank of the Savannah River near another bluff called Lower Amaira (probably the Yamacraw bluff of the early 18th century) where his Indian informants said "the Spaniard had in their Last returning from port Royall killed & taken away 22 Yamassie women" (Dunlop, 1687). Farther to the south, on Sapelo Island, Dunlop passed by

> very large plantations where we see the ruins of houses burned by the Spaniards themselves We see the Vestiges of a ffort; many great Orange Trees cut down by the Spaniards in sept^r last There was great plenty of ffigs peaches; Artechocks onions etc. growing in the preists garden his house had been of Brick & his small chappell, but all had been burned to Ashes last harvest by themselves; we see the remains & rags of old clothes wch some of our people know to have belonged to the Inhabitants of port Royall (Dunlop, 1687).

Based on the reference to the "remains" and clothes of the inhabitants of Port Royal (known by the Spaniards as Santa Elena) discovered by Dunlop at what may be presumed to be the former site of the Sapala mission, these were almost certainly Yamassee Indians who had once lived in the Santa Elena/Port Royal area, but who had resettled the abandoned town of Sapala as early as 1685 (see Overview). Since there is not even a single reference to raids on Yamassee towns during the August—September León raid the previous year (as was implied by Dunlop's Yamassee informants), the destruction of the Yamassee settlement on Sapelo Island was probably carried out during Francisco de Fuentes's expedition later that winter.[85]

Both of these attacks—one near Yamacraw bluff on the Savannah River and one on Sapelo Island—seem to have comprised part of Fuentes' effort to rid the coast of English-allied Yamassee Indians. It is also probable that St. Catherines Island, also settled by the Yamassee in 1685, was struck as well during Fuentes's return. In his letter of October 1686, Governor Márquez Cabrera indicated plans to "depopulate the said Island of Santa Elena and Santa Catalina, and the island of the Yamazes" (Márquez Cabrera, 1686), presumably referring to modern Parris

[Santa Elena] Island, its neighbor Hilton Head Island, as well as St. Catherines Island to the south. Although the majority of later references refer to Santa Elena as the primary target (Márquez Cabrera, 1687; Rocha, 1687), during his *residencia* the governor himself related that the mission was sent to the vicinity of Santa Catalina, "having certain news that the Scottish and the greater part of the Yamaze Indians had returned to settle the said Island of Santa Catalina and its neighbor," presumably referring to Sapala (Márquez Cabrera, 1688a). That same year, the governor certified regarding the military service of Francisco de Fuentes that he was sent "to dislocate the English from the said Island of Santa Elena and the Yamaze Indians, their friends, who inhabited the [island] of Santa Catalina, which he executed, without having news that they have returned to it up to the cited day of August 8, 1688" (Márquez Cabrera, 1688b). Evidently, although the Yamassee had indeed settled on both Santa Catalina and Sapala Islands in 1685 following the final retreat of Guale and Mocama (Gómez, 1685; also see Overview), the Fuentes raid of 1686 resulted in the depopulation of these islands for at least the next two years.

In a later letter to the governor of Carolina, Governor Márquez's successor recounted that the goals of the Fuentes expedition were different from those of the León expedition, and that more strict controls were imposed on the participants.

> the second voyage of one galliot and piraguas that my predecessor sent went only to the borders of this government in order to punish some Indians who were vassals of my King and Lord, having lacked in their obedience. They went to Santa Elena, an island of this presidio, and there [the Indians] gave resistance to the Spaniards, fighting with them. . ., and an order was given to this galliot that it should not go as far as that jurisdiction and border [Carolina], only to that which pertains solely to this presidio in order to punish within its boundaries its own vassals who have denied obedience to my King and Lord and who have done damage in its lands, without passing to the contravention of the treaties (Quiroga y Losada, 1687).

As related above, the Fuentes expedition was explicitly ordered to remain south of the legal bounds of Carolina, avoiding the type of controversy raised by León's plundering of Edisto Island that summer. This order, evidently followed to the letter by Captain Fuentes, may indeed have avoided direct retaliation by the Carolinans, who at the time considered the Spaniards to be "a cruell and inveterate Enemy" (Moore et al., 1686).[86]

Despite such restrictions, the Fuentes expedition was judged to be an unequivocal success by the Spaniards, inasmuch as the Yamassee seem to have been effectively (if only temporarily in the long term) pushed back from Spanish territory. In his later defense during his *residencia*, Governor Márquez Cabrera described the expedition, noting that Fuentes was sent "to dislodge the said enemies from the Island of Santa Catalina and its neighbor, as they did, killing the cattle, burning the houses and *milpas* [cornfields]" (Márquez Cabrera, 1688a). A later account mentioned killing both "cattle and pigs" (Royal *Cédula,* 1688). Not everything was destroyed, however, for upon the return of Fuentes' vessels in January of 1687, nearly 12,000 pounds of corn and 400 pounds of beans were delivered as spoils of the expedition to the landing at the mouth of the St. Johns River, suggesting that the Yamassee had been quite successful in their land settlements.[87] Rice was even mentioned as spoils in one of the governor's letters, although this may have been looted from Stuart's Town (Royal *Cédula*, 1688).

Intriguingly, during the Fuentes raid 37 fugitive Christian Indians were brought back, "and some gentile [pagan] Yamases who wanted to come and settle" (Royal *Cédula*, 1688). Very soon after the Fuentes raid a quantity of some 75 pounds of corn were given to "the Christian Indians that Captain Francisco de Fuentes brought from the provinces of Santa Elena, who went to settle at Tolomato," and later another 200 pounds were given to this same group of Indians brought back by Fuentes, described as "Christians settled in the village of Tolomato," for use as seed in planting their spring crops (Royes, 1687). Some of this group may have been members of the group of Yamassees who fled northward from Guale and Mocama after the 1683 pirate raid, settling on Hilton Head Island before the establishment of Stuart's Town in late 1684 (see Overview). How long these new settlements remained in Tolomato after 1687 is unclear.

In retrospect, the Spanish raids of 1686 effectively defined the extent of the vacant coastal buffer zone between Florida and Carolina, and ultimately set the stage for the Yamassee War of 1715. With the destruction of Stuart's Town by the León expedition, and the effective campaign against the coastal Yamassee towns by the Fuentes expedition, the early 18th-century social geography of lower Carolina was established. The Carolinans largely abandoned their rush to push settlement southward into debated lands, and the Yamassee settled en masse on the mainland north of the Savannah River mouth. This relationship was formalized in the early 1700s, but within a few short years the Yamassee would once again shift allegiances, rising up against the English and continuing their role as major players in the international struggle for the Georgia coast (Swanton, 1922; Crane, 1956).[88]

NOTES

1. The *galeota*, or galliot, was a small, oared vessel with a single sail which, due primarily to its speed and maneuverability, was frequently used by corsairs (and here by those who chased them). Galliots typically possessed some 17 oars, each manned by a single sailor. On this occasion, Captain León led his own galliot, one loaned from Havana under the command of Pedro Hortelano, and a galliot taken from the pirate Grammont by the Floridians, commanded by Joseph Juan (see below).

2. An incomplete list of the members of the León expedition (based on the testimony that follows) includes the following individuals:
—Galliot 1, *El Rosario* (of the coastal guards, sent from Havana)
  Captain Alejandro Thomás de León (expedition leader)
  Lieutenant Joseph Juan
  Sergeant Sebastián de Cojimar, age 36
  Diego Ruíz, age 30
  Bartholomé Rodríguez, age 25
  Juan Clar, age 27
—Galliot 2, *Nuestra Señora de Regla* (from Havana)
  Pedro Hortelano, age 37 (galliot leader, León's lieutenant)
  Alejandro Jorje, age 38 (Hortelano's lieutenant)
—Galliot 3 (captured from Grammont, based in St. Augustine)
  Thomás de la Torre (?)

3. Beyond this filing note written by 18th-century notary Castilla, the rest of this page was drafted as the cover sheet for the documents that follow, as such indicating the subject of the autos and listing the governor and his notary Solana.

4. Here the governor makes reference to the three major pirate attacks on Florida during the last few years (see above).

5. Governor Márquez Cabrera refers here to equipping and manning the presidio's galliot, taken from Grammont. The crew was most likely principally composed of free blacks and mulattos living in St. Augustine who had no official duties in the military structure of the presidio (see above). As discussed further below, one member of the crew was Thomás de la Torre, the mulatto slave (native to Martinique) of Captain Antonio de Argüelles. According to the later testimony of this escaped slave (who was apprehended by the Spanish in 1687) he volunteered for the corsair expedition in 1686.

> Governor Márquez Cabrera] having communicated about [Torre's] case with the stated [Alexandro Thomás de León], they agreed that this witness [Torre] would go with the said Alexandro Thomás, the said [León] assuring him [the governor] that he would arrange his not being free but rather a slave, and in the function that he went to perform at the settlement of San Jorje, if he [Torre] perished, he [León?] would pay his master [Argüelles], in which conformity he [Torre] embarked in the said piraguas, and being in the province of Guale, Adjutant Andres Hernández, lieutenant of the said province, got an order to apprehend him [Torre], and that he should come to this presidio, and the said Alexandro Thomás de León, in a letter that he wrote to the said Governor Don Juan Márquez Cabrera, who had dispatched the said order, assured his [Torre's] person, in which conformity he took him in his company up to the plantations of the said settlement of San Jorje (Torre 1687).

Argüello's slave Thomás was thus permitted to accompany the corsairs only under strict assurances that he would return, and that his value would be paid to Argüelles in case of his death.

6. The three galliots probably left St. Augustine within a few days of this *auto* dated August 5, 1686. The two remaining galliots returned on September 19, the date of the next *auto*. The dates of specific events during the month-long expedition are contained in the English account of the assault (Moore et al., 1686).

7. The following section of this document post dates the initial *auto* by a month and a half, and represents a follow-up to the departure of León's galliots. The rest of the *autos* and testimony in Document 11 relate to the arrival of the two surviving vessels with their prisoners and spoils.

8. The two individuals named here were the captains of the two galliots that survived and returned to St. Augustine.

9. The English account reveals that León's force landed just below Stuart's Town at noon on August 17, upon which

> the few inhabitants of that Towne having scarcely given the Alarum to their Neighbors by fyring great guns, when the Spanish came running thro' the woods, enter'd the Plancons and approached in Two bodyes ere the small number of people then there could gett together soe that not being above ten men and alltogether unable to oppose soe great a force as the Enemie apprared to bee they betook themselves to woods. The Spaniards immediately possessed themselves of the Towne where they continued 3 days and haveing plundr'ed the houses destroyed the Plancons killed a great quantity of Hoggs and cattle they burnt the Towne downe to

> the ground and took away two men and a boy prisonrs (Moore et al., 1686: 82).

The Scottish youth mentioned in Hortelano's account, a 17-year-old from Edinburgh named John Livingston, testified below. There was no mention of two men having been captured from Stuart's Town; the English account may have been in error, or the two prisoners might have been among the dead in the later wreck of the Spanish galliot *El Rosario*. A subsequent Spanish correspondence indicated that the English-allied Yamassee Indians, formerly from the island of Santa Maria (and thus probably under chief Altamaha), warned the Scottish settlers of the impending attack (Menéndez Márquez and Rocha, 1686). Although this same letter stated that the Yamassee fired several threatening shots at León's group from shore, none of the expedition's survivors made any reference to this.

10. Hortelano later testified in Havana that after sacking the Scottish settlement, they went "more to the windward of the said port [of Santa Elena], to a place called the Bay of Ostalon, in some plantations" (Hortelano 1686). The plantations in question were those of Governor Landgrave Joseph Morton and his secretary Paul Grimball, located at the mouth of the Edisto River (Crane, 1956), and indeed roughly 10 leagues south of Charles Town. The probable locations of these sites are labeled on a 1695 map of the region, in which "Grimballs" was situated on the northeastern end of Edisto Island, "Land[r] Morton" across the river and upstream along the North Edisto River drainage, and "Governor Morton" situated farther inland along the North Edisto drainage and closer to the English settlement of New London on the South Edisto River (South and Hartley, 1985). The contemporaneous English account of the Spanish invasion locates the Grimball plantation on "Edeston Island" and the "new" Morton plantation "near London," where the governor's slaves and servants were captured (Moore et al., 1686), suggesting that Governor Morton's slaves were taken from the latter site listed above on the 1695 map.

11. The disposition of the 11 slaves taken during León's raid would ultimately generate considerable controversy between the Carolinans and the Spaniards at St. Augustine. Based on a 1688 English petition for their return, the names of the men were Peter, Scipio, Doctor, Cushi, Arro, Emo, Caesar, and Sambo. The three women were listed as Frank, Bess, and Mammy (Dunlop, 1688: 4).

12. Declarations were taken below from the two English indentured servants, 19-year-old Catherine Havena and 20-year-old Samuel Yankey (taken from the plantations of Grimball and Morton, respectively). In his 1689 list of losses sustained as a result of the Spanish raid, Paul Grimball made a brief mention of "Keate Oats an English maid my sarvant by Indentors they cared away captefe & keepes hur" (Grimball, 1689: 236). The first name Keate (Kate) identifies this as the same individual who testified here, called Catherine. Her surname, rendered as Havena by the Spaniards and Oats by Grimball, is more difficult to reconcile. She was listed together with 16 head of cattle, all valued at 10 English pounds.

The English account states that Governor Morton was informed that "the Spaniards had been att his house, plundered it and taken Two white people Prison[rs]" (Moore et al., 1686: 83). This was probably a reference to Samuel Yankey and the Governor's brother-in-law Edward Bowell. The latter was killed in the wreck of *El Rosario*, and his "half burnt body" was later discovered by the English (Moore et al., 1686: 84). Bowell's remains were presumably burned when Pedro Hortelano set fire to the galliot's wreck.

13. The church of Santo Christo de San Román in Campeche was sacked by pirates in their earlier raid, during which time this candlestick was probably stolen. The fact that it ended up in Governor Morton's house provides strong evidence for his illicit negotiations with pirates.

14. This chasuble, a vestment worn by priests during mass, was later asserted to have been the one stolen by Yamassee raiders from the Timucuan mission of Santa Catalina de Ahoica in February of 1685 (Quiroga y Losada, 1687).

15. Later testimony in Havana revealed further details of this incident. As related by Pedro Hortelano (1686),

> with the design of passing on to San Jorge, a storm came up suddenly and routed them, and the piragua of the said Captain Alexandro Thomás was suspended out of the water and thrown more than an arquebus shot on land in some flooded scrubland [*paxonales anegadizos*], where the said Captain Alexandro Thomas and many other companions perished, and with the industry and labor of he who declares, they removed some shotguns and two *pedreros* [artillery pieces that fired stones] and the papers of the said Captain Alexandro, all while swimming in mud [*sieno*], and he set fire to what he could not get, seeing the impossibility of pulling out the said piragua.

Since Joseph Juan (1686) and others testified at the same time that León and the others drowned, it seems likely that *El Rosario* was thrown to shore after having capsized, and after its occupants had drowned.

The location of this wreck was at the Edisto Island plantation of Paul Grimball, since it was here that the English discovered the burned body of Governor Morton's brother-in-law on August 29 (Moore et al., 1686). As related later by Carolina Governor James Colleton, part of the spoils robbed by the corsairs were found at Grimball's plantation, "burnt in a perryauge or Galliott together with the late Governours Brother in Law who was bound or Irond in the Galleot which senior Alexandros men fired" (Colleton, 1688). The Spaniards had arrived there first on August 24, remaining for "5 days wasting Robing killing & desstroyeng sd Grimballs houses goods & catell" (Grimball, 1689). After the wreck of *El Rosario* on or about the 26th (when the hurricane struck the Carolina coast), the survivors cut new masts for the remaining galliots (Hortelano's vessel had to be refloated) and left prior to Saturday, August 29, when the English forces finally arrived (Hortelano, 1686; Moore et al., 1686). The raid on Governor Morton's plantation upriver probably occurred during the first two days after landfall on Edisto Island. Given that the galliot *El Rosario* was mired in a swamp and could not be withdrawn, the charred remnants of its hull may still lie buried in this vicinity.

16. Beyond the 11 black slaves and assorted loot from the plantations, León's force brought three young prisoners to St. Augustine: a Scottish boy named John Livingston from Stuarts Town, an English indentured servant girl named Catherine Havena from Paul Grimball's plantation, and another indentured servant from the Governor Morton's plantation, Samuel Yankey. Declarations were taken from all three (see below), but as yet there is no clear indication as to their fates. In the later controversy regarding the disposition of the 11 slaves and the silver robbed from the plantations, mention was made of five prisoners having been taken during the 1686 raids, with the accompanying demand for their return (Dunlop, 1688: 22–23), suggesting that they had not been turned over by that time. By 1689, the indentured servant Catherine (Kate) had still not been returned to Paul Grimball, who claimed her as a loss (Grimball, 1689: 236).

17. The term *atiqui* was the Timucuan Indian word meaning interpreter, and had been effectively adopted by the Spanish in St. Augustine.

18. Oostende is on the coast of modern-day Belgium.

19. A *queche*, or ketch, was a one-masted ship which might easily have been used interchangeably with the term *balandra*, or sloop (employed almost universally for the vessel that entered Guadalquini harbor).

20. They arrived at the port of Guadalquini, where they ultimately became involved in the pirate raid that destroyed both the missions on St. Simons Island (Asao and Guadalquini), forcing the removal of Guale province south of the modern Georgia border and resulting in the criminal prosecution of the provincial lieutenant (see Document 10).

21. Based on the testimony in Document 10, the phrase *las casas del Rey* undoubtedly refers to the aboriginal council house of the Guadalquini Mission. The use of the term "king" may signify the aboriginal cacique, but may also refer to the use of the council house as a public structure where visiting Spanish soldiers stayed (thus signifying the house of the King of Spain).

22. All other accounts of this incident (including that of the lieutenant himself) indicate that the lieutenant arrived only after the prisoners had been in Guadalquini three days, and was with them less than a day before the pirate ship arrived.

23. This testimony conflicts with that of Lieutenant Saturnino de Abaurrea in Document 10, who indicated that he had ordered the three prisoners to assist in sailing the sloop to the mainland on Saturday, and who mentions nothing about the prisoners being at or on the sloop when the pirate ship entered Guadalquini harbor the following Sunday morning, October 22. There is indeed testimony which suggests that shots were fired when the ship arrived, and it is possible that portions of the earlier testimony in Saturnino de Abaurrea's trial were uniformly falsified by witnesses in order to cover up facets of the lieutenant's negligence.

24. This figure, if accurate, would equal some 15,000 pounds of corn that was robbed from the storehouses at Mission Guadalquini.

25. The name of the frigate's captain was spelled differently each time it was written, but based on these renditions—Chacopal, Chachopal, Cahopal—and the fact that these were based on the oral testimony of a Flemish man speaking in English to a Spanish notary, along with other clues from English documents relating to Charles Town and the Carolina colony, this pirate has tentatively been identified as the notorious Dutch corsair Captain Jacob (Jacob Everson), who has been linked with another pirate, Captain Yankey, who may have also taken part in this raid (see below).

26. Siguate was another name for the island of New Providence in the Bahamas, which was assaulted twice during 1684 by Spaniards attempting to destroy the notorious pirate haven (see note 34, this section). Since Juan Clar was apparently left there late in 1684 or early in 1685, and worked some eight months on the island, it seems apparent that New Providence was not destroyed in 1684, and in fact had been reoccupied by the English by 1685. Captain León's raid late that year seems to have prompted yet another abandonment of the island, which is when Clar turned himself over to the Spaniards and began working as a crewman on the Havana galliot.

27. Thirty quintales equals roughly 3000 pounds of corn.

28. Although this has yet to be confirmed, evidently a number of Spanish slaves captured during the pirate raid on Vera Cruz had been sold in Charles Town, and were working on plantations in the interior.

29. Captain Thomas Jingle (the name was spelled in several ways) was the pirate cited by Andrew Ranson and his cohorts, captured early during the 1684 raid, as the leader of the six vessels who planned the invasion of St. Augustine (Wright, 1960), of which one was the frigate of Captain Jacob. Inasmuch as this name had been translated from English into Spanish, Herbert Bolton (1925) rendered its pronunciation as "Hinckley." Other documentary evidence suggests that this might possibly have been another infamous pirate named Captain Yankey, an alias for Captain John Williams, who seems to have sailed with Jacob Everson during this period (Haring, 1910: 254). The two pirates (Yankey and Jacob) were later reported to have entered Charles Town harbor illegally with "a Spanish prize" with the consent of Governor Moreton (Lords Proprietors, 1686). At least one of the two (Yankey) did participate in the earlier sack of Vera Cruz (Haring, 1910; Oexmelin, 1953; Juarez Moreno, 1972).

30. The 11 passengers on the sloop that had been captured by the Indians of Guadalquini seem to have been held prisoner on Captain Jacob's frigate until someone in Charles Town paid for their freedom, the excuse being that the pirates had freed them from their Indian and Spanish captors, and had provided passage up to Charles Town. This was undoubtedly one way to reap at least some profit from their largely unsuccessful raid on St. Augustine and the Mocama and Guale missions.

31. The prisoner was presumably to work four years in return for having his freedom from the pirates paid for.

32. This individual might have been one of a pair of Spanish prisoners captured during a June 1682 raid on the cattle ranch of La Chua in the Timucua province, who were subsequently deposited on the coast of Cuba (see Bushnell, 1978, 1994).

33. The English girl was evidently sold at the age of seven into indentured servitude in 1674 in the English colony of New Providence in the Bahamas, and from the tone of her testimony held little regard for her English masters (and thus might even have willingly gone with the Spaniards).

34. Known to have been a haven for pirates, New Providence was first assaulted by Spanish forces from Cuba in January 1684, and completely destroyed in a second assault later that year, perhaps in August (Craton, 1962: 75–76). Most of the survivors fled to Jamaica, although a few ended up in Massachusetts and, as is evident here, Charles Town.

35. The name Gombre from the Spanish text is undoubtedly that of Paul Grimball, Governor Morton's secretary, whose plantation was one of the two sacked by León's expedition. Catherine ("Keate") was the only servant mentioned on Paul Grimball's list of losses due to the Spanish raid (Grimball, 1689).

36. The Scottish youth later signed his name as John Livingston, and thus was the only one of the three prisoners who could write (he was also the only one who did not come to Carolina as an indentured servant).

37. This seems to have been the governor's first opportunity to interrogate an actual Scottish resident of the colony on Santa Elena Island.

38. Based on the contents of a March 1685 letter from the two leaders of Stuart's Town, Lord Cardross and William Dunlop (Insh, 1929), the 148 Scottish colonists sailed from Scotland in the 170-ton ship *Carolina Merchant* on July 21, 1684, and after a 10-week journey across the Atlantic, landed at Charles Town on October 2. After losing some of their number to illness during their month at Charles Town, the colonists arrived in early November 1684 to found Stuart's Town on Port Royal Island. The origin of the name Vuenbi, or Buenbi, is unknown.

39. This passage may refer to William Dunlop, who participated in the government at Charles Town (McCrady, 1897: 215–216).

40. This notorious incident has been described in some detail, and it is generally considered to have been the primary motive for the León raid of 1686. This slave raid, in which a group of some 50 Yamassee Indians under the leadership of their cacique Altamaha destroyed the Timucuan mission of Santa Catalina de Afuyca in February 1685, is discussed in the Overview.

41. The pirate Grammont had raided St. Augustine yet another time in the spring of 1686, but was engaged by León and defeated. His arrival in Stuart's Town to resupply in early July may have stemmed from this defeat.

42. Although the Scottish colonists had petitioned the Carolinians for cannons soon after their arrival, it was not until November 1685 that the colony's proprietors ordered five unmounted cannons from Charles Town to be sent to Stuart's Town (McCrady, 1897: 215–216; Insh, 1929: 79–80). Based on the testimony of John Livingston, it seems that they did receive at least three cannons for their fortification, although they do not appear to have been used in defense of the town during the León raid.

43. Although Livingston indicated ignorance of such plans, Cardross and Dunlop wrote in March 1685 that they "went near to Saint Catharina, which we hear the Spainards have desarted on the report of our setling here, and we desyre this summer to vew it and tak possessione of it in his Majesties name for the behove of the lords proprietors" (Cardross and Dunlop, 1685: 75). Although they stated that they would need a royal patent, recognizing that it had been Spanish territory, their plans seem to have specifically included Santa Catalina, as Governor Márquez Cabrera suspected.

44. Joseph Morton was installed as Governor in May 1682, and although he was replaced in April 1684, he was reinstated for a second term in September 1685 (McCrady, 1897: 194, 201, 210).

45. Like Catherine Havena, Samuel Yankey was also an indentured servant.

46. At least one ship originating out of Charles Town is known to have participated in both the 1683 Grammont raid and the 1684 Jingle raid (Wright, 1960: 136–137). This may have been the ship of either Captain Thomas Jingle or Captain Jacob Everson, both of whom were pirates who evidently had houses in Charles Town.

47. This matches the testimony of John Livingston, who reported that Grammont arrived to take on provisions two and a half months before (see above).

48. During the summer of 1685, Dr. Henry Woodward made his first trading journey to the Apalachicola province on the lower Chattahoochee River. Despite two Spanish expeditions dispatched from Apalache that fall and winter to catch the English traders, Woodward returned to the interior in the spring of 1686, and was indeed still in the interior at the time of this declaration (see Crane, 1956).

49. The returning Matheo must have run across León's ships on their northward journey from Guale, prior to having arrived at Stuart's Town. He then returned northward with them in one of the galliots.

50. Based on the formal petition of these Indians dated the same day (see note 51), the names of these Indians were Agustín, Domingo, Baltasar, Ventura, and Matheo.

51. The formal petition by these Indians identifies this Indian as Azencio, who had been the leader of those who originally set out from Guale in León's galliots.

52. The precise identity of this river is uncertain, but it may have been the Savannah, was one of the primary corridors of trade into the western interior. These traders might have been using the normal route, through Stuart's Town, with Woodward traveling farther over to the east in order to bypass another encounter with Lord Cardross at the Scottish settlement (Woodward had been delayed from entering the interior in April of 1685 by Cardross, who claimed Scottish domain over trade in the lower Savannah River region [Crane, 1956: 29–30]).

53. Referring to the emerging Lower Creek tribal confederacy, the term Uchise seems to descend from the late prehistoric name for the middle Ocmulgee River in central Georgia, Ichisi.

54. The phrase *mejillon de ostion* probably refers to a large oyster shell, since although *mejillon* is literally mussel, *ostion* refers to an oyster. Such shells were (and still are) common at campsites frequented by Indians in coastal regions, having been discarded after consumption. Unfortunately for the English traders, they did not consider this before leaving their captives for the night.

55. Cabeta, or Coweta, was one of the most important Apalachicola, or Lower Creek, towns on the lower Chattahoochee River. This town was one of those which had been burned by the Spanish lieutenant of Apalache, Antonio Matheos, the previous December due to their trading alliances with Dr. Woodward and the other Carolina traders (see Swanton, 1922; Bolton, 1925; and Crane, 1956).

56. This statement finally clarifies the passage in the 1688 royal *cédula* that Niquisaya was "he who passed and conveyed Captain Henrique and his companions." This last passage was used by Antonio de Arredondo (1742: 268) to assert that it was Niquisaya who "sold" Santa Elena to Henry Woodward in 1666 (see Overview). In fact, Niquisaya was only about 30 years old at that date, and could not have been the "old man" who placed Woodward on his "throne" (Sandford, 1666). Indeed, as discussed in the Overview, the earlier cacique of Santa Elena fled to Guale in 1667, probably turning Woodward over to the Spanish, and a cacique of Santa Elena (possibly the same individual) was said to have died there in 1672. The 1688 *cédula* actually referred to Niquisaya's 1686 assistance in gaining Woodward passage and trading access to the Apalachicola province of the deep western interior.

In March of 1685, Niquisaya was identified as a 50-year-old "pagan Indian native of the Yamasi nation," and as their "principal leader" (Márquez Cabrera, 1685b). Although at that time Niquisaya warned the Spanish about the Yamassee chief Altamaha's plans to attack the Timucua province, less than two years later Niquisaya was killed in Governor Márquez Cabrera's follow-up to León's raid on Santa Elena (see below). As recounted in the later royal *cédula* (1688), the governor stated in a March 6, 1687 letter to the crown that "Niquisalla" was a "principal Indian," and that he and his son and nephew were "the leaders [*caudillos*] of the Yguajas and Colones who had aggregated themselves to the English." Márquez Cabrera further elaborated that "this Niquisalla had sold them the lands with the ceremonies and writings that are done in such cases, uprooting plants and moving earth [*arrancar plantas y mover tierras*]." Referred to by the Spaniards as an untrustworthy, malicious liar (*cabiloso*), this enigmatic leader of the Indians of the Carolina/Florida frontier may well have periodically shifted allegiances in response to changing circumstances.

57. The petition of these Guale Indians, dated on the same day as this testimony, appears in other correspondence of Governor Márquez Cabrera (1686) to the King, and contains largely the same details described here. The formal petition indicates that Pedro Hortelano intended to hang the Indian Matheo upon their return to the Guale towns (perhaps as a former fugitive to the English), but was prevented from doing so by the *tunaque* Alonso (probably the Alonso Espinosa, *tunaque* of Tupiqui, listed in the 1685 Leturiondo visitation). Both Alonso, who remained sick in Guale, and his nephew Bernavé (probably the Bernabé Espinosa, *elesache* of Tupiqui, listed in the same visitation, and who later became the *mico* of Tupiqui), were listed as petitioners along with the earlier five Indians. The Indians were eventually granted all the spoils of their encounter with the English traders by the Governor.

58. The following *auto* effectively summarizes the evidence presented above, and sets forth the governor's decision regarding the disposition of the spoils.

59. The governor's source for this statement is unclear, for although the Scottish youth John Livingston testified that an Englishman had come from Charles Town to buy some of the Timucuan Indian slaves, he did not know how many. Governor Márquez Cabrera must have had other information, perhaps from other earlier depositions (which have yet to come to light).

60. The location of this declaration, apparently taken from the pirate captain whose galliot was captured at Matanzas and used by Governor Márquez Cabrera on the León expedition, was not discovered for this volume. The fact that two Carolina ships were outfitted for this expedition was additionally confirmed by the testimony of Juan Clar (above).

61. This passage may refer to the planned visit by Lord Cardross and William Dunlop to the Island of Santa Catalina in the summer of 1685 (Cardross and Dunlop, 1685). How Governor Márquez Cabrera knew about this is unknown.

62. This accord appears below.

63. Here Governor Márquez Cabrera made a very controversial decision, ordering the seizure of all the goods taken illegally by the León expedition within the bounds of Carolina. Although Márquez Cabrera provided for a full inventory to be made, and for copies to be given to León's surviving Lieutenant Pedro Hortelano, and also forwarded to Spain for a decision on the final disposition of the goods, the following documents reveal that this was a disputed command.

64. The accord signed by the royal officials effectively put the governor's decision into action, providing for the housing, feeding, and employment of the captured slaves, and for the notification of Pedro Hortelano.

65. This last passage of the formal notification is something of a departure from the normal course of events, inasmuch as Pedro Hortelano intended to dispute the Governor's decision (as was done in his letter below).

66. Although planning to dispute the seizure of the slaves and other goods, Hortelano nevertheless was obligated to turn them over while his complaint was being prepared and examined.

67. The following document is a handwritten letter from Pedro Hortelano to Governor Márquez Cabrera, and constitutes his formal petition for the suspension of the governor's decision to seize the booty of the León expedition. Hortelano was speaking on behalf of the rest of the corsairs who participated in the expedition. The text is written in a convoluted and sometimes confusing style, and thus was difficult to render into clear English.

68. Here Pedro Hortelano presents his petition for the suspension of the governor's *auto*, and provides his justification, stating that he was never consulted prior to the decision and its execution, as was his legal right as an interested party.

69. Here Hortelano makes reference to a royal *cédula* outlining the specific rights granted to corsair expeditions by the Spanish crown, a copy of which he seems to have had in his possession.

70. Hortelano argues here that the cited royal *cédula* only permits the initial investigation of returning corsair expeditions at the port where they first arrive, leaving any appeals and further legal actions for the jurisdiction of the Royal Audiencia to which that port pertains (in the case of St. Augustine, that of Mexico).

71. Here Hortelano requests a full copy of the documentation surrounding the seizure of the booty.

72. Here Governor Márquez Cabrera argues that inasmuch as the León expedition did not follow their instructions and orders not to push northward into Carolina, thus contravening previous royal *cédulas*, any *cédulas* which they might provide were of no bearing. By relegating the decision regarding the disposition of the slaves and other seized goods to the King himself, and not to the local Audiencia, Governor Márquez Cabrera effectively extended the amount of time needed for a final determination to a scale of years.

73. This passage makes reference to the governor's unwillingness to release copies of the prisoners' testimony to Hortelano, presumably based on the fact that these contained what amounted to secret intelligence information in 1686. Interestingly, due largely to the illegal sack of English plantations in Carolina, the testimony was never fully exploited by the Spanish, remaining secret for another three centuries.

74. Such slaves, labeled as troublemakers in Havana and banished to Florida in exile, were considered a dangerous influence on the captured slaves from Carolina.

75. Governor Márquez Cabrera here refers to the group of pirates captured early in the 1684 Jingle raid along the northern coast of Florida. The presence of their leader Andrew Ranson in the Franciscan convent, a product of a failed execution attempt followed by their taking sanctuary among the friars, was undoubtedly a continual thorn in the governor's side (see Wright, 1960).

76. Argüelles's slave Thomás disappeared during the León expedition, and ultimately aided the English against his former owners. The unexpected storm in Carolina, and the death of León (who had assured the governor of Thomás's conduct), set the circumstances for the slave's escape. His own account of the event is clearly mixed with substantial equivocation.

> [W]hile sacking [the plantations], one night a storm struck them that obligated the said piraguas to beach on land and abandon them on account of the weather, and during the dawn watch [*el quarto del alba*] this witness encountered the said Captain Alexandro Thomás and two Apalachee Indians of those that he had taken from this city, and wishing to cross an arm of a river in order to go to a plantation where part of his people were, by having gone that night to sack it, a quantity of Chiluque Indians surrounded them and apprehended them and took them to the army where more than two hundred Englishmen were together with as many again Indians, who had joined upon the alarm of their arrival eight leagues from the settlement, and having apprehended them they remitted them to the said settlement to the presence of its governor (Torre 1687).

Details were provided by a Spanish sailor who had spoken with Torre after his return to St. Augustine.

> he said that after the [galliot] was lost they went to take shelter in a place or ranch [*estancia*] that was near there, which they had already sacked, and at the time that they wished to arrive, they found an estuary that was there before arriving at the ranch, so full of water that they could not achieve it, and having seen this they took shelter in a forest because of the great cold and water, until such time as the water lowered in order to cross, and in this interim some enemy Indians attached to the English saw them and imprisoned them and carried them to the army of the said English and delivered the said mulatto and his companions (San Payo, 1688).

The slave's claim that he and Alejandro Thomás de León met after the wreck and were interrogated together as prisoners in Charles Town is clearly a lie, since all witnesses confirm that León was killed in the wreck of *El Rosario*. Based on other sources of evidence, Thomás de la Torre evidently made his escape with an Indian named Pedro during the storm and fled directly to the English, who at the time referred to him and his companion as "Two fugitives from the Spaniards" who had made depositions revealing the location of the invading galliots prior to August 29 (Moore et al., 1686). According to former Spanish prisoners of Captain Yankey (based in Charles Town), on whose ship they, Argüelles's escaped slave, and the Indian Pedro later embarked, Torre "fled and went to the said port of San Jorje, taking in his company three Indians who he said were his servants, two of which he sold there as slaves, and the other he brought in his company named Pedro" (Penate, 1688). The remnants of León's crew "presumed that he had fled to the settlement of San Jorje, which is also of Englishmen, in order to achieve his liberty" (Barios, 1688). Torre's later claims that he was captured against his will after becoming lost in the storm was clearly designed to conceal the truth of his flight (and the fact that he actively encouraged the Carolinians to assault St. Augustine, as noted below).

77. Here Pedro Hortelano complies with the original order by Governor Márquez Cabrera, listing all the goods seized by the León expedition. This list is more complete than that of the earlier visitation, although several other items were noted by other members of the expedition. All of these objects fall within the range of items listed by Paul Grimball (1689) as his losses during the invasion.

78. This is the largest number of plantations stated to have been plundered, inasmuch as other accounts (including those of the English) typically only mention those of Governor Morton and Paul Grimball.

79. This passage suggests that there were more goods taken than reported here, although the items of greatest value were probably all included in the manifest. Despite this, Paul Grimball's (1689) list of dozens of household items he claimed to have lost in the Spanish raid must have included items only damaged or destroyed by the pirates, since only a fraction of the items listed would have fit in the surviving vessels. Indeed, there seems good reason to suspect that many of Grimball's losses were a result of the hurricane that struck soon after the arrival of the Spaniards. A contemporaneous English description of the attack noted that "The

whole countrey seemes to bee one entire map of Devastation the greatest part of our houses are blowne downe and still lye in their ruine many of us not haveing the least cottage to secure us from the rigour of the weather the long incessant raines have destroyed almost all our goods which lye intombed in the ruines of our houses" (Moore et al., 1686).

80. Solana mistakenly wrote that Rodríguez signed the document, but corrected the error within the text.

81. Castilla squeezed this final note in on the margins of the last page of Document 11. The abrupt ending of this testimony, without any final summary or wrap-up, suggests that one or more last pages may have been omitted by Castilla when he removed the original, although their contents were probably of little historical interest.

82. In the residencia of Governor Márquez Cabrera, the 1073 pesos and 5 reales paid to these 18 men were imposed as a debt on the governor himself (Márquez Cabrera, 1688)

83. The exact quantity of corn is not readable on the microfilm copy of this document from Governor Márquez Cabrera's *residencia*, but it was either 150 or 250 (more likely the latter) *arrobas* (25 pounds each) of corn drawn from a total of 300 *arrobas* taken on the trip. The supplies were given to the force of 350 Indians in the village of Santa Maria (at that time on Amelia Island) by Captain Francisco de la Rocha (Reyes, 1687).

84. Fuentes's second in command was Captain Francisco Romo de Uriza, who led one of the piraguas during the expedition (Cabrera, 1687). Governor Hita Salazar (1692) later certified that Romo de Uriza fought "in the encounters that were offered with the rebellious Indians of the said settlement [of Sancta Helena]." The governor himself remained as the lieutenant of the *castillo* while Fuentes was away from his post (Márquez Cabrera, 1686, 1688).

85. The fact that the mud-plastered friar's house and chapel had been recently burned in 1687 suggests that Mission San Joseph Sapala was not burned in the pirate raids of 1684, and remained standing until it was occupied by Yamassee Indians in 1685.

86. The two governors (Quiroga y Losada and Colleton) who inherited the dispute between their predecessors (Márquez and Morton) effectively managed to avoid further escalation of hostilities, each denying responsibility for the earlier excesses of individuals under their government (see Bolton, 1925; Crane, 1956; and Bushnell, 1994). Colleton's predecessor Governor Morton was indeed on the verge of launching an assault against St. Augustine, apparently offering to add 300 men to pirate Captain Yankey's force of 200 (distributed on three vessels) for such an expedition (Torre, 1687). One major catalyst for this planned assault was the escaped slave Thomás de la Torre, who not only provided detailed information on the best route for such an attack, but also indicated a burning desire to personally strangle Governor Márquez Cabrera. As recounted by a former prisoner of the pirate Captain Yankey,

> the said governor of San Jorje found out that they had burned his brother in the said galliot that was lost in that coast, and that likewise the said mulatto [Thomás de la Torre] had insisted to the said governor that he should dispatch vessels in order to take the post of St. Augustine, Florida, facilitating him greatly and promising him to place them within the place without being noticed, carrying them through a river that he said was to the leeward of it, leaving the ships at the mouth of the river, and entering with the piraguas that had to navegate three days upriver, and at the end of [the three days] leave the piraguas in the said river and march across land another three days until falling upon [*amanecer*] the port of St. Augustine, Florida, and that if they did not achieve the said enterprise, he [Torre] would pay him [Governor Morton] with his head, and that he had to grasp the governor [Márquez Cabrera] and with his own hands he had to kill him, because he had held him fourteen years as a prisoner [?]being native to the island of Martinica, and he had his father in the same prison, and he was going to take him from it, all of which was public in the said port of San Jorje (Penate, 1688).

A later correspondence from Governor Colleton to Governor Quiroga y Losada of Florida confirmed that this fugitive slave had made formal depositions to the English (Colleton, 1688).

87. An entry in the books of the Royal Contaduría dated May 9, 1687, related that 466 arrobas (25 pounds each) and 12 pounds of corn and 15 arrobas and 15 pounds of beans had been remitted by Adjutant Joseph Rodríguez from the *embarcadero* of San Pablo, at the mouth of the St. Johns River (Rocha, 1687). These provisions were described as "those that Captain Francisco de Fuentes brought in the galliot of His Majesty from the province of Santa Elena from the settlement of the Yamazes." At six reales per arroba of corn and eight per arroba of beans, the total spoils amounted to nearly 3000 *reales*, or some 365 *pesos*.

88. The Yamassee War of 1715 resulted in a flood of refugees to St. Augustine, once again significantly altering the demographic profile of Florida's remaining mission communities (Hann, 1989).

DOCUMENT 12: ROYAL CEDULA TO GOVERNOR QUIROGA Y LOSADA, 1689

INTRODUCTION

The following royal *cédula* represents a second request by the Spanish Crown to the governor of Florida for information regarding the Island of Santa Catalina and the province of Guale, complaining that the first request (made in a *cédula* dated November 10, 1681) had never been fulfilled. Interestingly, the earlier order had indeed been complied with in June 1683 by Governor Don Juan Márquez Cabrera (1683) who dispatched a detailed map (still extant) of all of Spanish Florida drafted by Alonso Solana (Bushnell, 1994; and see the Overview). Whether or not this map had been misplaced by 1689 is unclear, but at that time the need for this material in the King's Junta de Guerra prompted the dispatch of the following *cédula* to the new governor of Florida.

As noted within the *cédula* below, a similar request was dispatched on the same day to the bishop of Cuba. Although nothing is currently known regarding Governor Quiroga y Losada's compliance with his *cédula*, through a long series of delays the requested ecclesiastical report was finally made in the early 1690s by the secular priest of St. Augustine, Alonso de Leturiondo (1701; and see discussion by Hann, 1986b:165–167 and Bushnell, 1994). This report has yet to be found, but Leturiondo's later memorial summarized some of the information contained in the earlier report (Leturiondo, 1701).

[f.1]
Year of 1689, Number 12[1]

The King

Don Diego de Quiroga y Losada, my governor and captain general of the city of St. Augustine in the provinces of Florida, or to the person or persons under whose charge might be its government. In view of what Don Juan Márquez Cabrera, your predecessor in that government, represented to me in a letter of the eighth of December of the past year of sixteen eighty[2] about the Indians having abandoned the Island of Santa Cathalina (which is in the province of Guale) due to the invasion which the English of the town of San Jorge and the Chuchumecos made against them, and the great suitability of settling it again, it being fertile and abundant in provisions, and the relief and aid of that presidio, I ordered the president of Canaria, by *cédula* of the tenth of November of the year of sixteen eighty-one,[3] to see to it that in the ships which go to Havana from those islands there should embark some families, aiding them like those who embarked or were ready to embark in the ships (*naos*) of Barlovento, having understood [f.1, vto.] that not because some of the said families might arrive at it [Havana] did they have to continue on to settle the Island of Santa Cathalina until they had my resolution for it, and that of the Junta de Guerra of the Indies, and so that I could determine if they were to settle or not, I ordered by *cédula* of the same day, the tenth of November of sixteen eighty-one, that [Governor Márquez Cabrera] should inform me of the district which all those provinces of Florida comprise, sending a map adjusted at the base with distances, of the situation of them, and of the said Island of Santa Cathalina, with all distinction and clarity of form which could be entered in the understanding of all its district and jurisdiction, and of that which relates to this province, explaining the benefits that would result from settling the island, and if they were looking after only the greater abundance of people, or in what consisted the suitability of its population, the fruits which it produces, in what quantity, and of what types, and if they are the same that are gathered on the mainland, and if they will be so necessary that without them they will not be able to sustain themselves, and if the island is at risk that foreigners might settle and fortify themselves on it; and by your predecessor not having made the said report up to now, it has seemed suitable to order and command you (as for the present I do) to do so immediately because it is greatly [f.2] needed, and by the Junta needing to have it present, and that you should remit it on the first occasion which offers itself to the hands of my undersigned secretary, expressing in it everything which occurs to you to say and prepare, so that with entire understanding of it a resolution can be taken once and for all on the settling of the said Island of Santa

Cathalina. By dispatch of the date of this one, the same report is requested of the Bishop of Cuba, for thus is suitable to my service. Signed in Buen Retiro on the twentieth of May, sixteen eighty-nine.

I, the King

By order of the King, Our Lord,
Antonio Ortíz de Halora

Duplicated

[paraph] [paraph] [paraph] [paraph] [paraph]

To the governor of Florida, ordering him to make immediately the report which was requested by *cédula* of November 10, 1681, about the settling of the Island of Santa Cathalina, because it is greatly needed.

Corrected [paraph]

Official

[f.2]

I made a copy of this royal *cédula* which remains placed in the archive of government under my charge. Florida, August 6, 1739.

Castilla[4]

Duplicated from number 75 of the third legajo.[5]

NOTES

1. Castilla made this note on the upper margin of the original *cédula*.
2. This letter appears in AGI SD 226.
3. The text of this *cédula* appears in AGI SD 839.
4. Here the 18th-century notary Francisco de Castilla placed his certification of having made a copy of this original *cédula*.
5. This filing note was placed vertically on the outside of the last folio of the *cédula* and refers to the specific filing location of the document.

DOCUMENT 13: ROYAL CEDULA TO GOVERNOR TORRES Y AYALA, 1693

INTRODUCTION

The following royal *cédula* was issued in 1693 in response to the continual war of attrition waged by the English colonists of Carolina against the Indians of Spanish Florida, and specifically the Guale and Yamassee Indians of the coastal regions and those of the Apalachicola province in the deep western interior. Citing the ineffectiveness of the efforts of the two previous Florida governors Quiroga y Losada and Márquez Cabrera (between 1680 and 1693) to recover these captive Indians and stem the tide of Carolinian aggression, the King issued a *cédula* permitting the new governor of Florida to act independently according to the local situation. Governor Torres y Ayala was not only directed to attempt the peacable recovery of captured Indians, but also, failing the success of diplomatic means, to launch retaliatory strikes against English subjects, capturing as many of them as the number of Indians who had been carried off from the Spanish domain.

This *cédula* established essentially an "eye for an eye" policy of retaliation between Florida and Carolina, giving the governor of Florida the power to use the means at his disposal, within the bounds of prudence, to combat the English aggression. The next year Governor Torres y Ayala was indeed prompted to launch such an attack, although the expedition was carried out by Apalachee Indians against English-allied raiders from Apalachicola (Bushnell, 1994). Some 50 prisoners were indeed taken, but the effect of such retaliation seems to have been negligible, inasmuch as during the first decade of the 18th century the Carolinans repeatedly struck bold, and ultimately mortal, blows to the mission provinces of Florida, enslaving hundreds of Indians and forcing the withdrawal of the remaining mission Indians to the protection of St. Augustine itself. Nevertheless, the following order reflects the frustration of the Spanish Crown with the continuing border wars on the northern fringe of the Spanish empire.

The King

Don Laureano de Torres y Ayala, to whom I have granted the reward of the duties of my governor and captain general of the city of St. Augustine of the provinces of Florida, or to the person or persons under whose charge its government might be: by two short [letters] which the Field Master Don Diego de Quiroga y Losada, your predecessor in that government, wrote me on February twenty-fourth and April first of sixteen eighty-eight,[1] and by the papers that he remitted to me with them, it has been on record that the governors and Indians of the town of San Jorge on the coast of those provinces have in the past on different occasions and times made prisoners of some Christian and pagan Indians of the Yguala and Yamas language[2] of the province of Guale, and likewise [they have made] slaves of those of the [province] of Apalachicole, seizing them and taking them to San Jorge, and although various tasks with those of San Jorge have been performed by the said governor and his predecessor so that they might be returned and delivered amicably to the persons who have gone for them, this has not been possible to accomplish, [the English] excusing themselves from delivering them with frivolous pretexts, giving them to understand that they have been captured by pirates and others not subject to that government, taking them to sell as slaves to the Islands of Barlovento, being Indians who have given me their obedience since their [f.1, vto.] discovery, from which extremely grave damages follow, since beyond the risk that the Christian Indians should leave the evangelical law and return to their errors, superstitions, and ancient idolatries, the pagans might not reduce themselves to our sacred Catholic faith, the Governors of San Jorge have been failing in this, in view of the peace and good correspondence which has always been observed with them by your predecessors in the execution and fulfillment of the treaties arranged between this crown and that of England, as they are charged; this having been seen in my Junta de Guerra of the Indies, along with what my fiscal of the Consejo has said and alleged, it has seemed [suitable] to advise you that in cases similar to this, you should endeavor to admonish the governor of San Jorge to observe, as is his obligation, the good correspondence that we endeavor to maintain on our part with him and the subjects of his King in consequence of the friendship and alliance that there is between this crown and that of England, and that if amicable means, tasks of courtesy, and reprimands are not enough for the correction of similar offences, you will move on to take reprisals against, and retain as many of their subjects as the Indians they took away from us, and have been captured and taken to their colonies, acting in this task with more or less resolution, according to the force with which you might find yourself in order to maintain that which you take in a manner that you do not remain less attended and successful, not being able to sustain that executed in the matter due to the English governor being superior in forces, in which I hope that you will act with the [f.2] prudence that is suitable and so important in order to conserve in all peace and defense those provinces, and of the receipt of this dispatch, and of what happens and what you execute with regard to its contents, you will give me notice in order to find myself informed about it, since thus is suitable to my service. Signed in Madrid on the twelfth of August, sixteen ninety-three.

I, the King

By order of the King Our Lord,
Don Juan de Larrea

[paraph] [paraph] [paraph] [paraph] [paraph]

To the governor of Florida preparing him for what he is to execute with the English of San Jorge in cases similar to that which is expressed above.

[paraph]

Official Registered

[f.2]

I made a copy of this royal *cédula* which remains placed in the archive of government at my charge. Florida, August 6, 1739.

Castilla[3]

From the fourth legajo. Number 23.[4]

NOTES

1. The latter is located in AGI SD 839.

2. The mention of the Yguaja (mistranscribed as Yguala) and Yamas languages refers to Guale and Yamassee Indians under the Spanish domain.

3. Castilla's note regarding the copy he made to replace this original document was placed on the back of the *cédula*.

4. This filing note refers to the location of this *cédula* in the St. Augustine archives.

DOCUMENT 14: INVESTIGATION OF THE LIMITS OF FLORIDA, 1726

INTRODUCTION

In 1721, nearly four decades after the effective abandonment of the Georgia coast by the Spaniards, English colonists from Charles Town established yet another fortification in Spanish territory, this time on the actual site of a former Guale mission. In July, a small wooden fort was constructed on the banks of the Altamaha River, precisely on the ruins of Mission Santo Domingo de Talaje, abandoned since 1661 (see Overview). This outpost, named Fort King George, proved to be the source of years of diplomatic controversy (see Crane, 1956: 235–247; Cook, 1990), and ultimately it was dismantled after only six years. Nevertheless, the dispute prompted the Governor of Florida Don Antonio de Benavides to initiate an investigation into the historical basis for Spain's territorial claims to the Georgia coast, and the documents that resulted appear below.

This original *auto* comprises testimony from six elderly veterans in St. Augustine, all of whom were questioned regarding their own knowledge and experience relating to the Spanish occupation of the coastal strip to the north of St. Augustine. The six men, their ages ranging from 60 to 82, provided an abundance of information regarding the Guale coast during the late 17th century, some of it remarkably accurate. Nevertheless, inasmuch as the following text is based on the oral testimony of old soldiers remembering both hearsay and personal experiences, this document must be viewed more as oral history than as a contemporary historical account. Consequently, there is some confusion in the testimony, and outright errors in fact, but the material nonetheless serves as a fascinating retrospect of the struggle for the Guale coast. In this sense, the 1726 investigation also foreshadows the Montiano *auto* of which it ultimately formed a part, displaying yet another facet of Spain's attempt to hold back the English onslaught in the diplomatic and legal realm.

Year of 1726, Number 14

Jesus, Mary, Joseph

Original investigation made in order to ascertain the limits and ownership of these provinces of Florida.[1]

Autos and declarations about the justification of where the jurisdiction of this presidio reaches to the north.[2]

[f.1]

Auto

In the city of St. Augustine, Florida, on the seventeenth of the month of September, seventeen twenty-six, the señor Don Antonio de Benavides Vasan y Molina, colonel of cavalry in the armies of His Majesty, exemplar of the Royal Guard Corps, and His governor and captain general of this stated city and the provinces of its jurisdiction, said that inasmuch as in a royal *cédula* dated in Madrid on the second of June of the current year His Majesty (may God preserve him) is served to command His Lordship again to place in execution the contents of the [royal *cédula*] which accompanies it, with the date of the twenty-second of June of the past year of seventeen twenty-five, in which are cited those of the tenth of the said month of June and the eighteenth of August of seventeen twenty-four,[3] each issued about the demolition of the fort that the English of Carolina have constructed in the dominions of His Majesty, and the settlement of the limits which pertain to that and this jurisdiction, and because before proceeding to the said task it is important to justify the extension of dominions which are subject to this government so that the reprimands and defenses might be made with clearer right against the governor of that colony [Carolina] in case he resists the just possession of those [dominions] that pertain to His Majesty, His Lordship was ordering and ordered to me, the notary, that immediately, and in continuation of his *auto*, an investigation should be made with all those persons who individually can give reason or notice [f.1, vto.] of the limits and jurisdiction of lands that His Majesty had and has to the north of this presidio, and those that in times past he previously occupied and posessed as his, with the rest that they might know in this matter; and having done as much as is sufficient, the steps will be taken by His Lordship which are indicated by His Majesty in the cited royal *cédulas*, and for this His Lordship thus provided, commanded, and signed, of which I, the notary, swear.

Don Antonio de Benavides

Before me,
Juan Solana
Public and Governmental Notary[4]

Declaration of
Captain Don Juan Ruíz Mexia

In the city of St. Augustine, Florida, on the sixteenth of the month of September of this year of seventeen twenty-six, His Lordship señor Don Antonio de Benavides Bazan y Molina, colonel of cavalry in the armies of His Majesty and exemplar of the Royal Guards, governor and captain general of this stated city and its provinces for the King Our Lord, before me, the notary, swore in Captain Don Juan Ruíz [f.2] Mexia, who is [captain] of infantry for His Majesty, and the stated did so before God Our Lord and a sign of the cross, according to legal form, and aware of it, he promised to tell the truth, and being questioned by the *auto* which is at the head, made for the effect, he said that the witness, being an infantry soldier in one of the companies of this presidio, was named in an armada of ships and piraguas which was made in this presidio in order to exterminate the English from Carolina, by that territory being of the jurisdiction of this government, and being ready to place it in execution in the mouth of the bar of the said Carolina, a north wind happened upon them which obligated all the vessels to seek protection in the Bay of Santa Elena, fifty leagues distant from this presidio, a little more or less,[5] in which Bay a presidio was established that existed for some time until it was demolished, passing the garrison to this [presidio] of Florida.[6] He who is testifying likewise says that being a soldier, he was detailed with twelve men on the Island of Santa Cathalina, which was settled by [f.2, vto.] Christian Indians of the Yguaja nation,[7] which owed obedience to this government for many years, like also the Island of Sapola, that of Azago, that of Guadalquina, that of Peraban, that of San Phelipe, that of San Pedro, Tupiqui, San Felipe, Santa Maria, and the Island of San Juan,[8] and that on all the islands referred to were settled Christian Indians with missionaries of San Francisco who administered them the sacred sacraments, and a garrison of soldiers on the Island of Santa Cathalina, as the head of the rest, which is forty leagues to the north distant from this presidio, and which with the hostilities that the said towns of Indians received from the English of Carolina, they came retreating down to the Island of Santa Maria, where they maintained themselves divided into three towns until the year of seventeen two, when the aforementioned English of Carolina besieged this post, and they retreated to this presidio, where they are settled at present.[9] It is certain to the witness that since he had use of reason, he knows all these [f.3] dominions up to San Gorge and its territory [as those of] the King Our Master and Lord, and what he has said and declared is the truth and what he knows and has seen, aware of the oath which he has made, in which he affirms and ratifies, and he will say so each time that he is asked, and he is of the age of eighty-two years,[10] a little more or less, and he signed it and His Lordship made his paraph.

[paraph]

Juan Ruíz Mexia

Before me,
Juan Solana

Public and Governmental Notary

Declaration of Sergeant Major Don Juan de Ayala

In the city of St. Augustine, Florida, on the seventeenth of the month of September of this year of seventeen twenty-six, His Lordship the señor Don Antonio de Benavides Bajan y Molina, colonel of cavalry in the armies of His Majesty and exemplar of the Royal Guards, governor and captain general of this stated city and its provinces for the King Our Lord, for the justification of the *auto* which is at the head, commanded to appear before him Sergeant Major Don Juan de Ayala, who before me, the notary, was [f.3, vto.] sworn in, and he did so before God Our Lord and a sign of the cross, in legal form, and having done so, aware of it, he promised to tell the truth, and being questioned by the *auto* which is at the head, he said that he came to this presidio forty-four years ago,[11] although he had news of it and its town much before, and that the lands that he has heard before and after he was here pertain and have pertained to the King Our Lord, may God preserve him, are from San Jorge, which is where the English are today, down to the head of Los Martires[12] to the south, and after he who is testifying was in this presidio, in the year of [sixteen] eighty-three, Sergeant Major Don Juan Márquez Cabrera governing [the presidio], the English nation began to move, and against reason and justice they cast out the Spaniards and settled on the Bay of Santa Elena,[13] which had a presidio of Spaniards there, and so ancient, before it happened that the royal officials of this post, going to pay the presidio of Spaniards that was there, [f.4] were killed by the Indians, for which reason the said presidio was suspended.[14] Afterwards, Don Francisco de la Guerra y de la Vega governing these provinces, the witness heard that the English had settled in the said places, and heard it said again that they had sent [ships] from this post to dislodge them, and they brought some prisoners, and that this is what this witness knows of the ancient times by having heard it.[15] And in the time of the referred Governor Don Juan Márquez Cabrera, he found out with evidence that they had settled where they found themselves in San Jorge, and he who is testifying knew with evidence what the said Don Juan Márquez Cabrera did as a result of this lamentable act to dislodge the English from Santa Elena, as he dislodged them and investigated all who came, and brought the prisoners and sent them to Havana,[16] and afterwards, in the said time, occurred the sack of Vera Cruz, and the ships which escaped and came to exit [the Bahama Channel] ascended up to the said Santa Elena and entered in its bay, and from then on [the English colony] has continued always growing and gathering [f.4, vto.] forces, and today is numerous in people and very settled with haciendas of livestock and cornfields of quality, and finds itself with much commerce, and this witness is certain of having seen all the province [of Florida] with his eyes, by having traveled across it by land and by sea, and now he has certain notice that the English of Carolina have newly constructed a fort in the dominions of the King Our Lord, and that it is very certain that from this presidio to the north all the islands and mainland were populated by Christian Indians with their ministers of the Order of San Francisco up to the said Santa Elena, which is fifty leagues distant from this presidio, a little more or less, and this is the truth and what he knows, aware of the oath that he has made, in which he affirms and ratifies, and he will say so each time he is questioned, and he is of the age of eighty years, a little more or less, and he signed it, and His Lordship made his paraph.

[paraph]

[Juan de Ayala][17]

Before me,
Juan Solana
Public and Governmental Notary

[f.5]

Declaration of Juan de Sandobal

In the said city on the said day, month, and year, the aforementioned His Lordship, the stated señor governor and captain general, for the justification of the *auto* which is at the beginning, commanded to appear before him Juan de Sandobal, a soldier of this presidio, who before me, the notary, was sworn in, and he did so before God Our Lord and a sign of the cross, according to legal form, and having done so, aware of it, he promised to tell the truth, and being questioned by the said *auto*, he said that the witness has been in this presidio fifty-six years serving His Majesty with the post of infantry soldier, and that on different occasions they named him to go in garrison to the Island of Santa Cathalina, forty leagues distant from this presidio, a little more or less, where he was six years in garrison, and that the said Island was populated by Christian Indians, and that there were another seven villages also populated by Christian Indians, with their missionaries, and that the witness recognizes and holds as the dominion of His Majesty the place where they say that the English of Carolina have made a fort, because the year that he who declares came to this presidio to serve His Majesty, Don Francisco de la Guerra y de la Vega governing it,[18] the pagan Indians allied to the English had depopulated the village of [f.5, vto.] Talaje, which is the same territory where the fort finds itself today,[19] and that due to the damages which they received from the opposing Indians, the witness is certain that thus the aforementioned Island of Santa Cathalina, and the rest which were populated, retreated to that of Santa Maria, where they were until, with the motive of the siege that the said English placed against this presidio, all the Indians retreated to it, and this is the truth and what he knows and has seen, aware of the oath that he has made, in which he affirms and ratifies, and he will say so each time he is questioned, and he is of the age of seventy-two years, and he signed it, and His Lordship made his paraph.

[paraph]

Juan de Sandobal

Before me,
Juan Solana
Public and Governmental Notary

Declaration of Adjutant Joseph Rodríguez Meléndez

In the stated city on the said day, month, and year, the aforementioned His Lordship, the stated señor governor and captain general, for the justification of the *auto* that is at the beginning, commanded to appear before him Adjutant Joseph Rodríguez Meléndez, *reformado* of this presidio, who before me, the [f.6] notary, was sworn in, and he did so before God Our Lord and a sign of the cross, according to legal form, and having done so, aware of it, he promised to tell the truth, and being questioned by the *auto* which is at the beginning, he said that the witness has been in garrison in the province of Guale in the village of Santa Cathalina, a population of Christian Indians, where the lieutenant of the said provinces was always maintained, and he was one of those named to go and depopulate the English who were in Carolina at that time, in a small armada [*armadilla*] which left from this presidio in order to eject them from that place, it being in the dominions of this government, and that being at the point of executing it, a severe storm struck the vessels, with which they ascended to the Bay of Santa Elena, where he who is testifying saw the formation of a Castillo of wood which the Spaniards made in early times when the said province was discovered,[20] and he who is declaring is certain from having heard it said that the royal officials of this presidio went to pay the infantry of the garrison of the said Castillo of Santa Elena, and on [f.6, vto.] one occasion, the said royal officials going to pay the infantry, they killed them on the road, and that the money that they were carrying for the said payment did not appear.[21] And [also] the fort that the English have today in Talaje, thirty-three leagues distant from this presidio, is constructed in the dominion of this government, because he who is testifying saw that land [*terreno*] populated by Christian Indians and missionaries of San Francisco who administered them the sacred sacraments, and he knew and saw the same in all the province of Guale, which was comprised of different villages, and that which was farthest from this presidio was at fifty leagues, until with the occasion of hostilities and the siege which the English of Carolina placed against this post all the Indians of the aforementioned province retreated, and this is the truth and what he knows and has seen, aware of the oath that he has made, which he affirms and ratifies, and he will say so each time he is questioned, and he is of the age of eighty years, and did not sign due to the impossibility of his sight, and His Lordship signed it.

Benavides

Before me,
Juan Solana
Public and Governmental Notary

[f.7]

Declaration of Adjutant Don Alonso de Avila

In the city of St. Augustine, Florida, on the eighteenth of the month of September of this year of seventeen twenty-six, His Lordship señor Don Antonio de Benavides Bazan y Molina, colonel of cavalry of the armies of His Majesty and exemplar of the Royal Guards, governor and captain general of this stated city and its provinces for the King Our Lord, for more justification of the *auto* which is at the head, commanded to appear before him Adjutant Don Alonso de Avila Saberda, *reformado* of this presidio, who before me, the notary, was sworn in, and he did so before God Our Lord and a sign of the cross, according to legal form, and having done so, aware of it, he promised to tell the truth, and being questioned by the said *auto*, he said that the witness has seen the villages of Christian Indians that there were in the province of Guale, and that all were with their missionaries, and he was on the Island of Santa Cathalina where the garrison of infantry was maintained with its lieutenant, and he is certain that in Santa Elena was [f.7, vto.] the first presidio of Spaniards until it was moved to this [presidio] of Florida,[22] and the witness has seen that before the English settled in San Jorge, vessels went to look for corn up to Santa Elena,[23] fifty leagues distant from this presidio, a little more or less, and from there to San Jorje there are about ten or twelve leagues, and regarding the place where the English have made the fort the witness knows that there was a town of Christian Indians that was called Talaje, thirty-three leagues from this presidio, a little more or less, and that from this presidio up to the place of San Jorge to the north the witness has recognized and recognizes as dominions of the King Our Lord until the year of seventeen two, when the English from the said San Jorge placed a siege against this presidio, and the towns of Christian Indians retreated to make their villages in the immediate area, where they maintain themselves today, and that all that he has said and declared is the truth and what he knows and has seen, aware of the oath [f.8] that he has made, which he affirms and ratifies, and he will say so each time he is questioned, and he is of the age of seventy-five or seventy-six years, and he signed it, and His Lordship made his paraph.

[paraph]

Alonso de Avila y Sababedra

Before me,
Juan Solana
Public and Governmental Notary

Declaration of Captain of Cavalry Don Francisco Menéndez Márquez

In the said city on the said day, month, and year, the aforementioned His Lordship, the said señor governor and captain general, for more justification of the *auto* which is at the beginning, swore in the Captain of Cavalry Don Francisco Menéndez Márquez, accountant for His Majesty, who before me, the notary, was sworn in, and he did so before God Our Lord and a sign of the cross, according to legal form, and having done so, aware of it, he promised to tell the truth, and being questioned by the said *auto*, he said that since he has had use of reason, he who is declaring knows and has seen that to the north of this [f.8, vto.] presidio from the Island of Santa Cathalina down to the Bar of San Juan del Puerto, there were towns of Christian Indians, each one with its missionary of the Order of San Francisco, on the islands as well as on the mainland,[24] and the cause for the occasion of the village of the said Island of Santa Cathalina having retreated to that of Santa Maria, and all the rest of the villages that were on the mainland, was that the pagan Indians allied to the English made them great hostilities,[25] and the witness knows that in Santa Elena, fifty leagues distant from this presidio, was the first presidio that the King Our Lord had, and the first conversions of the Indians,[26] and he has heard it said commonly that the cause of the garrison of infantry having retreated to this presidio of Florida was because the royal officials, having gone from this presidio to pay that of the said Santa Elena, they killed them on the road, and he is certain of having heard that where the fort of the English is found today, which is called the Bocas de Talaje, likewise thirty-three leagues distant from this presidio, the Yguaga Indians had their town with its missionary, and due to the hostilities that they received from the pagan Indians, they moved to the islands of the sea,[27] and he who is testifying has seen that with the occasion of the siege that the English of San Jorge placed against this presidio, the aforementioned Indians of the province of Guale left their villages and came to settle in the vicinity of this presidio, where they maintain themselves, and all that he has said and declared is the truth and what he knows, aware of the oath that he has made, which he affirms and ratifies, and he will say so each time he is asked, and he is of the age of sixty years, a little more or less, and he signed it, and His Lordship made his paraph.

[paraph]

Francisco Menéndez Márquez

Before me,
Juan Solana
Public and Governmental Notary

[f.9, vto.]

Certification

I, Ensign Juan Solana, Public and Governmental Notary of this city and presidio of St. Augustine, Florida, certify and swear in the form that best I can to those who read the present how it is on record to me, having heard it said by the old and ancient men of this presidio during my fifty-eight years in this place that the first town that His Majesty, God preserve him, had in these provinces was in Santa Elena, and the first conversions, fifty leagues from this presidio, more or less, and ten or twelve leagues to the north up to the place of San Jorgue, where the English find themselves settled, and that two causes motivated having passed the garrison and conversions to this [presidio] of Florida, one they say was due to the Bar of this port being next to the mouth of the [Bahama] Channel, because of worrying that enemies might impede the pass with great facility from the armadas of His Majesty which go to exit [the channel],[28] and the other [cause] was that the royal officials having gone from this presidio to pay the garrison of infantry of the presidio of Santa Elena, the Indians killed them on the road, and the place where the English today find themselves settled, which they call Carolina, was the province that we called [the province] of Escamaqu, [f.10] and [expeditions] went there from this presidio to look for fruits [of the land] in vessels by sea and by the rivers in piraguas, until the English settled it, governing these provinces Don Francisco de la Guerra y de la Vega, who, as soon as he found out about it, finding two vessels of His Majesty in this port, and one which had come to conduct the *situado* from New Spain, armed them for war.[29] They left and went to enter through the Bar of Santa Cathalina, where they armed eight piraguas[30] with the Indians of the province of Guale and some Spaniards, and the said vessels and piraguas having come forth by the rivers, being ready to execute [the attack] upon the very port of the said San Jorgue, a severe storm struck them so that the vessels could not maintain themselves, and the said dislodgement [of the English] was frustrated. And it is on record to me by having seen it that all the islands to the north of this presidio, which they called the province of Guale, were populated by Christian Indians with their missionaries of the Order of San Francisco, and opposite the said islands on the mainland three villages of Yguaja Indians, one called Satuache, another Tubique, and Talaje, which is where they say the English [f.10, vto.] have constructed a fort of wood.[31] And it is on record to me by the devastation that they are experiencing in this presidio from the said English that since the town of San Jorge began to find itself with some favored forces of the Indians allied to them, they have ruined and destroyed all the province of Guale in order to take possession of it, as is being experienced, it being on record to me to be land of the King Our Lord up to the said Santa Elena. And so that it is on record according to that ordered by His Lordship in his *auto*[32] of today, the date below, I give the present in Florida on the nineteenth of the month of September of this year of seventeen twenty-six, of which I swear.

Juan Solana
Public and Governmental Notary

[f.11]

Auto[33]

In the city of St. Augustine, Florida, on the nineteenth of the month of September, seventeen twenty-six, His Lordship señor Don Antonio de Benavides Varan y Moleño, colonel of cavalry in the armies of His Majesty and exemplar of the Royal Guard Corps, and His governor and captain general of this stated city and its provinces, said that not withstanding the superabundant justification that results from the investigation that has been made by virtue of the auto of the seventeenth of the current [month] about the districts that pertain to His Majesty and the jurisdiction of this government, His Lordship was commanding and commanded me, the notary, to certify what might be on record to me, and what I might know on the subject of the cited *auto*, and thus done, it should be gathered together and placed as a continuation of the principal [testimonies], and copies should be taken that are suitable to remit to His Majesty on the first occasion[34] and to base the remaining tasks which might have to be done about the definition of boundaries between this jurisdiction and that of Carolina, which His Lordship reserves for execution in his own time and in the form that His Majesty has ordered in the royal *cédulas* cited in the said *auto*, and for this His Lordship thus provided, commanded, and signed.

Don Antonio de Benavides

Before me,
Juan Solana
Public and Governmental Notary

NOTES

1. This cover sheet was drafted by notary Francisco de Castilla in 1739.

2. This summary title was placed on the outside of the folded bundle of folios comprising the original 1726 document.

3. This convoluted passage refers to four royal *cédulas,* all of which relate to the English fort of 1721. The most recent, and the direct cause of the present *auto*, is that of June 2, 1726, which evidently repeated instructions given in an earlier *cédula* dated June 22, 1725 (a copy of which accompanied the later order). This earlier *cédula* also made direct textual references to two other *cédulas*, dated June 10, 1725, and August 18, 1724.

4. Juan Solana was the son of Alonso Solana, the late-17th-century notary who penned Documents 10 and 11 under the governorship of Don Juan Márquez Cabrera. His handwriting displays many features similar to the script of his father, although in many ways it is somewhat more sloppy. Juan probably inherited the office of public and governmental notary from his father Alonso.

5. The preceding passage refers to the abortive 1670 expedition by Governor Francisco de la Guerra y de la Vega to attack the newly founded English colony at Charles Town (San Jorge). Had an unexpected storm not interfered with the small Spanish fleet, composed of 3 ships and 14 piraguas under Juan Menéndez Márquez, the fledgling colony might not have survived (Crane, 1956: 10; and Bushnell, 1994).

6. Here Ruíz Mexia refers to the late 16th-century Spanish colonial town of Santa Elena, uprooted in 1587 after the burning of St. Augustine by Sir Francis Drake.

7. Yguaja was the 18th-century equivalent for Guale. Ruíz Mexia was apparently one of the Guale garrison on St. Catherines Island during the turbulent last years of that province's history.

8. Here Ruíz Mexia cites from north to south the mission towns of the Guale and Mocama provinces post-dating roughly 1670 (although his declaration implies that all of these were islands, he actually cites individual missions on those islands). The towns of Santa Catalina, Sapala, Asajo, Guadalquini, San Phelipe, San Pedro, and San Juan reflect the pre-1684 distribution of Guale and Mocama, and the three towns of Tupiqui, San Felipe, and Santa Maria comprise the three aggregate towns on Amelia Island after that time (which, with San Juan, survived until 1702, as noted below). The identity of Peraban is problematic, but inasmuch as it is placed between Guadalquini on the southern tip of St. Simons Island and San Phelipe in the middle of Cumberland Island, Peraban may have been a native name for Jekyll Island, more commonly referred to by the Spaniards as the Island of Whales (see Appendix A).

9. The 1702 assault by Governor Moore of Carolina resulted in the final retreat of the Indians of Guale and Mocama to the safety of the Castillo's guns just north of St. Augustine. Hann (1989) discusses the mission towns during this period.

10. Born in 1644, Captain Ruíz Mexia undoubtedly witnessed most or all of the southward retreat of Guale and Mocama after the 1660s.

11. Ayala's testimony fixes the date of his arrival in 1682, at about the age of 36.

12. The Florida Keys, named Los Martires ("The Martyrs") by Juan Ponce de León in the early 16th century.

13. Here Ayala makes reference to the 1684 foundation of the Scottish colony of Stuarts Town on the Island of Santa Elena (see Document 11).

14. This reference is undoubtedly a product of local tradition, or myth, inasmuch as the described murder of the royal officials actually occurred in 1576, when three officials were murdered on Sapelo Island (Bushnell, 1981: 122–123). Although this act, and the associated uprising of the Indians around Santa Elena, resulted in the temporary abandonment of the fort, the final withdrawal a decade later had nothing to do with these earlier murders.

15. The previous passages relating to the presidio at Santa Elena and the term of Governor Guerra y Vega were based on hearsay, inasmuch as Ayala arrived in Florida during the term of Governor Márquez Cabrera. The last section seems to be a mixed reference to the establishment of Charles Town during the term of Governor Guerra y Vega, and the establishment and destruction of Stuarts Town during the term of Governor Márquez Cabrera more than a decade later.

16. As yet this is the only mention, contemporary or otherwise, known regarding the fate of the young prisoners brought back by the León expedition from Stuarts Town and Carolina in 1686 (see Document 11).

17. Ayala's signature is completely illegible.

18. Sandobal's testimony places the date of his arrival in St. Augustine between 1664 and 1671, when Governor Guerra y Vega was governor of Florida.

19. Sandobal makes it clear here that Fort King George was indeed built on the site of the former mission of Santo Domingo de Talaje, a fact confirmed by the testimony of all subsequent witnesses (see below). This passage also makes reference to the 1661 Chichimeco assault on Talaje, which resulted in its destruction and abandonment (prior to Sandobal's arrival in 1670, and during the term of Guerra y Vega's predecessor).

20. Here Adjutant Rodríguez describes in greater detail the events of Governor Guerra y Vega's aborted 1670 expedition against Charles Town. Intriguingly, Rodríguez also makes note of having seen the ruins of a wooden fort at Santa Elena, undoubtedly the late 16th-century fort San Marcos, noted as *la formazion de un castillo de madera que en lo primitibo yzieron los españoles quando se descubrio dha provinzia.* William Hilton's 1663 expedition to the Carolina coast had earlier discovered at Santa Elena "the Ruines of an old Fort, compassing more than half an acre of land within the Trenches," almost certainly describing the same structure (Hilton, 1664). When recently excavated by archaeologists, some of the cedar posts were still intact below the ground (South, 1991: 35–38).

21. Rodríguez also makes reference to the 1576 murder of the royal officials.

22. Although Santa Elena was one of the first two colonial towns established by Pedro Menéndez de Avilés in Florida, its establishment in 1566 actually postdated that of St. Augustine in 1565.

23. Here Avila makes reference to the frequent expeditions sent north from St. Augustine during the 17th century to barter corn and other provisions from the unconverted province of Escamaçu.

24. Francisco Menéndez Márquez, born around 1666, was too young to have been witness to the two Guale missions farther north of Santa Catalina (San Phelipe de Alave and San Diego de Satuache).

25. In addition to raids from the mainland by English-backed Indians, the pirate raids of 1683–1684 provided the final impetus for the southward retreat of Guale and Mocama (see the Overview).

26. Here Menéndez Márquez refers to the early conversion attempts around Santa Elena by Jesuit missionaries during the late 1560s and 1570s.

27. The phrase "Bocas de Talaje" could literally be translated as the "Mouths of Talaje," undoubtedly referring to the many channels at the mouth of the Altamaha River, on one of which was situated Mission Santo Domingo de Talaje (and the later Fort King George). After the 1661 Chichimeco raid that destroyed Talaje, Mission Santo Domingo was relocated to the northern end of St. Simons Island (see Overview).

28. In this passage Solana refers to a more accurate reason for which Santa Elena was abandoned in favor of St. Augustine after the burning of St. Augustine by Drake in 1586, specifically noting the strategic importance of the southern location at the mouth of the crucial Bahama Channel, through which the Spanish treasure fleets sailed during the colonial era on their return journey to Spain.

29. Here Solana provides a more thorough description of the failed 1670 Spanish assault on Charles Town.

30. Other sources give 14 as the number of piraguas (Crane, 1956; Bushnell, 1994).

31. Solana leaves out only Mission San Phelipe de Alave in his listing of the principal mainland missions of the Guale province during the mid-17th century (see Overview). Although its Indian inhabitants were known as Yguajas during the 18th century, the province itself still retained the name of Guale.

32. The *auto* ordering notary Juan Solana to append his own certification to the preceding testimony follows.

33. This *auto* was drafted prior to Solana's preceding certification, but was copied here at the end.

34. A copy of this original investigation was indeed sent to Spain, where it remains in AGI SD 844.

DOCUMENT 15:
PAST AND PRESENT PROVINCES OF FLORIDA, 1736

INTRODUCTION

This final document in the Montiano package was drafted only a few years earlier, prior to Governor Montiano's term but following the 1733 foundation of Georgia. By order of then Governor Don Francisco del Moral Sánchez Villegas, Captain Don Luis Rodrigo de Ortega drew up a list of all the Indian provinces and towns, including Christians and pagans, that had once been within the Spanish domain. By 1736, the far-flung mission provinces of Spanish Florida had been reduced to the immediate environs of St. Augustine, and increasing numbers of Indians in the northwestern interior were entering the English and French trading networks. Nevertheless, in an attempt to present the historical extent of Spanish rule in old Florida, Captain Rodrigo de Ortega outlined all the previous and present aboriginal provinces which had formerly rendered obedience to the Spanish crown (table 6).

It is unclear where Captain Rodrigo de Ortega obtained his information, for some of it (particularly his lists of the mission towns) dates to the late 17th century, and is quite accurate and thorough. In addition to a retrospective look at the now-abandoned mission provinces of Spanish Florida, Captain Rodrigo de Ortega also listed the major provinces of unconverted Indians living in the deep interior in 1736, providing yet another overview of western Georgia and Alabama during the early 18th century. Although detail is largely lacking, the list is nevertheless of interest.

Ultimately, the following document serves as a capstone to the rest of the Montiano packet, effectively summarizing the past and present (as of 1736) Indian societies which, in theory, made up Spanish Florida during the first Spanish period. What is perhaps most telling is the manner in which Captain Rodrigo de Ortega asserted the prior dominions of Spanish Florida, not using geographical features or lines of latitude, but rather former Spanish alliances with aboriginal groups living upon the landscape. In many ways, this illustrates the tenuous grip that the Spanish colonists actually held on the territory of Florida. To a large extent, the Spanish claim to Florida was fundamentally based not so much on actual Spanish control of the land, but more or less fragile relationships with the Indian societies who called it home.

Year of 1736 Number 15

Certification given by Captain Don Luis Rodrigo de Ortega about the limits and ownership of these provinces of Florida.[1]

[f.1]

Account sworn before God and the King (God guard), made by me, Captain of Infantry Don Luis Rodrigo de Hortega, by order of the señor Governor and Captain General Don Francisco del Moral Sánchez Villegas, who is [governor] of this presidio and its provinces for His Majesty, for the justification of the right and possession which His Majesty has, and has had, of the following provinces:

Firstly, this presidio of St. Augustine, Florida, and its provinces.

First province, the province of Mocama, which falls to the north, which was of Catholics; first town San Antonio, Salamototo,[2] San Juan del Puerto, Santa Cruz, Pirigiligua,[3] Gualiquini, San Simón.[4]

Second province that of the Higuajas,[5] which falls [f.1, vto.] also to the north, of Christians; Santa Maria,[6] Tupiqui, Santo Domingo, the village of San Phelipe, Asajo, Sapala, Santa Catharina.

And on the mainland to the west, eleven ancient villages of Christian Higuajas.[7]

From the Bar of Santa Elena to the south, I have always heard that it is terrain of our King, and from the Bar of Santa Elena to the north, of the English.

The province of Mayaca falls to the south of this presidio, which was of Christians; the first village is Mayaca, Malao, Atoquime, Tissime, Jororo, Abara, and Cahele.[8]

The province of Christians of Timucua falls to the west; the town of Santa Fé, Ebitanaia, San [f.2] Francisco Potano, Santa Catharina, the Ochocones,[9] Tarifica, Afuica, San Juan de Guacara, San Pedro, San Matheo, Machava, Asile.

TABLE 6
Rodrigo de Ortega List of Florida Provinces, 1736

Christian Provinces
Province of Mocama, to the north
San Antonio
Salamototo
San Juan del Puerto
Santa Cruz
Pirigiligua
Gualiquini
San Simón
Province of the Higuahas, to the north
Santa Maria
Tupiqui
Santo Domingo
San Phelipe
Asajo
Sapala
Santa Catharina
Eleven ancient mainland villages of Christian Higuajas
Province of Mayaca, to the south
Mayaca
Malao
Atoquime
Tissime
Jororo
Abara
Cahele
Province of Timucua, to the west
Santa Fé
Ebitanaia
San Francisco Potano
Santa Catharina
the Ochocones
Tarifica
Afuica
San Juan de Guacara
San Pedro
San Matheo
Machava
Asile
Province of Apalache, to the west
Bitachuco
the Chines
Ayuale
Capole
Ocone
Tomole
Espalaga
Pactale
Baququa
the Chacatos
San Luis
Escambe

TABLE 6—(*Continued*)

Pagan Provinces to the West–Southwest and Northwest
Province of the Ayavamos (French allies)
Province of Movila (French allies)
Province of the Uchises, 12 villages (Spanish allies)
Province of the Talapuses, 18 villages (Spanish allies)
Province of the Chicazaes (English allies)
Province of the Apuas (English allies)
Chicasas and Uches (English allies)
Pagan Provinces to the South
Province of Amagiro, 15 villages
La Costa

The province of Apalache, which falls to the west, of Christians; first town Bitachuco, Ayuale, Capole, Ocone, Tomole, Espalaga, the Chines, Pactale, Bacuqua, the Chacatos, San Luis, Escambe.

The provinces of pagans who have rendered obedience to our King (God preserve him), which fall to the west–southwest and to the northwest:

Firstly the province of the Ayavamos, which the French possess today.

The province of Movila, which the French possess.

The province of the Uchises, which is for [f.2, vto.] our King,[10] with twelve villages.

The province of the Talapuses, which is for our King, with eighteen villages.

The province of the Chicazaes, who are with the English.

The province of the Apuas, who are with the English.

Chicasas and Uches, who are with the said English.[11]

Villages of pagans to the south of this presidio:

Firstly, the province of Amagiro enters with fifteen villages of pagans, outside of the coastal towns of La Costa, which is another group [*gentio*].[12] And the shame is that of these provinces of Christians, with so many temples as they have had, where the sacred gospel was so resplendent, this English nation with all its allied Indians, [f.3] has depopulated them and all the rest of these provinces which I have covered, both of Christians and pagans serving His Majesty. And what I certify is that of all the provinces there are no lands like those of Apalache, of pagans and Christians, where there are many [types of] wood, of all manner of wild livestock [*ganados silbestres*], and so that it is on record where suitable, by order of His Lordship the señor governor and captain general, I give the present certification, sworn in St. Augustine, Florida, on the twenty-seventh of November, seventeen thirty-six.

Don Luis Rodrigo de Ortega

I left a copy of this certification written on three folios. Florida, August 7, 1739.

Castilla[13]

NOTES

1. This cover page was drafted by the notary Castilla to head Captain Rodrigo de Ortega's original certification.

2. The late-17th-century towns of San Antonio de Enacape and San Diego de Salamototo, located along the middle St. Johns River to the southwest and west of St. Augustine, were not at the time considered to be towns within the Mocama province, instead falling more within the political domain of the Timucua province extending to the west. By the early 18th century, however, the inhabitants of the St. Johns region seems to have become more closely affiliated with the coastal Mocama region, perhaps partly as a result of southward aboriginal population movements in the late 17th century.

3. This town is presumably equivalent to the Pirihiriba of the 1702 era, located on the south bank of the mouth of the St. Johns River (see Arnade, 1959).

4. Technically speaking, the Colon residents of Mission San Simón during the 1670s and 1680s were not a part of the Mocama province, nor did they speak the same language (see Overview). Nevertheless, perhaps due to the long proximity of this town to Mission San Buenaventura de Guadalquini on the southern tip of St. Simons Island, the refugees of San Simón seem to have attached themselves to the town of Santa Cruz, and thus may have been considered Mocama in retrospect by Rodrigo de Ortega.

5. Higuaja, or Yguaja, was the name commonly used during the 18th century to refer to the Guale.

6. Originally a Mocama mission town, Santa Maria was the aggregation site of several northern Guale towns during the pirate raids of the mid-1680s, and thus was included by Captain Rodrigo de Ortega as a Guale town.

7. This passage refers to the mainland mission towns of the Guale province, effectively abandoned by the last quarter of the 17th century (see Overview). Because only four principal mainland missions are known for the late 17th century, Rodrigo de Ortega may have been referring to the multitude of towns in that region during the early 1600s.

8. The province of Mayaca noted here was missionized during the last years of the 17th century, and included the missions of San Salvador de Mayaca, la Concepción de Atoyquime, San Joseph de Jororo, and Atissimi, including natives of Malao (Hann, 1991b).

9. The only other clear reference to this group yet known appears in a 1692 document discovered by John Hann (personal commun., 1991), which includes a petition by Marcos, the cacique of the Ocochunos, relative to establishing a new village near Mission Santa Catalina in the Timucua province. This last name is similar to Cotocochuni, the name used for the Yustaga province within the Timucua mission province during the first quarter of the 17th century (see Worth, 1992: 63–8).

10. Within only three years General Oglethorpe of Georgia recruited the assistance of these Lower Creek for his 1739 invasion of Florida.

11. The interior provinces noted above probably correspond to Alabama [Ayavamos], Mobile [Movila], Uchise, Tallapoosa [Talapuses], Abihka [Apuas?], Chickasaw [Chicasas], and Yuchi [Uches] (see Swanton, 1922, for a thorough treatment). The identity of Chicazaes (if not Chickasaw) is unclear, although the absence of the important Cherokee from the list of English allies might suggest one possibility.

12. Hann (1991a: 22) identifies the Amajuro/Majuro River as the Withlacoochee River on the western coast of central Florida. The cultural identity of these 15 villages of Amagiro Indians noted by Rodrigo de Ortega is unclear (the river was named as such as early as 1675 [Díaz Vara Calderón, 1675]). The Indians of La Costa lived along the southern Atlantic coast of Florida, evidently including the Keys; Costas was also a name applied during this period to the Alafay Indians of the Tampa Bay region (Hann, 1991a: 357–358; 1991b: 172).

13. The notary Francisco de Castilla here left his customary note stating that a copy of this original document had been archived in St. Augustine.

ADDENDUM: THREE ADDITIONAL ORDERS REGARDING GUALE, 1673–1700

INTRODUCTION

Soon after the August 14 completion of Governor Manuel de Montiano's formal report and package of appended documents, three additional orders relative to the same subject came to the governor's attention. Quickly penning a cover letter explaining the relevance of their contents, Montiano added the original orders to his final submission to Spain, dated August 18, 1739 (see Preface). Placed here as an addendum to the primary Montiano package, these orders date to 1673, 1699, and 1700, respectively, and provide additional details regarding the *repartimiento* labor draft during the 1670s, as well as references to two expeditions sent by Florida governors to deliver shipwrecked Englishmen to Charles Town. Governor Montiano's introductory letter is presented below, followed by the text of each order and with a brief introduction.

[f.1]

My Lord

I place in the sovereign royal understanding of Your Majesty that after having concluded the report of the 14th of the current [month], directed toward demonstrating and making known with evidence the direct dominion and ownership that without a shadow of confusion or doubt Your Majesty has to the provinces to the north of this post, some papers arrived in my hands that are the same [f.1,vto.] originals that I pass to the [hands] of Your Majesty, in which the following things are verified.

In the [document] number 1, duplicated, it is on record that in the year of 1673, by order of Governor Don Manuel de Cendoya, Adjutant Diego Díaz Mexia drafted fifty Indians from the villages of the mentioned provinces [of Guale], which at that time were the island and village of Santa Maria, the island of Guadalquini, the Yamase caciques, the village of San Phelipe, [f.2] the village of Asaho, Zapala, Tupiqui, and the villages of Santa Catalina and Satuache.

In the [document] number 2, duplicated, it is on record that in the year 1699 Governor Don Laureano de Torres dispatched Ensign Don Luis Rodrigo so that he should go to San Jorge to transport some Englishmen lost on the coast to the south of this post, giving him an order to take four soldiers from [this post] and two from the province of Guale, and at the same time [f.2,vto.] the experienced Indians who might be necessary from there, and that on the return from his journey he should leave the two soldiers of Guale in their destination.

In the [document] number 3, duplicated, it is on record that in the year 1700 Governor Don Joseph de Zuniga dispatched the aforementioned Ensign Don Luis Rodrigo so that he should go to San Jorge to transport some Englishmen and blacks who had been lost in the environs of this post to the [f.3] the north in a ship, and in the province of Guale in a launch, from which it can be concretely inferred that if the province of Guale was the residence of the English, it would not have been necessary to make use of the courtesy and friendship of picking them up from the accident suffered in their home and take them to their own home, because their very own servants would have had this care. This is as much about the matter as occurs to me [f.3,vto.] to place in the royal comprehension of Your Majesty, whose Royal Catholic person may God guard the many happy years that Christianity has need of. St. Augustine, Florida, August 18, 1739.

My lord,
Don Manuel de Montiano

ORDER 1: CENDOYA TO DÍAZ MEXIA, JANUARY 24, 1673

Providing an important addition to the series of five labor draft orders for Guale during the term of previous Governor Francisco de la Guerra y de la Vega (dating to the period 1665–1669), the following order reveals important demographic changes in late 17th-century Guale and Mocama. While the *repartimiento* orders during the late 1660s made explicit reference to the pagan Yamassee caciques in Guale and Mocama, the expected contribution of laborers was never specifically enumerated (see Overview; also see Document 5, Orders 3, 6, 9, 10, and 11). By 1673, however, some 24 laborers were enumerated for the two major clusters of Yamassee settlement within the old provinces of Guale and Mocama (on the islands of Guadalquini and Santa Maria), making up nearly half of the entire labor draft from these northern provinces. The influx of unconverted Yamassee into the coastal missions thus effectively doubled the labor pool available for St. Augustine, making up for the ravages of depopulation in the northern provinces.

[f.1]

Sergeant Major Don Manuel de Cendoya, governor and captain general of this city and presidio of St. Augustine, Florida and its provinces for the King our lord.

Inasmuch as it is suitable to the service of His Majesty to send to the provinces of Guale on matters pertaining to the conservation of this post, and for this it is necessary that a person of all satisfaction and care goes, and because I have [confidence] in Adjutant Diego Díaz Mejia, for the present I order that as soon as he receives this order he should leave this city and go to the province of Guale, in which he will comply with the instruction of mine that he carries with the care that I trust of his person, and I command all the caciques, *micos*, and *mandadores* of the villages where he might arrive to give him all the aid necessary for the complete fulfillment of what I order to the said Adjutant Diego Díaz Mejia, to whom I charge the good treatment of the natives, and the copy of this my order will be taken in the office of the secretary of government of these provinces. Given in the city of St. Augustine, Florida, on January 24, 1673.

Don Manuel de Cendoya

By order of the governor and
captain general, my lord,
Juan de Pueyo
His Secretary

Order to Adjutant Diego Díaz Mejia to go to Guale.[1]

[f.1,vto.]

The copy of this order on the other side by the señor Sergeant Major Don Manuel de Cendoya, governor and captain general of these provinces, was taken in the office of the secretary of government. Of this I swear,

Alonso Solana
Governmental Notary[2]

[f.2]

Sergeant Major Don Manuel de Cendoya, governor and captain general of this city and presidio of St. Augustine, Florida, and its provinces for the King our lord.

Adjutant Diego Díaz Mejia will take from the province of Guale the Indians cited here for the agricultural work in this presidio, from the following villages:

From the island and village of Santa Maria de los Yamazes	12
From the island of Guadaquini, from the Christians	4
From the Yamaze caciques[3]	12
From the village of San Phelipe[4]	2
From the village of Asao	4
From the village of Zapala	4
From the village of Tupiqui	4
From the villages of Santa Catalina and Satuache	8
	50

The said Adjutant Diego Díaz Mejia is to bring all the stated fifty Indians, with the distinction of those that he takes from each village, without disturbing them or pressing them with burdens, and if it is necessary to change [the quantity from] the villages he will do so, taking from each one according to the people there are,[5] and in case the caciques refuse to give the Indians he cannot press them to give them up by force, rather he will come without them, and in everything the said Adjutant will comply with the orders of His Majesty, for this is important to his royal service. [f.2,vto.] Given in the city of St. Augustine, Florida, on the twenty-fourth of the month of January, sixteen seventy-three.

Don Manuel de Cendoya

By order of the governor and
captain general, my lord,
Juan de Pueyo
His Secretary

Instruction that Adjutant Diego Diaz Mejia is to observe for the draft of the Indians of Guale.

ORDER 2: TORRES Y AYALA TO RODRIGO, MARCH 10, 1699

The last two orders in Governor Montiano's addendum relate to expeditions sent by the governors of Florida to Carolina, in each case delivering shipwrecked Englishmen to the governor in Charles Town. In the following order, a group of six Englishmen who survived a shipwreck along the Florida coast to the south of St. Augustine were to be delivered to the governor of Carolina. Only six Spanish infantrymen joined Ensign Luis Rodrigo[6] on the journey northward, and two of these were to be picked up from the garrison post in Guale (at that time in Mission Santa Maria on present-day Amelia Island). The trip actually served several purposes, since in addition to turning over the six Englishmen, Rodrigo additionally acted as a courier, bringing a letter from Governor Torres y Ayala to his counterpart in Carolina. One further task was intelligence-gathering by the Spaniards sent to Charles Town, indicating that such trips served as a good opportunity to pick up news from the English.

In sum, the official orders for these two expeditions to Carolina suggest that the hand-delivery of shipwrecked Englishmen to Charles Town served as a routine manner of maintaining communications between the two competing colonies (Florida and Carolina), and also provided the Spaniards with current intelligence regarding English activities, including associations with pirates.

[f.1]

Don Laureano de Thorres y Ayala, knight of the order of Santiago, governor and captain general of this city of St. Augustine, Florida, and its provinces for the King our lord.

Inasmuch as in a meeting of accord with the royal officials of the Royal Hacienda and coffer of these provinces, I have resolved to send to the settlement of San Jorje the Englishmen who were lost on the southern coast of this presidio, and for their transport I elect and name Ensign Luis Rodrigo, *reformado* of this presidio, to go as the head of the six infantry that must be taken as their guard, to whom I order and command that as soon as this my order is delivered to him, with six infantrymen—four of them from this presidio and two of which he will take from the garrison of the province of Guale—and the experienced Indians that he will need from the said province, he will make the journey to the said province of Carolina and deliver the six Englishmen who were lost on the stated coast to its governor, with the letter of mine for the governor that he is carrying, and in the discourse of the journey, including going, staying [in San Jorje], and returning, he will endeavor [to assure] that there are no dissentions or differences among the said infantry that he leads, but rather that they attend to guarding well both at night and during the day, as much in the canoes as on land, in such a manner that no mishap is experienced through a lack of vigilance. Regarding the stay in the said place of San Jorje, he will endeavor to stay the least time that he can, on account of the lack of infantry in this presidio, leaving on the return [journey] the two infantrymen in the said province of Guale, and with all guile, pretense, [f.1,vto.] and cunning he will endeavor to find out in the said settlement of San Jorje the news of Europe and whichever other [news] of hostilities that some pirates intend in these Indies, [and about] settlements that friendly or enemy nations intend to make in them, and on the contrary, he will endeavor that the infantry and Indians that he takes do not divulge any news in the said place about settlements or anything else, always being on guard against the Englishmen of the said settlement, in which preparations the said ensign will conduct himself with the wisdom and maturity that is required, and that I expect from his zeal, and I order and command the infantry that he takes with him and the rest of the Indians that they are all at the orders and dispositions of the said ensign, guarding them as my own, for thus is suitable to the service of His Majesty, for which I ordered the present dispatched, signed by my hand and endorsed by the undersigned public and governmental notary of these provinces, who will take a copy of this order in order to attach it to the *autos* made about this matter. Given in St. Augustine, Florida, on the tenth of March, sixteen ninety-nine.

Don Laureano de Torres y Ayala

By order of the señor governor
and captain general,
Juan Solana
Public and Governmental Notary

[f.2]

A copy of this order remains taken as is ordered in it. I swear,

Solana

ORDER 3: ZUÑIGA Y CERDA TO RODRIGO, OCTOBER 25, 1700

This final order provided for the delivery of an unspecified number of Englishmen and black people accompanying them (whether or not these were slaves is unknown), all of whom had shipwrecked north of St. Augustine, including some within the Guale province (on Amelia Island). As in the previous order, Ensign Rodrigo was instructed to deliver letters from Governor Zuñiga y Cerda to the governor of Carolina, although there was no explicit mention of intelligence-gathering by the Spanish visitors. In his 1739 cover letter above, Governor Montiano used this order as further evidence that the English did not originally own Guale, citing Governor Zuñiga y Cerda's statement that the Englishmen to be delivered to Charles Town had shipwrecked in the province of Guale, proving that the Spaniards, and not the English, controlled Guale in 1700.

[f.1]

Field Master of the Spanish infantry Don Joseph de Zuñiga y Zerda, governor and captain general of this city of St. Augustine, Florida, and its provinces for the King our lord.

Inasmuch as in virtue of an accord that I have celebrated with the royal officials of the royal hacienda and coffer of these provinces, it is resolved to send to the provinces of Carolina and port of San Jorxe the Englishmen and blacks who shipwrecked both in the province of Guale in a launch and those who were lost in a seagoing ship [*nabio de alto bordo*] four leagues to the north of the bar of this port, and it is suitable to name a person to go as leader in this errand, and that he should be of all satisfaction and experience, therefore, these and other qualities coinciding in Ensign Luis Rodrigo, *reformado* and resident of this city, and expecting from his zeal that he will conduct himself as he has until now, giving a good account of what he was ordered by me and my predecessors, I elect and name him to go as head of the eight infantrymen I have named him, and that with the English people and blacks who are turned over to him he should go to the port of San Jorxe and make a delivery of all of them to the governor of the said port, to whom he will deliver the letters of mine that he is carrying, during which errand and journey, including going, staying [in San Jorxe], and returning, he will conduct himself with the maturity and wisdom that is required, in such a form that [there is no] discord, but rather that they should go in peace and [f.1,vto.] friendship, not staying in the said port one hour more than what is essential to the charge that he has been given, bringing with him the piraguas and experienced oarsmen [*gente de boga*] and the rest of the infantry that he leads at his charge and care, having from the moment he begins the journey the guard, watchfulness, preparedness, and care that is required day and night so that some mishap does not occur through lack of vigilance and watchfulness, and I order and command to the said [ensign] that he go always in convoy, and in view of all the vessels in which he carries the stated shipwrecked people, in such a form that none gets ahead of the others, and neither should any be left behind or detained, and in everything he will act and proceed according to how the cases and occasions arise, and I order and command all the infantry and the rest of the people who go or come with the said Ensign Luis Rodrigo to have and hold him as their leader, and to obey, observe, and execute his orders as my very own, for thus is suitable to the service of His Majesty, for which I commanded the present dispatched, signed by my hand, sealed with the seal of my arms, and endorsed by the undersigned public and governmental notary, who will take a copy of this my order in order to attach it to the *autos* that have been made about the aforementioned shipwreck, and so that it is on record in [the *autos*] what I have ordered and commanded the said Ensign Luis Rodrigo about this remission. Given in [f.2] this city of St. Augustine, Florida, on the twenty-fifth of October, seventeen hundred.

Don Joseph de Zuñiga y Zerda
[seal]

By order of the señor governor
and captain general,
Juan Solana
Public and Governmental Notary

Order to Ensign Luis Rodrigo, reformado of this presidio.

NOTES

1. This note was written at the bottom of the order, serving as a title or filing note.
2. On the back of the order, the notary Solana certified that he had made a copy of the order, as instructed in its text.
3. This entry refers to the previous entry, indicating that these unconverted Yamassee caciques were situated on the same island of Guad-

alquini (St. Simons Island). This fact is confirmed by later descriptions of the island (see Overview).

4. The following five entries comprise the towns of the old Guale province, apparently in order from south to north. The placement of San Phelipe first, and before Asao (at that time located on St. Simons Island), suggests that it had already been relocated to its Cumberland Island location (see Overview). The fact that Sapala and Tupiqui are listed separately (while the aggregated towns of Santa Catalina and Satuache are combined into a single entry) implies that these two towns were not yet joined as of 1673 (although they seem to have been aggregated before 1675).

5. The officer in charge of gathering the laborers was normally given permission to adjust the numbers for each specific village without reducing the overall number from each province. In this way, as the demographic profile of villages and provinces changed, the labor draft could be adjusted.

6. This individual may well be Luis Rodrigo de Ortega, who penned Document 15 (this volume) some 37 years later (and was by that time a captain).

APPENDIX A
LOCATIONAL DATA FOR GUALE AND MOCAMA MISSIONS, 1655–1685

Introduction

Due to the fact that the research associated with the translation of Governor Montiano's 1739 submission to the Spanish Crown has resulted in a reevaluation of the previously accepted locations for several Guale and Mocama missions, the following essay is presented in order to provide locational data for the period 1655–1685 (see figure 7 and table 7). The arguments for the location of each primary mission town during the retreat and aggregation of Guale and Mocama are relegated to this appendix in order not to distract from the text of the Overview, and in order to avoid lengthy footnotes.

Locational essays are divided into each distinct site in which a primary mission town (or aggregate town) was located during the time range indicated, and when a single mission town was located in two or more separate locations under the same name, these will be designated with Roman numerals following the name (i.e. San Phelipe I, II, etc.; see table 8 for reference). Many of the arguments are interrelated, and the essays are cross-referenced for easy access to the data. Figure 6 in the Overview presents this locational data in graphic form, and the maps in fugures 1, 2, 4, and 5 display the actual predicted locations. Mission locations are listed from north to south. The standard conversion used for league distances during this period was 2.63 miles per league.

San Diego de Satuache (through ca. 1663)

The original site of the Guale town of Satuache was evidently abandoned around 1663, and thus the only solid contemporary evidence for its location derives from the 1655 mission list (Díez de la Calle, 1655, 1659). This list, which was apparently based on a mission visitation route (Worth, 1992: 70, 77), provides only relative distances between the missions, and thus the 1655 figure of 60 leagues from St. Augustine is far too great. A better idea of Satuache's location is provided by the distance of this town to its nearest neighbor to the south, Santa Catalina. Since the site of Santa Catalina has been soundly established (see below), it is possible to project the location of Satuache using the Wammassee Head site as a starting point.

San Diego de Satuache was evidently 10 leagues from Santa Catalina, and was the next and last stop on the visitation route to the north (see discussion below relative to San Phelipe de Alave). Furthermore, an important clue was provided in 1680 by Guale's lieutenant, who reported (citing the caciques of Santa Catalina) that "the villages of San Felipe, Satuahe, Tupique, [and] Asajo had moved from the mainland to settle these islands" (Saturnino de Abaurrea, 1680). This retrospective comment places the location of Satuache on the mainland, and not on the barrier islands of Ossabaw or Skidaway. Yet another important clue was provided in 1627 by Governor Luis de Rojas y Borja, who in reviewing the locations suitable for raising hemp, noted that "The pueblos of Satuache and San Phelipe in the province of Guale, are likewise adapted [for this], as they have fertile meadows drained by a river. Those places are forty leagues from this city and on the way to them there are six bars to pass over" (Rojas y Borja, 1627). Based on this information, combined with the distances noted in 1655, the location Satuache can

TABLE 7
Modern Equivalents for Late-17th-Century Spanish Geographical Names

Spanish Name	Modern Equivalent
Rio de San Juan	St. Johns River
Barra de San Juan	Mouth of the St. Johns River
Isla de San Juan	Fort George Island
Isla de Zarabay	Little Talbot Island
Barra de Santa Maria	Nassau Sound
Isla de Santa Maria	Amelia Island
Barra de San Pedro	Mouth of the St. Marys River
Isla de San Pedro	Cumberland Island
Barra de Ballenas	St. Andrew Sound
Isla de Ballenas	Jekyll Island
Barra de Guadalquini	St. Simons Sound
Isla de Guadalquini	St. Simons Island
Rio de Santa Isabel	Altamaha River
Barra de Asajo	Altamaha Sound
Barra de Ospogue	Doboy Sound
Isla de Sapala	Sapelo Island
Barra de Sapala	Sapelo Sound
Isla de Santa Catalina	St. Catherines Island
Barra de Azopo	St. Catherines Sound
Barra de Aguadulce	Ossabaw Sound
Bahia de Cruces	Wassaw Sound

be projected to be at or near the mouth of the Ogeechee river.

While the actual site of Satuache has yet to be identified, the mouth of the Ogeechee was indeed home to late Precolumbian aboriginal occupation ancestral to that of Guale (see Pearson, 1984). Although this town was missionized during the first half of the 17th century, and for decades remained the northernmost frontier town in the Guale mission province (bordering Escamaçu to the north), Satuache's last appearance as a distinct mission town was in April 1663 (Uçeda, 1663). Soon after this, its inhabitants abandoned the Ogeechee River location, probably fleeing south in response to the assaults of Chichimeco raiders along the Savannah River valley just to the north (see Overview). Satuache soon merged with Mission Santa Catalina de Guale, for beginning as early as 1666 it was listed together with Santa Catalina on the yearly *repartimiento* labor draft orders (Guerra y Vega, 1666, 1667a, 1668a). Both Satuache and a closely associated chiefly lineage named Faslica consistently appeared in association with Santa Catalina throughout the final years of the 17th century, indicating that the fusion of these two towns was a more or less permanent arrangement.

San Phelipe de Alave
(through ca. 1670)

As noted above, San Phelipe was a mainland mission situated in a fertile river valley (Saturnino de Abaurrea, 1680; Rojas y Borja, 1627). Beyond this information, the projected location of Mission San Phelipe de Alave is based principally on the original manuscript version of Juan Díez de la Calle's (1655) mission list, which appears to have been drawn from a visitation route through the missions of Florida (the printed version [Díez de la Calle, 1659] omits the author's notations regarding the order of the northern missions). This document provides not only the distances of each mission from St. Augustine, but also the order of visitation for the Mocama and Guale provinces. Importantly, although mission San Phelipe was stated to be 4 leagues farther from St. Augustine than Santa Catalina (54 leagues as opposed to 50 leagues), it was the ninth mission visited on a route that ran from San Joseph de Sapala (8th) to San Phelipe (9th) to Santa Catalina (10th), and finally to San Diego de Satuache (11th; see Appendix B). Consequently, although San Phelipe was stated to be at an intermediate distance between Santa Catalina (at 50 leagues) and Satuache (at 60 leagues), it seems to have been located on the mainland on a route between Sapala and Santa Catalina.

Based on the island locations of Sapala and Santa Catalina, it is possible to project that to get to Mission San Phelipe, the visitor traveled from Sapelo Island toward the mainland, canoeing up the narrow channels through the marsh as a shortcut to reach the South Newport River. From there, San Phelipe was situated several leagues upriver, fixing its location at an undiscovered site somewhere on the upper reaches of the South or North

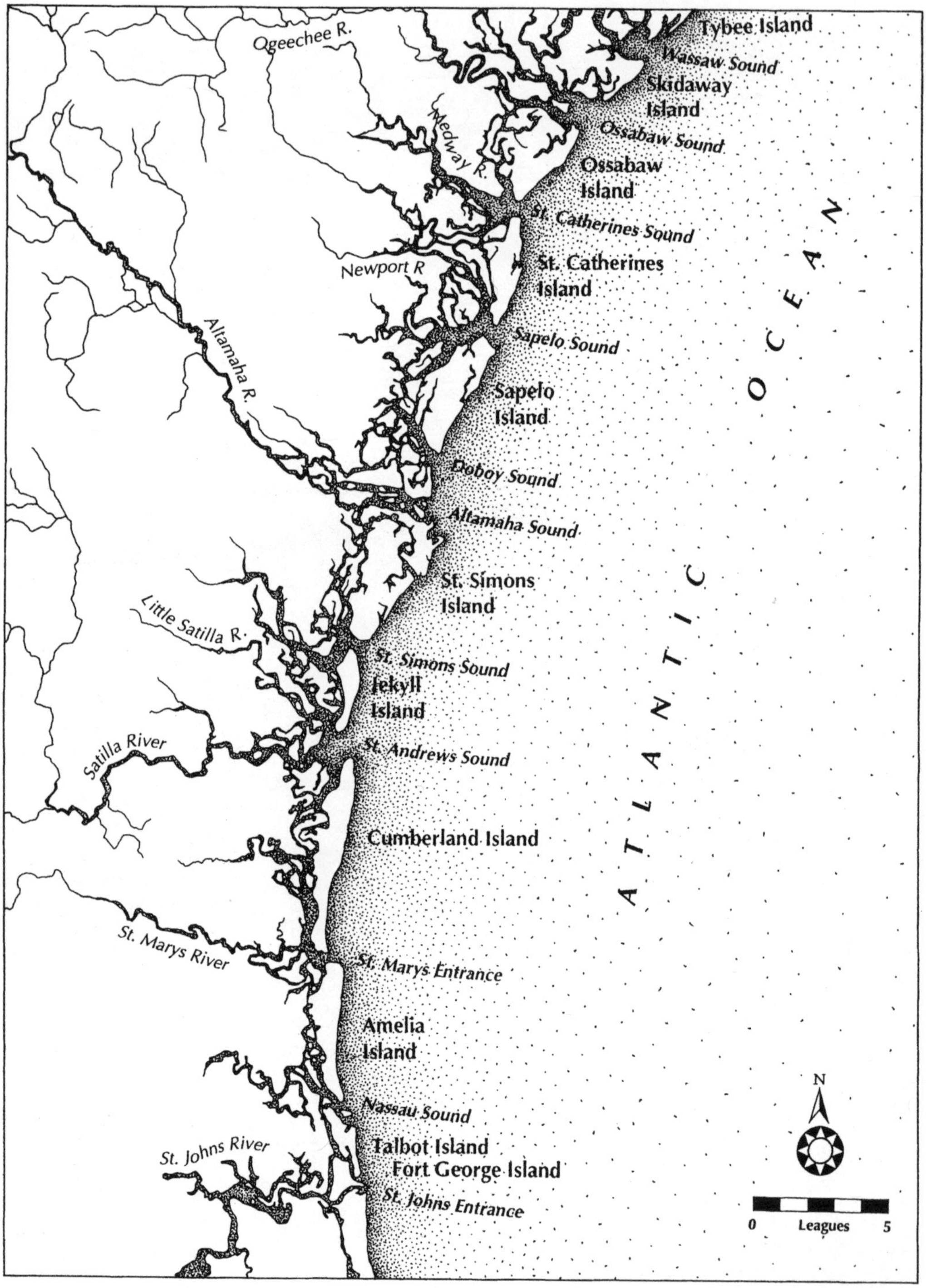

Fig. 7. Map of the contemporary Atlantic coastline of Georgia and northeastern Florida (see corresponding list of equivalent late 17th-century Spanish geographical names in table 7).

TABLE 8
Successive Locations for Guale and Mocama Missions

Mission Town	Physical Location
San Diego de Satuache I	San Diego de Satuache (through ca. 1663)
San Diego de Satuache II	Santa Catalina de Guale (ca. 1663–1680)
San Diego de Satuache III	San Joseph de Sapala (1680–1683)
San Diego de Satuache IV	Santa Maria (1683–1702)
San Phelipe I	San Phelipe de Alave (through ca. 1670)
San Phelipe II	San Phelipe de Atuluteca (ca. 1670–1684)
San Phelipe III	San Phelipe III (1684–1702)
Santa Catalina de Guale I	Santa Catalina de Guale (through 1680)
Santa Catalina de Guale II	San Joseph de Sapala (1680–1683)
Santa Catalina de Guale III	Santa Maria (1683–1702)
Santa Clara de Tupiqui I	Santa Clara de Tupiqui (through ca. 1670)
Santa Clara de Tupiqui II	San Joseph de Sapala (ca. 1670–1684)
Santa Clara de Tupiqui III	Santa Clara de Tupiqui III (1684–1702)
San Joseph de Sapala I	San Joseph de Sapala (through 1684)
San Joseph de Sapala II	Santa Maria (1684–?)
Santo Domingo de Talaje/Asajo I	Santo Domingo de Talaje
Santo Domingo de Talaje/Asajo II	Santo Domingo de Asajo
San Buenaventura de Guadalquini I	San Buenaventura de Guadalquini (through 1684)
San Buenaventura de Guadalquini II	Santa Cruz y San Buenaventura de Guadalquini (1684–ca. 1696)
San Buenaventura de Guadalquini III	San Juan del Puerto (ca. 1696–1702)
San Pedro de Mocama	San Pedro de Mocama (through 1660s)
Santa Maria	Santa Maria (through ca. 1665)
San Juan del Puerto	San Juan del Puerto

Newport River drainages (and well inland). From San Phelipe, the visitor descended some 4 leagues down the North Newport River (accounting for the placement of Santa Catalina at only 50 leagues from St. Augustine), taking a shortcut through the marsh to arrive at Mission Santa Catalina de Guale. Given that Mission San Phelipe was listed between Sapala and Santa Catalina in the 1655 list, even though its distance from St. Augustine was indicated to be greater than either of the latter missions, the upper Newport River drainages would seem to be the only logical site.

Although its northern neighbor Satuache retreated southward during or soon after 1663, the appearance of San Phelipe as a separate town on *repartimiento* labor draft orders from 1665 through 1669 suggests that it may have remained in its northern location until the early 1670s (Guerra y Vega, 1666, 1667a, 1668a, 1669). The fact that two rebellious Indians from Santa Catalina fled directly to San Phelipe in the late winter of 1665 provides further evidence that it remained Santa Catalina's immediate northern neighbor at least into the late 1660s (Guerra y Vega, 1665c). Nevertheless, by 1673, San Phelipe had moved far to the south, taking up residence on Cumberland Island, actually within the geographical extent of the Mocama province at that time (see below). Although the abandonment of its original location was most likely triggered by the English presence to the north, the extreme distance of San Phelipe's relocation (and its failure to aggregate with Santa Catalina like Satuache) may have more to do with internal political disputes within the Guale province (see Overview).

Santa Catalina de Guale (through 1680)

As a result of extensive archaeological investigations, the location for Mission Santa Catalina has been firmly established to be at the Wammassee Head site on the inland side of St. Catherines Island (Thomas, 1987). The 1655 list (Díez de la Calle, 1655, 1659) evidently places Santa Catalina 4 leagues downriver from San Phelipe, and 10 leagues south of Satuache (see discussion relative to San Phelipe de Alave). After the arrival of refugees from Satuache soon after the arrival of the Chichimecos along the Savannah River in 1663, Santa Catalina remained comparatively stable until the spring of 1680, when English-allied Indians led an assault that resulted in the burning of the mission and permanent abandonment of this original location (see Overview). After this time, although the identity of Santa Catalina was maintained throughout the rest of the 17th century, it occupied a series of distinct locations with different primary names (see below).

Santa Clara de Tupiqui
(through ca. 1674)

Although Tupiqui was listed by Lieutenant Saturnino de Abaurrea (1680) as one of the four principal Guale towns originally located on the mainland, its precise original location is difficult to determine based on only late-17th-century evidence. Since Tupiqui did not appear on the 1655 list (no resident friar seems to have been stationed there at that time), the mission town's original location must be derived from evidence dating to the early 1600s. Although Jones (1978: 207) indicates a Newport River location, the 1606 visitation of Guale makes it clear that Tupiqui's neighbor Espogache was situated at a point roughly equidistant from Talaje (near Darien) and Guale (at Wamassee Head), both located 6 leagues away. This information suggests its placement inland along the Sapelo River, perhaps at the Pine Harbor site. Such a location would indeed explain the long and close association between Tupiqui and Sapala, with the former situated on the mainland opposite the island town of Sapala. Tupiqui seems to have been maintained at this original location through the late 1660s, inasmuch as Fray Carlos de Anguiano of Santa Catalina was apparently ministering to Tupiqui in April of 1663 (Anguiano, 1663), and Tupiqui's later aggregation site of Sapala was listed separately at that time (Barreda, 1663). Furthermore, Tupiqui appears as a distinct town on the *repartimiento* labor drafts of the late 1660s (Guerra y Vega, 1666; 1667a; 1668a; 1669) and again in 1673 (Cendoya, 1673).

Nevertheless, Tupiqui was not named on either 1675 mission list (Arcos, 1675; Díaz Vara Calderón, 1675), and during the 1677–1678 Argüelles visitation the reason for this becomes clear, for by this time Tupiqui had aggregated to the island mission of Sapala (Argüelles, 1678), where it was to remain until the final withdrawal from the Georgia coast after the pirate raid of 1684 (see Overview). The abandonment of Tupiqui's original site on the mainland, and the relocation to Sapala, seems to date to around 1674, when the last of the mainland Guale missions was relocated to the barrier islands.

San Joseph de Sapala
(through 1684)

The general location of the Sapala mission on modern Sapelo Island is easily determined, although the determination of its precise location on the island is somewhat problematic. In 1655, Sapala was described as being some 9 leagues south of the mainland mission of San Phelipe, and 5 leagues north of Santo Domingo de Talaje (Díez de la Calle, 1655). Placing Talaje at the Fort King George site on the northern bank of the Altamaha River (see below), the distance of 5 leagues suggests the Bourbon Field site on the northern end of Sapelo Island (Larson, 1980).

Following the 1661 removal of Talaje to its St. Simons Island location under the name of Asajo (see below), subsequent descriptions with reference to the new Asajo mission confirm the location of Sapala on the northern end of the island at Bourbon Field. Using the more securely identified location of Asajo at Cannons Point on the northern end of St. Simons Island, San Joseph de Sapala is consistently placed at a distance of some 6 or 7 leagues to the north in mission lists dating between 1675 and 1683 (Arcos, 1675; Díaz Vara Calderon, 1675; Fuentes, 1681; Barbosa, 1683). Furthermore, the two lists above predating the 1680 abandonment of Santa Catalina place Sapala only 2 leagues south of Santa Catalina, agreeing with accounts dating to the time of its abandonment (Hita Salazar, 1680a; Cigarroa, 1681).

Sapala was joined by immigrants from Tupiqui between 1673 and 1675 (see above), and as late as 1677 there seems to have been some dispute as to the preeminence of Tupiqui over Sapala (Argüelles, 1678). More refugees arrived in 1680, when the inhabitants of Santa Catalina and its aggregate Satuache fled to Sapala after the English-sponsored assault on Mission Santa Catalina. Consequently, between 1680 and 1683, the site of San Joseph de Sapala was home to no fewer than four separate mission towns on the northern frontier of the Guale province. While Santa Catalina and Satuache removed in 1683 to the southern mission of Santa Maria (see below), Tupiqui remained with Sapala until the fall of 1684, when the planned relocation of both was interrupted by the pirate raids that forced the final abandonment of the Georgia coast. The ruins of Sapala apparently were still standing as late as 1686, when the Yamassee Indians living there were routed by Spanish forces (see Document 11).

Santo Domingo de Talaje
(through 1661)

The original location of the Talaje mission was undoubtedly at the Fort King George site near modern Darien, on the northern bank of the Altamaha River near its mouth (Thomas, 1987). When the English fort was constructed in 1721, the Spaniards were very clear in explicitly identifying its location on the original site of Mission Santo Domingo de Talaje (see Document 14). Furthermore, late-17th-century documentation only serves to confirm this location, including the 1655 description of Talaje as being situated 5 leagues south of Sapala and 8 leagues north of San Buenaventura de Guadalquini on the southern tip of St. Simons Island (see below). Based on the fact that Talaje was originally a mainland mission (Saturnino de Abaurrea, 1680), these distances place Talaje squarely at the mouth of the Altamaha. Furthermore, the description of Talaje as the first Guale mission struck by the Chichimeco raiders during their descent of the Río de Santa Isabel (the Altamaha) backs up this assertion. Indeed, documentation from the early 17th century provides perhaps even better evidence for this location (Jones, 1978).

Talaje was, however, the first Guale mission to fall victim to English-sponsored raids from the north, and after being overrun and dismantled by Chichimeco warriors in 1661, its inhabitants removed to a more secure location on the barrier island to the east (see below).

Santo Domingo de Asajo
(1661–1684)

The mission village established by the refugees from Talaje following the destruction of their mainland village at the mouth of the Altamaha River was situated on the northern end of St. Simons Island, most likely at Cannons Point (Larson, 1980). This island was known as the Island of Guadalquini, named for the long-standing northernmost Mocama mission of San Buenaventura de Guadalquini, but it became a major aggregation point on the frontier of Guale and Mocama during this period. Although distinct but paired towns during the turn of the century, by the late 17th century Talaje and Asajo seem to have largely fused into a single principal mission town. Perhaps only in retrospect after the 1661 relocation to St. Simons Island, the original location seems to have been more consistently referred to as Talaje, whereas the later island location was almost universally referred to as Asajo (or Asao). Consequently, the post-1661 location of the original town of Talaje will be referred to as Asajo for this essay.

Noted to have two friars in 1663 (Campana, 1663; Fernández, 1663), Asajo did not show up on the *repartimiento* labor draft orders for Guale until 1669, suggesting that its inhabitants were given a special dispensation for some eight years after the Chichimeco attack, perhaps in order to permit the rebuilding of the town and its store of provisions. Noted between 1675 and 1683 to be some 6 or 7 leagues south of Sapala (Arcos, 1675; Díaz Vara Calderon, 1675; Barbosa, 1683), with a travel distance of perhaps 8 to 9 leagues between the two (Fuentes, 1681), Asajo was the northernmost of four Indian villages on St. Simons Island during the late 1660s and 1670s.

Asajo's nearest neighbor, some 2 leagues to the south, was the refugee village of San Simón, populated by pagan Colones, and another league beyond the pagan Yamassee village of Ocotonico (Arcos, 1675; Fuentes, 1681). Based on the Solana map of 1683 (figure 3), San Simón was located on the inland side of the island, probably at the later site of Fort Frederica. Some 3 leagues south of these pagan refugee villages was the mission of Guadalquini, located on the southernmost tip of the island (see below).

Like its neighbors to the north and south, Santo Domingo de Asajo was occupied until the fall of 1684, when Asajo was burned to the ground by pirates in early October. Interestingly, the mission of Asajo seems to have dispersed after this time, most of its inhabitants fleeing north to join the English-allied Yamasees. Only in the late 1680s and mid 1690s does the name Asajo re-appear in the Guale province (Ebelino de Compostela, 1689; Pueyo, 1695), suggesting that there may have been some continuity throughout this period, perhaps only submerged beneath the more well-represented aggregate towns.

San Buenaventura de Guadalquini
(through 1684)

The location of the Guadalquini Mission has been one of the most consistently misunderstood facts of modern research into the Mocama and Guale province. Almost universally presumed to have been located on Jekyll Island (Swanton, 1922; Jones, 1978; Thomas, 1987; Hann, 1987, 1990; Bushnell 1994), Guadalquini was actually located on the southern tip of St. Simons Island, probably near the modern lighthouse. Jekyll Island, currently known in print as the Island of Guadalquini, was actually known by the Spanish as "Isla de Ballenas," or the Island of Whales. St. Simons Island was in fact the Island of Guadalquini, and not the Island of Asao (which actually does not appear in Spanish documents of the period). The reasons for this confusion are many and complicated, but the presumption seems to proceed from a combination of the slightly ambiguous distance measurements in the 1655 and 1675 mission lists, the previous misunderstanding of the shift in locations for Talaje/Asajo during the late 17th century, and the natural assumption that Jekyll Island should have a major mission like all the rest of the larger islands on the Guale/Mocama coast.

Despite the long-standing acceptance of a Jekyll Island location for Guadalquini, the evidence for its actual location on the southern tip of St. Simons Island is substantial and essentially unequivocal. Perhaps the best proof is provided by the 1681 Fuentes census presented for the first time in this volume, in which Guadalquini is noted to be the southernmost of four Indian groups on modern-day St. Simons Island, and is explicitly described as being situated "on the southern point of this stated island at a distance of three leagues," and directly on the Bar of Guadalquini. Furthermore, both the 1675 Arcos mission list and the 1683

Barbosa census note that in traveling to Mission San Phelipe on Cumberland Island some 6–8 leagues southward, *two* bars are crossed (the Bar of Guadalquini and the Bar of Ballenas), corresponding to St. Simons Sound and St. Andrew Sound respectively, on either side of Jekyll Island.

Beyond this, the documentation surrounding the 1684 pirate raids on Guale (see Document 10) indicates that Guadalquini and the village of San Simón were within walking distance, and indicate that Guadalquini, San Simón, and Asajo were the three villages situated on the Island of Guadalquini at that time. This conclusion is strongly supported by the Solana map of 1683 (figure 3), which shows three Indian villages, two Christian and one pagan, on the Island of Guadalquini, and in precisely the expected positions for the three villages noted above. Moreover, the unnamed island between Guadalquini (St. Simons) and San Phelipe (Cumberland) is portrayed as unoccupied, as expected for Jekyll Island. That Jekyll Island was in fact the unoccupied "Isla de Ballenas" is further demonstrated by Antonio de Arredondo's 1737 map, which gives the name "Ballenas" to the island immediately south of St. Simons (Jekyll) (Bolton, 1925).

Until 1661, then, San Buenaventura de Guadalquini, and thus St. Simons Island, was the northern frontier of the Mocama province, fronting on the southernmost Guale town of Talaje on the mainland. Only after the 1661 Chichimeco raid did the Guale province extend southward to the northern end of St. Simons, effectively pushing the linguistic/cultural frontier between Guale and Mocama to the middle of the island itself, where pagan refugees soon settled (see Overview).

San Phelipe II (de Atuluteca) (ca. 1670–1684)

Probably during the early 1670s, the aboriginal inhabitants of San Phelipe de Alave removed far to the south, settling on the northern part of the abandoned Cumberland Island, former home of mission San Pedro de Mocama on the southern end of the island (see Overview). The fact that San Phelipe's labor draft quota had been reduced to only 2 laborers in 1673 (after years with a quota of 4) might imply that their relocation was recent at that time, and that they were given a special dispensation in order to establish the new town (Cendoya, 1673). In 1675 San Phelipe was noted to be some 6 or 9 leagues south of Guadalquini, and this distance was refined to 8 leagues in 1681 and 1683 (Arcos, 1675; Díaz Vara Calderón, 1675; Fuentes, 1681; Barbosa, 1683). To the south, San Phelipe was variously described as 3 leagues from the northernmost settlement of the "Island of Mocama," or Amelia Island (Arcos, 1675), 3 leagues from Mission Santa Maria, on Amelia Island (Díaz Vara Calderon, 1675), 2 leagues from a Yamassee village on Cumberland Island located 3 to 4 leagues north of San Pedro (Fuentes, 1681), and 3 leagues from the abandoned Yamassee town at San Pedro (Barbosa, 1683). Yet another description of Mission San Phelipe's location was given by Guale's Lieutenant Saturnino de Abaurrea in 1684, when he noted that San Phelipe was scheduled to relocate to the abandoned site of San Pedro, only 4 leagues to the south.

Given the better-known locations of Guadalquini and San Pedro, both on the southern tip of their respective islands, the above information suggests that San Phelipe relocated to a site perhaps in the vicinity of Table Point or Brickhill Bluff on the inland side of Cumberland Island. Although the name San Phelipe was retained, the native component seems to have been changed from Alave to Atuluteca. This almost certainly resulted from the 17th-century Mocama name for Cumberland Island, which seems to have been Atuluteca. San Pedro to the south was also occasionally referred to as San Pedro Atulteca (e.g., Rojas y Borja, 1630), although its more common name was San Pedro de Mocama, in reference to its position at the head of the overall Mocama province during the early 17th century. Nevertheless, despite the fact that San Phelipe adopted the native name of the earlier mission of San Pedro, the two were unquestionably in distinct locations (see Overview).

San Pedro de Mocama (through 1660s)

The important early mission of San Pedro de Mocama was almost certainly located on the inland side of the southern end of Cumberland Island, at the Dungeness Wharf site (Milanich, 1971, 1972). In 1655 the mission was placed some 8 leagues north of San Juan del Puerto, and 12 leagues south of San Buenaventura de Guadalquini (Díez de la Calle, 1655, 1659). Although this once important Mocama mission seems to have been abandoned during the early 1660s, perhaps fusing with the nearby Mocama mission of Santa Maria before its own disappearance soon thereafter, the name San Pedro remained attached to the bar and river between Cumberland and Amelia Islands for years to come. When the old mission site was reoccupied by pagan Yamassee before 1681, it was noted to be some 4 leagues north of Santa Maria (Fuentes, 1681), a distance confirmed by a subsequent reconnaissance two years later (Barbosa, 1683). San Pedro was typically described as being 3–4 leagues south of the relocated Guale mission of San Phelipe during this same period (Fuentes, 1680; Barbosa, 1683; Saturnino de Abaurrea, 1684).

Santa Clara de Tupiqui III (1684–1702)

The third location for the Tupiqui Mission was on the northern tip of Amelia Island, probably on the abandoned site of an earlier Yamassee Indian town (see the Overview). During the 1685 Leturiondo visitation, the largely depopulated Tupiqui was noted to be 3 leagues from Santa Maria (and for this reason its inhabitants were required to come there for a formal visitation). Naming this mission Azao in 1689, Bishop Ebelino de Compostela (1689) noted it to be the northernmost town on the Island of Santa Maria, but in 1695 and 1697 Spanish officials referred to it again as Santa Clara de Tupiqui, locating it 3 leagues north of San Phelipe in 1697 (Pueyo, 1695; Menéndez Márquez and Florencia, 1697). That same year the Englishman Jonathan Dickenson (1697) located this town 2–3 leagues north of St. Philip's (San Phelipe), although he referred to it as Sappataw [by 1695 the cacique of Sapala was indeed located in Tupiqui (Pueyo, 1695)]. These distances correspond well with the 1675 description of Arcos's Island of Mocama, which situated the island's northernmost Yamassee village 3 leagues north of La Tama (the later San Phelipe III), and some 3 1/2 leagues north of Santa Maria (see below).

The fact that the Santa Clara de Tupiqui Mission received not one but three distinct designations between 1685 and 1697 (Tupiqui, Asajo, and Sapala), returning to Tupiqui in 1701 (Zuñiga y Cerda, 1701), probably reflects a further aggregation of towns here during this final period, and may be a response to the fact that the population of Tupiqui was severely reduced by 1685 (see Document 9, and the Overview). The 1689 mention of Asajo at this mission, along with the listing of its cacique at Mission Santa Maria in 1695, suggests that some of the inhabitants of the old Asajo mission had returned from among the English-allied Yamassee by that time (although they never again seem to have formed a distinct town). Late in 1702, Tupiqui III was burned by English forces under the command of Carolina Governor James Moore.

San Phelipe III (1684–1702)

The third distinct location for San Phelipe was established following the final removal of the Guale and Mocama missions from the Georgia coast after the pirate raid of 1684. San Phelipe seems to have been established on the then-abandoned site of the ca. 1675 Yamassee town of La Tama (Arcos, 1675), which was described at that time as being roughly 3 leagues south of the northern tip of the island (2 leagues south of Ocotoque, which was 1 league south of the northernmost Yamassee town on the island). San Phelipe was visited immediately after Santa Maria during the 1685 visitation of Domingo de Leturiondo (1685), and in 1689 was listed as the middle town on the Island of Santa Maria. In 1697, both the Spanish (Menéndez Márquez and Florencia, 1697) and English (Dickenson, 1697) lists place San Phelipe only half a league north of Santa Maria. Using the known location of Mission Santa Maria (see below), these distances place San Phelipe III on the inland side of Amelia Island, probably at or near the site of modern Amelia City. San Phelipe was finally abandoned and burned during the 1702 Moore raid.

Santa Maria (through ca. 1665)

The physical location of the mission town of Santa Maria is known with some degree of certainty based on recent archaeological excavations, and has been found to be on the inland side of Amelia Island (Saunders, 1992). Nevertheless, the occupational record of this site is quite complex, extending from the early mission period until the final removal of the Guale and Mocama missions to St. Augustine. As noted in the Overview, the original Mocama mission of Santa Maria seems to have lasted until at least 1665, when the cacica Juana replaced Clemente Bernal, the dead cacique of the entire Mocama province at San Juan. Although not noted in the 1655 Díez de la Calle list due to the lack of a resident friar, the location seems relatively certain using both earlier and later documentary references. Sometime after 1665, Mission Santa Maria seems to have been abandoned, perhaps when the cacica Juana relocated to San Juan. Nevertheless, the mission site was reoccupied before 1673 by immigrant Yamassee refugees, and thus remained a Yamassee town until their flight after the 1683 Grammont raid.

During the Yamassee occupation of Santa Maria (pre-1673–1683), its location was variously described as 6–7 leagues north of San Juan del Puerto, and between 6 and 10 leagues south of mission San Phelipe (Arcos, 1675; Díaz Vara Calderón, 1675; Fuentes, 1681; Barbosa, 1683). The fact that Santa Maria was but one of as many as four Yamassee settlements on Amelia Island during this period seems to have contributed to a considerable degree of confusion in the documentary descriptions of Santa Maria's location. The 1675 Arcos list provides perhaps the best detail regarding the mission's location with respect to these other towns, and from this information it becomes clear, for example, that in 1675 Bishop Díaz probably lumped the four Yamassee towns on the Island of Santa Maria together, noting only the distance from the southernmost town to San Juan and from the northernmost to San Phelipe (Díaz Vara Calderón, 1675).

Following the reoccupation of the abandoned Yamassee town at Santa Maria by the Guale towns of Santa Catalina, San Diego de Satuache, and San Joseph de Sapala between 1683 and 1685, its location was described as being approximately half a league south of San Phelipe and just over 3 leagues south of Tupiqui on the northern end of Amelia Island (Leturiondo, 1685; Menéndez Márquez and Florencia, 1697; Dickenson, 1697). The newly reoccupied Santa Maria was also noted by these sources to be approximately 6 leagues north of both San Juan del Puerto and Santa Cruz y San Buenaventura de Guadalquini. This mission was finally abandoned and burned in the 1702 Moore raid.

Santa Cruz y San Buenaventura de Guadalquini (1684–ca.1696)

In yet another case of mistaken identity, the site of the relocated Guadalquini mission town has long been believed to be only 3 leagues north of St. Augustine on the inland waterway (Hann, 1987, 1990). This seems to stem from the paucity of documentary information on this mission, and thus the exaggerated importance given to the erroneous placement of this name by the Englishman Jonathan Dickenson (1697). Mission Santa Cruz was actually located near the mouth of the St. Johns River, and the town long assumed to have been Santa Cruz was none other than Nuestra Señora de Guadalupe de Tolomato.

First, the evidence for the actual location of Santa Cruz y San Buenaventura de Guadalquini is comparatively clear. In 1685, following the relocation of the burned Guadalquini mission on St. Simons Island, Santa Cruz was noted to be only 6 leagues from Mission Santa Maria, placing it in the vicinity of San Juan del Puerto (Leturiondo, 1685). Furthermore, when Sergeant Major Leturiondo was ordered to proceed directly from his visitation of Apalachee and Timucua to Guale and Mocama, he apparently traveled down the St. Johns River from Salamototo (where he received his orders), and held the first visitation (including the general *auto* of the entire visitation of Guale and Mocama) in the town of Santa Cruz y San Buenaventura (see Document 9). From there he proceeded northward to Santa Maria and San Phelipe, and finally to San Juan on his way south to St. Augustine along the coast.

The 1689 Ebelino de Compostela list (1689) placed Santa Cruz directly between San Juan and the Island of Santa Maria, with only Tolomato falling between San Juan and St. Augustine. During the 1695 visitation of Guale and Mocama, Captain Pueyo proceeded directly southward from the northernmost mission of Santa Clara de Tupiqui, passing San Phelipe and Santa Maria on his way to Santa Cruz, which was visited prior to his arrival in San Juan (Pueyo, 1695). Soon after this visitation, the cacique of Guadalquini Don Lorenzo de Santiago relocated his village from Santa Cruz to the nearby San Juan, and in 1697, the royal officials did not include Santa Cruz in their list (Menéndez Márquez and Florencia, 1697). Only in 1701 does it become clear that Don Lorenzo had become the cacique of San Juan upon his relocation (Zuñiga y Cerda, 1701; also see Overview).

The above information is supplemented by other references, all of which suggest that the location of Santa Cruz was on the northern side of the St. Johns River, on the mainland about a league west–northwest from Mission San Juan. In March of 1685, Governor Márquez Cabrera noted that the newly relocated towns of Guale and Mocama were situated in three locations: one on the Island of Santa Maria, one on the Island of San Juan, and "the other one league from the said Island [of San Juan] on the mainland" (see Overview). Furthermore, when Captain Pueyo ordered the inhabitants of Santa Cruz to relocate to Mission San Juan, he noted that Governor Quiroga y Losada was worried about "the endangered that they are in the said village of Santa Cruz of being infested with enemies by the mainland" (Pueyo, 1695), indicating that the final relocation of Santa Cruz between 1695 and 1697 was a strategic move from its mainland location to the sheltered nearby island location of San Juan. The mainland location of Santa Cruz is also confirmed by documents relating to the 1702 English assault on St. Augustine (Arnade, 1959).

Indeed the only document that suggests that Santa Cruz was located farther south was the relation of the shipwrecked English sailor Jonathan Dickenson, who noted a village he called "Santa Cruce" 2–3 leagues north of St. Augustine (Dickenson, 1697). The fact that Dickenson's relation fails to mention the Tolomato Mission, which Spanish authorities uniformly described as being in the precise location of the Englishman's "Santa Cruce" (even during that same year) indicates that Dickenson was simply in error, or was somehow mislead by his Spanish guides. The latter possibility might be implied by Dickenson's (1697) comment that his party was forced to walk across Fort George Island in order to depart from Mission San Juan, despite his belief that they could have traveled by boat, saying "the Spaniards were not willing to discover the place to us."

San Juan del Puerto (through 1702)

Mission San Juan was the only town in Mocama and Guale that remained in its original location throughout the entire 17th century. Archaeological evidence has confirmed the location of this mission on the inland side of Fort George Island at the mouth of the St. Johns River (see Thomas, 1987: 90–91). During the late 17th century, San Juan was generally described as being about 12 leagues north of St. Augustine (Díez de la Calle, 1655, 1659; Díaz Vara Calderón, 1675; Dickenson, 1697; Menéndez Márquez and Florencia, 1697), and was variously placed between 3 and 7 leagues south of Mission Santa Maria (Arcos, 1675; Díaz Vara Calderón, 1675; Fuentes, 1681; Barbosa, 1683; Menéndez Márquez and Florencia, 1697), or some 8–11 leagues south of San Pedro de Mocama (Díez de la Calle, 1655, 1659; Fuentes, 1681; Barbosa, 1683). Soon after 1665, San Juan may have been joined by the inhabitants of the former Mocama mission of Santa Maria (and may also have been host to those of San Pedro), and between 1695 and 1697 San Juan was aggregated with Santa Cruz y San Buenaventura de Guadalquini (see Overview). The mission was abandoned following the 1702 Moore assault.

APPENDIX B
LATE-17TH-CENTURY MISSION LISTS FOR GUALE AND MOCAMA

1655 Díez de la Calle list

Nuestra Señora de Guadalupe (3rd)
–3 leagues north of St. Augustine
San Juan del Puerto (4th)
–12 leagues north of St. Augustine
San Pedro de Mocamo (5th)
–20 leagues north of St. Augustine
San Buena de Boadalquibi (6th)
–32 leagues north of St. Augustine
Santo Domingo de Talege (7th)
–40 leagues north of St. Augustine
San José de Zapala (8th)
–45 leagues north of St. Augustine
San Phelipe (9th)
–54 leagues north of St. Augustine
Santa Cathalina de Guale (10th)
–50 leagues north of St. Augustine
Chatuache (11th and last to the north)
–60 leagues north of St. Augustine

1663 Franciscan letters (Guale only)

Santo Domingo de Asajo
Tupiqui
San Joseph de Sapala
Santa Catalina de Guale
San Phelipe de Alave
San Diego de Chatoache

1666–1668 Guale and Mocama labor quotas

Guadalquini (5 laborers)
Santa Catharina and Satuache (8 laborers)
Sapala (4 laborers)
Tupiqui (4 laborers)
San Phelipe (4 laborers)

1669 Guale and Mocama labor quota

Guadalquini (5 laborers)
Asao (4 laborers)
Santa Catharina (4 laborers)
Satoache (4 laborers)
Zapala (4 laborers)
Tupiqui (4 laborers)
San Phelipe (4 laborers)

1673 Guale and Mocama labor quota

Santa Maria de los Yamazes (12 laborers)
Christians, Island of Guadaquini (4 laborers)
Yamazes, Island of Guadaquini (12 laborers)
San Phelipe (2 laborers)
Asao (4 laborers)
Zapala (4 laborers)
Tupiqui (4 laborers)
Santa Catalina and Satuache (8 laborers)

1675 Díaz Vara Calderón list

La Natividad de Nuestra Señora de Tolomato
–2 leagues from St. Augustine
San Juan del Puerto
–10 leagues from Tolomato
Santa Maria
–6 leagues from San Juan
San Phelipe
–3 leagues from Santa Maria

San Buenaventura de Guadalquini
—9 leagues from San Phelipe
Santo Domingo de Asajo
—6 leagues from San Buenaventura
San Joseph de Zapala
—6 leagues from Santo Domingo
Santa Catalina
—2 leagues from San Joseph

1675 Arcos list

Santa Catalina, with Satuache aggregated
—northern frontier
—140 persons
San Joseph de Sapala
—2 leagues from Santa Catalina, crossing one Bar
—50 persons
Santo Domingo de Asao
—6 leagues from San Joseph, crossing the Bar of Aspogue and the Bar of Asao
—30 persons
San Simón, pagans
—2 leagues from Santo Domingo
—40 persons
Ocotonico, [pagans]
—1 league from San Simón
—120 persons
Guadalquini
—1.5 leagues from Ocotonico
—40 persons
San Phelipe
—6 leagues from Guadalquini, crossing the Bar of Guadalquini and the Bar of Ballenas
—36 persons (some pagans)
Yamazes, pagans
—3 leagues from San Phelipe, first village on the Island of Mocama
—60 persons
Ocotoque, pagans
—1 league from Yamazes
—40 persons
La Tama, pagans
—2 leagues from Ocotoque
—50 persons
Santa Maria, pagans
—.5 league from La Tama
—40 persons
San Juan del Puerto
—3 leagues from Santa Maria, crossing the Bar of Santa Maria
—30 persons
last village in the province of Guale [Tolomato]
—by navigable rivers from the Bar of St. Juan

1677–1678 Argüelles visitation

Santa Catalina
—caciques of Satuache and Faslica noted
San Joseph de Sapala
—mica of Tupiqui noted
Santo Domingo de Asao
—cacique of Yfulo noted
San Buenaventura de Guadalquini
San Felipe
Santa Maria, village of the Yamasees
San Juan del Puerto
Nuestra Señora de Guadalupe de Tolomato

1679–1680 Barreda patent

Tolomato
San Juan del Puerto
San Phelipe
Ubadalquini
[Asao]
San Joseph de Çapala
Santa Catalina de Guale

1680 Márquez Cabrera list

Santa Catalina de Guale
San Joseph de Sapala
Santo Domingo de Asao
San Buenaventura de Guadalquini
San Phelipe de Atuluteca
San Juan del Puerto

1681 Fuentes census

Satuache/Santa Catalina/Sapala/Tupiqui
—northern frontier, on the Island of Sapala and Tupiqui
Yamazes, pagans
—2 leagues south, on the southern tip of the island
Asajo (Bar and village)
—6–7 leagues south–southwest by boat
Colones, pagans
—in Asajo and in the middle of the island
Yamazes, pagans
—aggregated to the Colones and to Guadalquini
Guadalquini (Bar and village)
—3 leagues south, on the southern tip of the island
San Phelipe
—8 leagues south
Yamazes, pagans
—2 leagues south, on the Island of San Phelipe
San Pedro, pagan Llamazes (Bar and village)
—3–4 leagues south
Santa Maria, pagan Llamazes (Bar and village)
—4 leagues southwest
San Juan del Puerto (Bar and village)
—6–7 leagues south

1683 Barbosa census

San Joseph de Zapala, with Tupiqui, Santa Catalina, and Satuache
 —northern frontier
Asahao
 —7 leagues from San Joseph, crossing two Bars
Guadalquini
 —4 leagues from Asahao by land, 6 leagues by water
San Phelipe
 —8 leagues from Guadalquini, crossing two Bars
San Pedro, abandoned by the Yamazes
 —3 leagues from San Phelipe
Santa Maria, abandoned by the Yamazes
 —3 leagues by land and water (4 leagues in crossing)
San Juan
 —6 leagues from Santa Maria, crossing the Bar of Santa Maria and the Island of Zarabay (3 leagues long)

1685 Leturiondo visitation

Santa Cruz y San Buenaventura
 —6 leagues from Santa Maria
 —caciques of Utista, Pisocojolata, Samomo, Utinajica, Napofaie also present
Santa Maria
 —caciques of Santa Cathalina, San Joseph de Sapala, and San Diego de Satuache also present
San Phelipe
 —caciques of Aleste, Talapo, Ospoque, Fasque also present
Tupiqui
 —3 leagues from Santa Maria
San Juan del Puerto
 —caciques of Santa Lucia, Nebalasa, Chololo also present
Nuestra Señora de Guadalupe de Tholomato
 —visitation held in town of Otax

1689 Ebelino de Compostela list

Tolomato
 —25 families
San Juan del Puerto
 —25 families
Santa Cruz de Obadalquini
 —60 families
Santa Catalina
 —on the Island of Santa Maria
 —30 families
San Phelipe
 —on the Island of Santa Maria
 —20 families
Azao
 —on the Island of Santa Maria
 —25 families

1695 Pueyo visitation

Santa Clara de Tupiqui
 —caciques of Zapala and Santa Catalina also present
San Phelipe
 —caciques of Ajiluste/Aluste, Taljapu, Juzpo, and Fazqui also present
Santa Maria
 —caciques of Santa Catalina, Tulafina, Azajo, and Fuslique, Yfulo, and Azpogue also present
Santa Cruz de Guadalquini
 —cacique of Colon and a Yamase cacique present
San Juan del Puerto

1697 Menéndez Márquez and Florencia list

Tholomato
 —3 leagues by water north of St. Augustine
San Juan (village and Island)
 —10 leagues by land from Tholomato
Santa Maria (village and Island)
 —6 leagues by water from San Juan
San Phelipe
 —.5 league, on the Island of Santa Maria
Tupiqui
 —3 leagues from San Phelipe, 22 leagues from St. Augustine, on the Island of Santa Maria

1697 Dickenson relation

Santa Cruce
 —2–3 leagues from St. Augustine by water
St. Wans
 —from Santa Cruce 2 leagues by canoe, 5 leagues to sentinel house, 4 leagues along shore to inlet, 2 miles by canoe
St. Mary's
 —from St. Wans 1 mile by land to sound, then by canoe
St. Philip's
 —1 mile by water
Sappataw
 —2–3 leagues by water

1701 Zuñiga y Cerda visitation (Guale only)

Santa Maria
 —caciques of Santa Cathalina, Tulufina, Fuslico, and Yfulo also present
San Phelipe
 —caciques of Aluste, Tarapu, Jospo, and Aytiniti (aggregated) also present
Tupiqui
 —cacique of Sapala also present

REFERENCES

PRIMARY SOURCES

Unless specifically noted below, all transcriptions and translations of primary Spanish documents were taken from original documents in the Archivo General de Indias (AGI) in Seville, Spain, or from microfilm copies, photocopies, and recently digitalized copies of these originals. Although many of the microfilm copies are located in the P.K. Yonge Library of Florida History at the University of Florida in Gainesville, other documents were discovered and copied on recent trips to the Archivo, and thus many copies remain solely in possession of the author. Although handwritten, typed, and printed transcriptions and translations made by other investigators exist for a number of the following documents, preference was always given to the original handwritten manuscript versions unless otherwise indicated.

Abbreviations for sections of the AGI are as follows: Audiencia of Santo Domingo (SD), Indiferente General (IG), Escribanía de Cámara (EC), Mexico (MEX), and Contaduría (CD).

Finally, since many of the documents cited below form enclosures within a larger documentary package (such as testimony taken as a part of legal proceedings), references are frequently "nested" (one citation refers the reader to another), since the full citation appears only once due to space constraints.

Agustín, Domingo, Baltasar, Ventura, Matheo, and Bernabé

1686. Petition to Governor Juan Márquez Cabrera, 9-27-1686. SD 227A.

Alcayde de Cordoba, Martín

1660. Testimony, 5-2-1660. In Ranjel, 1660.

Aluste, Diego, and Juan Chicasle

1699. Letter to the crown, 3-1-1699. SD 234.

Anguiano, Carlos de

1663. Certification regarding the state of Guale, 4-6-1663. *In* Montiano, 1739. *See* Document 6, translated for present volume.

Aranda y Avellaneda, Pedro de

1684a. Letter to Governor Juan Márquez Cabrera, 10-3-1684. *In* Aranda y Avellaneda, 1688.

1684b. Letter to Governor Juan Márquez Cabrera, 10-5-1684. *In* Aranda y Avellaneda, 1688.

1684c. Letter to Governor Juan Márquez Cabrera, 10-6-1684. *In* Aranda y Avellaneda, 1688.

1684d. Letter to Governor Juan Márquez Cabrera, 10-8-1684. *In* Aranda y Avellaneda, 1688.

1688. Case against Governor Juan Márquez Cabrera. EC 156C. Transcriptions in Jeanette Thurber Connor Collect., P.K. Yonge Library of Florida Hist., Gainesville.

Aranguiz y Cotes, Don Alonso de

1659a. Letter to the crown, 11-9-1659. SD 839.

1659b. Auto concerning proposed infantry post in Apalachee, 10-21-1659. SD 839.

1661a. Letter to the crown, 11-15-1661. CD 965.

1661b. Order to Captain Antonio de Argüelles, 6-29-1661. *Transcribed in* Argüelles, 1662.

1662a. Letter to the crown, 9-8-1662. SD 225.

1662b. Order to Captain Matheo Pacheco y Salgado, 10-24-1662. *Transcribed in* Pacheco y Salgado, 1698.

1663a. Order to Captain Antonio de Argüelles, 3-24-1663. *Transcribed in* Argüelles, 1662.

1663b. Order to Captain Antonio de Argüelles, 1-23-1663. *Transcribed in* Argüelles, 1662.

1663c. Order to Captain Antonio de Argüelles, 1-12-1663. *Transcribed in* Argüelles, 1662.

Arcos, Pedro de

1672. Testimony, 3-22-1672. *In* Cendoya, 1672.

1675. Mission list for Guale and Mocama, 7-1675. SD 839.

Argüelles, Antonio de

1662. Petition to the king. SD 23.

1678. Record of the visitation of Guale and Mocama, 1-1678. EC 156B.

Arredondo, Antonio de

1742. Demostración historiographica del derecho de España a Nueva Georgia. SD 2593. *Transcribed in* Bolton, 1925: 221–325.

Avila, Diego de

1606. Account of the visitation of Bishop Juan de las Cabezas Altamirano to Florida. SD 235.

Barbosa, Francisco de

1683. Census of Guale and Mocama, 6-7-1683. *In* Márquez Cabrera, 1683.

Barios, Salvador de

1688. Testimony, 4-25-1688. MEX 616.

Barreda, Jacinto de

1663. Certification regarding the state of Guale, 4-10-1663. *In* Montiano, 1739. *See* Document 6, translated for present volume.

1680. Patent concerning the death of Fray Sebastián Martínez, 1679–1680. *In* Montiano, 1739. *See* Document 6, translated for present volume.

Bernal, Clemente
1660. Testimony, 5-16-1660. *In* Ranjel, 1660.

Campaña, Juan Bauptista
1663. Certification regarding the state of Guale, 4-14-1663. *In* Montiano, 1739. *See* Document 6, translated for present volume.

Cardross, Lord (Henry Erskine), and William Dunlop
1685. Letter, 1-10-1685. British Public Records Office, Colonial Entry Book, vol. 21.

Cendoya, Manuel de
1671. Order to Captain Matheo Pacheco y Salgado, 7-12-1671. *Transcribed in* Pacheco y Salgado, 1698.
1672. *Auto* concerning the testimony of Diacun, 3-22-1672. SD 839.
1673. Order to Adjutant Diego Díaz Mejia, 1-24-1673. *In* Montiano, 1739. *See* Addendum, Document 1, translated for present volume.

Cigarroa, Salvador de
1681. Certification concerning Governor Hita Salazar's actions following the abandonment of Santa Catalina, 1-9-1681. EC 156A.

Clar, Juan
1686. Testimony, 9-23-1686. *In* Márquez Cabrera, 1686.

Colleton, James
1688. Letter to Governor Diego de Quiroga y Losada, 4-1-1688. SD 839.

Cruz, Juan Bauptista de la
1660. Testimony, 5-13-1660. *In* Ranjel, 1660.

Diacun
1672. Testimony, 3-22-1672. *In* Cendoya, 1672.

Díaz Vara Calderón, Gabriel
1675. Letter to the crown, 11-20-1675. SD 151.

Díez de la Calle, Juan
1655. Memorial of the principal settlements, churches, and doctrinas that there are in the conversions of the provinces of Florida at the charge of the missionaries of the order of San Francisco, who are the only ones that serve in them in the conversion and indoctrination of the Indians. Photostat in Mary Letitia Ross Collection, Georgia Department of Archives and History, Atlanta.
1659. Noticias sacras y reales de los dos imperios de las Yndias Occidentales desta Nueva España. *Selection transcribed in* M. Serrano y Sanz (ed.), Documentos historicos de la Florida y la Luisiana, siglos XVI al XVIII, pp. 131–133. Madrid, 1912.

Dickenson, Jonathan
1697. Narrative of a shipwreck in the Gulph of Florida. *Transcribed in* Swanton, 1922: 92–93.

Dunlop, William
1687. Journal of the mission to St. Augustine, 4-1687. *Transcribed in* Dunlop, 1929a.
1688. Journal of the mission to St. Augustine, 6–7-1688. *Transcribed in* Dunlop, 1933.

Ebelino de Compostela, Diego
1689. Letter to the crown, 9-28-1689. SD 151.

Echagaray, Martín de
1684. Petition to the crown, 1-30-1684. MEX 616.

Escovedo, Andrés de
1675. Testimony, 5-23-1675. *In* Hita Salazar, 1675.

Estevez de Carmenatis, Nicolás
1669. Petition to the crown. SD 233.

Fernández, Gabriel
1663. Certification regarding the state of Guale, 4-8-1663. *In* Montiano, 1739. *See* Document 6, translated for present volume.

Florencia, Matheo Luis de
1682. Petition to the crown, 8-11-1682. SD 234.

Fuentes, Francisco de
1680. Testimony concerning the resettlement of Santa Catalina, 10-27-1680. *In* Hita Salazar, 1680c.
1681. Census of Guale and Mocama, 7-1-1681. *Transcribed in* Montiano, 1739. *See* Document 7, translated for present volume.

Fuentes, Joseph de
1708. Petition to the crown, 1-7-1708. SD 848.

Gómez, Manuel
1685. Letter to Governor Juan Márquez Cabrera, 11-12-1685. SD 839.

Guerra y Vega, Don Francisco de la
1665a. Order to Adjutant Bartolomé Sánchez de Entonado, 1-17-1665. *Transcribed in* Montiano, 1739. *See* Document 5, translated for present volume.
1665b. Order to Captain Martín Alcayde de Cordoba, 1-17-1665. *Transcribed in* Montiano, 1739. *See* Document 5, translated for present volume.
1665c. Order to Captain Antonio de Argüelles, 3-4-1665. *Transcribed in* Montiano, 1739. *See* Document 5, translated for present volume.
1666. Order to Adjutant Alonso de Alvarez, 2-1-1666. *Transcribed in* Montiano,

1739. *See* Document 5, translated for present volume.
1667a. Order to Adjutant Francisco de Aispiolea, 1-10-1667. *Transcribed in* Montiano, 1739. *See* Document 5, translated for present volume.
1667b. Order to Captain Alonso de Argüelles, 8-18-1667. *Transcribed in* Montiano, 1739. *See* Document 5, translated for present volume.
1668a. Order to Ensign Juan Domínguez, 1-21-1668. *Transcribed in* Montiano, 1739. *See* Document 5, translated for present volume.
1668b. Order to Captain Antonio de Argüelles, 4-22-1668. *Transcribed in* Montiano, 1739. *See* Document 5, translated for present volume.
1669. Order to Adjutant Francisco de Aispiolea, 1-16-1669. *Transcribed in* Montiano, 1739. *See* Document 5, translated for present volume.

Hilton, William
1664. A relation of a discovery. *Transcribed in* Salley, 1911: 31–61.

Hita Salazar, Don Pablo de
1675. *Auto* concerning English depredations, 5-23-1675. SD 839.
1677. *Auto* concerning San Jorge, 3-22-1677. SD 839.
1680a. Letter to the king, 5-14-1680. SD 839.
1680b. Order to Captain Lorenzo Joseph de León, 7-22-1680. *Transcribed in* Montiano, 1739. *See* Document 5, translated for present volume.
1680c. *Auto* concerning the resettlement of Santa Catalina, 10-19-1680. EC 156A.
1680d. Order to Sergeant Manuel Gómez, 5-17-1680. *Transcribed in* Montiano, 1739. *See* Document 5, translated for present volume.
1680e. Order to Captain Don Enrique de Ribera, 5-26-1680. *Transcribed in* Montiano, 1739. *See* Document 5, translated for present volume.
1680f. Order to Captain Nicolás Estebedes de Carmenatis, 5-23-1680. *Transcribed in* Montiano, 1739. *See* Document 5, translated for present volume.
1680g. Order to Captain Francisco de Fuentes, 6-18-1680. *Transcribed in* Montiano, 1739. *See* Document 5, translated for present volume.
1680h. Response to charges in *residencia*, 12-1680. EC 156A.
1681. Certification of the service of Captain Francisco de Fuentes, 1-27-1681. IG 135.
1683. Letter to the crown, 5-20-1683. SD 226.
1687. Certification of the service of Captain Juan Saturnino de Abaurrea, 11-12-1687. IG 135.
1692. Certification of the service of Captain Francisco Romo de Uriza, 8-9-1692. SD 234.

Horruytiner, Don Pedro Benedit
1652. Investigation of the hacienda of Asile, 3-1652. *In* Governors Benito Ruíz de Salazar Vallecilla, Nicolás Ponce de León, and Pedro Benedit Horruytiner, *Residencia.* EC 155B.

Hortelano, Pedro
1686. Testimony, 12-2-1686. MEX 616.

Jesús, Francisco Alonso de
1630. Letter to the crown, 3-11-1630. SD 235.

Juan, Joseph
1686. Testimony, 12-2-1686. MEX 616.

Leturiondo, Alonso de
1701. Memorial regarding the condition of Florida. *Translated in* Hann, 1986b: 165–225.

Leturiondo, Domingo de
1685. Record of the visitation of Guale and Mocama, 12-1685. *In* Montiano, 1739. *See* Document 9, translated for present volume.

Livingston, John
1686. Testimony, 9-23-1686. *In* Márquez Cabrera, 1686.

Lords Proprietors
1686. Instructions for Governor James Colleton, 3-3-1686. British Public Records Office, Colonial Entry Book, vol. 22.

Lorenzo, Cacique
1685. Testimony, 1-7-1685. *In* Márquez Cabrera, 1685c.

Luna, Pedro de
1686. Petition to the crown, 9-1686. SD 235.

Márquez Cabrera, Don Juan
1681. Letter to cacica Merenciana, 1-30-1681. SD 226.
1683. Letter to the crown, 6-28-1683. SD 226.
1684. *Auto* about the settlement of the province of Guale, 8-1684. SD 227A.
1685a. Letter to the crown, 3-28-1685. SD 227A.
1685b. *Auto* concerning the Yamassee cacique Niquisaya, 3-22-1685. SD 856.
1685c. Criminal case against Captain Don Juan Saturnino de Abaurrea, 1-1685. *In* Montiano, 1739. *See* Document 10, translated for present volume.
1686. *Autos* concerning the return of the galliots of Captain Alexandro Thomás de León, 9-1686. *In* Montiano, 1739. *See*

Document 11, translated for present volume.
1687. Letter to the crown, 10-6-1687. SD 839.
1688a. *Residencia.* EC 156C.
1688b. Certification of the service of Captain Francisco de Fuentes, 8-8-1688. IG 135.

Matheo
1686. Testimony, 9-27-1686. *In* Márquez Cabrera, 1686.

Medina, Bernardo de
1678. Declaration, 10-17-1678. SD 839.

Menéndez, Don Alonso, Don Francisco de Ybarra, Don Juan de Zapala, Bernabé de Aluste, and Don Thomás de Yor
1657. Letter to the crown, 10-16-1657. SD 235.

Menéndez Márquez, Antonio
1673. Petition to the crown, 3-20-1673. IG 124.

Menéndez Márquez, Thomás, and Joachín de Florencia
1697. Certification of the friars, doctrinas, and villages of Florida, 4-15-1697. SD 230.

Menéndez Márquez, Thomás, and Francisco de la Rocha
1686. Letter to the crown, 10-4-1686. SD 230. *Translation provided by* John H. Hann.

Montiano, Don Manuel de
1739. Documentary package concerning Guale and Mocama, 8-18-1739. SD 2584. Translated for present volume.

Moore, James, Thomas Gibbes, Robert Gibbes, Andrew Percival, Bernard Schenckingh, Joseph Morton, John Godfrey, Joseph Morton, Jr., William Dunlop, and John Farr
1686. Letter, 9-1686. *Transcribed in* Dunlop, 1929b: 81–89.

Oré, Luís Geronimo de
1936. Relación historica de la Florida, escrita en el siglo XVII. A. López (ed.). Madrid.

Pacheco, Francisco
1672. Letter to Manuel de Cendoya, 3-1672. *In* Cendoya, 1672.

Pacheco y Salgado, Doña Lucia and Doña Maria
1698. Petition to the crown. SD 848.

Penate, Simón
1688. Testimony, 4-25-1688. MEX 616.

Pesquera, Alonso de, Gregorio de Movilla, Francisco Pareja, Alonso Ortíz, Estéban de San Andrese, Francisco Fernández.
1621. Petition to the crown, 9-1-1621. SD 26.

Ponce de León, Don Nicolás I
1651a. Order to Captain Antonio de Argüelles, 5-17-1651. *Transcribed in* Argüelles, 1662.
1651b. Order to Captain Antonio de Argüelles, 6-20-1651. *Transcribed in* Argüelles, 1662.

Ponce de León, Don Nicolás II
1675. Order to Captain Don Matheo Pacheco y Salgado, 1-6-1675. *Transcribed in* Pacheco y Salgado, 1698.

Pueyo, Don Juan de
1695. Record of the visitation of Guale and Mocama, 2-1695. EC 157A.
1701. Certification of the service of Captain Juan Saturnino de Abaurrea, 2-28-1701. IG 135.

Pulido, Blas
1722. Petition concerning the friars of Florida, 10-5-1722. SD 842.

Quiroga y Losada, Don Diego de
1687. Letter to Governor James Colleton, 11-2-1687. SD 839.

Ranjel, Don Diego
1660. Governor Don Diego de Rebolledo, *Residencia.* CD 963–964.

Rebolledo, Don Diego de
1656. Order to Captain Nicolás Fernández de Goyas, 4-20-1656. *Transcribed in* Montiano, 1739. *See* Document 5, translated for present volume.
1657. Letter to the crown, 10-18-1657. SD 839.
1658a. Title to Nicolás Estevez de Carmenatis, 5-10-1658. IG 128.
1658b. *Auto* concerning the lieutenants of Apalachee and Timucua, 9–11-1658. *Transcribed in* Ranjel, 1660.

Reyes, Gaspar de los
1687. List of expenses to Indians in 1687, 12-31-1687. EC 157A.

Rocha, Francisco de la
1687. Record of the delivery of corn and beans, 5-9-1687. *Transcribed in* Márquez Cabrera, 1688.

Rodríguez Tisnado, Juan
1685. Letter to Governor Juan Márquez Cabrera, 3-16-1685. SD 856.

Rojas y Borja, Don Luis de
1627. Letter to the crown, 2-13-1627. SD 225. *Translation in* Mary Letitia Ross Collection, Georgia Department of Archives and History, Atlanta (original not in cited legajo).
1630. Investigation concerning the petition of Fray Francisco Alonso de Jesús, 4-1630. *Transcribed in* Governor Benito Ruíz de Salazar Vallecilla, *Residencia.* EC 155B.

Royal *Cédula*
1680. Royal *cédula* to Manuel de Espinosa, 9-3-1680. SD 2529.
1688. Royal *cédula* to Governor Don Diego de Quiroga y Losada, 8-14-1688. *Transcribed in* SD 2591.

Ruíz de Salazar Vallecilla, Benito
1646. Order to Ensign Antonio de Argüelles, 1-27-1646. *Transcribed in* Argüelles, 1662.

San Payo, Sebastián de
1688. Testimony, 4-25-1688. MEX 616.

Sánchez de Urisa, Juan
1672. Certification of the service of Juan Francisco de los Santos, 3-28-1672. *In* Santos, 1672.
1675. Certification of the service of Captain Antonio de Argüelles, 10-1-1675. IG 125.

Sandford, Robert
1666. A relation of a voyage on the coast of the province of Carolina. *Transcribed in* Salley, 1911: 75–108.

Santiago, Cacique
1685. Testimony, 1-7-1685. *In* Márquez Cabrera, 1685c.

Santos, Juan Francisco de los
1672. Petition to the crown, 3-1672. SD 234.

Saturnino de Abaurrea, Juan
1680. Letter to Governor Pablo de Hita Salazar, 11-1-1680. *In* Hita Salazar, 1680c.
1684. Letter to Governor Juan Márquez Cabrera, 9-12-1684. *In* Márquez Cabrera, 1685a.
1685. Confession, 1-9-1685. *In* Márquez Cabrera, 1685c.
1696. Petition to the crown, 4-28-1696. SD 228.

Torre, Thomás de la
1687. Testimony, 12-15-1687. MEX 616.

Uçeda, Juan de
1663. Certification regarding the state of Guale, 4-7-1663. *In* Montiano, 1739. *See* Document 6, translated for present volume.

Westbrooke, Caleb
1685. Letter, 2-21-1685. British Public Records Office, Colonial Entry Book, vol. 21.

Woodward, Henry
1674. A faithfull relation of my westoe voiage. *Transcribed in* Salley, 1911: 130–134.

Ybarra, Pedro de
1604. Record of the visitation of San Pedro and Guale. *Transcribed in* Serrano y Sanz, 1912: 164–193.

Zuñiga y Cerda, Joseph de
1701. Record of the visitation of Guale, 2-1701. SD 858.
1702. Letter to the crown, 11-5-1702. SD 858.

SECONDARY SOURCES

Arenas Frutos, Isabel
1991. Expediciones franciscanas a Indias, 1625–1650. *In* Actas del III Congreso Internacional sobre Los Franciscanos en el Nuevo Mundo (Siglo XVII), La Rábida, 18–23 de septiembre de 1989. Madrid: Editorial Deimos.

Arnade, Charles W.
1959. The seige of St. Augustine in 1702. Gainesville: Univ. of Florida Press.

Bolton, Herbert
1925. Arredondo's historical proof of Spain's title to Georgia. Berkeley: Univ. of California Press.

Bushnell, Amy Turner
1978. The Menéndez Márquez cattle barony at La Chua and the determinants of economic expansion in seventeenth-century Florida. Florida Hist. Q. 56: 407–431.
1981. The king's coffer: proprietors of the Spanish Florida treasury, 1565–1702. Gainesville: Univ. of Florida Press.
1989. Ruling "the Republic of Indians" in seventeenth-century Florida. *In* Peter H. Wood, Gregory A. Waselkov, and M.Thomas Hatley (eds.), Powhatan's mantle: Indians in the colonial Southeast, pp. 134–150. Lincoln: Univ. of Nebraska Press.
1994. Situado and sabana: Spain's support system for the mission provinces of Florida. Anthropol. Pap. Am. Mus. Nat. Hist. 74.

Connor, Jeanette Thurber
1926. The nine old wooden forts of St. Augustine. Florida Hist. Q. 4: 103–111.

Cook, Jeannine
1990. Fort King George: step one to statehood. Darien, GA: The Darien News.

Crane, Verner W.
1956. The southern frontier, 1670–1732. Ann Arbor: Univ. of Michigan Press.

Craton, Michael
1962. A history of the Bahamas. London: Collins.

Deagan, Kathleen A.
1978. Cultures in transition: fusion and assimilation among the eastern Timucua. *In* Jerald T. Milanich and Samuel Proctor (eds.), Tacachale: essays on the Indians of Florida and southeastern Georgia during the historic period, pp. 89–119. Gainesville: Univ. of Florida Press.

Dunlop, J.G.
1928. Paul Grimball's losses by the Spanish invasion in 1686. The South Carolina Hist. and Geneaological Mag. 29: 231–237.
1929a. Capt. Dunlop's voyage to the south-

ward, 1687. The South Carolina Hist. and Genealogical Mag. 30: 127–133.
1929b. Spanish depredations, 1686. The South Carolina Hist. and Genealogical Mag. 30: 81–89.
1933. William Dunlop's mission to St. Augustine in 1688. The South Carolina Hist. and Genealogical Mag. 34: 1–30.

Gannon, Michael V.
1965. The cross in the sand: the early Catholic Church in Florida, 1513–1870. Gainesville: Univ. of Florida Press.
1981. The conflict between church and state in Spanish Florida: the administration of Juan Márquez Cabrera, 1680–1687. Paper presented at La Rabida, Spain.

Geiger, Maynard J.
1937. The Franciscan conquest of Florida. Washington, DC: Catholic Univ. of America.
1940. Biographical dictionary of the Franciscans in Spanish Florida and Cuba (1528–1841). Franciscan Stud. 21. Paterson, NJ: St. Anthony Guild Press.

Granberry, Julian
1993. A grammer and dictionary of the Timucua language. Tuscaloosa: Univ. of Alabama Press.

Hally, David J.
1986. The identification of vessel function: a case study from northwest Georgia. Am. Antiquity 51: 267–295.

Hann, John H.
1986a. Translation of Governor Rebolledo's 1657 visitation of three Florida provinces and related documents. Florida Archaeol. 2: 81–145.
1986b. Translation of Alonso de Leturiondo's Memorial to the King of Spain. Florida Archaeol. 2: 165–225.
1987. Twilight of the Mocama and Guale aborigines as portrayed in the 1695 Spanish Visitation. Florida Hist. Q. 66: 1–24.
1988a. Florida's terra incognita: west Florida's natives in the sixteenth and seventeenth century. Florida Anthropol. 41(1): 61–107.
1988b. Apalachee: the land between the rivers. Gainesville: Univ. of Florida Press.
1989. St. Augustine's fallout from the Yamassee War. Florida Hist. Q. 68: 180–200.
1990. Summary guide to Spanish Florida missions and visitas with churches in the sixteenth and seventeenth centuries. The Americas 46: 417–513.
1991a. Missions to the Calusa. Gainesville: Univ. of Florida Press.
1991b. The Mayaca and Jororo and missions to them. Florida Anthropol. 44(2–4): 164–175.
1993. Visitations and revolts in Florida, 1656–1695. Florida Archaeol. 7.

Haring, C.H.
1910. The buccaneers in the West Indies in the XVII century. Hamden, CT: Archon Books.

Hoffman, Kathleen
1991. The archaeology of the Convento de San Francisco. Florida Anthropol. 44(2–4): 139–153.

Hudson, Charles
1990. The Juan Pardo expeditions: exploration of the Carolinas and Tennessee, 1566–1568. Washington, DC: Smithsonian Institution Press.

Hudson, Charles, Marvin T. Smith, and Chester B. DePratter
1984. The Hernando de Soto expedition: from Apalachee to Chiaha. Southeast. Archaeol. 3: 65–77.

Insh, George Pratt
1929. Arrival of the Cardross settlers. The South Carolina Hist. and Genealogical Mag. 30: 69–80.

Jones, Grant D.
1978. The ethnohistory of the Guale Coast through 1684. *In* David Hurst Thomas, Grant D. Jones, Roger S. Durham, and Clark Spencer Larsen, The anthropology of St. Catherines Island: 1. natural and cultural history. Anthropol. Pap. Am. Mus. Nat. Hist. 55(2): 178–210.

Juarez Moreno, Juan
1972. Corsarios y piratas en Veracruz y Campeche. Seville: Escuela de Estudios Hispano-Americanos.

Lanning, John Tate
1935. The Spanish missions of Georgia. Chapel Hill: Univ. of North Carolina Press.

Larsen, Clark Spencer (ed.)
1990. The archaeology of Mission Santa Catalina de Guale: 2. biocultural interpretations of a population in transition. Anthropol. Pap. Am. Mus. Nat. Hist. 68.

Larson, Lewis H., Jr.
1980. The Spanish on Sapelo. *In* Daniel P. Juengst (ed.), The Sapelo papers: researches in the history and prehistory of Sapelo Island, Georgia, pp. 35–45. Carrollton: West Georgia Coll. Stud. in the Soc. Sci. 19.

Lyon, Eugene
1976. The enterprise of Florida: Pedro Menéndez de Avilés and the Spanish conquest of 1565–1568. Gainesville: Univ. of Florida Press.
1987. The revolt of 1576 at Santa Elena: a failure of Indian policy. Paper presented to the Am. Hist. Assoc., Washington, DC.

McCrady, Edward
1897. The History of South Carolina under the Proprietary Government, 1670–1719. New York: Macmillan Co.

Milanich, Jerald T.
1971. Surface information from the presumed site of the San Pedro de Mocamo Mission. Pap. Conf. Hist. Sites Archaeol. 5: 114–121.
1972. Tacatacuru and the San Pedro de Mocamo Mission. Florida Hist. Q. 50: 283–291.

Milanich, Jerald T., and William C. Sturtevant
1972. Francisco Pareja's 1613 confessionario: a documentary source for Timucuan ethnography. Div. of Arch., Hist., and Rec. Management, Florida Dep. of State, Tallahassee.

Oexmelin, Alexandre-Olivier
1953. Historia de los aventureros-filibusteros y bucaneros de América. C. Armando Rodriguez (translator). Trujillo: Editora Montalvo.

Pearson, Charles E.
1984. Red Bird Creek: late prehistoric material culture and subsistence in coastal Georgia. Early Georgia 12(1–2): 1–39.

Reitz, Elizabeth J.
1991. Evidence for animal use at the missions of Spanish Florida. Florida Anthropol. 44(2–4): 295–306.

Salley, Alexander S., Jr., ed.
1911. Narratives of early Carolina, 1650–1708. New York: Charles Scribner's Sons.

Serrano y Sanz, Manuel
1912. Documentos históricos de la Florida y la Luisiana, siglos XVI al XVIII. Madrid: Libreria General de Victoriano Suárez.

Smith, Marvin T.
1987. Archaeology of aboriginal culture change in the interior southeast: depopulation during the early historic period. Gainesville: Univ. of Florida Press.

South, Stanley
1991. Archaeology at Santa Elena: doorway to the past. South Carolina Instit. of Archaeol. and Anthropol. Popular Series 2. Columbia.

South, Stanley, and Michael O. Hartley
1985. Deep water and high ground. *In* Roy S. Dickens, Jr. and H. Trawick Ward (eds.), Structure and process in southeastern archaeology, pp. 263–286. University: Univ. of Alabama Press.

Swanton, John R.
1922. Early history of the Creek Indians and their neighbors. Bur. of Am. Ethnology Bull. 73. Washington, DC: Gov. Printing Office. Reprint, Johnson Reprint Corporation, 1970.

Thomas, David Hurst
1987. The archaeology of Mission Santa Catalina de Guale: 1. search and discovery. Anthropol. Pap. Am. Mus. Nat. Hist. 63(2).

Worth, John E.
1992. The Timucuan missions of Spanish Florida and the rebellion of 1656. Ph.D. diss., Dep. of Anthropol., Univ. of Florida, Gainesville.
1994. Late Spanish military expeditions in the interior southeast, 1597–1628. *In* Charles Hudson and Carmen Chaves Tesser (eds.), The forgotten centuries: Indians and Europeans in the American South, 1521–1704, pp. 104–122. Athens: Univ. of Georgia Press, Athens.

Wright, J. Leitch, Jr.
1960. Andrew Ranson: seventeenth-century Pirate? Florida Hist. Q. 39:135–144.

INDEX